The Communicator's Handbook
Tools, Techniques and Technology

Third Edition

MAUPIN
HOUSE

The Agricultural Communicators in Education (ACE) is an international association of communications professionals who prepare and disseminate knowledge concerning natural resources, agriculture, and the food industry using a wide variety of traditional and electronic media. Most of the 700 members are faculty and staff at land grant and Sea Grant universities throughout the United States and in similar institutions in other nations. Others are employed by the federal government, associated agribusinesses, and at international agricultural development centers around the world.

Their stock in trade is scientific information for scientists and the food and fiber industry and problem-solving information for consumers, businesses, and the media. For more information about ACE, contact the headquarters office at 352-392-9588.

Third Edition

Published by
Maupin House
P.O. Box 90148
Gainesville, FL 32607
http://www.maupinhouse.com

Copies may be ordered from
Maupin House
1-800-524-0634

Created in Quark Express and Adobe Photoshop by David and Lawrence Dishman

Cover design: Lawrence Dishman

Copy editor: Candace Nelson

Cover photography: Thomas Wright

Library of Congress Cataloging-in-Publication Data
The communicator's handbook : tools, techniques, and technology / Patricia Calvert, editor. – 3rd ed.
      p.   cm.
      Includes bibliographical references and index.
      ISBN 0-929895-16-9
      1. Communication—Handbooks, manuals, etc. I. Calvert, Patricia.
P90.C63465   1996
302.2—dc20   96-26243
                                     CIP

Printed in the United States of America.

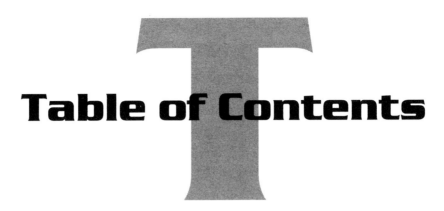

Table of Contents

Chapter 10

Posters

Want an inexpensive way to publicize an item or event? Choose a poster – but understand how to design and use it well.

Chapter 11

Slides and Slidetapes

Slides and slide-tape presentations can combine audio and visual elements to communicate a message quickly, effectively, and inexpensively. The equipment is portable and readily available, and shows can be revised and duplicated easily.

Chapter 12

Designing Visuals for Presentations

Visuals make presentations more memorable. They carry information, and they increase the amount of information an audience remembers. Plan, prepare, and present slides, overheads, and computer visuals that are easy to understand and amplify the impact of an oral presentation.

Chapter 13

Effective Meetings

As the world becomes more "high-tech," people crave "high-touch" opportunities. Face-to-face meetings provide such a forum to share ideas, generate enthusiasm, and accomplish committee tasks.

Chapter 14

Public Speaking

A well-prepared and delivered speech hits the mark with an audience. The art of public speaking can be learned if the speaker follows the easy steps this chapter outlines..

Chapter 15

Media Relations

How effectively does your organization deal with the media? A full-service approach to media relations goes a long way toward building creditability with your audiences – and with the gatekeepers. Included are hints for media interviewees and their media relations consultants

Chapter 16

Campaign Communications: Public Information Campaigns

What do floods in Missouri, a new apple variety in Minnesota, gardening in Oregon, and agricultural disasters in Georgia have in common? They each would make a fine topic for a public information campaign. The versatility and creativity of a public information campaign offers the communicator unique opportunities to deliver an intensive educational message over a specific period of time. .

Chapter 17

The ABCs of Working with Volunteers

Even during today's busy times, people care enough to volunteer. And they make a difference. Learn how to care and manage your special volunteers..

Chapter 18

Radio

With the help of the mind's eye, radio unlocks a world larger than life, brighter than brilliant, and more intense than anything the physical world can deliver. What's more, it's efficient and cost-effective when compared to other methods of direct mass communication. The challenge in radio is to understand what it can do for you..

Chapter 19

Television News

Television news is a proven – and often unforgiving – medium. Along with the intended message, an unblinking camera captures cracks and wrinkles of your presentation technique. Take the utmost care in planning and delivering a television news production. It pays off..

Chapter 20

Video Productions

Television and video permeate every aspect of today's media life. Learn how to make the most of this dominant force in entertainment, education, news, elections, and the national culture

Introduction

Communications – creating the future! The Third Edition of *The Communicator's Handbook* reflects the fast-paced, rapidly changing world where communications professionals live and work.

In 1996, the members of Agricultural Communicators in Education (ACE) who wrote this resource actively participate in the global village – communicating at the speed of light with colleagues and clients, using technologies and tools that were virtually unknown when the first handbook was published in 1989.

As businesses and organizations downsize and reinvent their mission and purpose, this new edition brings a simple and profound message: communications – and communicators – remain central to survive and thrive.

Collaboration and cooperation are hallmarks of today's new communications order, an era created by limited resources, expanded and diverse audiences. The new order promotes shared ideas, opinions, programs and professional expertise.

More than 35 authors worked collaboratively to bring the best of their research and experience to this edition. Many others were involved in its graphic design, publication, and marketing.

With topics ranging from the art of writing well and navigating the Internet to strategic communications planning, organizational marketing and emerging communication issues, the handbook itself testifies to the power of teamwork.

The team who worked on *The Communicator's Handbook* offer it as help from professionals to professionals. Through communication and collaboration we work together to create a successful future for our businesses and organizations!

Patricia Calvert
July 1996

Effective Communication: Practical Lessons from Research

Communicators in the final decade of the 20th century often may have found themselves overwhelmed with burgeoning technology and talk of the "information age" and "information superhighway." Astonishing increases in the amount of information and the number of channels through which it may flow pose a danger of leaving us dazed and bewildered. But in the final analysis the communication challenge is unchanged. The communicator's role still is to get information to people, ideally through the most effective and efficient channels.

That never has been an easy task. There is enormous competition. To get your specific message seen and heard – much less have people remember and respond to it – requires your best efforts. We know that people today are inundated with messages – mass media and interpersonal, intended and unintended. They select only a small fraction to which they pay attention. One estimate, for example, is that worldwide, fewer than one percent of messages on radio and TV are attended to by their potential audiences.

Even when people do pay attention to what they read and hear, they are likely to retain only a small portion. A study of television news showed that only 30 minutes after viewing an evening newscast, half of those surveyed could not recall a single thing they saw.

Finally, of those messages people pay attention to and understand, few result directly in changes in behavior or attitudes. Only after years of reports on the relationship between smoking and increased chances of lung cancer was there any significant change in smoking habits.

Communicators must be conscious of the fact that there are many obstacles in their efforts to reach audiences with information. The "information superhighway" is filled with potholes and lined by exits. But on the whole, roadblocks faced by communicators are not new. The communication process is likely to fail today for the same reasons it was likely to fail in decades past. These include:

Failure to share meaning. Some years ago a cartoon showed an educator opening the head of a student and pouring in the appropriate measure of knowledge. Such direct communication of knowledge would be nice, but it simply is not possible. Human beings always must communicate indirectly by first converting experiences or knowledge into symbols (words or gestures). These then must be interpreted, or decoded, by the receiver of the message. Language, an ambiguous gesture, or the absence of a shared culture can doom communication to failure. A "drinking fountain" in New York is a "bubbler" in Milwaukee. An "intestinal parasite" to an agricultural researcher is a "worm" to a farmer. Such semantic "noise" in communication often leads to misunderstanding.

Field days offer the advantages of face-to-face demonstrations and multi-media coverage combined in a single package.

Failure of communication channels. There frequently is physical "noise" in communication, as well, caused by anything from a smudge on the newspaper page to static in radio signals or line failure in a cable television system. Inability of audience members to hear or see at a meeting can result in ineffective communication. The expectations audiences bring to various media also may affect their success as communication channels. We expect to be entertained by television. How does this affect the use of TV as an educational medium?

Lack of attention to or lack of interest in the message. Communicators typically assume that people who buy newspapers do so because they want news. Yet studies have shown that many other motives are involved (habit, the desire for entertainment, etc.). People often view television with other people or while they are doing other things. The typical TV news viewer also may be reading a newspaper, chatting with a spouse, or calming rambunctious children at the same time he or she watches the broadcast.

Given all the potential pitfalls, then, what are the communicator's prospects for success? Given the advances in communication technology and the knowledge gained through communication research, they may be better today than ever before. This chapter presents nine "lessons learned" from research into the communication process in recent decades. These lessons can help communicators better understand and use both mass media and interpersonal processes to reach audiences effectively. No attempt is made here to be comprehensive; rather, the focus is on the practical implications of research results. A suggested reading list is provided at the end of this book for those wishing to read more in any of the nine areas.

Communication is a long and difficult process

Not surprisingly, research tells us that people tend to seek out information that interests them. During the Persian Gulf War, for example, the frequency of newspaper readership increased significantly. Dramatic gains in audience numbers were enjoyed by media channels such as Cable News Network, C-SPAN, and National Public Radio. Studies also show a parallel increase in public knowledge about the war.

Newspaper readers, according to audience research, tend to remember more stories than broadcast audiences do.

But what about situations in which the public is not predisposed to seek out information? Two examples are informative. One was an effort to educate residents of five Midwest communities about energy topics, ranging from home energy conservation to nuclear power. Over a four-month period, major newspapers in each of the five communities printed 14 half-page articles on specific topics. The total number of words printed was approximately 50,000, or about half a small book. Results

showed that knowledge about energy had increased over the period, but only by 2.8 percent. Such results are typical of single-medium efforts to increase knowledge among general populations.

A more comprehensive effort is represented by an earlier project of the Stanford Heart Disease Prevention Program in California. In one community, residents received an intensive two-year barrage of mass media messages in newspapers and on radio and television. A second community received the same intensive media coverage, but also included personal contact between health experts and community residents. Results showed that knowledge of heart risk factors increased by 26.5 percent in the first community and 36.0 percent in the second community.

Why is learning so slow and limited? We often imagine a public heavily tuned in to mass media, and that image may be quite accurate. But research has shown that different media have different effects. For example, audiences recall stories they read in the newspaper or on the computer screen better than they remember stories they get through radio or television broadcast. This fact, coupled with decining newspaper readership (particularly among younger age groups), has important implications for communicators.

Studies also show that while most people spend extensive amounts of time viewing television, viewing patterns have been affected significantly by growing access to cable. The growth of cable has been paralleled by dwindling viewer numbers for network news, though local news audiences often are affected to a lesser extent.

These results suggest that while increases in knowledge about most public issues are possible, intensive multi-media coverage over long periods of time is necessary. Although these figures can be discouraging to some, they must be kept in perspective. Compared to the number of people who might be reached through personal communication, vastly larger audiences still may be reached effectively through mass media. A 1992 study of young farmers' sources of information about sustainable agriculture identified mass media as the most prominent source, with more than 80 percent of respondents reporting frequent use of mass media to gain information on the subject.

Two practical implications follow from this discussion. First, be realistic in setting goals for increasing knowledge among target groups. A 10 percent increase in knowledge in a community of 50,000 represents a substantial change. Second, use a multi-media approach. Because many people are not regular television viewers, radio listeners, or newspapers readers, messages must be repeated in different forms over time to be understood. Getting your news in a front-page story in your local newspaper is an important step forward in effective communication, but it is not enough.

The rate of learning by an audience is uneven

Information offered by mass media or interpersonal channels does not diffuse evenly to audiences. Beginning with the classic diffusion study about hybrid seed corn in Iowa, and continuing through hundreds of other studies about the way new ideas and practices are adopted, there is clear evidence that some people learn well ahead of others. The different rate of learning sometimes may be explained by differences in such factors as education, income, and age. Higher education generally encourages the gathering and processing of information. Younger persons often are more oriented to adoption of new ideas. And those with higher incomes often are in a better position to act upon what they learn.

Conferencing by telephone network can be an effective way to reach specific, clearly identified audiences.

A 1990 study in Ohio showed that the level of residents' knowledge about school issues and the extent to which they trusted media reports about the school system were related to such factors as education level, race, gender, and general political disaffection. This means, again, that what audiences bring to the communication process has much to do with its effectiveness.

A majority of studies about how people get information finds that "gaps" in knowledge are created whenever new information arrives. An exception to this occurs only when the information is very important and when virtual saturation coverage of news about a given situation occurs. In this case, those with the least information often catch up to those who already know. But this usually is only temporary. As the event dies down again, those who originally knew more again begin to move ahead in knowledge.

Thus, when we think about communicating with audiences on most topics, we should expect that those who already know the most about a topic will be the first ones to learn more. Further, unless heavy emphasis is placed on the topic, those with little knowledge are not likely to learn much. This has important implications for those who are concerned about information equity.

Communicators often must consider ethical issues associated with the potential impact of differing levels of knowledge available to different groups. But avoiding the creation of knowledge "gaps" may require a heavy investment in communication resources to reach older, more isolated, or other disadvantaged audiences, for example. And investments in reaching these groups can be frustrating because group members require more time to learn and have fewer resources with which to act upon the information even if they receive it.

We learn more from people we know less well

In a study of how people first hear about new jobs, it was found that the most valuable contacts came from those the job-seekers did not know well, rather than close acquaintances. This makes sense when we recognize that the information we get from groups with which we associate often is not new – we know much of it already. The main function of groups we belong to is to provide support and socialization rather than to teach new information. When we want truly new information, therefore, we are likely to get it from those we know less well.

Researchers have become much more interested in recent years in the analysis of "communication networks" – the complex interpersonal communication links that connect individuals to groups and groups to one another. Today, computer networks connect vast numbers of individuals who may never meet face-to-face but who may share information on a daily basis. Research indicates that much valuable and new information comes to groups through "bridge" roles – people who are members of more than one group and share information between groups. Here, again, computer networks readily facilitate such sharing. Also valuable are people who don't belong to groups, but relay information from one group to another by having contact with group members.

The practical significance of this finding for the communicator can be found both in information seeking and sending. When you want to learn what people in a community know or think about an issue, don't focus on contacting people you know. You probably have a good sense of what they know and think. Much more valuable knowledge will come from contacts with people you know less well and come into contact with less frequently. In terms of information sending, studies suggest that communicators will have the most impact when they have contacts with new audiences, rather than those with whom they usually work. Thus, the common practice of building a list of clientele on whom one focuses regularly tends to restrict total impact, even though it might involve a highly receptive and supportive group.

Knowing what motivates people to communicate is important

With the explosion of communication technology in recent decades has come an increasing awareness that most people have a number of choices about communication channels. As early as the 1970s, researchers had learned a great deal about why people use media and what they expect to find when they do use media. Researchers found that such motives as surveillance of one's environment, a desire to escape or simply to "kill time," or the need to be entertained could be used by different individuals to explain reading the same newspaper item.

Television has the potential to reach large audiences, with more and more specialized programming opportunities afforded by expanding cable systems.

The motives also are likely to differ by age or level of maturation. A young child watches a television commercial because of its bright colors, fast motion, and music. An older child watches the same advertisement to see an irresistible product he or she simply must have. An adult tunes in to the commercial to see how an advertiser tries to persuade people to buy a product they might not need.

Which medium is best for the following purposes?

• To keep up with the way the government is doing its job? newspapers, magazines, commercial and public TV.

• To kill time? Commercial TV, magazines, radio, recorded music.

• To learn about myself? Friends, books.

• To obtain information about daily life? Newspapers, friends, magazines, books.

• To overcome loneliness? Friends, recorded music, radio.

• To get to know the quality of our leaders? Newspapers, public TV, magazines.

• To be entertained? Recorded music, film, radio.

• To feel I'm involved in important events? None best.

• To release tension? Recorded music, radio, friends, film.

• To get away from usual cares and problems? Film, recorded music, friends, books, radio.

Most of the time, people seek out media or interpersonal sources of information for entertainment, not to solve a particular problem. However, research shows that about 90 percent of adults conduct at least one learning project each year, spending anywhere from seven to 100 hours on the effort. The average adult conducts five learning projects in a year. This tells us that when people do have specific problems or interests, they are willing to seek out a considerable amount of information on topics of interest from many different sources.

Another aspect of motives for using media has to do with characteristics of media channels. Research shows that certain media are preferred for specific types of information. For example, newspapers, magazines, and television are the media of choice to keep up with government news. To kill time, commercial television, magazines, radio, and recorded music are most likely to be chosen. This suggests that certain media may have an advantage in meeting specific information needs, either because of the nature of the medium or because of expectations people have developed about what they will find in a particular medium.

Radio is among the most flexible media, and typically is readily available to communicators who need to repeat their messages through a variety of channels.

Clearly, all members of a communicator's audience do not have the same motivations when they choose to use media or engage in interpersonal communications. But to the extent that a communicator can anticipate people's motives, he or she can be more effective by supplying what is needed. Educators have long talked about finding the "teachable moment." Audiences are most interested in problems of domestic violence at the height of media coverage of a case involving celebrities and want to know about planting a garden when beautiful spring days arrive. If different motives and needs among audience members can be identified, media can be tailored more closely to their varying needs.

For example, a 1991 study of farmers' sources of information about environmental issues showed a preference for field demonstrations and meetings. The reason? Complex environmental rules and regulations may affect different farmers in different ways. Field demonstrations and meetings allow for two-way communication, in which individuals can frame questions in terms of their own respective situations.

On the whole, studies of extension audiences reveal that printed materials are their best source of information. This may be because the bulk of resources have been spent in the past on this medium. But, in part, it also may be that printed materials are sought out by people because they expect this medium to provide answers. They may not have the same expectations of radio or television, even though those media could carry the same information.

Information seeking is additive, not substitutive

A well-worn saying about media selection, when considering new ideas and practices, is that mass media are most useful to make people aware of new ideas and give them information about those new practices, but interpersonal communication channels are most important when evaluating a new practice or making a decision. The practical recommendation has been to use mass media in the early stages, and then switch to interpersonal channels. Recent adoption-diffusion research and re-analysis of older studies indicate that this saying needs to be modified.

Newer research suggests that when people are just beginning to hear about a new practice, they do not seek much information actively about it. If mass media carry the message, they likely will hear about it from these sources. If friends know, they will learn interpersonally. As a person learns more about an innovation and becomes seriously interested in the possibility of adoption, information-seeking tends to increase across all channels. That is, people tend to talk to friends, listen to media, and read all they can about it. Mass media's highest use comes at this point, as does the highest level of interpersonal communication. Thus, the use of media and interpersonal sources is additive across the adoption process, rather than substitutive (with one medium being the best at one point in time and other media preferred at other times).

What this means for communicators is that rather than using the mass media only to make people aware, they might assign media a continuing role across the adoption process. The medium you choose to make people aware of a new idea should depend on how the local communication system works.

In Silicon Valley, for example, most people first learned about computers from other people, rather than mass media. This may be because computers were such an important part of the business and lifestyle of the region. For hybrid seed corn, the mass media were the first source for most farmers. But no matter how people first learn about a new idea or innovation, once they become interested, they will search for relevant information from any available channel. Information providers should be prepared to flood both mass media and interpersonal channels with information once an audience is interested.

Research also shows that at least for complex innovations such as computers, information seeking of all types continues at a high level after adoption has occurred. The same post-adoption need for information probably occurs in areas such as nutrition. Once a person has been convinced to alter his or her diet to improve health, there will be a high future need for information on nutrition. Thus, communication planners should consider the need to allocate substantial communication resources to post-adoption needs.

No set order to bring about change

We often imagine that if we want to change people's agricultural, health, or other practices, we must start by giving them information that causes them to have positive attitudes about the change and that this results in a change in behavior. However, research suggests that any of these three − knowledge, attitudes, or behavior − may occur first. Psychologists have found that if one could change people's behavior, they would come to believe that what they were doing was right (behavior first, then information and attitudes). A study of farmers' adoption of computers in the 1980s showed that farmers tended to seek information first, then change behavior, and finally readjust attitudes (positively) to match what they had done.

Printed matter still is preferred by extension audiences, who count on print material as a reliable source of information.

The implication? Depending on the communicator's situation, flexibility is possible in bringing about change. When a communicator can change behavior directly (for example, by getting people to eat new foods at a demonstration), interest in information and attitude change may follow. In other situations, information may be delivered first. Changing attitudes, according to research, is generally a difficult process, although one can take advantage of attitudes that already are formed to encourage information seeking or changes in behavior.

Communicators also must be keenly aware of the importance of societal or community values as they relate to change. Group norms may make individuals resistant to innovations or new ideas.

Learning information is often a group activity

While most communication models tend to assume one "sender" talking to one "receiver," it is common that other people and groups are involved. For example, when a family makes a decision about buying an expensive new car or about developing new eating habits, it is unlikely that one person makes the decision alone. A rather complex chain of communication messages is likely to occur.

Thus, communicators should consider whether a persuasive message is likely to result in communication among several individuals. Sometimes, the interrelationships that result are surprising.

Exhibits, particularly when they can be staffed, are a good way to provide highly technical information.

Nutritional communicators, for example, had focused on reaching the wife in a family, since they assumed she traditionally took on the role of cook. However, research showed it was the husband's nutritional knowledge, not the wife's, that made the difference in the family's overall nutritional pattern.

Why? They found that the wife was serving foods she knew her husband would like. If he practiced good nutritional habits and ate a variety of nutritional foods, the family would have a good level of nutrition. If his nutritional knowledge was limited, however, and he ate only a few foods, the wife would not serve other foods even though she knew they would be good for the family. From a communication point of view, failure to reach the husband as well as the wife doomed much effort to failure.

Research in decision making within families supports the common observation that even in cases where one spouse makes a decision, he or she is likely to talk about it with the other spouse. Even an individual activity such as reading a newspaper, when placed in a household context, becomes a shared venture. Whether a person reads a given newspaper article may depend not only upon the individual's interest, but also upon his or her knowledge that the spouse will be interested. Similarly, studies of television viewing also support the common experience that what one member of the household is interested in influences what others watch.

This research tells communication planners they need to consider who the important targets for information are, and how those target individuals are likely to interact (or not interact) with others. In nutritional information campaigns, for instance, efforts have been made to design communication components to encourage interaction and discussion by couples. This can be as simple as requiring both spouses to fill out questionnaires or track diet over time.

Even when you don't communicate, you do

There are two elements to a message. First, there are the words or pictures that are used. Second, and less obvious, are the unstated "rules" that go along with any message about how that message is to be valued and interpreted. For example, a large newspaper headline means "important story." Similarly, when a teacher puts a transparency up on a projector, its content is seen as a major point (students begin taking notes).

Imagine a large green interstate highway road sign that says, "Please disregard this sign." The message is to pay no attention to the sign, but the sign itself is based on the unstated communication rule that says, "Big signs are important." This idea of rules about communication has been subject to research that makes a vital point: In any communication situation, but especially in interpersonal situations, how a person says something may be as important as or more important than what he or she actually says. Some refer to this as "nonverbal" communication. However, the fact that we develop "rules" about such behavior suggests that it is something more.

Research centering on the communication process often concerns these "rules." Studies about television, for example, suggest that technical editing, graphic display techniques, panning, or cutting from one part of an interview to another may mean one thing to a journalist and quite another to audience members. To the journalist, cutting from one point in an interview to another is a necessary technique to focus a response. To a viewer, however, the perception may be that what was seen was the entire interview.

Likewise, a young child does not recognize what part of a television segment is a commercial and what part is program. The child has not yet learned the "rules" surrounding the advertisement – a sudden change in music, a change in who is portrayed, etc. Even the words, "We'll return to 'X' after these messages," may not be enough.

Newspapers are not immune to this confusion, either. While a journalist knows that an editorial is the reasoned opinion of the editorial board of a newspaper, many readers believe letters to the editor, columns, and editorials to be the same thing.

These differences in perceptions and comprehension of rules generally can be found between professionals of any type and the audiences they serve. When the communicators and audiences are of different cultural, age, or gender groups, the probabilities of miscommunication due to different understanding of the rules increase.

Although communicators commonly pretest messages to see if they are clear, they less often consider how audiences perceive the rules governing communication channels. Given the increasing diversity of available channels as well as of audiences, understanding what people expect from them is becoming more important.

New communication technologies pose difficult problems for communicators

As communicators moved into the 1990s, they could hardly avoid a perception that they were caught up in a new technological revolution. Those who made full use of the new technologies, it appeared, might reap gratifying successes. Those who failed to comprehend all the new possibilities might be left behind. The new technologies seemed to dominate the communication workplace. Videocassette recorders, satellite receiving dishes, teletext, videotex, CD-ROM, electronic mail, and the microcomputer became common tools of the modern communication society. Modems delivered copy to far-flung media terminals, while advances in both software and hardware paved the way to easy manipulation of graphics as well as their integration with text. Simple remote control units in the hands of viewers made it much more challenging for television programers to retain stable audiences. And few among us would predict that the pace of technological advances is likely to slow down much in the foreseeable future.

But communicators never must lose sight of one fact: Communication is a human activity. It begins and ends with people. Everything that comes between merely facilitates – or hinders – the process.

The technologies are tools that, used appropriately, can make communicators' work easier and more effective. Tools both affect and are affected by the society into which they are introduced. Some of the ways in which the new technological tools affect communicators have nothing to do with the messages they carry.

One major effect of television and computers, for example, has been that adopters of these technologies get less sleep than they did before. Many of the effects are complex and somewhat contradictory.

Television is an impersonal mass medium, broadcasting the same message to millions. Yet studies show that this same medium often finds itself listed as a "companion" sitting across the viewer's dinner table.

The microchip that frustrates ATM bank card users when the machine refuses to do their bidding is the same chip that lets children discover themselves in the world of interactive computing. Likewise, digital technology that enhances graphic capabilities can be used to alter photographs in deceptive and unethical ways.

The new communication technologies have not replaced the old. Just as radio did not replace newspapers and television did not replace radio, electronic mail through computer networks has not replaced the telephone. And satellite receiving dishes and sophisticated teleconferencing systems may never replace face-to-face meetings. New media struggle to find a niche, while older media adjust and have their uses redefined.

Typically, when new communication technologies are introduced, futurists talk enthusiastically about their vast potential. It was predicted, you may recall, that microcomputers would lead to "the paperless office of the future." During this early period, media are full of stories and examples of how the new technologies have been introduced and how they may improve communication.

Later, media coverage declines, and articles become more realistic about what the new technology can do. Computers have become vitally important, but they have increased rather than decreased the amount of office paperwork.

New technologies do pose some difficult problems for communicators. One problem has to do with equity. Those who already are informed best tend to be the first to have access to new communication channels nourished by advancing technology. Another problem is the sheer number of channels from which potential audiences have to choose.

In response to both of these challenges, communicators must be aware of the frequent need to package and send essentially the same message along a variety of channels – new and old. At the same time, however, they must be wary of spending too much of their time adapting and rewriting information for different channels and not enough time gathering and analyzing what is worth sending.

They must never lose sight of the fact that the information

they disseminate must be accurate and worthwhile, otherwise their credibility is open to question and they may have no reason for being. Technology, no matter how inviting, must not be allowed to compromise the reliability and effectiveness of information.

Communicators must remember that new technologies, almost always holding great promise, need to be tested over time. New tools don't always live up to expectations. In the worst instances, they may fail completely.

In the best instances, they still may require communicators to spend more time checking to make sure their information is being communicated and keeping themselves up to date on new systems being installed by information recipients.

Technological advancements hold wonderful promise to enhance the work of the communicator, even beyond the progress they assure most other segments of society. But they cannot replace the human being who creates the message, and they must not become crutches upon which communicators lean as substitutes for their individual commitment to responsibility.

Conclusion

The communicator who wants research information to help guide his or her work has a wealth of information on which to draw. The body of research knowledge about the communication process is large and growing. It can help the communicator understand how communication works and offer direction in communication planning and strategy decisions.

Research findings about messages, channels, and audiences are reported in a number of books that are available readily. New research conclusions are the subject of journal articles that appear almost daily.

The new communication technologies are changing the way in which communicators relate to audiences. The impact of expanding technologies will continue to be explored by researchers.

Research, like technology, cannot supplant the talent and dedication of the individual communicator. But it may help provide an advantage in a setting marked by increasing numbers of challenges and growing competition.

The Art of Good Writing

Writing is part of many communication media. And it's challenging for most people. Think of a scholar agonizing over a research paper as the publishing deadline nears; a reporter constructing a breaking story for the next news program; a person searching for the right words for an electronic mail message while the end of the business day approaches.

Putting together sentences and paragraphs that convey an easily understood message is an achievement. Doing it under time pressure is more remarkable. This is true whether you're preparing a get-well card for a friend, or writing a book or for newspapers, magazines, radio, television or the information superhighway.

Techniques for writing effectively do vary somewhat with the medium. For example, if you're writing a script for a video, you need to think visually. Words should complement visuals. Radio requires writing for the ear. This chapter focuses on writing for readers. But many of the principles apply to all mediums. Writing for viewers and listeners is covered in other chapters.

Who is your audience?

Many beginning writers make the mistake of not thinking enough about their audiences. In large part, you will succeed as a writer to the degree that you know your audiences' ages, occupations, educational and income levels, limitations, prejudices, interests and dislikes. Without this kind of information, you're like an inexperienced hiker wandering in a forest of tall redwoods without a compass.

This adage is worth remembering: "Readers fail to understand us when we fail to understand them."

Write for easy reading

Because your goal is to be understood, consider these ideas about easy-to-read writing.

Be conversational. Most people like this style. They don't care if you end a sentence with a preposition. You convey a clear message with common, everyday words. Everybody uses

contractions when speaking. Sprinkle them in your written messages and watch your writing spring to life.

Try short, familiar words. Two out of three words in the Gettysburg Address have one syllable. Only occasionally will longer words serve you better. Language expert Rudolph Flesch uses syllable counts to measure readability. His guide is worth repeating: 100 to 130 syllables per 100 words for easy reading, 131 to 160 for standard reading, 160 and above for difficult reading. Gauge a sample of your writing. Many who do are surprised to learn that they're writing well above the reading capability of many of their audiences.

Use personal words. You'll find a gold mine in "I," "you," "we" and other personal pronouns. Personal words involve readers. Syllable, word and sentence counts mean little if you aren't personal.

Use short sentences. People find them easier to read. The best average length is 17 words. That doesn't mean you should carefully meter out 17 words for every sentence. Your readers will get bored. It's okay to string out some sentences. But short sentences, or long, -keep the meaning clear.

Create short paragraphs. Long sentences and long paragraphs are a cure for insomnia. Good writing often comes in neat little paragraphs of two to four sentences.

Don't ask readers to unscramble your ideas. Place thoughts in logical order. State your major point in one sentence. Tell why it's important, then list other appropriate information.

Common grammatical pitfalls

Nobody expects you to know all the rules of grammar. But if you expect others to read what you write, and to respect your efforts, you must know some basics. Here are some common misuses of grammar. In each example, the first sentence is incorrect, the second correct.

Inconsistent or mixed tenses. "The farmer seeded oats in three fields and has plowed the back forty." "The farmer seeded oats in three fields and plowed the back forty."

"She is writing for working mothers and presented her information to meet their needs." "She writes for working mothers and presents her information to meet their needs."

"Mary walks outside, then started to weed the flowers." "Mary walked outside and started to weed the flowers."

Dangling modifier. "Coming over the hill, the building was seen." "Coming over the hill, she saw the building."

"To profit from a long meeting, the seats must be comfortable." "To profit from a long meeting, we need comfortable seats."

Repetition. "Market gardeners annually produce tons of fresh produce each year." "Market gardeners produce tons of fresh fruits and vegetables each year."

Redundancy. "Students evaluated the importance of the course." "Students evaluated the course."

"Beautiful hills and valleys add to the beauty of the area." "Hills and valleys make the area more beautiful."

Excess baggage. "The nursery owner blamed low rainfall and a lack of soil moisture for causing the poor landscapes." "The nursery owner blamed the drought for the poor landscapes."

Hem-hawing. "Apparently the test seemed to indicate the new battery was evidently defective at purchase." "The test showed the new battery may have been defective."

Circling. "The project all of the City Council selected was the downtown renovation project." "The City Council selected the downtown renovation project."

Back door approach. "This trip will not cost employees any money." "This trip is free to employees."

Words can't think for you

If words could do our thinking, writing would be simpler. But words are tools. Used correctly, they work for us. Used incorrectly, they work against us. Remember that most of us will skip over words we don't understand before we will reach for a dictionary.

One of our worst mistakes is using words that contribute little to our messages. These are lazy words, words that don't pay their way. Examples are forms of "there is."

"There has been an increase in the amount of pizza consumed by teenagers" contains several idle or lazy words. Shake out the lazy words and you get: "Teenagers are eating more pizza."

Few writers have sorted out idle words and used the precise words better than Mark Twain. He said that the difference between the right word and almost the right word is the same as the difference between lightning and the lightning bug.

Some forget-me-nots

Start well. Because you want to attract readers, make your first two or three sentences count. Give them oomph! Continue to engage your readers. Language analysts have found that most people who read would rather be doing something else. One bad paragraph can break the sometimes shaky engagement you have with a reader.

Make the declarative statement routine. "The declarative sentence ends in a period." is a declarative sentence.

Keep it simple. Avoid excessive mechanical roadblocks that cause readers to back up and restart. Commas, semicolons and colons should clarify, not confuse.

Trim the fat. Reject such sentence openers as "Needless to say..." and "Hopefully...." It's hard to kick the "unnecessary word" habit, but you can do it. Learn to spot obvious trimmers. For example, people don't "scream loudly" or "murmur quietly."

Look it up. In writing, ignorance isn't a sin. Laziness is. Keep a dictionary close by. You will know that "linage" means newspaper advertising space and "lineage" means your family tree.

Send up trial balloons. Let others read your copy. Don't fret if you hear, "I don't quite follow you," or, "This needs more work." Writers need thick hides.

Removing the fog

Wordiness causes problems for many writers. It can't be emphasized enough that trimmed prose is more palatable to readers. To improve wordy sentences study these examples and apply what you learn to your writing.

"The discussions became quite heated at times, which was an indication that members themselves determined the goals of their club."
Better: "Occasional heated discussions proved that members set their club's goals."

"There are many weaknesses in writing that can be detected if your material is carefully reread."
Better: "Rereading helps you detect your writing weaknesses." Removing the fog leaves a simple seven-word sentence.

"The horticulturist pointed out that the homeowners in his section of town wanted nice, green lawns but weren't willing to apply enough fertilizer needed to reach their goals."
Better: "The horticulturist said many local homeowners won't apply enough fertilizer to have good lawns." This cuts in half a 28-word sentence.

Too many prepositional phrases fog over a sentence, too:

"The essay contest is sponsored locally by the Central Electric Supply Company in cooperation with the Roberts County Extension Office."
Better: "The Central Electric Supply Company and Roberts County Extension Office sponsor the essay contest."

Good transition phrases help to clarify and to show readers the relationship between what they've read and are about to read. Examples are "Later that year," "After the game," "Despite that problem," and "Meanwhile, the other class...."

Stick with active voice

Don't use passive voice sentences as your mainstay style. They immediately tag you as a lazy writer. You can spot passive voice simply by watching for "am," "is," "was," "been," "are," "were" and "be." When such words serve as auxiliary verbs – "is featured" or "was liked" – you've got passive voice. Some examples of passive and active voices:

Passive: "An ordinance that extended swimming pool hours on Saturdays was passed today by the City Council after it was pressured by a group of parents."
Active: "Pressured by parents, the City Council today extended swimming pool hours on Saturdays."

Passive: "A scaled-down highway improvement plan was approved today by the State Legislature."
Active: "The State Legislature today scaled down the highway improvement plan."

Someone wrote that active voice sentences get attention and passive voice sentences get cold shoulders. An exaggeration, perhaps, but the active voice does strengthen writing.

Weak: "A wide range of learning experiences is provided under the guidance of a volunteer 4-H leader."
Strong: "Volunteers guide 4-H members through many learning experiences."

Weak: "The clothing drive for flood victims was conducted by the Business and Professional Women's Club."
Strong: "The Business and Professional Women's Club collected clothing for flood victims."

To improve, read about writing

Practice makes perfect. Well, that's not quite true in writing. No writer ever attains perfection. But gaining experience and reading what experts say can help any writer improve.

Writing for Newspapers and Magazines

News articles written by communicators at non-profit agencies, universities, businesses and public relations firms face special challenges. Those writers know that preparing good articles does not by itself assure use by major dailies. Big papers depend less on stringers and canned news and more on their own reporters and news wire services.

Electronic delivery makes a difference with some editors, however. Many agency, university, and organization news gatherers are using rapid delivery technology to reach the pages of big dailies, wire services, and some magazines. Some smaller weeklies may even use electronic delivery to minimize typing or keystroking. Weekly editors usually invite news from sources other than their own staffs.

Some basics

What is news? Many definitions exist, but Mitchell Charnley's in *Reporting* are among the better ones: "News is tomorrow's history done up in today's neat package.... News is the best record we have of the incredible meanness and the magnificent courage of man.... News is the timely, concise, and accurate report of an event; it is not the event itself."

News editors consider an item news if it is timely, has local interest, carries a sense of importance, involves conflict, is about progress (or lack of it), is unusual, or contains a human interest appeal. For a fuller discussion of news traits, consult Chapter 4, "Writing skills short course."

The lead. Learning to write a lead is important. Practice writing leads that use striking statements, quotations, questions, and other attention-getters. Readers sense enthusiasm in a writer and react accordingly.

After writing a one- or two-sentence lead, expand your article. Add facts or statements in descending order of interest and importance. This classic, inverted triangle news writing format is still the standard.

Be local. Editors may reject articles lacking local interest or impact. Almost any story idea you have can be localized, but it takes a little digging sometimes. Try to use local names, no matter what the topic. For example, let's say your subject is a new business marketing approach that is sweeping the country. An article about a local business person who uses the strategy to improve earnings and who reveals his or her secrets would please most editors.

Be correct. Get the facts and spell them correctly. Nothing is so embarrassing as an agency or organization release with poor spelling or an unchecked fact. If you have to guess on a name or a fact, hold the item until you're sure.

Be neat. Submit clean copy You have no excuse for sending marked up copy to an editor, especially if you use word processing. Correcting copy on computers is a snap.

Write tight. Before mailing the article, apply the imaginary scissors test: Will it make sense if it is cut from the bottom? Make sure the answer is yes.

Stay In touch. Maintaining good relationships with editors and reporters is important. Visit editors to learn what they want and when they want it.

Be local. Be correct. Be interesting. News editors consider an item news if it meets these and other criteria.

Advance and follow-up stories

Editors label news stories and features by several names: advance, follow-up, color, sidebar, interpretive, descriptive, and investigative. The advance and follow-up probably head your list.

Good advances and follow-ups take work and sometimes imagination. It is easy to give time, place, speakers, and topics in an advance. But you can't afford to rely on your readers to supply the interest without some help from you. A good advance has a built-in interest factor. Check these examples:

First lead – A meeting on crop marketing outlooks will be held Wednesday at 8 p.m. at Gordon High School. Interested parties are invited.

Second lead – Skidding commodity markets may attract several producers and local business people to Gordon High School Wednesday, when university economists peek into the future. The meeting starts at 8 p.m.

That's more like it. Both leads give facts, but only the second gives a reason for producers and local business people to attend. Stories about meetings need a "why" angle.

The educational payoff of a meeting may be in the follow-up article. You can remind those who attended of the highlights, reinforcing the learning process. A follow-up also reaches people who did not attend the marketing outlook meeting.

Don't start a follow-up article with attendance figures, or note that "an interesting time was had by all," or list speakers and their subjects. Instead, give the reader some useful information.

Did the economists predict better markets? Or did they see more of the same? You owe it to your reader and editor to follow through on coverage. Remember, by printing an advance, the editor saw this as a newsworthy event deserving additional coverage.

Features and columns

Features usually deal with people. They have a touch of the unusual, the unknown, or the unrecognized. These articles are excellent teaching tools when they focus on specific but unusual achievements or events.

Columns, on the other hand, are a journalistic hybrid – part article and part feature. They usually consist of reading material topped by a readily identifiable standing headline.

The feature. Look for people with interesting work or hobbies who are willing to talk. Their enthusiasm will shine through their words and will make your feature sparkle. Use direct quotations to dress up even a modest feature.

Interviews are key to features. Questions built around "how" or "why" attract better responses than do questions requiring only a "yes" or "no" answer. Search for human interest angles in feature writing. Nothing stirs heartstrings quite so

much. Probe beneath the surface. A writer once interviewing a couple asked, as an afterthought, about their children. Imagine her astonishment when she learned that all eight children had graduated from the same university. That made the story.

The column. The column can cover several short items or only one subject. Use the arrangement that seems to work for you. Editors generally have only one major requirement of a column – that it attracts readers and keeps a following in the paper. If readers ask for it when the editor goes a week without using it, the column has a home. One easy way to build readership is by printing names. Use them naturally so they fit in with the flow.

A column is a place for opinions. Most columnists can give personal views with no constraints except for the laws of libel, the dictates of good taste, and the willingness of the editor to print them. Educators, science writers, and public relations professionals, however, have much less freedom in column-writing.

Writing a weekly column is a commitment. The well can run dry. You may recognize at 2 p.m. on Monday that the column must be in the hands of the editors just two hours later, and you haven't written the first word.

To help prime your creative pump, keep a folder of ideas. File questions you get daily. Cut out articles. The contents of a new publication or a research result may deserve attention. Read unusual publications that deal with topics you don't normally bother with. Sometimes ideas come from strange sources.

Write your column as though you are writing a letter to a good friend or a favorite relative. This will give it personality.

Don't overlook fillers

Most newspapers carry small items at the bottom of some news columns. Editors call them fillers. Although not related to other items in the column, fillers serve a vital role. Page paste-up workers don't have to scurry for type to fill space that scheduled news items didn't occupy.

Newspaper syndication services, and commercial concerns, public relations, information and education offices provide fillers for publications. Brief sets of facts about programs and people in your organization will make excellent fillers.

Tailor-made and exclusive

You probably send news items to all magazines in your area. Yet, special occasions may dictate you send to just one magazine. This may be one that demands exclusivity. The key is learning what its editor wants.

If you plan to target an item to a certain editor, check in by telephone or through a personal visit first. The editor may suggest length and a story slant. That could save you the frustration of producing an article containing many unwanted words.

Some information offices mail out media alerts to call attention to a possible news story or to an upcoming event. If the idea of a tip sheet appeals to you, always include the names and phone number of persons to contact.

Whatever you can do to maintain contact with editors, do it. Editors may accept more items or suggestions from people they know.

Remember that you do not need to be a subject matter authority to produce an informative article. Don't let your lack of knowledge about a particular subject keep you from writing about it. Let your readers learn as you do.

When you use statistics, make sure they are correct. And then state them simply: "Three out of four people" is better than "74.6 percent of the population."

How to help a reporter get the story

Reporters are often imagined as all-seeing, all-knowing people who have a spiderweb of informants keeping them apprised of every new development. The truth is not quite that glamorous, but the best reporters do have networks of sources that tip them to good stories.

You can be one of those sources by understanding how the media work. As a communicator for a non-profit organization, you probably often function as a news middleman or liaison between your institution and the media.

Many reporters grow to rely upon credible communicators at universities and non-profit agencies almost like field correspondents. They count on their sources to keep them abreast of the latest trends and steer them to front-page stories. But the operative word here is *credible*.

How do you gain credibility with the media? First, by understanding what makes news. Second, by knowing what the media needs to deliver news to the public. And third, by using your imagination and creativity to find new ways of ensuring that the media knows about your organization.

Before establishing contacts with the media, it's also smart to be a good reporter within your own organization. Find out what kind of media profile your organization would like to pursue. What areas does the organization wish to highlight? Are members willing and able to be available to the press? How would the organization deal with the possibility of negative stories?

After you devise a plan for dealing with the media, you can develop ways to spread the word about your organization. Writing a news release and sending it to newspapers is still the most effective way of getting into the news network.

As stated before, computers link universities, public relations firms, and non-profit agencies to news associations such as the Associated Press. Since the Associated Press serves most newspapers, television, and radio stations, the wire service offers the most convenient and effective route to newspaper front pages and newscasts. But there are other ways of stimulating media interest that are often overlooked or underestimated.

Here's a list designed to win you a special place in a reporter's Rolodex:

Know your media gatekeepers. Know the editors, reporters, and news directors in your area. Read the newspapers, call newsrooms, and consult media directories to learn the reporters, editors, and news directors most likely to be interested in your organization. Remember to include reporters from cable television stations, newspaper and television editorial writers, and newspaper columnists. Some institutions hire a newspaper clipping service to clip articles mentioning their organization. A clipping service can help you gauge the effectiveness of news releases and also help learn which state and national reporters cover your organization.

Know who you are. You must know how to introduce your organization to the media. Don't assume that a reporter, editor, or news director knows enough about your organization. Send introductory letters accompanied by a business card and a brochure, pamphlet, or magazine describing your organization. One non-profit organization created a facts-at-a-glance sheet that describes the organization's mission to reporters. Other groups have drafted telephone directories listing organization members who are willing to serve as experts for the media. Tools like these serve as ice-breakers with new members of the media and updates for experienced reporters.

Respond promptly. Know the needs of the media. Answer all telephone calls promptly and know reporters' deadlines. More important, help them meet the deadlines. All reporters are attracted to a good story, but each has a somewhat different way of covering it. A newspaper or magazine reporter will generally interview sources in person or on the telephone, looking for photographic possibilities or statistics for an eye-catching piece of graphic art.

Know how to brief the media. The best way to be prepared for an onslaught of media interest is to have a written news release ready to give or send to reporters. That way, reporters can refer to the release when they are back at their keyboards. A written release ensures that your organization's view or version of events is clearly stated. Some organizations also offer a videotaped version of their news release to broadcast reporters. Others create press packets that include photographs, graphs, diagrams, and even artwork to accompany a news release. Aside from news releases, some institutions publish news tip sheets, which suggest ideas for feature stories to the media.

Be aware of trends and experts. Reporters have an endless need for experts able to answer their questions at a moment's notice, especially for in-depth and feature stories. Cultivate a reputation as a communicator who has access to the experts, and reporters will always know your telephone number.

For example, a flurry of articles about pesticides may prompt reporters to take a renewed interest in biological controls or natural alternatives to chemicals. Communicators at many universities have steered reporters to biocontrol experts, who have been quoted in articles across the country.

The best communicators know how to spot trends in the making. Better yet, they know how to generate compelling story ideas that showcase the expertise of their organization's members.

Know how and when to hold a news conference. The news conference is a tool for making news. The best time for a news conference is around 10 a.m., which is early enough to meet the deadlines of broadcast reporters and reporters from afternoon newspapers. But it's not too early for reporters for morning newspapers, who work late and don't usually arrive in their offices before 10 a.m. Make sure that chairs, handouts, and press packets are available for every reporter.

At many news conferences, the people meeting the media leave too early, before reporters have had enough time to digest their press packets and ask all their questions. A good news conference leaves reporters feeling stuffed with information and satisfied they will be able to write their stories with confidence. Don't leave them hungry for more.

Know all the ways to reach the media. Don't overlook opinion columns and letters to the editor as an effective way of publicizing your organization's views on a given issue. Columns and letters are effective ways to win column inches.

The care and handling of reporters

Much of successful writing for newspapers and magazines hinges on personal interaction between you and the editor. Many people approach a meeting with a reporter with all the trepidation they reserve for an encounter with their dentist. But an interview with a reporter doesn't have to be a messy, painful affair if you know some of the of following Do's and Don'ts for dealing with the media:

- Don't ask a reporter to go off-the-record. Requesting a reporter to withhold information is a risky proposition that can easily backfire. Assume the reporter is going to quote everything that is said; and make sure everyone knows that in advance.
- Don't ask a reporter for a copy of a story in advance. Some reporters will be insulted by this. What you can suggest diplomatically is that the subject of an interview would be happy to help the reporter check facts or answer any additional questions once a draft is written. Give the reporter business and even home telephone numbers to make calling back later easy.
- Don't assume the reporter is an expert. Start off simply with the basic premise of the story and gradually add on layers of information.

- Do treat the reporter with courtesy. It sounds corny and obvious, but manners go a long way with the media. Keep appointments with reporters and make them feel welcome. When members of your organization grant interviews to a reporter, they should try to be as forthcoming and informative as possible.
- Do ask the reporter about the story. Find out what angles the story will take and what visuals would enhance the article. Be willing to help a reporter reach and set up interviews with people in your organization.
- Do keep in contact with the media. But don't harass reporters with meaningless, "What can I do for you today?" telephone calls or visits. Cultivate a reputation that tells a reporter a compelling news story is waiting every time you call.

Writing Skills Short Course

Lesson 1: What is news?

News is a report of something new.

News depends upon:

Timeliness. Immediate or near the present – the first reason for a news story. Without timeliness a news story is either history or prediction.

Promimity. Close physically and/or psychologically to the audience and point of publication or broadcast. Editors prefer "local" stories.

Importance. How "big" and important is the idea, event, situation, or person.

News involves at least one of these factors.

Conflict. All kinds of struggles: man versus his environment, man versus man, etc.

Progress. Improvements made by man: research developments, better production methods, education, new equipment, improvements in living standards or human relations.

Unusualness. Rare, odd and sometimes unforeseen ideas, events or situations.

Human interest. Ideas, events, or situations which touch human emotions. Human interest events may arouse only casual curiosity, but they may incite anger or fear or elicit joy, sadness, compassion, or some other feeling.

Lesson 2: How do you report news?

Use the 5 Ws and an H!

(Who, what, where, when, why, how)

Who? Who said it? Who is it about?

What? What happened? Importance counts.

Where? Where did it happen? Remember proximity makes it news.

When? When did it happen? Remember timeliness.

Why? Why is it important? Remember proximity.

How? How did it happen? Was there anything unusual about it?

Make it readable

The best way to improve your writing readability is to use:

Short sentences. This is the best and easiest technique to improve readability. For today's mass audiences, news stories averaging less than 15 to 20 words per sentence are considered easy reading. Sentences longer than 30 words are usually difficult to understand. The best way to shorten sentences is to use periods. Lots of them. Close together. Punctuation––such as dashes and colons, also help to break long sentences into bites that are easier to swallow.

Short paragraphs. Keep paragraphs short. And vary their length from a few words to three to five average sentences. Remember, a 100-word paragraph looks quite long in a narrow newspaper column. Editors don't like them. Neither do readers.

Easy words. Use short, simple words in place of longer, many-syllable words with the same meaning. When a technical or difficult word must be used, explain it as simply as possible.

Personal words. Words like "you," "we," a name, a direct quote., give your copy more human interest. Admittedly, this kind of personalization is more often used in feature rather than hard news stories. But it is still a good technique for holding reader interest.

Active verbs. Active verbs keep a story moving and grab the reader more than "to be" verbs, which show little action.

Get to the point...fast!

Put the most important points first.

Most people whiz through newspapers, reading headlines and maybe the first paragraph or two of stories that catch their eye. So, get your important facts into the first paragraph; the first sentence is even better.

Editors chop stories to make them fit available space — usually from the bottom. So if you've got something essential to the story at the bottom of your copy, it might not make it into print. News writers usually use the <u>inverted pyramid</u> style

In otherwords, they place most important points first;
the second most important point next;
and so on, down to the
least important.

Lesson 4: Write a better sentence

Polish your style

There's always a better way to write it. Any time you rewrite something, you will probably improve it. Try your hand at simplifying words and phrases.

When you rewrite, try to shorten sentences and give them more action. In doing so, consider the context of your article. You may have a different "answer" than we do for the following because you thought of the sentence in a different context than we did. That doesn't mean you're wrong. But your sentence should be easier to read than the original. And it should contain an active verb.

Lesson 3: Style

Put one or more easy words in each blank.
(Possible answers follow.)

Note: Sometimes two simple words are better than one complex word.

deficiency _____   remainder_____

equivalent to _____   approximately_____

construct _____   illustrate _____

insufficient _____   beneficial _____

Empty phrases. Rid your writing of these cliches.

Change to something simpler.

so as to allow _____

make plans for _____

in order to _____

disposed of on the market _____

list a description of _____

are suspected of having _____

it is advisable to begin _____

more uniformly shaped _____

with the exception of _____

keep in mind _____

adjacent to _____

at the present time _____

Complex words: (Answers)

deficiency -- shortage, lack

remainder -- what's left, rest

equivalent to -- equal to, same as

approximately -- almost, about

construct - build

illustrate -- show

insufficient -- not enough

beneficial -- helpful, good

Empty phrases: (Answers)

so as to allow -- to allow

keep in mind - remember

make plans for -- plan

adjacent to -- next to, beside

in order to -- to

at the present time -- now

disposed of on the market -- sold

list a description of -- describe

are suspected of having -- might have

it is advisable to begin -- begin

more uniformly shaped -- alike

with the exception of -- except

Active verbs show action. You can find good examples on sports pages (hit, smash, ran, boot) and in recipes (mix, stir, baste, whip).

Rewrite the following sentences, simplifying them and using action verbs. Answers follow.

1. Example: **Poor**: Your consumption of milk should be a quart daily.

Better: Drink a quart of milk a day.

2. Poor: Strict adherence must be given to safety precautions when using these insecticides.

Better: _____

_____

3. Poor: Elimination of these pests calls for a strict insect control program.

Better: _____

_____

4. Poor: The right fertilizer must be used for high corn yields.

Better: _____

_____

5. Poor: Each pint carton should be labeled, and this label must be recorded on the information sheet for the laboratory.

Better: _____

_____

6. Poor: Evaporation of liquid takes place.

Better: _____

_____

7. Poor: When an application of wax is made to this surface a brilliance is imparted to it.

Better: _____

_____

8. Poor: When application of pressure is employed by the operator, the machine is activated.

Better: _____

Possible answers

2. Better: Observe safety precautions carefully when using these insecticides."

3. Better: Follow a strict control program to eliminate these pests.

4. Better: Use the right fertilizer for high corn yields.

5. Better: Label each pint carton and record it the laboratory information sheet.

6. Better: It dries.

7. Better: It shines when waxed.

8. Better: Push to start.

Lesson 5: Getting the facts

When writing a news story, make sure you have all the pertinent facts and that they are accurate. Think back to *who*, *what*, *where*, *when*, *why*, and *how*. Most news stories contain all of these. Sometimes you can omit one or more, such as *why* or *how*, if they are implied or already understood by your audience.

In the beginning...

The most important part of a news story is the first paragraph, the lead. It should contain the most important information in the story. Consider who, what, when, where, why and how when writing that first paragraph. Most leads contain more than one of these. Below are some examples of leads that feature at least one of the five Ws or the H in each, followed by one that contains all six elements.

Who: Dr. Norman E. Borlaug, 1970 Nobel Peace Prize winner, will speak Tuesday at the Memorial Union.

Why: To help more computer users boost their efficiency, the community college will be expanding the Computer Literacy Program.

How: Cooking meats in bags made of recycled paper can be toxic, warns a home economist.

What: Changing federal regulations in home health care are opening up new business opportunities in the Southeast.

When: May 6 is the deadline for Midtown's summer Little League baseball program, Columbia County Parks and Recreation officials announced today.

Where: From an oat field in southeast Michigan, the cereal leaf beetle has spread throughout most of the grain producing areas of the Midwest.

Who, What, When, Where, Why, and How:

       (who)   (how)

Midcity Mayor Georgia Smith announced her

 (what)   (when)

candidacy for governor Wednesday at a news

 (where)   (why)

conference in City Hall, saying she was "tired
of old-guard politics running the state."

Lesson 6: You're on your own

Okay, you've got the basics. Now write a news release from the facts given below. Remember, use short sentences, short paragraphs, and get to the point fast. Write for your local newspaper. Our version is in the next column. Don't peek before doing your story.

Think! What is most important to readers in your town: who, what, when, where, why, or how? Do not go on until you have written your release.

1. John R. Roberts is mayor of Metropolis.

2. The National Mayoral Association's (NMA) annual conference will be held next week.

3. Mayor Roberts will attend the National Mayoral Association's conference to report on the really neat utilities plan that your town has.

4. There are 2,300 members in NMA.

5. The utilities plan reduced your town's use of electricity by 50 percent last year.

6. The plan employs the use of solar collectors.

7. The NMA's conference is being held in Washington, D.C.

8. I.M. Incumbent is the president of the National Mayoral Association. He personally invited Mayor Roberts to the conference to talk about his plan on Thursday.

Now remember what we said about the inverted pyramid. Decide which things are most important, then get them into the story as quickly as possible. After you do your story, check your version with ours on this page.

NEWS RELEASE HEADING
(Name and address of your organization)

Contact: (Name)

             (Phone)   (Date)

RELEASE: Immediate

Roberts to report on utilities plan at mayors' conference

Mayor John R. Roberts will report on the Metropolis utilities plan at the National Mayoral Association's (NMA) annual conference Thursday in Washington, D.C.

Better: "I.M. Incumbent, president of the 2,300-number NMA, personally invited Mayor Roberts to make the presentation."

The Metropolis utilities plan, which uses solar collectors, reduced the city's use of electricity by 50 percent last year.

Note the release format above. The information at the top should show the editor where the release came from and where more information can be obtained. Leave two to three inches at the top for the editor to mark the copy for a headline, size of type, etc. Copy should be double spaced (actually, 1.5 is enough).

The most important facts in this story are *who* (Mayor Roberts) and *what* that person is going to do. This information should be in the first paragraph of your story.

Essentially, the information in our second and third paragraphs embellishes what appears in the first. You could reverse paragraphs two and three without being wrong. The main thing are to get all the essential information into your story and to get to the point as quickly as possible.

One other note: You'll notice we eliminated "really neat" from the description of the utilities plan. Expressing such an opinion is editorializing and is proper in a news story only when the comment can be attributed to someone, preferably by using a direct quote. As you read the news stories in this book or in newspapers, note the attribution ("Roberts said," "she claimed," etc.). A story containing editorial comments without attribution should never appear in a newspaper unless: (a)it's in a column (then the information can be directly attributed to the author of the column) or (b)it's on the editorial page (when the information is labeled as an editorial).

The meeting story

Routine meetings are easy to do, once you get the hang of it. You must get who, what, when, where, why, and how down on paper so your prospective meeting goer gets the message.

Try your hand at writing a routine meeting story from the following. Our version follows. Note: For the purpose of this exercise, you may save time by just inserting the words "program details" in your story where the information in No. 7 should appear.

1. The annual meeting of the Missouri Association of Consumers will be held Saturday (March 4) in Columbia, Mo.
2. This is a public meeting.
3. Registration is 9-9:30 a.m.
4. Registration is at the Flaming Pit Restaurant.
5. Cost of registration is $6.00. (That includes a noon lunch.)
6. At the meeting, media representatives will comment on their investigative reporting of consumer fraud.
7. The program is as follows: 9:30 a.m.–Panel on "Investigative Reporting in the Consumer Interest" moderated by Don Keough, Capital City correspondent for the Columbia Daily Tribune. Panel members will include media representatives from Missouri's major metropolitan areas.

   Noon–Luncheon address on legislative action by James L. Sullivan, director, Department of Consumer Affairs, Regulation and Licensing. After the address will be a presentation of the annual "Friend of the Consumer" Award. Last year's award went to James Mulvaney, then chairman of the Missouri Public Service Commission.

1:15 p.m. – Panel on "The Media's Responsibility to the Consumer." Panel moderator is Roy Fisher, former dean of the University of Missouri School of Journalism. Panel members are news and editorial writers and broadcasters who will comment then respond to consumers' questions.

8. The source of all this information is Mrs. Carolyn Leuthold, arrangements chairperson. She says, "It's a public meeting, and anyone who registers will have a chance to confront media representatives on consumer issues." She also says that anyone who wants to make an advance registration for the sessions can do so by writing to the Missouri Association of Consumers, Post Office Box 2353, Jefferson City, Missouri 65101, or by contacting her at 1501 Ross Street, Columbia, 65201 (Phone: 449-1358).

Joseph J. Marks
News Director

IMMEDIATE RELEASE
Mailed February 22

Media to rap with consumers on Saturday

COLUMBIA, Mo.- Media representatives will comment on their investigative reporting of consumer fraud, Saturday March 4, at the annual meeting of the Missouri Association of Consumers.

"It's a public meeting, and anyone who registers will have a chance to confront media representatives on consumer issues," said Carolyn Leuthold, arrangements chairperson.

Registration is 9-9:30 a.m. at the Flaming Pit Restaurant. Cost: $6 for registration and a noon lunch.

The program starts at 9:30 with a panel on "Investigative Reporting in the Consumer Interest" moderated by Don Keough, Capitol City correspondent for the Columbia Daily Tribune. Panel members will include media representatives from Missouri's major metropolitan areas.

James L. Sullivan, director, Department of Consumer Affairs, Regulation and Licensing, will deliver the luncheon address on legislative action.

Following his address will be a presentation of the annual "Friend of the Consumer" Award. Last year's award went to James Mulvaney, then chairman of the Missouri Public Service Commission.

At 1:15 p.m., Roy Fisher, former dean of the University of Missouri School of Journalism, will moderate a panel on "The Media's Responsibility to the Consumer." News and editorial writers and broadcasters will comment then respond to consumers' questions.

Advance registration for the sessions can be made through the Missouri Association of Consumers, Post Office Box 2353, Jefferson City, 65101, or by contacting Mrs. Leuthold, 1501 Ross St., Columbia, MO 65201 (Phone: 449-1358).

Note: In our meeting story, we include important news elements in the first paragraph then add details. Only the most interested persons will read beyond the first paragraph or even beyond the headline. By the way, it's not a bad idea to put a headline on your story when you submit it. Headline writers will probably have to change the headline to suit the space available, but including a tentative one is a quick way to tell the editor the essence of your story.

The award story

Names make news. And everyone likes a winner. Put those two facts together, and you have the award story.

These stories are quite easy to do. Once you figure out the system, you can literally "fill in the blanks" and do your own.

Check the following examples. With a few modifications, you can adapt the same format to almost any award story.

Morris named scholarship winner
(last name)

MIDTOWN, Mo. Patty Morris
                    (name of winner)

Vandalia, has been named winner of the Dennis Gallup
(hometown)

4-H Memorial Scholarship. Morris , daughter of Kenneth and
                                        (winners last name)

Gloria Morris, Route 2, was presented the scholarship,
     (parents names and address)

Wednesday, May 20, by the Missouri 4-H Foundation
     (day, date)

The scholarship was presented for her 4-H and
community activities during the last eight years.
                    (reasons)

The rest of the story details the winner's accomplishments and, may include, comments from the recipient on how the scholarship will be used.

(Name of County) County Scouts win state awards

MIDTOWN, Mo.–(Number, county) youths were among 124 Great River Council boy scouts presented Eagle Scout awards (Day, date and place)

Then, list the award winners along with their ages, their parents' names (if you have them), and their addresses. Generally, it is best to list each person in a separate paragraph. However, if you have more than one winner from the same town, you can put two or three in the same paragraph, providing this doesn't make the paragraph too long. It's a good idea to underline the names of towns to help the editor localize the story. For example:

Area award winners were:

John Jones, 16, son of T. Alvin and Julia Jones, 112 North St., Oakdale.

Don and Ron Davis, both 15, sons of Victoria Davis, 112 Woods St.; and Anthony Rossi, 15, son of Elvin and Eleanor Rossi, 112 Pine St., Firdale,

"The Eagle Scout Award is presented to fewer than one percent of Missouri's boy scouts each year," said H.H. Schwarts, Great River Council leader. "To win the award, the scout must have earned 24 merit badges, completed a community service project, spent at least three years in scouting and performed in a leadership capacity for at least six months."

The "how-to-do-it" story

Let's say you have a job like that of an extension specialist or some other community service person. You want to provide information in an appealing form.

First, let's see if it's appropriate to use the mass media to do this.

Think of your audience. If only a few people will be interested, you just as well might send them a letter, call them on the phone, send them an e-mail message, or have them come over to your house. If the audience is larger then you'll want to write a "how-to-do-it" story.

Consider what you want to tell this audience and how you can make the information appealing. Will this information save the readers time or money or make them happier or sexier?

Then, figure out how to address your audience as personally as possible. "You can save money by...", "Do-it-yourself auto mechanics can save time by..."

In the following example, an engineer is quoted. It is important that you attribute the information to a person, agency, etc., to give the information credibility.

Remember, be direct, personal, and appealing.

Insulate that water heater; save $15 - $30

BILLINGS, Montana–You can save $15 to $30 a year by putting a couple of inches of insulation around your hot water heater, claims Richard Phillips, Montana State University agricultural engineer.

"Most heaters have only about one inch of glass fiber insulation in their walls," says Phillips. "That's not enough to keep some of the heat in the tank from escaping."

Phillips recommends insulating with two-to-four-inch-thick unfaced glass fiber bats and securing them to the tank with tape or string.

"Insulation should be held in place firmly but not compressed when installed," he says.

Montana State University studies show that two inches of insulation will save about $25 a year on an 80-gallon tank; 4 inches, more than $30. Savings will run $15 to $20 annually if you put two or three inches of insulation around a 40-gallon tank, says Phillips.

Lesson 7: Be your own editor

Check your copy closely before you finally submit it for publication. If possible, have someone else check it too.

Listed below are some common grammatical mistakes. You can avoid most of these by following the KISS formula: "Keep It Simple, Stupid!" The less flowery the language the more likely you'll communicate effectively. And that's what this course is all about.

Common grammatical mistakes

Too many prepositional phrases.
Don't avoid these phrases completely, just remember too many make reading difficult. (Prepositions in the following example are in italics.)
Bad: The sales meeting was conducted *by* the sales manager *of* the company *in* the conference room.
Better: The company's sales manager conducted the sales meeting in the conference room.

Mixed tenses.
Wrong: He walked the dog and works with the horses.
Right: He walked the dog and worked with the horses. (Or: He walks the dog and works with the horses.)
Wrong: The women cleared their tables, grabbed their coats, and were going home.
Right: The women cleared their tables, grabbed their coats, and went home.

Dangling modifiers.
Wrong: Walking through the rows, the potato bushes nearly filled the rows.
Right: Walking through the rows, I noticed the potato bushes nearly filled the rows.
Wrong: To benefit fully from a long concert, the seats must be comfortable.
Right: To benefit fully from a long concert, you must have a comfortable seat.

Redundancy.
Wrong: Mary was wearing the same identical hat as Sue.
Right: Mary's hat was identical to Sue's.
Wrong: The two agencies cooperated together for a period of two weeks.
Right: The two agencies cooperated for two weeks.

Non-agreement.

This can be tricky. To check, think: Which one has correct noun-verb agreement?
Wrong: A bowl of apples, peaches, and bananas make a nice centerpiece.

Right: A <u>bowl</u> of apples, peaches, and bananas <u>makes</u> a nice centerpiece.
Wrong: Which one of the following sentences have correct noun-verb agreement?
Right: Which <u>one</u> of the following sentences <u>has</u> correct noun-verb agreement?

Careless repetition.
Wrong: You want to emphasize a point, so you repeat it, using different words for emphasis.
Right: You want to emphasize a point, so you repeat it using different words.

Mixed construction or faulty parallelism. Check for this in a series with elements compared and contrasted.
Wrong: We were told to write in ink, that we should use only one side of the paper, and we should endorse our papers properly.
Right: We were told to write in ink, to use only one side of the paper, and to endorse our papers properly.

Lesson 8: Writing features

A good feature writer is imaginative, curious, nosey, attentive, unconventional, witty, and is usually not above "borrowing" a good writing idea from someone else.

He or she does a good job of digging out information then is clever enough to twist even dull data into interesting and sometimes amusing prose.

What is a feature?

A feature differs from straight news in one respect—its intent. A news story provides information about an event, idea, or situation. The feature does a bit more. It also may interpret or add depth and color to the news, instruct, or entertain.

How to write It

The feature usually doesn't follow the inverted pyramid style of the news story. In fact, the hard-news-story lead based on one of the five Ws (who, what, when, where, why) or the H (how) is seldom appropriate for a feature story. The feature lead "sets the stage" for the story and generally cannot stand alone. A feature lead must interest the reader. It's the "grabber" that gets the reader into the story and keeps him or her going.

Many rules for news writing do apply to feature writing: short sentences, easy words, personal words, active verbs. But feature stories can be more fun to write because you can be more creative.

When the feature?

A feature is a better alternative than a news story when you want to accomplish one of the purposes cited above. When educational material is hard to swallow, a feature can be the "spoonful of sugar that helps the medicine go down." Remember, features are generally longer than news stories. Make sure the editor will give you the space for one before you write it.

What makes a feature go?

"Easy" writing makes for easy reading. That means short sentences, simple words, active verbs, and personal words, plus:

Transitions: So the article always keeps moving forward. They are used to add to, illustrate or extend a point.

They usually begin with words like "and," "also," "or," "nor," "moreover," "along with," etc.

They summarize: "at last," "so," "finally."

They link cause and effect: "as a result," "that produced," "consequently."

They refer back: "they", "those," "these," "that," "few," "who," "whom," "except for."

They restrict and qualify: "provided," "but," "however," "in case," "unless," "only if."

Interest-building devices: Personalize the people you are writing about and what they are doing: quote human interest words.

"Kicker": While the lead or "grabber" at the beginning gets the reader into a story, the kicker at the end of a feature should have a punchline that helps the reader remember the story.

Test your features

Write features and get opinions from others, especially editors. Check the feature below for style and feature writing devices.

> **She "saw" the way**
>
> Barbara Snell, 8, awoke in her back bedroom with the heavy smell of smoke around her. She knew she could find her way to safety, but could her mother and brother?
>
> Barbara awakened her 12-year-old brother, Paul. Then she hurried through the dense smoke to her mother's bedroom, keeping her brother close to her side.

> Mrs. Snell roused herself, groggy from the smoke. She started for the door she thought led outside. It was the door to the bathroom.
>
> "This way," cried Barbara, as she led her mother and brother to safety.
>
> She had no trouble finding her way. Barbara Snell is blind.

The feature thinking/writing process

Feature stories start in the mind. You have something you want to tell others. You would like to make it at least as interesting to your readers as it is to you.

Imagine this: You are asked to teach feature writing to people with little or no formal background in writing. You want to give them some personal examples close to their field. You begin searching through their regularly produced newsletters that they have brought to class as examples.

Mostly you find straight information summarized from university or agency publications then up pops an item that hits your eye immediately. My goodness! There are human interest words like "I" and "my" in the item. You know instantly that a feature can't be far away.

Study the original newsletter item . After you read the material in the box, look at some of the alternate leads that can be developed for writing the feature story. The end product follows. No Pulitzer Prize winner, but it has more effect on readers than a straightforward, "You-should-be-careful-of-kitchen-fires-because" story.

> (Original newsletter item)
>
> I'm reluctant to admit it, but last Thursday, I had my first kitchen fire. Although the fire was small and easily extinguished, the experience was frightening and certainly carried several messages that we all know well and need to review for our own safety. Of course one is controlling heat and keeping a check on the cooking process. When attention is diverted, it may be only for a moment, but that moment can be disastrous.
>
> In my experience, I was amazed at the voluminous amount of smoke from three strips of bacon. I made the error of removing the lid and, believe me, the smoke was excruciating and promptly resulted in a coughing siege and irritation in the throat.
>
> I could go on, but I did want to share some of the experience as a reminder to us that a home safety program can be an important part of our total housing program. Dave Baker, extension agricultural engineer and safety specialist, is an excellent resource person. I was interested that he indicated there was no good method of putting out a

fire such as mine, but had I carried the skillet with the lid on to the out-of-doors, I would have had less of a smoke problem.

From: Lois M. Deneke
State housing and
interior design specialist
Lincoln University

P.S. Dave Baker says the best bet for keeping kitchen fires from getting out of control is to have a multi-purpose or chemical extinguisher handy. Baking soda works, too, especially on grease fires. If a fire occurs in a pan, says Dave, put the lid on. If a fire starts in the oven, close the oven door, and turn off the gas or electricity. Open a door or window and use a fan to draw smoke out of the house. The vent fan above the stove can be helpful, too. Act fast and, above all, don't panic.

Now, here are some alternate leads from the above.

They say nothing teaches like experience. But in Lois Deneke's case, the lesson was almost too hot to handle.

or

It's amazing what three strips in the kitchen will do, especially if the strips are bacon — and they catch on fire. It all began when . . .

Now observe the original information in the form of a new feature article:

Homemaker Has Hot Time

Lois Deneke had a hot time in her kitchen last week.

She was pretty "smoked up" at what happened then. But now she's cool and ready to share her experience with those who suddenly find themselves in a spot too hot to handle.

You see, Lois is a state housing and interior design specialist with Lincoln University. One of her jobs is to design homes to be safe and convenient. But she got a firsthand lesson in safety last Thursday when she experienced her first kitchen fire.

"The fire was small and easily extinguished," she said.

But I was amazed at the amount of smoke from three strips of bacon!

"I made the error of removing the lid and, believe me, the smoke was awful! I ended up having a coughing siege and a sore throat."

Because of what happened, Lois contacted Dave Baker, extension agricultural engineer and safety specialist at the University of Missouri-Columbia, to find out the best way to handle kitchen fires.

"I was interested to learn that there was no good method of putting out a fire such as mine," said Lois. "But had I carried the skillet with the lid on out-of-doors, I could have had less of a smoke problem."

She said Dave Baker's advice is:

—Keep a multi-purpose dry chemical fire extinguisher handy (or at least a good supply of baking soda).

—If fire starts in a pan, put the lid on, if you can.

—If the fire is in the oven, shut the door and shut off the gas or electricity

—Take care of the smoke.

"You'll just have to fan it out," Dave told Lois. "You can do that by opening a door or window and using a fan to draw the smoke out of the house. The vent fan above the stove can help remove smoke."

Dave said it's important to act fast and not to panic.

In other words...in case of fire, stay cool!

Lesson 9: Keep on writing!

The best way to test your skill as a feature writer is to write feature stories. Then get opinions from readers and writers. Note the writing techniques used in the following.

He hob nobs with the best of corn'n cobs

COLUMBIA, Mo.—If you'd like to hobnob with corncobs, or find the world's toughest cornstalk, or breed your own corn hybrid, see Marcus Zuber.

The University of Missouri-Columbia agronomy professor, one of the world's leading corn breeders, has added four more inbred lines to his list of "specialty corns."

That gives him 43 lines. Count 'em...43.

One of his earlier lines, Mo17, is the parent of corn hybrids that account for one-seventh of all the corn grown in the United States.

Geneticists say developing hybrids is child's play compared to developing an inbred line. Inbred lines are the basic blocks from which breeders build better plants.

Of Zuber's 43 lines, 30 are "specialty corns."

Some are high in lysine, the amino acid essential for animal and human growth.

Some are high in amylose, the starch used for making film and similar products.

Some are "high waxy types" and contain a paste used in making adhesives.

Some are known for their stalk strength. Since 1960, Zuber has more than doubled the stalk strength of some of his corn hybrids, making them more resistant to lodging – so they won't topple and fall in bad weather. That lodging resistance could save farmers up to 25 percent in yield losses in some years.

And some of Zuber's corn gets puffed by hundreds each year. It ends up as corncob pipes.

See, all the corncob pipes in the world are produced in three factories in Missouri – two in Washington and one in St. Clair. They produce 25 to 30 million pipes annually, most from corn known for its cobs.

Zuber developed seven inbred lines and four hybrids especially for this industry.

"The pipe people like cobs with a minimum diameter of 1-7/8 inch, enough wood tissue to make a bowl," Zuber said. "They also want that wood free from fractures so it doesn't crack."

What with all the corn lines and hybrids he's developed and all the uses of corn, Marc Zuber's research touches millions of humans and animals each day.

And that's no pipe dream!

Publications

Even in an electronic age, publications remain a primary delivery system for information. Nothing has proven more user friendly than timely, well-written, well-designed, neatly produced publications.

Publications retain this favored position because there are times when you need to give specific instructions for reaching an objective, to provide more details than can be handled easily through other media, or to supply information for future reference.

Publications can accomplish these things with relative speed, comparatively low cost per contact, and the expectation of a good result. Studies show that audience penetration with a message is good and that readership and use of content are high when a publication is provided in response to a direct request for information.

Many of the polished publications seen today require a high degree of professional skill in writing, design, and production. It is possible, however, for someone with little experience to do a good job of producing simple publications.

This chapter will acquaint you with the major steps in the process and will provide simple guidelines to help you through them. When you prepare a publication from a manuscript, you move through these three major stages:

Planning. Consider the purpose, audience, message, and outline of the publication.

Writing. Decide on a basic style for the manuscript, draft it, rewrite it, then edit and polish it.

Production. Determine the format and design, prepare camera-ready copy or output, and print it.

Planning the publication

Planning is the thinking-through process that helps you organize your publication. Unfortunately, it is a step that often is passed over lightly or bypassed altogether, even though it has been proven to save time and money.

It is the time when you ask yourself these basic questions:
- Who is my audience?
- Who am I trying to reach?
- Why is a publication needed?
- What do I want my audience to learn from the publication?
- How can I best say what I want them to know?

If you successfully answer each of these questions in the planning stage, you will know who the audience is, understand your purpose for the publication, know what the message is, and have a master plan to follow as you write.

Audience

A time-honored maxim of communications is, "Know your audience." This emphasizes the need to think carefully about whom you want to reach.

To get to know the members of your audience better, write down as much information about them as you can. Include basic points such as their ages, genders, occupations, incomes, and places of residence. Also include how they think and feel and what they may need to know about the subject of your proposed publication. Too often, we don't communicate well because we write for ourselves or our co-workers instead of for a clearly defined audience.

Purpose

Publications are the workhorses of communication, but they may not be the best method to use every time you want to communicate a message.

The first step in the planning process is to determine which channel of communication will do the best job of getting your information to an audience. Several other chapters in this book discuss the merits of the various media.

Once you have determined that a publication is right for your use, try to define its purpose on paper. The ability tomake the purpose of the publication clear to yourself is a test of whether you will be able to make it clear to your readers.

It also is important to keep the purpose realistic and of manageable size. Don't set out to accomplish more than you comfortably can in the space of the publication. Remember that people say they are more likely to read publications that are short, simple, and to the point.

Message

Only when you know your audience can you decide what information is essential to achieving your purpose. The basic goal is to keep the message as short as possible without overlooking important facts.

Initially, list all the information your publication could cover. Then review the list and remove what your reader doesn't need to know or can get by without knowing right now. Check the list for points you can assume the reader knows already and cross these off too.

Look at the points remaining and ask yourself what facts or concepts the reader will need to learn in order to understand them. Add these, being sure that each will be clear to the reader as it stands. Missing links in information can play havoc with the reader's ability to use it.

At this step also consider whether some points you list can be made better with illustrations than with words.

The outline or master plan

A good outline can provide you with a master plan for your publication. While some people have negative feelings about outlining from their school days, it still is a vital step in publication planning. You must see the organization of your publication well enough to construct a clear outline if your reader is to see the message clearly too.

> **Here's what an outline does for you:**
> • keeps you organized, which helps your audience follow you better
> • saves time in writing
> • helps you stay focused on each point and ensures that you cover the important ones
> • keeps you from backtracking and from writing aimlessly

The form of the outline itself is of less importance than having one that is simple and is right for the subject, one that will result in a publication organized from the reader's viewpoint.

The strict rules for outlining you may have learned in school need not be applied to informal publications. Not all sections must be structured the same. It is acceptable, for example, for one section of the publication to have second-level headings and another to have none. Any section that has one subdivision, however, also should have at least a second one.

Simply put, publications have three basic parts: a beginning, a middle, and an end. Within this simple framework, the outline for each may vary, depending on the form you want the publication to take.

The outline may be sequential or chronological first-this, next-that order. It can be in a cause and effect order-here's-the-problem, here's-what-to-do, and here's-how-to-do-it. It also can be arranged in order of importance most-important-point-to-least-important-point, or vice versa.

Writing the publication

As you draft your manuscript, keep in mind that you are writing to be read. Your goal for the manuscript should be clear, simple, easy-to-read writing. Strive for an easy, conversational tone to help achieve this.

Often we hesitate to write in simple language because we think we may lose our audience. Research shows, however, that with well-written materials, just the opposite occurs. As reading levels go down, interest and comprehension go up for all groups. It is not simplicity that turns off the audience, but rather too little new information.

As an added point in favor of simplicity in writing, remember that such critically acclaimed and popular writers as John Steinbeck and Ernest Hemingway wrote on the fourth- and fifth-grade levels.

Guides to simple writing

Sometimes we don't simplify our writing because we aren't sure how to go about it. These techniques may help you:

- Keep sentences short. While sentences should vary in length for the sake of variety and a natural rhythm, the average length should be only about 15 words.
- Work for greater clarity through the use of exact words.
- Choose simple forms over complex. A complex form often is important to clear expression, but in most cases complex ideas should be presented in simple terms. If you must use complex or technical words, find a way to explain them.
- Prefer the familiar word. Astute writers draw on large vocabularies only to give exact meaning to their work, never to impress.
- Avoid unnecessary words. Usually you can cut your work in half without affecting meaning and understanding. The "deadwood" can be edited out as you work toward a final draft.
- Use active verbs. They make your writing more readable by making it more interesting, livelier, and shorter.

Balanced treatment

As you write, be aware of the need to give fair, accurate, and balanced treatment of the sexes and minorities. Unless the information is specific to one sex or group, keep several guidelines in mind.

- Avoid man-words where substitutes can be used without making your writing awkward. For example, use *synthetic* instead of *manmade*, *human beings* instead of *mankind*, and *salespeople* instead of *salesmen*.
- Specify gender only where it serves a legitimate purpose. Rather than contend with the *he/she* or *him/her* dilemma, rewrite a sentence using the plural pronouns *they* or *them*.
- Treat both sexes as full participants in the action.
- Use job titles that fit both sexes equally well.
- Where illustrations show people in action, show them in non-stereotyped roles.
- Avoid using singular male pronouns as universal pronouns. Traditionally in English they have served to refer to either sex, but that usage is no longer accepted. For a thorough discussion of effective writing, see Chapters 3 and 4.

Producing the publication

Production of the publication encompasses the work that takes place after the manuscript is completed. It includes deciding on a format, designing the pages, preparing camera-ready copy, and printing or copying the publication.

Format

Format refers to the finished size of the publication and the number of columns per page. It also has to do with the typeface and paper used, the method of binding used, and the overall look of the publication.

> The finished size is governed by the content and the equipment on which the publication will be printed.
>
> - Is it to be primarily text or will it include illustrations that need special space consideration?
> - How many pages will it have?
> - Will it be delivered to the reader as a handout, sent in an envelope, or treated as a self-mailer?

In printing terms, a sheet of paper is different from a page. A sheet is a piece of paper that has two sides when not folded. A page is one side of a piece of paper. Therefore, a sheet of paper has two pages when not folded, and four pages when it is folded once.

An 8-1/2 by 11-inch sheet of paper is very functional, and many publications are printed on this size. Sheets usually are flat, though they can be folded in half to make 5-1/2 by 8-1/2 pages. Sometimes a 9 by 12-inch sheet is folded to create a 6 by 9 finished publication, or folded into thirds to form a 4 by 9-inch finished publication.

Depending on the size paper you select, you usually will use one, two, or three columns per page. An 8-1/2 by 11-inch page can handle any of these choices, but you should avoid a single column on this size because the lines of text would be too wide to be easily followed by the reader's eye. The maximum width visible by the eye is 1-3/4 to 2-1/4 inches; minimize the number of stops the eye must make as it travels across the page. If the paper is folded to become a 5-1/2 by 8-inch page, however, a single column could be the best solution.

Design

The quality of the information and clarity of presentation are of first importance in a publication. However, a well written and well edited publication is improved by good design. Problems with design often arise because the producer does not have a clear plan or becomes too ambitious.

Simplicity and consistency are keys to achieving easy-to-read pages that will attract and hold the reader's attention.

Designing a publication is like most things – there's a right way and a wrong way to do it.

Letting each page take its own shape and form is the wrong way. Giving each page a similar structure so that there is a sense of cohesion and character is the right way.

Grids

The use of a design tool called a grid can help you achieve simplicity and consistency. It also can save time and money and take the guesswork out of how your publication will look.

A grid is a means of organizing material using a pattern of horizontal and vertical lines that divide a page into uniform sections called modules or columns. Text and illustrations are fitted into these sections. The modules remain the same from page to page, making the layout of the publication consistent from one page to another.

Professional designers find that grids aid in the creative process and save time. Grids also can help the amateur more quickly achieve a neatly designed publication with a professional touch.

You can use standard graph paper as a basic sheet on which to construct a grid. Keep in mind that the more modules in the grid, the greater your freedom in design. The larger the modules, the less freedom you have in working within them.

Visualization

Earlier in the planning process, you considered the possibility of illustrations for the publication. In the design and layout steps, however, you get to the basics of visualizing specific points.

Using illustrations where possible often helps get your message across to the reader. Never add illustrations simply to "dress up" the publication; good visuals are always an integral part of the message itself.

The printing method you choose and the graphic skills or resources you have will influence the type of illustrations you use. Simple line drawings, charts, and graphs can be used with almost any printing method. They also can be produced faster and less expensively than photographs.

You can gather drawings from other publications or from commercial collections of ready-to-use drawings. Check local art-supply or book stores for other available clip-art books. Many companies also offer electronic clip-art. When you use art created by someone else, be sure to observe all copyright rules.

Charts or graphs should be simple. If you produce them yourself using a computer software program or if you draw them by hand, be sure lines are straight, letters are properly spaced, and the text is easy to read.

Even though equipment and staff constraints may dictate a simple approach to illustrating your publication, you still can display some parts of it in a different way to achieve a stronger visual sense.

One section of the text, for example, may lend itself to being "boxed" as a separate item. Simply make this text a bit narrower than the rest, add a heading and place, a box around the information. Lists also work well in boxes.

You might handle another section as a short article, or sidebar, which is related to the whole but is displayed under a separate title. A general publication on gardening, for example, might include a *sidebar* on annuals that perform best in your area.

In summary, here are six basic design pointers to guide you:

- Keep it simple, clean, and functional.
- Remember the audience you want to reach, the content of the publication, and how the publication will be distributed.
- Aim for a design that you or your staff can produce.
- Know the limitations of the printing equipment you'll use and stay within them.
- Limit the number of typefaces to avoid clutter. Your typesetter or your desktop publishing system may offer a variety, but a good standard to follow is to use one face for the text and another one in varying sizes for headings.
- Be consistent within the publication in column width, margins, spacing, headings, and illustration labels.

Type

A few fundamentals about type may be useful in preparing your manuscript for printing. The different types available are called "faces" and usually come in a range of sizes from 6 to 72 points (72 points equals an inch) and with a complete font in each size. A font is a full set of characters in any one size and style of type.

There is a wide array of typefaces today, each with individual characteristics that influence its readability and legibility.

Classes of type

Type falls into classifications such as *oldstyle* (Garamond), *modern* (Times), *sans serif* (Helvetica), and *script* (Commercial Script). The two classifications that may be most useful to you will be modern and sans serif.

Oldstyle and modern typefaces are based on ancient Roman inscriptions. They have endured over the centuries because they have a classic quality and high legibility. These typefaces are designed with a distinct contrast between thick and thin strokes of the letters. Letters also have *serifs*, thin "feet" or "tails," that finish the strokes. Their open, round design also adds to their readability. As a result they are a good choice for text.

The sans serif classification includes contemporary faces, many of which came into vogue in the 1970s. They have remained popular and successful for use in headings, smaller blocks of reading matter, and for posters and advertising. The letters have a clean, modern look with no serifs and little contrast in the thick and thin strokes of the letters.

While other classes of type have areas of special use, they are not good "text" faces and should be avoided in publications. Script, for example, is designed to look like handwriting. While it is traditionally used for formal invitations and announcements, the letters have little contrast in strokes and no serifs and seem to run together. Text letters such as Old English are designed to approximate the hand lettering of the early illuminated manuscripts. Use them sparingly in diplomas and certificates.

Some typefaces, particularly those widely used, have many variations in weight and style that together make up a "family" of type. For example, Helvetica, a popular sans serif face, is available in light, medium, bold, and extra bold versions. There also are italic, expanded, and condensed versions.

With these variations in a range of available sizes, you can prepare a publication that uses only one typeface, yet has the variety in weight and style needed to set off content effectively. If you want the variety of a second face, it could be used for headings.

For example, you can use a modern typeface such as Times for the text to provide good readability and legibility. You might use a larger, bolder sans serif face such as Helvetica for contrast and good visibility in the headings.

Methods of producing type

There are several methods of producing type. The three that may be most available to you are *typewriter* or strike-on composition, *desktop publishing* with a personal computer, and *typesetting* by a print shop.

Helvetica Light   Helvetica Regular   Helvetica Bold   Helvetica Italic

Some typefaces, especially those widely used, have a variety of weights and styles (called a "family"). These include light, regular, bold, and italic.

Electric typewriters can be used as simple typesetters to provide clean, even text or to prepare stencils for mimeographing. In combination with neatly applied press-on transfer or machine lettering for headings, the result can be quite acceptable. You also may want to purchase headline lettering from a local print shop.

Typesetting systems (phototypesetting) make use of three elements to produce type: a master character image, a light source, and a photo- or light-sensitive material. Most of these systems are found in print shops.

Many office computers are equipped with desktop publishing software to create near-typeset quality camera-ready pages. The integral parts of desktop publishing systems are a personal computer, word processing and/or page layout software, and a laser printer equipped with a page-description programming language called PostScript.

Guides for typesetting

If you don't have desktop publishing equipment and want to typeset your publication, you need to provide the text to a print shop. Work with the typesetters to learn if they want the text on disk in word processing files or on paper (even if you provide word processing files, include a copy of the text).

If you provide the information only on paper, you may find these pointers helpful.

- Type the information on standard 8-1/2 x 11-inch white paper.
- Double-space the copy and allow margins of at least 1-1/4 inch all around. Be sure to keep a copy in case the original is lost.
- Underline words in your manuscript only if you want them set in italic type. If you want to emphasize a word, draw a wavy line under the word or words and mark "bf" in the margin. It will then be set in boldface type for emphasis.
- Identify each manuscript page at the top with the title and page number.

- Number each sheet consecutively. After the last line on the last sheet, type "end."
- Make any corrections after the manuscript is typed above the line and in ink.

To keep costs as low as possible, carefully edit and double-check your manuscript before delivering it to the typesetter. Double check all facts and all spelling, punctuation, and capitalization. Typesetters must set copy as it is sent to them even though they may suspect that something is incorrect. You will be charged for changes to correct your mistakes.

You also will need to instruct the typesetter about specifics of your publication: the typeface and type size, the amount of leading (space) between lines of type, the width of the lines, how to indent paragraphs, and other points. The process of marking these instructions is called specifying the type instructions.

Ask your typesetter for instructions on how to mark the type specifications for the style you want.

If you are unable to prepare camera-ready copy in your office, a commercial typesetter is one option.

Basic formats for type

There are several basic formats for setting type. For example, you can set the text so it is justified (straight or "flush") on both the right and left sides. Or you can set the type so that it is flush on the left and "ragged" (uneven) on the right. Studies show that ragged right is more readable than justified text.

Both styles usually have indented paragraphs and use hyphenation as needed. Either modern or sans serif typefaces are used. Headings may be centered or may start at the left margin (flush left).

Layouts

If a typesetter is setting type and laying out pages for you, all you need to supply are the words, illustrations, and full-scale rough drawings (dummies) or an example of how you want the pages to look.

If you are producing camera-ready pages on a desktop publishing system or a typewriter, you only will need to give them to the printer numbered in the order they are to appear.

Offset printing or copier layout

When you print by the offset method or by photocopier, you need to prepare a ready-to-use "camera-ready" layout to make a printing plate or to photocopy. This involves deciding precisely where you want type, headings, and illustrations and aligning them on a sheet of white paper just as you want them to appear in the printed publication.

Artistic ability and special training are helpful but not essential to this process. Organization, neatness, a "good eye," and appropriate tools are essential.

Preparing camera-ready pages

A T-square, triangle, and masking tape are good tools for aligning your copy. If the paper isn't straight, your text won't be straight either. Use a T-square on the edge of a table. Tape the paper to the table after it is parallel to the T-square. Another solution is to use a clear plastic ruler with crosshatch markings; when you place the ruler over your copy you can see through it and align the copy with the markings.

Rubber cement or hot wax help prepare a smooth, wrinkle-free paste-up and allow you to move an item once you have placed it. Art supply shops have waxers that apply a coat of wax to the back of your paper. The wax then holds the copy in place on the layout page.

For simple publications, clear plastic (matte finish) tape may work equally well and is easier for many people to handle. You must be careful to apply it only on the edges of the paper, not over the type.

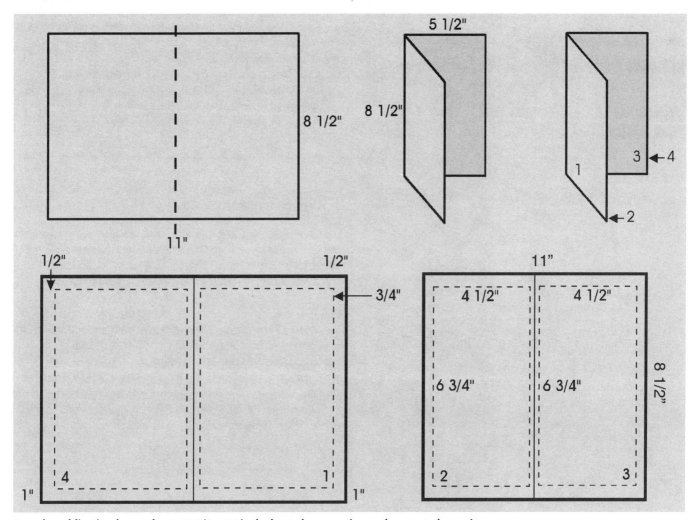

Sample publication layout for an 8 1/2 x 11-inch sheet shows paging and suggested margins.

Spacing and margins

Consistency is important in the spacing and margins of the publication, not only for appearance but for successful printing.

As a rule of thumb, the widest margin is always at the bottom of the page. Side and top margins may be alike, or the top margin may be a bit wider than the side margins. On facing pages, the inside margins (called the gutter) are narrower, but may need allowance for three-hole punching.

If you produce a four-page publication from an 8-1/2 by 11-inch sheet folded, the finished size of the publication will be 5-1/2 by 8-1/2 inches. You would treat the front and back pages (pages 1 and 4) as single pages and the inside pages (pages 2 and 3) as facing pages.

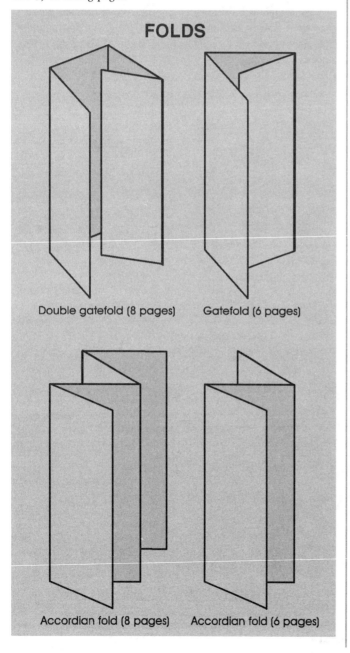

FOLDS

Double gatefold (8 pages)   Gatefold (6 pages)

Accordian fold (8 pages)   Accordian fold (6 pages)

The margins for pages 2 and 3 could be 1/2 inch at the inside edges (gutter), 3/4 inch at the top, 1/2 inch on the outside, and 1 inch at the bottom. All type and illustrations would be within an image area 4 1/2 inches wide by 6 3/4 inches deep proportionately, the same shape as the full page.

On pages 1 and 4, the outside margins could be 1/2 inch, the bottom margin 1 inch, and the top margin 3/4 inch. The top margin on page 1 might appear larger because you probably would use larger type for the title of the publication and allow extra space around it. If your type is prepared on a desktop publishing system or by a commercial printer, larger or contrasting headings can be created as a part of the typesetting process. If you rely on a typewriter, you will have to achieve these qualities by using all capitals, underlining the heads, or both.

A better solution might be to use rub-off (transfer) letters available in art supply stores or machine lettering if such a system is available to you.

If your illustrations are black-and-white line drawings, they may be cut and pasted on the layout sheet or drawn directly on the sheet.

Photographs are not pasted on the layout, but the space they are to occupy must be carefully indicated. Label the photos to correspond with the space assigned so that the printer can match up picture with location. Do not write on the back of the photo itself because this could damage the emulsion in a way that would show in the printed publication. If you provide photographs, write the caption on a label and tape it to the back of the photo. If you scan the photo, identify the file name and include it with your text files.

If you produce publications often, you may want to investigate courses in your community that cover design and layout.

Layouts for mimeographing

If you will be using a mimeograph machine to print your publication and you have an electronic stencil-maker available, prepare the layout much as you would for offset printing. The electronic stencil-maker scans each page and reproduces the light and dark areas on the stencil.

If you do not have such a machine, use a typewriter to cut the stencil. Type the copy exactly where and how you want it to appear on the page. You can either type in the headings or, with the use of a stylus and lettering guide available at a mimeograph or art supply shop, create larger, bolder headings for contrast.

Consult your mimeograph supplier for pointers on the most effective use of the equipment.

Printing the publication

The biggest expense in production is the cost of printing. You will want to know enough about the more frequently used processes to make an informed decision on the system to use (when there is a choice).

The methods most readily available probably will be offset printing, electrostatic (photo) copying, electronic laser printing, or mimeographing.

Offset presses can produce thousands of impressions per hour.

Offset presses

There are many types of offset presses, ranging from simple to sophisticated. They range from one color with limited numbers of impressions per plate to those that can handle multiple colors and produce thousands of impressions per hour.

All offset presses have inking and dampening systems and three printing cylinders the plate, blanket, and impression. The system operates on the principle that oil and water don't mix. The flexible plate with the image to be printed is clamped to the plate cylinder. When this cylinder rotates, it comes in contact with the dampening rollers, then the inking rollers. The dampeners wet the plate so the non-printing area will repel ink. The inked image is then transferred to the blanket cylinder, which "offsets" the image onto paper as it passes between the blanket and impression cylinders.

The offset method requires minimal preparation time, is adjustable to allow good alignment (register) of materials, and is flexible enough to handle a wide range of papers and ink colors.

The preparation of plates for offset presses includes "stripping" negatives.

The offset method requires minimal preparation time including touch-ups.

Copiers and laser printers

Photocopiers offer fast, convenient, and economical means of making multiple copies of a wide range of documents. They are used extensively in offices, in-house printing departments, and quick printing shops. Visit with the operators to learn about the equipment before preparing your publication.

Since 1960, the electrophotographic method of copying has dominated the copier scene. These copiers use electrophotographic coatings to produce the images in the copier. Such materials have the property of holding an electrostatic charge in the dark and losing the charge when exposed to light reflected from the white areas of an original layout. The image areas that remain charged are developed with an oppositely charged dry powder or liquid toner that is then fixed to paper by heat, pressure, or solvent vapor.

Electronic laser printers produce an original image, not a copy, from electronic images sent to the printer. Because many laser printers produce images at 300 or 600 dots-per-inch, they can reproduce black-and-white photos reasonably well. Some electronic laser printers also have the capability of scanning, storing, and printing from a camera-ready original.

Color copiers also are available, but generally are not meant for quantity reproduction.

Mimeograph and duplicators

Mimeograph machines and offset duplicators are old equipment but still used by some offices. A mimeograph machine uses a stencil made of thin, tough paper with a waxy coating that is "cut" using a typewriter. The stencil is fastened to the outside of a duplicator cylinder. Ink from inside the cylinder is pressed on the cylinder surface. As the paper moves through the machine it comes into contact with the stencil, and an image is transferred from stencil to paper.

Digital duplicators often resemble a photocopier. They often have several options, but frequently print on a variety of kinds and sizes of papers, use different colors of ink, and reproduce photographs. Some duplicators resemble small printing presses.

While many improvements have been made in mimeograph and duplicators, the quality of the products they print usually does not compare with those from offset presses, laser printers, or photocopiers.

Electronic laser copying offers fast, convenient, and economical means of making multiple copies.

Ink and paper

Selecting inks and papers is similar to buying paint. The choices seem almost endless. Papers are sold and labeled by weight and type – 60-pound offset, for example, or 20 - pound bond. At the economical end of the line are newsprint-like papers (newsprint itself, however, can be used only on a type of printing press called a web press). At the expensive end of the line are a wide variety of special paper stocks with many different finishes.

The basic decision on ink is whether to use one or more colors. In printing terms, single color means that only one color ink is used throughout the publication. It can be black or another color, though black or very dark colors are the most readable. In most cases, color ink costs more than black ink.

Process or four-color printing is used to reproduce color photographs. Because this uses four ink colors, the printer must make four negatives and four plates. The act of dividing a color photograph into four negatives is called color separating. When these four separations are printed together (yellow, magenta, cyan, and black), the illusion of full color is presented. Because printing of the four negatives is difficult (the images must align perfectly), it is an expensive process requiring sophisticated printing equipment.

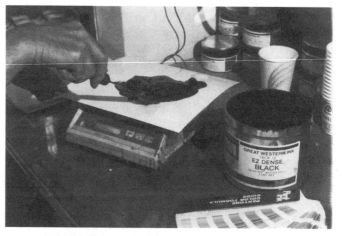

Selecting ink color is essential in the final stages of the offset printing process.

Ink usually is mixed according to a predetermined color formula guide. Work with your offset printer to select an ink color to enhance your publication.

You can create the illusion that more than one color of ink has been used by screening the single ink color to create several tones of the one color. If you're working with commercial printers, you can ask them to place a screen tint in front of your artwork or blocks of text when making the printing plate. This screen has a dot pattern representing a percentage of the darkness of the original art or text that you want. Keep in mind that tints of less than 10% tend to disappear when printed and tints of more than 70% tend to look solid.

If you're producing camera-ready copy with desktop publishing equipment, most software programs routinely provide screen tints. (You also can achieve this same effect by using rub-off pattern sheets on camera-ready pages.)

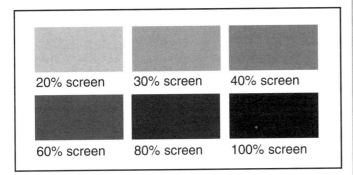

| 20% screen | 30% screen | 40% screen |
| 60% screen | 80% screen | 100% screen |

While using screens can dress up a publication, be sure the reproduction method handles the screen well. If you are preparing camera-ready copy from a laser printer, the dots usually are too close together to reproduce well. However, if you provide the printer with an electronic file for high-resolution output (such as 1200 dpi), the reproduction will be excellent.

Consult your printer about papers and inks for the publication, taking into account the equipment on which it will be printed. Their swatch books offer dozens of choices the paper and ink colors options to best suit your publication and your budget.

Newsletters

Nothing beats face-to-face communication. But a close second is the letter. It can be a warm, friendly, personal means of finding out information.

Those same characteristics can make the newsletter a valuable means of communication, too. Newsletters can keep us informed of such things as changes in company policy, job opportunities, and upcoming meetings. They can satisfy our curiosity about who is doing what, stroke our ego when we see our names in print, and provide humor and stimulation.

A newsletter also can provide income. Some people have gained fame and wealth through their newsletters. An entrepreneur who has the corner on some specialized type of information can make money selling that information in the form of a subscription newsletter. There appears to be no limit to the subjects – from how to enter recipe contests to tips for traveling around the world cheaply.

The looks and the form of newsletters keeps changing as more people become adept at desktop publishing and electronic, paperless ways to send messages. But the need for the newsletter remains strong.

Not all newsletters are perceived as vital, though. Many are either tossed away at first glance or banished to the "to-be-read-later" pile. However, with planning and commitment, your newsletter can avoid either fate.

Know your audience

The first step in planning a newsletter is too often overlooked: Know your audience. Who are they exactly? What are they interested in? What is their educational level? Age? Gender? What do they have in common?

People who do newsletters for profit have a pretty good handle on this knowledge, otherwise they wouldn't be able to sell their product.

But people who do newsletters for free sometimes get carried away with what they want to say rather than what the audience wants to read.

As a newsletter editor, you will have to devise a means for finding out about the audience. This may involve personal inquiry, surveys, focus groups, market research or all of the

above. This knowledge will determine how you write, select topics and put together your newsletter.

Define your purpose

After you have described your audience, the next step is to define your purpose. What is it that you want people to do after reading your newsletter? Think this through and commit your ideas in writing. This may help you sharpen your focus. The narrower the purpose, the better. For example, you may be planning a newsletter for the people who volunteer at a hospital. Your plan might look something like this:

<u>People who do volunteer work at Baton Rouge General Hospital</u>

- recognition for their work with generous use of photos and names

- inspiration through testimonials from staff and patients who have been helped

- information about the kind of volunteer work needed and what it will involve.

You might want to start a for-profit newsletter for people who are good at crafts and want to make money at it. Your audience and purpose might look like this:

<u>People in Louisiana who want to do a better job of marketing their crafts</u>

- dates, times and places of crafts shows in the state and region

- costs and commitment involved in different types of marketing strategies

- pricing information based on time involved in production

- first-hand accounts of mistakes and successes of artisans.

Another audience might be part-time farmers with small operations learning to use computers to make their record keeping and management more efficient:

<u>Part-time farmers with small operations</u>

- costs and features of computer equipment

- costs and features of software packages for small businesses

- success stories from farmers who implement computer-assisted management.

The more specific your purpose, the easier it will be to prepare your newsletter. Your mind becomes tuned in to bits of information that could make good articles. Make note of these in a file. Each time you go to put the newsletter together, all you have to do is dig in that file for the material and ideas you need.

Pick a format

Your audience and purpose will determine the frequency, length, and format of your newsletter. If your audience needs the information for monthly planning, then the frequency should be monthly. If the audience uses electronic mail and they need the information fast, then use an electronic format. If you want to impress your clients with the kind of work your company is doing, then you may want a slick publication with color photos sent out quarterly.

Newsletters tend to fall into three categories: bullet sheet, news/letter and the magaletter.

Bullet sheet. This type of newsletter, usually one page, front and back, includes short articles no more than a paragraph or two in length. There may or may not be headlines. The first few words of the article simply may be underlined or set in boldfaced type.

The bullet sheet is meant for a quick read of vital information. The reader wants the information quickly. Time is of the utmost importance.

This style works well for some electronic newsletters. As people scroll through the pages on their computer screen, they can grasp the information readily. Starting your electronic message with headlines is helpful. For example, Educom's "Edupage" newsletter starts out with a list of headlines called "Top Stories" and then follows with "Also" for another set of headlines. The newsletter then follows with the stories, none of which is usually more than a paragraph.

News/letter. This type of newsletter is a more complete, longer version of the bullet sheet. It usually involves an 11-inch by 17-inch sheet of paper folded to a four-page format. There is typically a long article on the front page, termed the "lead" article. This article will take up most of the space on the front page and may jump to an inside page.

There are regular features in the newsletter that may have the same headings, such as "From the President," "Job Openings" or "News Briefs," and appear in the same place every issue. For example, a calendar with events may always appear on the back page.

Magaletter. All newsletter publishers want their product to impress. But this type of newsletter is almost a magazine. The magaletter has fewer pages than a magazine, usually eight to 12, and shorter articles. But it includes full-color photos and illustrations and is usually printed on a high-quality slick paper. It also has regular features that are like "departments" in magazines that readers easily can turn to for specific types of information. For example, a newsletter for college alumni may include a department with alumni news listed by decades of graduation.

Writing for newsletters

Writing for a newsletter must be informative yet chatty. After all, it is a "letter" with "news." Think of it as writing to someone you know with the latest "scoop."

That does not mean it is any easier to write a newsletter than something else. It may be harder. You need to write to express your ideas in a clear, crisp, simple manner. You have to go back over your initial writing and edit to eliminate excess words and rephrase to streamline the flow. Space is a premium. Paper costs money, so you do not want to use any more of it than you have to. Time costs money, too. Your reader wants to get the message as quickly as possible, otherwise he or she will turn to some other item of business.

Take journalism to heart

Not only must you be a careful writer for your newsletter, but you also must be a good reporter. A journalistic approach to writing a newsletter is what you want. You must be methodical and precise in gathering your information. You must adopt these two premises of journalism:

Completeness. Get all the facts. Find out the answers to *who*, *what*, *when*, *why*, *where* and *how* – known as the five Ws and the H in journalism. Make sure your articles don't raise more questions than they answer.

To get the information you need, you will have to do research and interview people. This means you will have to call and visit people with a prepared set of questions. You may have only one chance to get the answers. The interviewee may not be available later when you are up against your publication deadline. You need to get it right the first time. Ask for more than you will actually use. It is always better to cut out information than to try and scramble later for more. As a back-up measure, be sure to check with the person you interview whether it is all right to call back and, if so, where this person might be reached.

Accuracy. Get all the facts straight. Make sure names are spelled correctly. Make sure you get the correct titles for people. If you have any questions as you read back over your copy, call the source and confirm the details. Your credibility and the credibility of your newsletter is at stake. If people cannot trust the information in your newsletter, they will stop reading it.

Write to be read fast

Start off with a bang. Don't beat around the bush. Get to the point. Newsletter articles don't need flowery introductions. So adopt the concise writing style of newspaper journalism.

Use the familiar and shorter word. Write to express, not impress. Why say "utilize" when "use" will do?

Write at a level slightly below what your audience is capable of reading. Readers appreciate this because reading goes faster, and this saves them time. Even such stellar publications as the *Wall Street Journal* don't exceed a high school reading level. Take the fog out of your writing by keeping your average sentence length between about 12 and 15 words and by cutting down on the number of words with three or more syllables.

Edit. Editing invariably improves writing. But it is difficult to edit your own words. You get attached to them and defensive about eliminating them. If possible, have at least one other person edit the copy for you. If you have no one else, let the copy sit over night. The next day you can go back and get rid of verbiage and clean up for clarity.

Headlines can make or break your newsletter

When people read a newsletter, what they really do is scan the headlines. Their eyes stop when something catches their attention. Write headlines that will arrest the eyes of your audience.

Writing good headlines can be a struggle. It may take more time than writing the article. But what you will find is that as you write the headline, you cut through to the essence of the article. You may then want to go back and rewrite the first part of the article. Headline writing helps you make the point as concisely as you can. Here are a few suggestions for good headline writing:

Snare those lively words. Verbs like "grab," "strike" and "stir" can attract attention. Stay away from static verbs like "is" and "are." Use attention-getting labels like "Hell and High Water" for your article on flood damage.

Keep the verbs in present tense. This is the style readers are used to in newspapers. Present tense usually takes up less precious space.

State what the article is about. Cleverness captures interest. But don't get so carried away that you deceive the reader. The headline should lure the reader and state the point of the article. For example, the headline of an article on how to write a good, concise resume was titled, "Don't let a resume cramp your file." This is a clever play on words yet tells, what the article was about.

Give the best articles the biggest headlines. When you look at a newspaper, the most important stories have the biggest headlines. Follow suit with your newsletter.

Use upper and lower case letters. It is difficult to read headlines in all caps, unless they are one or two words. Some designers choose a style that capitalizes the first word only in a headline.

Write about the right stuff

When you want tangible results from your newsletter, such as subscription sales, you are highly motivated to write about what your audience wants and needs. But if your newsletter is an information piece from an organization, you may fall into the trap of writing more about you than them. No matter what kind of newsletter you write, always think in terms of what will interest the audience. Think about these five needs that everybody has and which needs might be appropriate to appeal to with your newsletter:

People like recognition. Use names in your newsletter. People like to read about themselves first, then about people they know, and finally about people who are famous. Take advantage of that need. Incorporate names whenever you can. Offer examples of people who do the things you wish to promote in your newsletter. For example, an extension specialist in Missouri did a newsletter for people who sew professionally and those who want to develop this talent. In each issue she used the name of someone who had asked her a question or who had provided her with a valuable tip. Another Missouri extension specialist used the same technique in the newsletter he did for the farm families in his county. He would find farmers doing the kind of practices he wanted to promote and use their names.

People like to increase their wealth and save money. There's a bottom line to just about every venture. The whole purpose of your newsletter may be to help people make money. But, if not, your audience will appreciate any information you can provide that will help their financial situation.

For example, in a newsletter for farmers learning to use computers, you might want to include information about bargains on software. You might want to review software and suggest to them the programs that provide the most value for the least money.

People like to feel safe, secure, and healthy. Include safety or health information in an article or have a department on tips. Feature someone who has lost weight or somehow benefitted from a company health program, for example.

People like to save time. Just about everyone has far more to do than there are hours in the day. This is true especially of newsletter audiences. That's why they read newsletters. Easy-to-read tips on saving time can endear your newsletter to your readers. You might want to feature people who have enhanced their lives through time-management techniques.

People like to have fun. When authors approach their newsletter as a means to communicate with a friend, they are more likely to think of something funny to say every once in a while. And that is an ingredient lacking in too many publications – humor. If you can bring a smile to someone's face, you have won a friend. Add a little humor to your newsletter. Don't be so serious all the time. Write a clever headline. Include a poke-fun department. Pass on a funny situation that someone solved successfully.

One administrator wrote a newsletter for his staff and regularly included a "Turkey of the Month" feature in which he admitted some error. This endeared him to his readers.

You can have fun with the name of your newsletter, such as these newsletters did: "The Whale Street Journal" for the employees at San Diego's Sea World; "No Bull Udder Facts" for dairy farmers; "The Inner Sole" for the employees at a shoe factory.

Find out if anybody's reading

Even though you may be armed with a clear-cut audience and purpose, you are still not ready to launch a new newsletter until you have figured out an evaluation plan. You need to find out if anybody out there is reading you. Coming up with a plan before you start publishing will help assure that you stick to your audience and purpose and not get off track.

There are three levels of evaluation:

Level 1: Get feedback on a regular basis.

Write at least one article per issue that calls for some response from the reader. Examples might be:

- Include an order blank and ask readers to send in the names of acquaintances who might like to receive the newsletter.

- Publicize a publication you have in quantity and see how many requests you get because of the article.

- Solicit questions from readers and include question-and-answer articles in the newsletter. An enterprising extension specialist in Missouri started a newsletter called "Beginnings" for newly married couples to help

them get their financial feet on the ground. One issue included this article:

What do "you" do?

How do the two of you handle money and bills? Are you happy with your present system? If you would like to share your system with others, drop me a line or call. I'll include it in next month's "Beginnings."

In an issue of the national newsletter "Communications Concepts," the author asked for readers to send in puns so he could give "fun in the pun awards" to the worst and best. This also provided some humor for the newsletter.

Level 2: Do a survey,

Do this once a year. Ask what the audience reads and does not read, likes and does not like about your newsletter. Use this information to improve your newsletter.

You will waste your time, though, if you don't design the survey the right way. There is an art to doing it. Here are a few tips:

- Ask only what you want to know and nothing extra.

- Keep the survey form as short as possible – no more than one 8-1/2 x 11 - inch sheet. The back of a postcard is best.

- Make it easy for people to return. Include a self-addressed, stamped envelope. A self-addressed, stamped postcard has advantages because it can be inserted in one of your issues.

- People are turned off by questions on age and income. If this information is vital to you, don't ask it first. Let them warm up to your survey first. Then when you do ask it, provide ranges, such as an age between 30 and 39 or an income between $30,000 and $49,999 per year.

You don't have to ask everybody. If you have a random sample, you can extrapolate the results to the whole population. Pick every tenth name from your mailing list, for example.

It is also essential to do a dry run before committing your survey to the mail. Test the survey on a handful of people to make sure your questions are understandable.

Level 3: Find out if anybody is doing something differently because of your newsletter.

This is the most difficult level of evaluation. It has to be carefully orchestrated. Figure out one thing you want to campaign for in your newsletter and then quickly find out if your campaigning did any good. Here are the steps:

- Promote something. You may want to use two or three or more issues to do this.

- Find out if anybody is doing it because of your newsletter.

- Remember to find out fast. They may start doing it. But they will forget they got the idea from your newsletter unless you time your evaluation and the campaign close together. Ideally, the timing should be within 30 days of the end of your campaign – or certainly within three months. For efficiency's sake, you may want to include this evaluation with your yearly survey.

- What you choose to campaign for depends on your audience and purpose. If your newsletter promotes your college, you may want to campaign for contributions. If your newsletter goes to newly married couples, you may want to campaign for them to set up a budget. You might want to campaign to help weight watchers keep off weight, smokers to stop smoking or farmers to adopt certain soil conservation practices. A hospital employee newsletter conducted a campaign to promote courtesy in elevators.

Whatever it is, if you find that people have changed their lives because of your newsletter, that's quite an accomplishment. Those kinds of results might help you get a raise or more subscribers. Either way, you've set yourself up for newsletter stardom.

Develop a style

Paris fashions have style. Cary Grant had style. Your newsletter should have style, too. But style in the publishing business refers to consistency in the way you express certain things, such as abbreviations, numbers and people's titles. This makes your newsletter easier to write. It also makes it easier to read.

For example, you may decide that for your newsletter, the style will be no titles for people. On first reference, you refer to the person's full name, such as John Smith. On second reference, he is Smith and not Mr. Smith or Dr. Smith.

At the University of Missouri, the style was for the second reference to be MU or Mizzou and not U of M.

With numbers, your style may be to spell out until 10 and then use numerals. This is a typical style used in journalism and promoted by the Associated Press Stylebook, a common one used at many newspapers.

For dates, you may decide to use abbreviations for months when they are part of a date, such as Oct. 13, 1997, and spell out when they are not.

Unlike grammar rules, there is no right or wrong about style choices. Just decide and then stick with it.

In this three-column format, the outside column is narrower than the other two. You can use this narrow column for shorter articles and lists, such as the list of the inside contents.

Design a winner

A well-designed newsletter will draw readers to it. To borrow a phrase from computer technology, it will be "user – friendly." People can easily find what they need to know. The elements to design in a newsletter include the nameplate, masthead, text, departments, charts and graphs, art and photographs, and color. All work together to give a newsletter a distinctive and unified look. All contribute to helping the newsletter be easy to read and useful.

Nameplate

The nameplate is where the name of the newsletter is. Sometimes called the "flag," the nameplate is usually at the top of the first page of the newsletter. But it doesn't necessarily have to be at the top. It can also be along the side, in the middle, or at the bottom. The nameplate consists of the name, the subtitle, the origin of the newsletter, and the date.

Name. Avoid using "Newsletter" in the name. After all, no one names a newspaper "Newspaper" or a magazine "Magazine."

Also avoid "Informer" and "Update." These are tired titles. Think of something descriptive of the purpose for your newsletter. For example, the name of a newsletter on ethics in journalism was "The Fine Line."

Whatever your name, let it be bold and dominate the page. The name should be one or two words.

Subtitle. To keep your name short, you may want to have a subtitle to explain more about the name. For example, the subtitle for the newsletter "Silver Threads" is "News for Senior Citizens." Subtitles can help clarify who, the audience is.

Origin. Make it perfectly clear where the newsletter is coming from. Don't make readers hunt for who is putting it out. Address and subscription information can be saved for the masthead. But always include who is responsible for the newsletter in the nameplate.

Date. Newsletters need a date. Some authors also like to keep track of volume numbers for ease in binding later.

If you can't afford to have your newsletter professionally designed, at least try to get your nameplate designed by a professional artist. The cost for this is relatively minor compared to the benefits of a better looking newsletter.

Text

You will need to select the font or style of typeface, the size of that type, and number of columns on a page. You also will need to decide if you want the column justified and if you want the words hyphenated at the end of the lines.

Font. Stick with one similar to what you see in newspapers or magazines. Your goal is ease in reading and not an unusual style that may be hard to read. Note that the typefaces in popular publications are usually "serif" typefaces, with little feet. Experts say the little feet help lead the eyes along for faster reading. Sans serif typefaces, those without little feet, are good for headlines and shorter pieces of body copy, such as cutlines for photographs.

Size. Look to newspapers and magazines for a readable size, usually 9 or 10 point type. You don't want to get too small. Some experts consider 8 point type too small for most people. Some experts prefer 11 and 12 point type.

The space in between the lines of type, called "leading," should be two points larger than the typeface size. Space larger than this starts to interfere with readability. This may be all right for short blurbs but could be a problem for more substantial copy blocks.

Use the same font and size through the text of your newsletter. A professional designer knows how to mix fonts and sizes and make a newsletter look good. But it's difficult to do this unless you have that expertise. To simplify your life and make your newsletter easier to read, stick with one.

Number of columns. Bullet sheet newsletters tend to use a one-column format. The type goes clear across the page. For best results with this format, keep the left and right margins at least an inch wide so the readers' eyes don't get weary traveling back and forth. Also, because of the line width, keep the typeface a little larger, usually 12 points.

Most other newsletters use a two- or three-column format. Some desktop publishing programs include grids to help you set up the correct spacing for formats.

One format that works well for newsletters is a five-column grid that allows you to have two wider columns (each two

In a four column format, you can set your text over one or two columns. To place copy in a box, you will need to set it slightly narrower so there's breathing room between text and rules.

columns wide) and a third narrower one (only one column wide). Keep the narrower one to the outside and use this for lists of names or sidebars for your articles. Some designers place mug shot photos in this narrower column.

To justify or not to justify. Some people like the more informal look of columns that are ragged on the right and unjustified. Others feel strongly that the columns should be justified so they match the straight lines of the pages and photos. They feel this is a cleaner, more formal look.

If columns are justified, usually you want hyphenation of words. Otherwise, you can create some odd spacing between letters that can interfere with readability.

If you use a ragged right style, then you don't need to use hyphenation. The ragged right style is designed to allow for more natural spacing between letters so hyphenation at the end of a line seems contradictory.

Departments

Newsletters can have departments just as magazines and newspapers do. These are the regular features given a certain place and look so they are easy to identify and find. For example, *Time* magazine has departments called "Milestones," "People" and "Essay." Southern University's employee newsletter has a department called "Ovations" in which honors and recognitions bestowed on faculty and staff are listed. Having departments makes newsletters easier to read.

A department can be as simple as a table of contents box on the first page luring readers to look inside. An employee newsletter for an oil company featured a question-and-answer department called "The Pipeline."

Having departments also makes your newsletter easier and faster to put together. You replace old articles with new articles in your layout and make minor adjustments for length.

Charts and graphs

Charts and graphs experienced a boost in popularity when the newspaper *USA Today* first came on the market. In an effort to be more appealing to television watchers, this newspaper incorporates many colorful charts and graphs.

The newsletter is a perfect place to use charts and graphs. They can make complicated, tedious information easier to grasp. When they are well-designed, they can brighten the look of your pages. Rather than using only words to explain how a piece of machinery works, develop a chart instead. Rather than listing a bunch of numbers, group them into a graph.

Photographs and illustrations

Photographs and illustrations can add flair to your newsletter and entice the reader. They can help communicate your message.

A five column format allows you versatility in your layout. You can set your text across one, two or three columns. Leaving a narrow column on the outside provides a place for lists, short items or cutlines.

To be effective, though, photographs must be clear and well-composed or they do more harm than good. If the photo is blurry and you can't identify the people in it, don't use it. It will make your whole newsletter look bad.

Action shots are best. But most newsletters are obligated to use "grip-and-grin" photos. These are the ones where you line up all the scholarship winners, for example, and they "grip" their checks and "grin" at the photographer.

Instead of grip-and-grins, try to plan these photo opportunities around the subjects. For example, if you want to honor a scholarship winner, then show the person doing something that made her worthy of the scholarship.

Always use cutlines, also known as captions, with your photos. A cutline provides a valuable opportunity to impart information to the reader and even entice the reader to find out more by reading the accompanying article. This opportunity is lost if the photo is just stuck in to make the layout look interesting. Even if the photo is just a facial shot of someone, commonly called a mug shot, have the person's name printed underneath. Don't assume that everybody reading your newsletter knows who that person is.

The best position for a cutline is underneath or along side the photo. You confuse the reader if you group cutlines with arrows pointing in the direction of the photo they describe.

Illustrations may be difficult and expensive to obtain depending on your access to professional artists. However, there are ample choices of clip-art books and CD-Roms for sale. Unfortunately, much of the art may be overused and outdated. Using it in your newsletter may detract from its appearance. Use art as you do photographs – only to help communicate your message.

Color

There are two things to consider with color in a newsletter: the paper and the ink. The most readable combination for many people is black ink on white paper. That provides the most contrast. If you choose otherwise, stay as close to white with your paper as you can and as close to black with your ink as you can. The darker the paper and the lighter the ink, the more you compromise readability.

Black ink on white paper also will make your black and white photographs look crisper. If you vary from that, the same rule applies stay with a dark ink and a light paper. It can be quite disconcerting, for example, to look at bright blue or green people in photographs.

Using a bright color ink in addition to the dark color you select for your text can add life to your newsletter. Two additional colors beyond the color you choose for your text can add even more excitement. However, the cost goes up with each additional color. And, unless you are a trained artist, trying to design a newsletter with two spot colors can be overwhelming.

The rule to guide you with the use of spot color is restraint. Keep in mind that "less is more". The price is the same whether you use a lot or a little. But it's best to use only a little. That way the spot color can add emphasis without looking too busy. Some suggested places to use spot color include:

The nameplate. Some people have their nameplate printed in quantity in one color. Then they duplicate the body of their newsletter on those pre-printed sheets with the equipment in their office. This can save money.

Large initial letters. A common design technique is to make the first letter of an article extra large. Doing this in color can add interest to the page.

Blurbs. These are short, provocative quotes pulled out from the article and set in a slightly larger type. They are also called pull quotes. Blurbs help break up a long article.

Tops of pages. Some newsletters have bars or lines printed in a spot color across the tops of pages.

Screened boxes. You can use a percentage of your spot color, usually 10, 20 or 30 percent, to create what's called a screen. Text can be superimposed on these screens to create an eye-catching box. It's usually not a good idea to use spot color

in headlines, however. This would be overusing spot color and would take away from its effectiveness. Your headlines already have emphasis due to their larger size.

Masthead

The masthead provides a place to include the names of all who contributed to the newsletter so they get credit for their work. It also provides the place for subscription information. Pack the masthead full of the details, and always put it in the same place for each issue of your newsletter. Some people like to place it at the bottom of page two. Others like to put it on the back of a four-page newsletter.

A typical masthead includes a miniature version of your nameplate for a unified look to your newsletter and this information:

- Authors and contributors
- Address, phone number, and the newsletter's place of origin
- Date and volume number
- Subscription information.

Two placement suggestions

Armed with knowledge of your audience and the purpose for your newsletter, you're ready to place all the articles and information you have pulled together for your newsletter. Here are some things to keep in mind:

The best goes first. Your front page is your most expensive real estate. Use your newsiest and most timely article there. Don't waste this space on more mundane matters, such as your calendar of events or letter from the CEO.

Avoid jumps. If the article doesn't fit the space you have allotted for it, then it's usually better to cut it than to jump the article to another page. If there is substance in the article that simply can't be cut, then you may want to package it into one or more additional articles. Tell the reader at the end that for more information, they can turn to another page.

Publishing a newsletter can be a gratifying experience. Readers like newsletters. They appreciate getting timely information in an easy-to-read manner. Once a routine is established, assembling a newsletter can be done in a relatively short period of time.

But like anything, to be done well, a newsletter takes dedication to excellence. This dedication will be rewarded by loyal readers. They may indeed throw away your newsletter – but only after they have read it.

Photography 7

Although the ways in which we capture and reproduce photographs is rapidly changing, still images in color or black-and-white remain an essential element in communicating our institutional messages or conducting educational programs. Whether for a slide presentation, a newsletter, a video, or an exhibit, photographs can illustrate a concept, attract attention, and document activities in a clear, compelling manner.

This chapter is written for the person who wants to communicate with photos. It will cover selecting a camera that's just right for you, adjusting the camera, making your pictures visually appealing and informative, employing special photographic techniques, and buying and using camera accessories.

A camera is an important tool for communicators. But don't forget that the photographer, not the camera, is the most important instrument for taking good pictures.

With creativity, practice and determination, you can take exciting photographs. Properly selected equipment will help you concentrate on taking pictures that convey a clear message instead of fumbling with the camera mechanics.

Selecting the camera

Today's photographer can choose between a simple, relatively inexpensive camera which consistently delivers correctly exposed, reasonably sharp photographs, or a more complex, adjustable camera offering full control over the picture-taking process.

No camera is perfect for every purpose. You must decide which features, such as ease of use, you are willing to trade for others, such as versatility and quality. Your choice should depend on the kinds of pictures you will take, how often you will be using the camera, and the extent of your commitment to learning about photography. For example, if you use photographs on a regular basis for a variety of purposes you should select a camera different from one you would use to take illustrations for an occasional office report.

Also, consider how many people will use the camera and how much they know about photography in general. If the camera will be used by several people who have little photographic background, select a simple and durable model. Extra features add flexibility, but only if you know how to use them.

Camera types

Cameras can be grouped on the basis of their design, the size of film they use, or their viewing system. For the sake of simplicity, we'll discuss film size and viewing systems. First, film size. Photographers refer to this as film format, and it includes such widely used and available film sizes as 35mm, 120, and 220. How you intend to use the pictures will determine which film format you need.

The 35mm camera, the nearest thing available to an all-purpose camera, employs the smallest film format that we recom-

You should select a camera and accessories based on how you plan to use the pictures you take.

mend for communication purposes. It's the most popular choice for color slides and for photographs to be used in all types of publications. With the new films now on the market, 35mm negatives can be enlarged to 16x20 inches with sharp results.

The new generation of compact 35mm cameras (now more commonly referred to as point-and-shoot cameras) offers features to suit almost every need and pocketbook. These cameras do almost everything for you automatically, from loading and advancing the film to setting exposure, focusing, firing the flash, and rewinding the film. As the price tag climbs above $150-$200, the cameras may offer modest zoom capabilities, close focusing, and other specialized focusing and exposure features. These cameras do not have interchangeable lenses, time exposure, or manual override features.

To exercise more control when taking pictures, you need to consider an adjustable camera. (If you are using an automatic camera, skip to the section on composition, "Creating pictures with impact.")

To maximize your ability to take quality photos, you will need a fully adjustable 35mm single lens reflex camera, or SLR. These cameras allow you to view the picture through the lens for better composition control, especially with wide angle, telephoto and close-up lenses. In addition, on an SLR you can adjust the shutter speed and lens opening for full control of stop action and depth of focus and, because you can easily remove the lens from the camera body, you can choose from a range of specialty lenses.

Professional photographers making pictures for publications or exhibits often use a medium format camera, such as a 120, which makes a 6 x 6 centimeter negative (2-1/4 x 2-1/4 inches). This camera is not much larger than a 35mm, yet produces a negative nearly twice as large. (Other medium format negative sizes are 6 x 4.5 cm and 6 x 7 cm.) The larger your negative, the sharper your picture will be. Medium format cameras are expensive and generally used by individuals and communication offices that have a serious need for and commitment to photography.

Instant cameras produce a finished photographic print within minutes of the film being exposed. Recent improvements in instant picture cameras have increased their popularity. However, most newspaper and publication editors won't use instant photographs because the lenses in these cameras are generally too inferior to produce sharp pictures. In addition, the layers of color emulsion in instant color prints prevent the edges of objects in the picture from looking sharp and crisp.

Filmless Cameras

The filmless camera revolution is well underway in the world of photography. The filmless camera is one that records images electronically rather than on film. Currently two types of filmless camera are available, the still video camera and the digital camera. The still video camera records images on a video floppy disk. Up to 50 images can be stored on a single

disk in some of these camera models, and for viewing you can plug the camera into a television set and see your pictures on the TV screen. The digital camera stores images in the same way that computers store information in internal memory or on floppy disks. To view digital images you plug the camera into a computer, open the proper program and view away. Of course, you must have a computer that is compatible with the digital camera and the appropriate software. It all adds up to a lot of cost and that's why the filmless camera revolution hasn't reached everywhere yet.

Prices for the electronic cameras range from $500 to over $10,00. Still video camera models are available from Sony an Canon. Digital cameras are available from Apple Computer, Kodak and Fuji. There are lots of add-ons that go with these models like video digitizers, memory cards and memory card processors. Include the computers and software needed for digital cameras and the costs of electronic images tend to skyrocket. Also, be aware that the higher price of the camera, the higher the quality of the images it produces. The low-end electronic cameras produce images that lack the sharpness and definition of traditional pictures captured on film and printed on photographic paper.

Looking beyond the high costs, the advantages of electronic photography are obvious: no waiting for pictures to come back from the lab and, with a computer program like Adobe Photoshop, you can manipulated digital images in more ways that you can imagine. Since a digital image is basically a digital file as far as a computer is concerned, you can send it electronically anywhere that you send other such files. The only limitation is that digital image files are usually very large and can take a lot of transmission time.

Viewing systems

The viewing system refers to the small window and associated assemblage that you look through to compose and focus your photograph. The simplest viewing system, and the one found on compact, or point-and-shoot cameras, is the viewfinder. On these cameras, the viewfinder is located above or to one side of the lens. Usually the viewfinder has lines in it to indicate the area that will be included in the photograph.

Viewfinder cameras are excellent for general photography of scenery and people. They are easy to use and convenient to carry. However, because the viewfinder and the lens see the subject from slightly offset viewpoints, there is a difference between what you see and what will be recorded on film. This is referred to as parallax error, a problem that is most noticeable when taking extreme close-ups.

With a viewfinder camera, your control over picture composition is limited compared to other types of cameras and, except for the most expensive models, you cannot use different lenses.

Single lens reflex. The SLR viewing system employs a complex system of mirrors that allows you to view the image

Viewfinder

directly through the lens. A hinged mirror behind the lens reflects the subject into the eyepiece. When you click the shutter release, the hinged mirror swings up just before the shutter opens to allow the light to fall on the film at the back of the camera. While the mirror is up, you cannot see the subject. This moment of blindness when you take your picture usually is not a problem at normal shutter speeds. Because they are more complex than other viewing systems, SLRs are more expensive than viewfinder cameras.

SLR or single lens reflex

The 35mm single lens reflex is by far the most popular and versatile camera for communication purposes. Several medium format cameras also employ the SLR system. The twin lens reflex is a variation of the SLR that uses two identical lenses, one for viewing, the other to expose the film. The twin lens reflex represents an older technology; few companies manufacture them today. However, many older models are still in use.

Camera features

Once you have selected the format and viewing system, you'll find a variety of features on the cameras in the category you have selected. Each camera has a slightly different technique for loading the film, focusing, determining exposure, and advancing the film. These are explained in the instruction book that comes with the camera. With practice, you can usually adapt to any system. The instruction book is an important document that should be kept with the camera or accessible to people who will use it. Above all, do not throw the instruction book away.

Here are a few features about cameras that you should consider carefully: interchangeable lenses, lens speed, exposure meter, and automatic exposure control.

Interchangeable lenses. All 35mm SLR cameras allow you to replace the normal lens with a specialty lens, such as wide-angle or a telephoto. Remember, only a few compact 35mm cameras permit you to do this, and they're at the high end of the cost range. Lens interchangeability is a valuable feature that lets you expand your photographic system as your needs and finances dictate

Lens speed. There also can be some variation in the lens you buy with your camera. For example, one option may be a 50mm, f/2, another a 50mm, f/1.4. The f-number in the lens description tells you how wide the lens will open at its maximum setting. The wider the opening, the more light gets through the lens to the film. In this example, the f/1.4 will let in more light than the f/2. Because it lets more light come through, the f/1.4 can be used in situations where there is little light, or it allows you to use a faster shutter speed in low light situations. As a result, the f/1.4 is referred to as a faster lens than the f/2. (See section on f-stops.)

Some people believe that because the faster lens costs more, it's a better lens. This is not necessarily the case. In fact, the f/2 lens may produce a sharper image in all but the poorest lighting conditions. Unless you are interested in doing much low-light photography, you can save money buying the slower lens in this example, the f/2.

Exposure meter. Built-in meters have made hand-held meters a thing of the past for most photographers (except for specialized needs such as metering flash exposures with a flash meter). Meters on most 35mm SLR cameras read directly through the camera's lens.

Some meters measure only a portion of the subject being photographed, others measure the entire picture area. On sophisticated cameras, the meter may have the capability to analyze the scene and make tricky exposure decisions for you. Through-the-lens meters are especially useful because they give accurate exposure readings no matter what lens or attachment you use (although exposure compensation may be needed with some filters).

To set the correct exposure, look through the viewfinder and adjust the shutter speed or lens opening until the indicator system for your camera shows the shutter speed and lens aperture are letting in the proper amount of light.

Automatic exposure control. Automatic exposure cameras are quite popular. They are convenient and usually produce acceptable pictures under standard conditions. However, automatic cameras can also produce poor photographs if you don't understand their limitations. (See section on exposure.)

If you decide to buy a fully automatic camera, be sure it also provides manual controls so you can still use the camera when the batteries are dead. Most automatic cameras use an electronic rather than a mechanical shutter, so they depend entirely on batteries to function.

You also should find out how much replacement batteries cost. They can be expensive. If you do select an automatic camera, avoid using it in extreme cold and always carry spare batteries.

Selecting the film

The film you use will depend on the kind of pictures you want to take. In the past, the choice was between color or black-and-white, and prints or slides. Advances in film technology and computerized reproduction of photographs have made the use of black-and-white film less essential for publication purposes. Thanks to computerized scanning technology, color prints can provide good quality black-and-white images for newsletters and extension publications. Black-and-white film is required primarily for high quality publication reproduction and for exhibit prints.

If you need black-and-white prints, use black-and-white negative film such as T-Max. If you want color photographs, you should use color print film, which always carries the word "color" in the name such as Kodacolor II. If you want color slides, look for the word "chrome" such as in Ektachrome or Fujichrome.

Sensitivity to light. Once you decide on the type of film you need, you must decide how sensitive the film should be to light. If you are taking pictures indoors without a flash or outdoors in the evening, you won't have much light. Conversely, a sunny day by the lake will be very bright. To accommodate such different conditions, film is rated with a number that indicates its sensitivity to light. This number is called an ISO (International Organization for Standardization) number; it used to be referred to as ASA (American Standards Association) in the United States. In Europe, the film rating number was referred to as DIN (German industrial standard). These numbers have been combined with the DIN number distinguished by a o sign: ISO 125/22o with the first number representing the old ASA, the second DIN. In the United States, you pay attention to the first number in this example, 125.

The higher the film speed number, the more sensitive a film is to light. An ISO 100/21o film will be fine outdoors on a sunny or cloudy-bright day. But you most likely will have to use a flash to get properly exposed pictures indoors. For example, T-MAX film is available in three different speeds: ISO 100, ISO 400, and ISO 3200, giving you a range of choices depending on the lighting conditions you expect during your photo shoot.

The ISO number should be set on your camera when you load the film. Most 35mm film cassettes have a bar code printed on them. And most newer 35mm cameras have a feature called DX film speed setting that reads the bar code and sets the proper film speed automatically.

Films with high ISO ratings (ISO 400 and up) can sometimes look fuzzy or grainy even though pictures may be in perfect focus. If you're taking pictures in bright sunlight, you won't need a highly sensitive film, so try to use a film with a lower ISO rating for a finer grained picture.

If you use color film, you also must take into account the type of light that will illuminate your picture. Most color films are balanced for daylight, which includes light from an electronic flash. If you use daylight film under fluorescent lights commonly found in offices and research labs, your photographs will have a greenish-yellow cast that many people find undesirable. Photos taken with daylight film under tungsten light will have a reddish-yellow cast. This off-colored cast can be reduced by using an electronic flash or a corrective filter.

Read the instructions

Too often film instructions are dropped into the nearest trash can without so much as a glance. With many films, the instructions have been getting briefer in recent years, and if you'll take a few minutes to read them you'll probably take better pictures.

The instructions will tell you the film's ISO rating, If your camera does'nt have an automatic DX film-speed-setting feature, be sure you set the ISO on your camera and don't change it until you load it with another roll of film. Failure to set the proper ISO will result in pictures that are under- or over-exposed.

Some instruction sheets tell you approximate exposure settings for different lighting conditions. The instruction sheet may also explain how to take flash shots and difficult or unusual scenes, such as a stage show. If you use the film under unusual lighting conditions, it will tell you which filter to use.

Finally, the instructions urge you to keep film out of hot places, especially the glove box or dashboard of your car. Film is sensitive to heat and light, and a few hours in a hot car can ruin your pictures.

Don't buy out-of-date film. While the film may still be good after the expiration date, outdated film is subject to color shifts that will make your photographs unusable. Your time is more valuable than the few cents you save on expired film.

For short-term storage, refrigerate unopened film in moisture-proof plastic bags. Keep it on the refrigerator door, where it is away from spills. Before using the film, let it sit at room temperature for at least three hours before opening the box.

How to hold the camera

The quickest way to assure sharp, clear pictures is to hold your camera correctly. Practice with an unloaded camera and hold it as if you're taking a picture.

Often people grasp the camera at each end and stick their elbows out. They put their feet together, lock their knees, and hold their breath before pushing the camera lever. Most of the time, this causes a slight downward jerk at the moment the picture is taken, causing a blurred picture or cutting off heads. No wonder film processors say that 90 percent of bad pictures are due to camera movement.

Always support the camera in the palm of your left hand, with the thumb and index or middle finger on the focusing grip of the lens. This gives the camera firmer support.

You can steady your camera by becoming a human tripod. Use your left hand as the tripod base; hold the camera as if it had been dropped into your hand palm up. Wrap your thumb and forefinger around the lens with the base of the camera resting on the palm of your left hand.

To complete the tripod, move the camera to your eye and let it rest on your cheekbone and nose. Operate the shutter release (and the film advance, if your camera doesn't do it automatically) with your right hand. This stance pulls both elbows close to your body and away from bumps. In this position, it's only natural to spread your feet apart and relax your legs.

If you want to take a vertical picture, turn the camera in your hand with the shutter release down, not up. This keeps your elbows at your sides, where they belong. Holding the camera in this manner allows you to support most of its weight on the palm of your left hand, leaving your other hand free to push the shutter release button and, if necessary, operate the film advance.

For vertical shots, turn the camera, with the camera lens resting in the palm of your left hand and your right elbow still against your side.

For extra support you can lean against a tree or a building. If you use a car for support, turn the engine off. You don't need the extra vibrations.

Frame your picture carefully in the viewfinder and you are ready to shoot. Relax. Keep both eyes open when you look through the viewfinder. Just before you snap the picture, take a breath and then let it out. This is much more relaxing than trying to tighten your chest enough to keep the air in.

As you release the shutter, keep a firm grip on the camera body. Move only your index finger in a slow, squeezing motion. If camera movement blurs your pictures, try resting your chin on top of your left-hand palm. This might feel a little ridiculous at first, but you'll soon see how much steadier it makes your hands.

Adjusting the camera

The camera is a miniature darkroom. It keeps the outside light away from the film in the camera until you press the shutter. When the shutter is released, light travels through the lens to the film and exposes it. The film reacts to the light and records an image. For the image to be usable, the film must be exposed correctly.

Exposure is controlled by two adjustments on your camera: the shutter speed, which controls the duration of the exposure, and the aperture or f-stop, which controls the intensity of the exposure. The indicator in the viewfinder tells you when the combination of these two settings is correct.

Each number on the shutter speed dial is twice as large as the number on one side and half as large as the number on the other side. These numbers represent fractions of a second, although the fractional numerator (1/) is left off. A 250 setting lets light pass through the lens twice as long as a 500 setting.

The shutter speed is calibrated in fractions of a second: 1/30, 1/60, 1/125, 1/500 and so on. Each speed is half or twice as long as the one next to it. So changing the shutter speed one interval will halve or double the amount of light reaching the film. Shutter speed controls the appearance of movement in the final image. Slower speeds allow moving objects to create a trace on the film, resulting in a blur. Faster shutter speeds tend to freeze movement.

Because you cannot hand hold a camera with perfect steadiness, you need to use a high enough shutter speed to prevent the effects of camera movement. The recommended minimum hand-held speed is 1/125. For telephoto lenses, the recommended minimum shutter speed is 1/focal length (1/500 for a 500mm telephoto).

The aperture or f-stop is controlled by a diaphragm inside the lens that can reduce or enlarge the light path through the lens. When the diaphragm is fully open, a maximum of light passes through to the film. When closed down, less light reaches the film. At first, the aperture scale seems like a strange series of numbers: f/2, f/2.8, f/4, f/5.6, f/8, f/11, f/16 and so on. Actually, these numbers are a series of ratios indicating the cross-sectional area of the light path. Changing the aperture a full interval (e.g., from f/4 to f/5.6) cuts the cross-sectional area in half, so only half as much light passes through the lens.

Because the aperture numbers represent fractions (f/2 = 1/2, f/4 = 1/4), small numbers indicate larger light path areas and higher numbers indicate smaller areas. The smaller the

The aperture or f-stop numbers follow the same principle as the shutter speed dial. The larger numbers let in less light, and each opening is half as large as the one before it.

number, the more light gets through. The problem with thinking of them as fractions is in the math (f/11 doesn't seem to be twice the size of f/16, but it is). This is because the lens opening numbers refer to the diameter of the circular lens opening divided into the distance from the lens to the film plane.

Rather than figuring the math, just remember that the aperture scale is set up exactly like the shutter speed dial. An f/11 lens opening lets in twice as much light as an f/16 and one-half as much light as an f/8.

This makes changes in the camera setting simple, once you get the hang of it. Say you are taking pictures at 1/125 and f/8. Suddenly you need to change 1/500 to stop action. You have cut the length of time light can pass through the lens in half twice (1/125 to 1/250 to 1/500). To get the same total exposure, you need to compensate by increasing the amount of light that comes through the lens by the same factor (f/8 to f/5.6 to f/4), so you move the lens opening from an f/8 to an f/4.

Depth of field. In addition to helping control exposure and allowing you to use different shutter speeds, the aperture also influences the sharpness of a photograph. That is, it has a major effect on depth of field, the area in a photograph from foreground to background that is in reasonably sharp focus.

Basically, the smaller the aperture (i.e., higher numbers: f/8, f/11), the greater the area in front of and behind your subject that will appear sharp. Other factors influencing depth of field are distance from camera to subject (The closer you are, the less the depth of field.) and the focal length of the lens. (Telephotos have less depth of field.) wide angle lenses have more.

If you are taking a picture of a man vaccinating an animal, you may want both the needle and the man's face to be in focus. That's no problem if both are about the same distance from your camera. More likely though, the camera is closer to the needle than to his face. Then you need sharpness not just at one distance but through a range of distance from foreground to background. You gain this depth of field by using a small lens opening, or f-stop.

Most lenses have a depth-of-field scale engraved on the barrel. This scale consists of a set of aperture or f-stop numbers which appear on each side of the focusing mark. By looking at the f-stop number you have selected on both sides of the scale, you can see the range of distance which will be in focus.

For example, say the man's face is seven feet away. By using a lens opening of f/16, you'll be able to focus on everything from five feet to about 12 feet, including the needle, which may be at 5.5 feet.

On an f/l6 setting, the depth of field scale tells you that everything between the two 16s (5 to 11 feet) will be in focus, so both the needle and the man's face are reasonably sharp.

Your next picture may be of just the needle without emphasizing the man's face. To take this picture you use an f/4 or f/2.8 aperture. At this setting, the depth of field is much smaller. If you focus on the needle at 5.5 feet, the face at seven feet will be outside this depth of field and out of focus.

But as you look through your camera, you may not be able to see this depth of field, even after you've set the smallest lens opening. This is because your camera lens remains all the way open until the split second you take the picture. When you press the shutter release, the diaphragm in the lens closes down to the selected f-stop just before the shutter opens to expose the film.

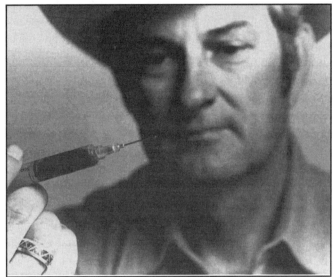

With an f/4 lens opening, only the area very close to your point of focus will appear sharp. This means the man's face will be out of focus if you focus on the tip of the needle.

Cameras with a depth-of-field preview button allow you to close the lens down to the preselected setting and permit you to check the focus on the man's face and the needle. Closing (or stopping) down the lens can make the viewing screen quite dark, so you do it only while you check the depth of field, Then, before taking the picture, release the depth-of-field preview button to allow careful viewing of the scene.

Exposure

With an automatic camera it's easy to take exposure determination for granted and leave all the control up to the camera. Automation works fine for average subjects, but it can lead to poor pictures if the subject is extremely dark or light, or if the lighting is contrasty.

For example, if you photograph a snow-covered landscape, following the meter will produce an underexposed picture. That's because the meter, fooled by the whiteness of the snow, will measure more light than is actually in the scene. We know from experience that snow reflects about two stops more light. The same goes for scenes in which your subject is surrounded by large areas of shade or dark colors. The meter will interpret those dark areas as requiring more light than is actually needed and will produce an overexposed photo.

With light or dark subjects or contrasty lighting, try to base your meter reading on the area in which you want to record significant detail, rather than on the entire scene. You may have to make a close-up reading or a substitute reading off the palm of your hand to get the correct result. This is especially useful in extremely bright situations, such as a snow scene.

To make a substitute reading, just hold your hand with the palm facing your camera in approximately the same lighting conditions as your subject. Set your exposure for the light reflected from your palm, but then open your lens one f-stop more than that indicated by the meter. (Since your thumb is pointing up, you can always remember to open up the lens one stop.)

For example, if your off-the-palm reading suggests using f/8, you should open the lens to f/5.6, before taking your picture. This technique takes longer to explain than it does to use in practice, but it's a very helpful technique for difficult exposure conditions.

Bracketing your exposure is another technique that professional photographers use when faced with unusual lighting conditions. Bracketing means shooting a series of pictures at different exposures, rather than making just a single exposure of your subject. Begin by making your first exposure at the setting recommended by your meter or best guess. Take a second picture, increasing the exposure by one stop and a third, decreasing your exposure by one stop less than your first. This process gives you three chances of getting a suitable exposure, instead of just one. For critical work with color slide film, bracket in one-half f-stop increments rather than whole stops. This process requires you to use more film, but it's the best guarantee of getting a good photograph.

Automatic exposure control

There are a variety of automatic exposure control systems in which the exposure meter and shutter and aperture mechanisms are linked. These systems can be classified under three main headings: program mode, shutter priority mode and aperture priority mode.

In program mode, the camera automatically selects both the shutter speed and the aperture for you. Some cameras have more than one program mode so the camera will automatically choose a faster shutter speed to stop motion or a smaller aperture to give greater depth of field.

The shutter priority mode lets you set the shutter speed and the meter adjusts the aperture for proper exposure at the shutter speed you've selected. The advantage of this system is that you can select the shutter speed you need to freeze or blur the action. The disadvantage is that the camera may select an f-stop that gives you either too much or too little depth of field for the composition you desire.

The aperture priority mode works just the opposite. You

select the f-stop or aperture for the desired depth of field, and the camera selects the shutter speed to give you the right exposure. The disadvantage is that the camera may drop your shutter speed below the speed at which you can successfully hand-hold the camera. It's difficult to hold the camera still below 1/30 of a second, especially with a telephoto lens.

Any of the automatic exposure modes will give you properly exposed photographs. But you should be aware of the settings the camera has selected. If you aren't, your automatic camera could give you properly exposed "blurs," or pictures with a distracting depth of field. And remember, there are tricky situations that might not give you the exposure you want. Then you should switch to manual mode and measure the exposure yourself or bracket.

Estimating exposure. If for some reason you can't use an exposure meter, use settings suggested on the film's instruction sheet if provided, which is not always the case.

You can also try the "Sunny 16 Rule." This rule of thumb works with any kind of film for outdoor shots. The rule is: When shooting under bright sunshine, simply set your f-stop or lens opening on f/16. Then adjust your shutter speed to the speed closest to the ISO of your film.

This means that with ISO 400 film, you would set your lens opening on f/16 and use a 1/500 shutter speed. With ISO 100 film, again use an f/16 lens opening with a shutter speed of 1/125.

Creating pictures with impact

A photograph can be an exciting, dynamic visual statement or simply a dull record of what was happening when the shutter was released. The difference is usually not because of luck or the quality of the camera, but rather with the creativity and motivation of the photographer. To make photographs that communicate effectively, the photographer must know how the pic-

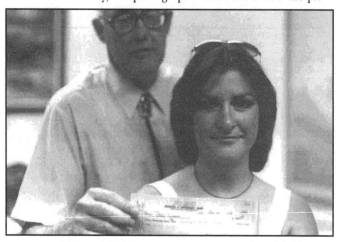

One solution is to move in close to catch the reflection of the winner's face in the mirror. You can read the plaque and see who won it at the same time. The photographer who took this Picture improved it's impact by placing the student in front of the donor, in shap focus.

ture is to be used and what is to be communicated. An attention-getting photograph for an exhibit, for example, may have very different requirements than a photograph accompanying a news story, yet both pictures probably could be made at the same location.

News photos. To illustrate a news article, keep the picture simple and get as close as possible to your subject. Try to avoid handshakes and shots of people holding trophies. If the photo is to report on someone receiving an award, take a picture of the recipient doing whatever he or she did to earn the award, rather than a picture of the award ceremony.

Arrange news photos to include as few people as possible and select a camera angle that shows faces. Check with managing editors in advance about deadlines and the type of film or finished photographs they prefer. For example, find out if they will accept color prints processed at a local one-hour processing house. Some newspapers may agree to develop your film for you.

One solution is to move in close to catch the reflection of the winner's face in the plaque. You can read the plaque and see who won it at the same time.

Displays and exhibits

Photographs are a good device for calling attention to exhibits and displays. The story should be evident at a glance, so select pictures that are simple and have dramatic compositions. Unusual camera angles, dramatic action, and extreme close-ups are sure eye-catchers. The larger the pictures, the

The extreme close-up, coupled with the out-of-focus face, conveys a complete story. The selective focus keeps the face from drawing attention away from the grasshopper. The fingers holding the grasshopper help draw the viewer's eye to the picture.

better. Use nothing smaller than 8 x 10 inches. (11 x 14 inches and 16 x 20 inches are ideal.) Both color and black-and-white prints are effective. Because of the overwhelming use of color photos, black-and-white prints can attract attention with of their rarity. Prints should have a matte finish so they are not shiny and reflective.

Reports and records

Photographs often illustrate various points in a report better than words. If the report isn't to be printed, use spray adhesive to attach the print to the page. Avoid using photo-mount corners; they usually fall off with handling. Also avoid water-base glue which will cause the print to buckle.

Composition

When you pick up a camera and click the shutter, you will record an image on the film. How well that image communi-

Faces almost always make strong centers of interest. You can strengthen the impact of a photograph in some cases by including enough surrounding area to allow for an off-center placement of your subject.

cates depends on how you organize the subject through the viewfinder. We call this organization *composition*. While there are no hard and fast composition rules, the following guidelines usually will improve your pictures.

Center of interest. When you look at a photograph, your eyes should immediately recognize one thing as the most important element of the picture. That element is called the center of interest. Remember that your eye will always gravitate toward the lightest, most sharply focused area in the photograph. Try to compose your picture with the center of interest in a well-lighted area and be sure your subject is in focus. Keep the picture simple; leave out all unnecessary details, which is easier said than done.

Rule of thirds. Try dividing the viewfinder into thirds using vertical and horizontal lines. Compose your picture so the center of interest falls where two of these lines cross; it usually will be more interesting to look at than if it were centered. Try to keep the horizon line in the upper or lower third of your picture and not through the center. Try to arrange your subject

Mentally divide your viewfinder into thirds, both horizontally and vertically. Compose your picture so the center of interest lies where these lines intersect, rather than dead center. This will usually give your pictures a more dynamic and exciting

matter for balance, but not necessarily symmetry.

Depth. You can create a feeling of depth by composing a picture with an object closer to the camera than the center of interest. For instance, framing through tree branches or placing another object in the foreground adds depth to a landscape picture.

Foreground which surrounds the subject can have a framing effect.

Action. Keep people busy, and they will appear more relaxed and natural. Don't have your subject stare directly into the camera unless it's a formal portrait. A few interesting props give the subject something to work with and help create a natural feeling.

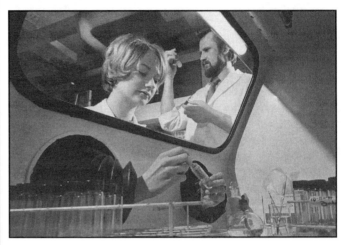

Keep people busy, but be sure you can see most of their faces.

Camera angle. An unusual camera angle or viewpoint can add a great deal of interest to an ordinary subject. Photographed from below, a person seems strong and dominating. But with the camera above and looking down, a person appears meek, submissive, even childlike. Perhaps that's why school children giggle spontaneously when they see a picture of their teacher taken from above.

Background. Unless it definitely tells part of the story, keep the background plain. Avoid extremely light or dark backgrounds.

Timing. Timing is one of the most important techniques used by professionals and yet it is often overlooked by amateur

Foreground helps put the subject into context. By crouching in the wheat field, the photographer was able to get a low, strong angle of both the wheat and the farmer.

photographers. Try to get your picture at the most dramatic moment, the one that symbolizes the event you're photographing. This is just as important when taking a picture of someone working as it is when photographing a sporting event. With practice and concentration, you can train your instincts to respond to the most significant moment when you are taking pictures of someone. It often requires shooting several pictures rather than just one or two.

Lead-in lines. Lines that converge at a particular point can draw the viewer's eye directly toward the subject of the photo and increase impact. Called lead-in lines, they lead the viewer's eye into the photo, acting like a pointer. They also connect the foreground with the background and can impart a sense of scale.

An f/4 lens opening knocks the house out of focus and emphasizes the pump.

The impact of this scene is increased when the photographer adds creative lead-in lines.

Selective focus. Selective focus can change the message of a photograph by deliberately emphasizing one element and de-emphasizing another. Use of a soft focus for the background often removes distracting elements and strengthens the composition.

Formal portraits. These pictures often are produced in a studio. Lenses ranging from 85mm to 105mm are good portrait lenses for a 35mm camera. If you have flash equipment, a simple setup involves a diffused electronic flash held above and to one side of the subject. Also consider taking portraits outdoors on an overcast day. The clouds diffuse the light, creating shadowless illumination. Don't overlook the possibility of making a portrait of your subject in a natural setting. Natural light, such

If you have flash equipment, you can make a simple studio setup with a diffused electronic flash held above and to one side of the subject.

as light normally present in a room through a window or from a lamp, conveys a feeling of atmosphere that can personalize the subject.

Lighting the scene

The world is full of light sources for your photographs. You can use a campfire, a light bulb, the moon, a candle, reflected light from a white wall – the list is almost endless. Of course, the sun is the most common source of photographic light, and its quality changes almost hourly from the soft luminescence of predawn to the hard brilliance of noon and the orange glow of sunset. The same scene shot at various times during the day can take on a completely different look.

High speed films (ISO 400 and higher) make it possible to take indoor shots without using a flash. For the most natural look, try to arrange for side lighting, possibly from a nearby window or open door. And, remember, color photos taken with film intended for daylight use will be affected, perhaps objectionably, by tungsten and fluorescent light.

This low-light shot was taken with only the room and lamp light.

Camera setting for flash

When using an electronic flash, you need to set the correct shutter speed on your camera unless it automatically sets the shutter speed for you. If you set a shutter speed faster than the correct one, the shutter will close before the flash reaches maximum intensity and part of your photo will be unexposed.

Most cameras indicate on the dial the proper shutter speed to use with a flash.

To determine the correct lens opening, follow the directions for your flash unit. Many flash units have automatic exposure features that eliminate the need for continuous exposure adjustments. When the flash unit is set on automatic and the camera is operated in program mode, the camera will measure the light reflected from the subject and control the duration of the flash.

Using flash outdoors

In bright sunlight or when the existing light is excessively contrasty, a flash can reduce deep shadows and lighten the subject. This is called fill flash. The more sophisticated and expen-

sive camera-flash combinations will perform the fill flash function for you. Otherwise, determining the proper exposure is tricky and best mastered by extensive experimentation and bracketing.

Here's one way to figure the correct exposure. Remember, you must use the shutter speed that synchronizes with the flash. Check the light meter reading for the lens opening at that shutter speed. Then adjust your distance from the subject until the lens opening agrees with the opening suggested by the scale on your flash.

Flash accessories

The most common placement of the electronic flash is on the camera's hot shoe, which carries the electric impulse directly between the flash and the camera without the use of a cord. While this placement is convenient, it often produces a picture that looks flat and unnatural, and the constant use of frontal lighting can give a boring regularity to photos taken with a flash.

In nature, subjects are rarely lit from the front, but almost always from the top or the side. To make your subject look natural, try to light it from a side angle. Side lighting also will be more comfortable for your subject and will eliminate red eyes on your subjects.

You can purchase a bracket to hold your flash to the side and slightly above the camera. This requires a connecting cord from flash to camera but helps provide better lighting effects. You also can solve the problem of harsh, unnatural shadows by

The hot shoe attachment is the most convenient place for the flash, but the picture often loses the soft gray tones needed.

Make your own inexpensive diffuser by taping several layers of white tissue over the flash. Open the lens one-half f-stop per layer of tissue.

By using a side bracket and bouncing the light off a white card, you can keep the gray tones, making the picture more normal.

using a diffuser, or by bouncing the light off a reflective surface.

A plastic diffuser fits over the flash's reflector to soften the light. Diffusers are available with various grid patterns for use with a normal, wide-angle, or telephoto lens.

You can make your own inexpensive diffuser by taping several layers of white tissue or matte acetate over the flash unit. A rule of thumb to figure your exposure for a manual flash unit is to open one-half f-stop per layer of tissue.

If you have a flash unit with a tilting head, another way to diffuse light is to bounce the flash off a nearby white or almost-white wall or ceiling. While there are formulas to figure the exact lens opening when you "bounce" the flash, in general, open your lens two f-stops to compensate for the decreased illumination.

Of course, the bouncing technique is much simpler if you have a computerized, automatic flash unit.

Camera accessories

Protecting your camera

The first camera accessories you need are those that will protect your investment. These include protective filters, cleaning supplies, and protective bags.

Protective filters. Filters protect lenses from scratches, bumps, and dents. Because lens paper can often scratch the lens, buy a filter with each lens so you rarely have to clean the lens. Instead, you will clean your protective filter when needed.

Protective filters can be purchased under various names, including haze, ultraviolet (UV), or skylight. These filters also will cut haze or ultraviolet light reflections.

Cleaning supplies. To get the most benefit from your camera system, you always must keep it clean. Carry a supply of lens tissue and fluid. Don't confuse this with eyeglass tissue, which will scratch the lens. The silicone material contained in eyeglass tissue will also ruin the anti-reflection coating on your lens. Carry a soft brush to wipe away dust and an ear syringe or a can of compressed air to blow dust from the internal parts of the camera.

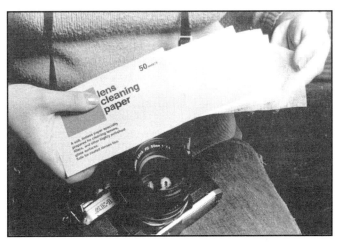

The only paper you should ever use to clean your lens is the type designed for photographic lenses.

Protective bags. Inexpensive gadget bags will protect and organize your equipment. These spacious bags often have compartments for lenses, film, and accessories.

A photographer who travels extensively or who works in extremely dusty situations needs a good case, preferably foam-lined. While these cases are heavier and don't carry much equipment for their size, they are a valuable protective device.

Many photographers who always plan to carry a gadget bag or carrying case find they don't need to buy the tight-fitting leather camera cases.

Filters

Other filters, in addition to the protective ones can improve your photographic results when, shooting under certain conditions.

A polarizing filter will help reduce unwanted glare and haze, darken blue skies to make the clouds stand out, reduce reflections in glass, and make the colors appear richer. This filter is valuable for both black-and-white and color photography.

When you are using color film, three filters will interest you.

No. 80A gives correct color rendition when you are using daylight film with regular tungsten lighting.

No. 80B makes it possible to use daylight color film with photo lamps 3400 Kelvin or with tungsten lighting.

When you are using tungsten-balanced film indoors with a flash or outdoors without a flash, use an **85B filter**.

There are six common types of fluorescent light, and each requires different filter combinations for optimum results. For less critical work you can use an FLD filter with daylight film. If you add an FLD filter, open your lens one stop. (If your camera's exposure meter reads the light through-the-lens, it will make the compensation for you.)

There are various special-effect filters you may wish to try. A starburst filter will create four-pointed stars on any bright point of light. A neutral density filter allows you to use high speed film in bright light.

Lenses

Lenses are generally classified as normal, wide-angle, and telephoto. A normal lens has a focal length approximately equal to the diagonal of the film negative. For a 35mm camera, a 50mm lens is considered normal, and for a 2-1/4 x 2-1/4 inch camera, 85mm is considered normal. A normal lens provides an image that most closely approximates the world as seen by the human eye.

Lenses with a focal length shorter than the diagonal of the negative is considered wide-angle while those with focal lengths longer than its diagonal is called telephoto. Telephoto lenses take in a narrower angle of view and compress the apparent distance between the foreground and background. Shorter focal-

length lenses take in a wider angle of view and tend to distort subjects near the camera. Wide-angle lenses distort less when the film plane of the camera remains parallel to the subject. The more the film plane is tilted in relation to the subject, the more severe the distortion will be.

As a general rule, the slowest shutter speed you can safely hand hold equals the lens length. This means that for a 200mm lens, you should use a shutter no slower than 1/250 when hand holding.

Zoom lenses are lenses with variable focal lengths, and they often appear to be the perfect compromise. But while these lenses may be fun to use, they often are too heavy and bulky to carry permanently on a camera. In addition, except for the most expensive ones, zoom lenses have small maximum apertures that get even smaller as you zoom out to the telephoto range. Because they are limited in their ability to let light come through the lens, you may have to use shutter speeds that are

The main difference between various lenses of the same brand is the focal length — the effective distance between the lens and the film when the lens is focused at infinity. For 35mm cameras, a 50mm lens is standard. Any lens with a focal length longer than this is called a telephoto lens and will bring the subject closer, while any shorter than 50mm is considered a wide-angle lens and will take in more of the scene.

slower than desirable, or faster ISO film, or a flash.

Lens selection. When selecting lenses, try to limit your choice to as few as possible. This will save money, extra weight, and indecision over which lens to use. Most experienced photographers settle on one or two favorite focal lengths for the majority of their work and reserve other focal lengths for special purposes. For photojournalism, a moderate wide-angle and a telephoto lens are most useful. In a 35mm format, this would be a wide-angle of 28mm focal length and a telephoto of 200mm focal length.

The wide-angle lens is ideal for pictures of two or three people engaged in a common activity and for pictures in which you need extra depth of field. The shallower depth of field inherent in the telephoto lens makes it possible to throw backgrounds out of focus, concentrating your viewers' attention on the main subject.

Another lens to consider is a macro lens. This is a lens designed to take extreme close-ups without having to use close-up attachments. Basically, a macro lens has a focusing range from extremely close up all the way to infinity. Just to keep things confusing, macro lenses are sometimes referred to as micro lenses.

Once you have a range of lenses, you may find that you use the normal lens so seldom that it hardly pays to own one. In fact, if you're purchasing a new camera, you may want to consider buying just the camera body with the moderate wide-angle and the telephoto and not buying the normal lens at all.

> **Tip**: Use a lens shade on any lens that is not deeply recessed in the lens barrel. The shade prevents glare and protects the lens from bumps.

Other accessories

Extra batteries. Only a few fully mechanical 35mm SLR cameras are manufactured now. The batteries in most newer cameras operate not only the exposure meter, but also the shutter release. Unless the camera has a mechanical shutter release for emergencies, a dead battery means no pictures.

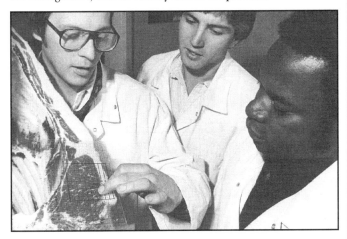

A midrange wide-angle (35mm) works well in tight quarters with little distortion.

A superwide-angle 16mm or fisheye takes in a very wide view of this biochemical lab, yet tends to distort everything near the edge of the picture and near the lens.

Lights. You need these for copy work and indoor shooting. Clamp-on lights with reflectors are inexpensive and flexible. Copy stands offer even more versatility, although the need to copy flat art is rapidly passing into the domain of the computer.

Tripods. These steadying devices permit the use of slow shutter speeds and small lens openings for greater depth of field. Tripods are also used for copy jobs. Select a sturdy tripod that's easy to set up and adjust. It should have a center post for quickly changing camera height and an easy-to-operate, positive-locking pan-tilt head. Metal tripods are generally more rigid and durable than those with plastic parts. Stability is the crucial feature here. You often will need a cable release to keep from moving the camera when you release the shutter. A monopod (a one-legged tripod) also may be used to steady a camera.

A telephoto lens (135mm in this case) compresses the scene, accentuating the closeness of the houses to the farmland.

Film holders and protectors. If you'll be using several rolls of film in one outing, film canisters on your camera strap will help you keep your hands and pockets free. They also protect against misplaced or damaged film.

A lead-shielded film bag is a good idea for photographers who frequently pass through airport X-ray checks.

Close-up photography

Close-ups add greatly to the impact of a slide show and can be a valuable teaching tool as well. Close-up photography isn't difficult but does require some additional equipment and practice.

Close-up devices

The best way to take close-up photos with an SLR is a macro lens. Another approach is to increase the distance between the lens and the film plane by using extension tubes or bellows.

The advantages of a macro lens:

- They are small, light, and easy to carry in the field.
- With through-the-lens metering, they require no exposure compensation.
- They operate like any other lens on an SLR.
- They also function like a normal lens, so you can use them for regular photographic purposes as well as for close-ups.

Extension tubes and bellows. Because they are inserted between the lens and camera to increase the lens-to-film distance, extension tubes and bellows can be used only on cameras with interchangeable lenses. The greater the extension, the closer the camera will focus.

Extension tubes are rigid metal rings that can be used separately or in combination to achieve varying amounts of extension. When used with a 50mm lens, tubes are best suited to photographing subjects one-inch high or larger.

The advantages of extension tubes:

- They are less expensive than bellows.
- They are fairly compact and rugged, making their use in the field feasible.
- The more expensive units retain the automatic diaphragm operation of the lens.

Bellows consist of an accordion-pleated cloth tube mounted on a geared track. With a 50mm lens, bellows work best for subjects one-inch high or smaller. Bellows are larger and heavier than other devices but allow more flexibility for small objects.

The advantages of extension bellows:

- They are faster to adjust than extension tubes.
- The amount of adjustment is infinitely variable.
- Bellows permit greater image magnification than extension tubes or macro lenses.

Because extension devices increase the lens-to-film distance, the light intensity reaching the film decreases. To compensate, you must increase the exposure in proportion to the amount of extension used. Directions for calculating this exposure factor are supplied with the instructions for these devices.

Camera steadiness is crucial in close-up work because any camera movement is magnified as much as the image is. A sturdy tripod is recommended, when it can be used. Unfortunately, most tripods can't be set low enough for many natural subjects. A bean bag, boat cushion, or rolled-up jacket can be a low angle camera support. A cable release is also recommended.

Lighting is often a problem in the field as many subjects are in the shade or in partial sunlight. A small electronic flash unit is a handy accessory to supplement natural light. A few tests in close-up situations will help you determine the correct close-up exposure with flash.

A reflector made of white posterboard or aluminum foil is useful for pumping light into shadow areas. Place the reflector as close as possible to the shaded side of the subject without getting it into the picture area. A reflector also can be used with a flash to lighten the harsh shadows created by direct flash.

Backgrounds can be a problem when the subject blends into the background so well that it becomes indistinct or when bright, out-of-focus areas distract from the subject. Artificial backgrounds can be made from cardboard or cloth. Natural colors, such as brown or green, tend to complement most natural subjects. Bright colors will give the photograph a studio appearance and may conflict with the colors in the subject. Keep the background distant enough so it remains out of focus (generally, not a problem because depth of field is extremely limited in close-ups) and remains free of shadows. Make sure the background is large enough to cover the entire picture area.

Document copying

Most graphic and title slides are now made with a computer rather than a camera. Graphics from a variety of print sources can be scanned, manipulated by a computer, and made into a slide on a computerized film recorder. But if you don't have access to the computer equipment, effective lecture slides still can be produced by photographing existing illustrations and graphics from textbooks, magazines, or other existing sources. However, beware of copyright violations.

A 35mm camera equipped with a macro lens is ideal for copying documents. Copying is easiest if you mount the camera on a copystand. This is simply a vertical pole with a mounting plate for the camera. The height is adjustable, and the camera always stays parallel to the base. A photoflood light mounted at a 45 degree angle on each side of the base will provide glare-free illumination.

Although it can be awkward with the camera pointed straight down, you can also use a tripod for copying. If you use a tripod, make sure the legs do not cast shadows on the material being photographed.

A sheet of 1/4 inch plate glass is helpful to flatten documents that may be wrinkled or to hold magazine pages flat. Just place the glass over the document and shoot through it. To keep your camera from reflecting in the glass, mask the camera with a piece of black cardboard. Cut a hole in it for the camera lens and hold directly beneath the camera when you're making the exposure.

When copying material that's very light in tone, such as printed data on a white background, your camera's meter will read the white background as gray, and your slides will be underexposed. Make substitute readings off the palm of your hand or off a gray card rather than directly off the document.

Warning: Most printed material is copyrighted and therefore illegal to reproduce.

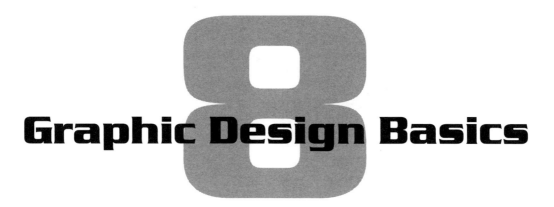

Graphic Design Basics

Long before the intricacies of modern language evolved, graphics were the key element in communication. Visual symbols were fundamental to man's understanding of a message. When words failed, pictures would communicate. In fact, such visual symbols became the basis for written language. Letters of the earliest alphabets were nothing more than symbols conveying a concept understood by the reader.

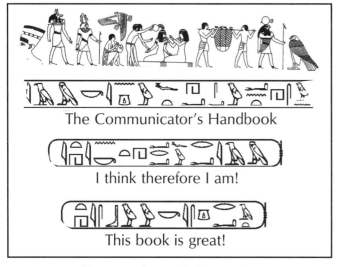

The Communicator's Handbook

I think therefore I am!

This book is great!

Letters are nothing more than symbols conveying concepts.

Much has been written on the impact of graphics on the evolution of man and his ability to communicate effectively. As important as it seems in a historical context, graphic design is every bit as important today. Visual elements show us how to open packages, how to wash clothes, how to assemble goods, and how to communicate with our computer. Graphics tell us which doors to enter and where to exit. Imagine driving a car without the help of graphics. Everything from which gear you're using, where to turn, and when to stop is communicated graphically.

If your goal is to communicate successfully, understanding the principles of graphic design is helpful. Whether you are writing a newsletter, designing a magazine, laying out a newspaper ad, making a poster, or delivering a speech, the use of graphics can make the difference in your effectiveness. Graphics

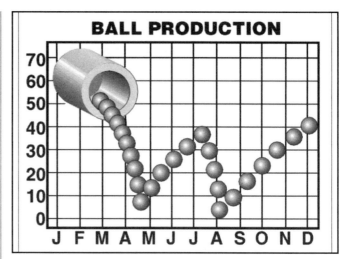

The use of graphics can make your presentation more attractive, clarify your message, and increase retention.

can make your product or production more attractive, clarify your message, and increase retention by your audience. This happens only when design principles are understood and followed. However, bad graphics can have just as much impact, though it won't be necessarily a favorable impact.

Students of graphic design, even those blessed with abundant talent, spend years perfecting their skills. This chapter will not impose unrealistic goals on those who protest "I can't draw a straight line even with a ruler." You won't have to struggle with tasks for which you lack aptitude. You simply need to understand, remember, and implement the principles if you want graphics to enhance your message.

The design process: keep it simple

As with other communication professionals, a graphic designer begins by asking specific questions. "What do I have to say and who needs to hear it?" When objectives are clearly understood, you can focus on solutions. Whatever the message might be, and whomever the audience might be, the visual must support and clarify that message. It doesn't matter which medium is used to convey the message. The principles remain the same.

Consider your audience carefully. Accommodate any peculiarities they present to you. Let's assume that you're designing a newsletter. If your audience is quite young, the use of visuals increases your chances of delivering a message to this group, which is not usually fond of extensive reading. If you're addressing an older audience, you'll want to consider larger type to compensate for possible vision problems. If you wish to reach researchers, graphs conveying data are useful. Though these approaches seem obvious, they too often are overlooked.

Learn from good examples

So you don't know where to begin? Look around you. What advertisements catch your attention in the magazines you read? What visual image remains clear in your mind from this morning's paper? Which poster stands out on a bulletin board? Study such examples of effective use of graphics. You can learn so much by observing techniques and solutions employed by others.

Learn from good examples. Look around you. Start paying attention to graphic designs in magazines, television, posters, billboards, etc.

Your overall design and use of visuals must not be complicated. The competition for the eye's attention is fierce. If your design and your visuals are clean, simple, clearly stated, and harmonious with the message, then you're helping your audience. You must assume that your audience doesn't understand what you're saying. You might as well assume, too, that your audience won't be generous in giving you time to say much. Keep everything very simple. Don't use visuals for mere adornment. Make them work for you. Don't overdo it, either. If one visual works in relating the message, you don't need more.

You'll notice how simplicity prevails. The poster with a few words well-placed and readable and with one strong, supportive visual is the one that works. The page that makes nice use of space, headlines and sub-heads, without too much text crammed into it, is the one you stop to read.

Start paying attention to such things and you'll see the style of good graphic designers. A casual observer or reader seldom realizes how much thought and planning goes into the design of a printed piece or into the graphics flashed on a television screen. The style is intended to catch your attention, to clearly state a message, and to have that message retained. That's the style you need to achieve. With a planned, balanced use of space, good selection of type, and clearly understood visuals supporting the message, your style can be effective.

Beginning to take shape

One of the design standards we need to understand first is the actual layout of a page. What determines the actual format of your page design? The problem is the allocation of space to the elements you wish to include. It's very much the same problem that you face when you begin placing furniture in an empty room.

Begin with a plan or a format. In designing newsletters, posters, brochures and other printed materials, you'll want to know that there are industry standards when it comes to sheet sizes. For economic reasons, standard page sizes exist worldwide. The paper mills and the manufacturers of printing and copying equipment have made the 8 1/2 x 11-inch page a universal common denominator. Even high-end digital printers and output devices follow this standard.

Though less common, 8 1/2 x 14-inch, or legal sheets, also are readily available. The other standard sheet, 11 x 17-inch, is really just a way to get four pages of 8 1/2 x 11-inch on a single sheet folded in half. Save yourself money and aggravation and do your design with those sizes as your standard. They are still very flexible and workable sizes.

Accordingly, let's consider designing a page to be printed on an 8 1/2 x 11-inch sheet. What format are we going to follow? The concept of columns of type (as in a newspaper) instead of words all the way across the page (as in a letter) serves many useful purposes. Of course you can get more words on a page this way.

The best reason, however, is that your audience is benefitted with quicker and easier reading. (Remember, always to make things easier for your audience.) Research reveals that people read faster and retain more when reading from columns. The eye doesn't have to scan all the way across the page for every line down the page.

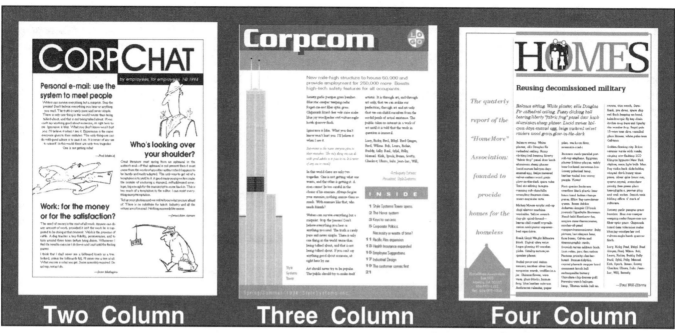

Decide which column format best fits your graphic needs.

Consider the equipment you use. Other factors need to be considered in determining a format. If columns are going to be used, are there going to be two or three columns on a page? You need to consider the source of your typed columns. Are you using a typewriter, your computer, or commercially set type? What are your limiting factors?

Don't design beyond your capabilities. Even if you have nothing more than a typewriter, chances are you have access to a copier that enlarges and reduces. Don't feel limited. (A copier is also a good solution for making your type darker if your printer or typewriter comes out too light.)

A two-column page is an easy format to work with, but three columns give you a little more flexibility in your design. (More than three columns on an 8 1/2 x 11-inch sheet probably won't give you enough column width to have many words per line. You don't want to hamper your reader with too many columns.)

Putting your ideas on paper

Your tools. Nothing short of actually performing the task can convince you that you can do it. There are plenty of sophisticated tools for the graphic designer. Unless you plan to design a lot of material, you don't need to spend much money to get the job done right. If you don't have a drafting table, use a desk top, dining table, or an old door set up as a table. You'll need a T-square, a triangle, a rule, some scissors or a knife blade, masking tape, and rubber cement. Drawing pens and pencils also will be used. A visit to an art-supply store will acquaint you with much better tools to use, of course, but you can get by with these.

Your T-square is placed on the left or right of your table, opposite the hand with which you draw. Tape your sheet down on the table, making sure the top edge of the sheet is parallel with the T-square. You only need to tape down the corners of the sheet to keep it in place. Your triangle is to draw vertical lines and angles.

Designers quickly learn not to use the T-square or triangle as a cutting edge. Nicks prevent you from making clean, straight lines. Also, always keep these tools clean on both sides. If you use your triangle or T-square for doing ink lines, place some masking tape just in from the edge around all sides of the triangle and under the T-square. By placing the taped side down, the triangle is elevated enough to keep ink from smearing or running.

If you are designing on a computer using word processing or desktop publishing software, you should use the same design techniques. Desktop publishing software uses tools such as T-squares, rules, and lines which are built into the software program.

Also, the flexibility of desktop publishing software allows you to do rough layouts which can be saved in different computer files. The files can be used as rough designs to update existing designs or to make quick changes to accommodate client needs.

Establish margins on all four sides of your page. Allowing at least a one-inch margin all around usually will be a safe solution. A cramped page is not an inviting one. Also, printing limitations usually require specific minimum margins. Know these things before you start.

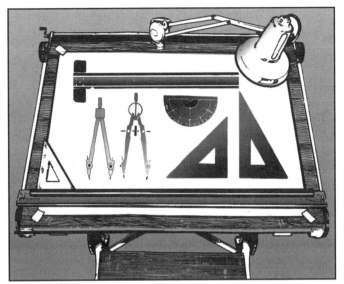

You'll need a T-square, a triangle, a ruler, scissors, rubber cement, a drawing board, and masking tape.

Design the format. Now let's design a three-column newsletter format. A designer begins making his or her layout as a rough pencil sketch to show where each column, each headline, each visual, etc., should fit. Mark your margins first. Within that space you'll "package" your message. With a one-inch margin on each side, we have 6-1/2 inches across within which we'll work. We can make three two-inch columns with a 1/4-inch space separating each column. Pencil these in to establish a grid which allows your eye to visualize space available.

Having done this, you now have a basic pattern to use. This grid will be the basis for every page of the particular job at hand. This consistency gives your newsletter, or whatever the assignment might be, its unity. Now you can have the manuscript set in type. Our grid tells us we want the words to be set in columns that are two inches wide.

Typefaces

To the uninitiated, the world of typefaces may seem overwhelming. It's not. It's true that there are hundreds of styles of type. They all have different names, come in different sizes, and can be bold, light, or medium. But the distinctions are actually subtle. All typefaces can be classified into two basic groups: serif and sans serif. A third group is decorative type. They are, as the name implies, used more for ornament and novelty and have relatively little application. Decorative types might be used on certificates or invitations, for instance, but they are generally harder to read.

Serif and sans serif. A serif type refers to letters which have small horizontal parts attached to the top and bottom of the letters. Frequently called flags and feet, these serifs, or horizontal edges on letters, are the feature which distinguish a typeface from the sans serif (without serifs) group.

In ancient Rome, when letters were commonly chiseled into walls of buildings, the straight-edged letters often resulted in cracks and fissures developing in the wall. To avoid that problem, they began putting horizontal edges on the top and bottom of the vertical lines forming the letters. Rounding off the letter in this way changed the direction of the stress, eliminated cracks, and introduced the concept of a serif typeface to western civilization.

Though considerable research has been done on the merits of serif versus sans serif type, most of it is contradictory. No definitive study prevails. The selection of one over another is usually arbitrary and the result of individual preference.

However, if you are designing information for mediums such as CD-ROM and the World Wide Web, special care should be taken when choosing typefaces. Remember that in both instances the type will be viewed primarily on a computer screen. Certain typefaces such as decorative or thick/thin serif typefaces are not highly readable on computer screens. Use a typeface that is neither too bold or too thin with equal thickness on vertical and horizontal lines.

Type selection. Individual preference doesn't mean you can select any typeface for any function and be effective. Common sense should help you. Study various typefaces in magazines and other printed pieces. Each typeface has its own personality. Some are formal, some whimsical, and some are easier to read. Consider your message and your audience and select a typeface that suits each. A helpful lesson can be learned from studying the various typefaces used by corporations for their logos or trademarks. Graphic designers carefully select a type that reflects the image a corporation wishes to project. You can do the same thing when selecting a typeface.

A serif type refers to letters which have small horizontal parts attached to the top and bottom of the letters.

Keep the design simple with typeface selection, too. You'll want to use an easily read typeface for the body copy, or the bulk of your text. Don't change typefaces within your text. If emphasis on a particular word is needed, bold or italicized letters may be used, but make these exceptions sparingly. Your headings, subheads, and captions under photos or illustrations ought to contrast with the body copy. Do this by using a bolder face of the same type, by using a larger size, by using sans serif type for text and a serif type for the headings, or some similar scheme. Be aware that using all uppercase (capital) letters is very difficult to read. Avoid that syndrome.

More than anything, you must remember to keep it all simple, clean, and clear. A page with a mixture of types is cluttered and ends up competing with or distracting from your message.

Visuals and spacing

The spacing between letters, between lines, and between text and headlines is also an important consideration. In most cases, technology controls those factors for you. Whether you're using a personal computer, a typewriter, or purchasing type from a professional typesetter, you want to think about how you space the elements. Good use of space allows your message to "breathe" and usually makes reading easier. However, be careful that you don't put too much space between a visual and its caption or between a subhead and the text relating to it.

Make sure your reader knows which elements relate to what. As unscientific as it sounds, your eye can usually tell you whether you are using space wisely. If you are using hand-set letters, such as transfer type available at office supply and art stores, you need to know that not all letters and numbers require the same space between them. In fact, it looks awkward and is less readable if exactly the same space is used between each letter. The shape of the letters dictates how you space them. For instance, the parallel lines in an uppercase A and an uppercase W require that they be placed closer together when in sequence. The same concept applies when lettering by hand.

> **Word Spacing** → ← → ← **Character Spacing**
> ## Alcalde Center Funding
> **Line Spacing**
> Smaller growers of eleven north-central New Mexico counties have been getting some help in the form of agricultural expertise from New Mexico State Univerity's Sustainable Agricultural Science Center at Alcalde, just north of Espanola.
> **Paragraph Spacing**
> The Rural Agricultural Improvement and Public Affairs Project, or RAIPAP, based at Alcalde, has

Be sure you think about the spacing between letters, lines, text, visuals, and headlines. Good use of space allows your message to "breathe."

Keep the design simple when using computers, too. As mentioned earlier, the use of personal computers with word processing and desktop publishing software has minimized the problems of determining appropriate space between letters. The computer, however, doesn't solve all of the design problems. In fact, the advent of desktop publishing systems made it even more important for people to understand the basic principles of graphic design. Now that more people have access to systems that set type in many different faces, that create borders and symbols, etc., the tendency is to use them all at once.

Don't give in to the temptation to use all the typefaces, borders, and symbols available on your computer.

There is probably an application for every feature a system can do; otherwise it wouldn't be included. Don't give in to the temptation to use it all on the same page, or in the same newsletter. Remember that initially your reader needs to be attracted to the piece. The same reader needs to be able to comprehend your message without having to weave in and out of a catalog of computer tricks.

Using photos and other visuals

Take time to select a good visual that supports your text. If the reader isn't helped by using the visual, you may be better off using blank space (also called white space or negative space).

Illustrations. If you have drawing skills, do a clean, simple line drawing to illustrate a point. If you're designing something for a church, social group, or your business, you might find someone else who can draw and is willing to help you. The value of original art is that you can make it exactly the size of the space you wish to fill and also you need only include that which clearly supports your text.

Photos. If a good photo exists, use it. A frequently used trick of graphic designers is to set up or stage a pose demonstrating a process or concept and to take an instant photo of it. By placing tracing paper over the photo, you can trace the outline of the important components of the photo and eliminate what isn't needed. You end up with a line drawing that will reproduce nicely when your piece is printed. This tracing technique also solves the problem of a photo that won't reproduce well because it's too dark or lacks contrast, for example.

Reproducing a photo in a printed document introduces several new challenges to consider. It costs more than a line drawing, for instance, and requires some extra work in the layout stages. Also, a photo won't always reproduce well on a copy machine. Color photos are much more expensive and require technical knowledge beyond the focus of this chapter.

There's reason to use a good photo, though, if a good one exists and helps clarify your message. If the subject of the photo is in focus, if it has good contrast (sufficient distinctions between the blacks, the grays, and the whites), and if it helps the reader understand what you are trying to communicate, it will work for you. Details for accommodating a photo into your brochure or newsletter will be discussed later.

The use of clip-art can reinforce your message, and there are a number of royalty-free clip-art images available on CD-ROM.

Clip-art. There are good sources of clip-art for sale that provide you with reproducible illustrations in a wide variety of topics. For that matter, you can cut art from a number of sources. Do not use art from a copyrighted work, however, without the publisher's permission. Many useful drawings such as famous landmarks or historical figures appear in old books printed so long ago that the copyrights have expired. Such works in the public domain are free to use. It might be worth a visit to your public library to photocopy drawings from an old reference book. Most U.S. government publications are not copyrighted and have good illustrations.

Above all, remember that the visual has to help the reader understand your message. Don't use one just to have one. Make it work for you. Don't overdo it, either. Whether it's a photo, a drawing, a graph or chart, or just a subhead with large decorative type, don't junk up your design with overkill.

The layout process

Now comes the fun part. With a format established, with type set, and good visuals, you now can fit the pieces together. All of the earlier work is just to prepare you for the final step in conceiving your finished piece. You'll want to experiment with all of the elements before you decide, so make photocopies of everything to play with and save your good drawings, photos, and type for the final layout.

Cut your type into columns. Your headlines and subheadings should be larger and can be cut into words or phrases. By moving the columns of type on the grids of your layout sheet, you'll determine how much space your message requires.

Your headlines deserve more space. Experiment with several options. Leave open space above ior beside them; move them to the left margin or to the right. Take advantage of the opportunities that three columns give you. Your headline might work in one column. You can extend it across two or all three columns.

What looks interesting? What attracts the reader? Also consider which visuals relate to text on that page. What size do you want the visual to be? Where do you place the visual? Though illustrations and photos need to be closely situated to the text they support, it's more important to consider how balanced the page looks. You always can relate visuals to text by using Figure 1, Figure 2, and so on, in the caption to the visual and then refer to that figure number in the text itself.

Balance. In attempting to achieve balance in your design, you must realize that elements such as illustrations, photos, and headlines, by their size and boldness, will carry more "weight" than the rest of the text. This means that the eye is more readily attracted to that space by its dominance. You achieve a balanced look by spacing these elements with careful consideration of their relationship with everything else on the page. Imagine your page as a plane balanced on a central point.

As you place a bold heading in one corner, for instance, the opposite corner will need something to balance that weight or dominance. Don't always think that symmetry is the solution to balance. It isn't. All of the visuals could be placed in one column and still have a balanced look.

It's important in laying out consecutive pages in a newsletter, brochure, etc., that you consider the balance on one page with the balance on the page opposite it. A reader sees both pages at once when looking at an opened magazine. That whole look must be balanced to be attractive.

Don't forget that blank space can be used visually to create balance. The contrast of small type surrounded by white space is going to draw attention to that space, for example. Don't be afraid of leaving blank space if it helps to balance everything. Your eye is a good judge of what is visually interesting and exciting. Experiment. Notice what designers do in popular magazines.

Nothing usually happens by chance with good graphic design. Balance is planned and the elements are ordered carefully and intentionally. Use logical order to bring the reader's attention to information in proper sequence. By leading your reader's eye from point to point in an orderly sequence, you'll help the reader's comprehension and encourage subject matter retention. Don't disrupt or confuse the flow of information by using poor design.

Mock-up or dummy. When your design looks right to your eye, tape all of the elements on your grid sheet. It doesn't need to be precise. It will show you if sections of the text need to be shortened or expanded. It will show you if you need to enlarge or reduce your visual. It also will serve as a good model to submit to anyone who needs to approve your concept. And it enables your printer to estimate production costs for you. This step is called your mock-up or dummy.

Put your plan into action

Using your dummy as a guide, you are now ready to make a final paste-up. In commercial printing, this final paste-up is photographed to make the plates for the offset printing press. This is also called a camera-ready layout. At this stage, everything must be neat and precise. Trim your columns of type and headings closely and carefully. Using the same grid as your dummy, your type and drawings will be secured by using a thin coat of rubber cement on the back side of the type. Some designers use tweezers or an X-acto knife to lift the cemented type into place. Secure it into the position indicated by your dummy. Avoid smearing and smudging. You must be neat. Rubber cement is usually easy to clean up and allows you to move the type around after you put it into place. Use your T-square and triangle to make certain that the columns are within the designated

To help you decide how to crop photos, make two pieces of L-shaped cardboard to use as frames.

grids and that the type is aligned. Use a cover sheet of tracing paper to press everything neatly in place.

You can't be too careful at this stage of your production. The way it ends up on your layout sheet is the way it is going to print. Designers use light blue non-photo pencils, available from art - and office-supply stores, to establish guidelines within which they can work. The pencils are called non-photo because their light markings are not perceived by the camera when the printer begins production. Any other marks on your layout, however, will be reproduced. Be careful!

Working with photos in the layout

If you're using photographs or drawings that need to be enlarged or reduced from what is available, there are some steps you should take. Remember that you want the photo to help the reader understand the point you're demonstrating. The photo must show clearly what is needed for the reader to comprehend. There may be other aspects of the photograph you would prefer to eliminate. There may be only one segment of the photo that relates to your message. Designers use cropping in these situations.

Cropping photos. To crop a photo means to zero in on your subject and eliminate what isn't needed. Make two L-shaped pieces of cardboard to use as frames around the photo. Move them in and out until you get just the portion of the photo that you want. In the margins of the photo, mark lines where you want the photo cropped horizontally and vertically. This achieves the same effect as taking the scissors to everything you don't want without actually cutting your photograph. You must realize that the shape of the photo after cropping is the space you must allow in your layout.

Sizing photos. You'll probably need to know how to enlarge or reduce the size of the photo. It's seldom when an available photo or piece of art exists in exactly the size you ultimately need. There are tools, such as proportion scales, which can help you figure what percentage the enlargement or reduction will be. They are inexpensive and readily available at art-supply stores. However, as long as you understand how shapes change proportionately, you can get by without this purchase.

To illustrate this concept, consider that you have a photo that you've cropped to 3-1/4 width and a two-inch height. The space that you have allowed for the photo in your layout is 6-1/2 inches wide. You will be enlarging the photo to twice its original size. You must realize that when you make that photo twice as wide, you are automatically making it twice as high. Accordingly, you must make your space available in the layout to fit both dimensions. This process is called scaling. The formula is simply the ratio that follows:

$$\frac{\text{original height}}{\text{original width}} \quad X \quad \frac{\text{adjusted height}}{\text{adjusted width}}$$

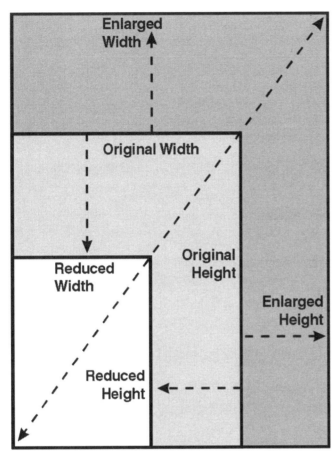

If you have trouble with algebra, you can draw your own diagonal scale illustrated above.

ings, the image is converted to a series of dots in a tightly spaced pattern. This is called a halftone negative. Look at a photo in your local newspaper and you'll see that it's a dot pattern.

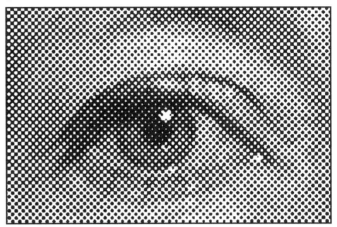

Because of the variations of gray tones in a photo, the image is converted to a series of dots in a tightly spaced pattern called a halftone.

Measure the width and height of your original image. Draw a box with those dimensions. Extend a diagonal line from the lower left corner through the upper right corner. Determine which is the critical dimension according to your layout space requirements. It doesn't matter if it's width or height. Let's use the earlier example. Your original image is 3-1/4 inches wide. You want to enlarge it to 6-1/2 inches wide. Extend the base line of your diagonal scale to the 6-1/2-inch mark. If you draw a perpendicular line up from that 6-1/2-inch mark, the point where it intersects the diagonal line will tell you what the enlarged height will be. The distance from your base line to the diagonal is the enlarged height. The same principle will tell you reduced heights or widths.

Confusing? It shouldn't be. Don't hesitate to check with your printer for help. As long as you explain what you want, the printer will help you get it right.

Halftones. There is one other point to make about preparing a camera-ready layout that involves a photo. Recall that the photo will cost extra to reproduce in your printed piece. That is because it will require a special negative to be developed by the printer. Because of the variations of gray tones in a photo, unlike the stark blacks and whites of your type and line draw-

In order for the printer to reproduce the photo accurately showing the range of gray tones, the halftone negative is made. When you make your camera-ready layout, you will not be gluing the actual photo down on your layout sheet. You will indicate the space where the photo is to go by using a solid box in that space. Professionals use rubylith, a red adhesive film, that can be trimmed right in the space where your photo will go. When your camera-ready layout is processed by the printer, the negative will show a transparent window where the rubylith was. A halftone negative of your cropped photo is made to the size you've indicated it should be. The halftone negative is then placed into that window. Your photo is printed reasonably close to the quality of your original.

More details

Any other directions you may have for the printer should be written down and securely attached to your camera-ready layout. Discuss all of your requirements extensively with the printer. Don't hesitate to seek advice on paper and ink combinations.

Papers and inks. Paper selection can be tricky. There are many colors, many finishes, and many weights to consider. Few selections will work for any given application. If you intend to mail your printed document, don't forget that more weight means more postage. Perhaps a trip to a mail center with samples of your printed document and paper can help determine if your document meets postal regulations. It may be useful to rely on a graphic designer or printing professional to help you make a decision. If your application and your budget are understood, it's easier for professionals to give good advice.

What about ink color? It must contrast with the paper. But don't overdo it. Your message, your visuals, your audience, and your budget need to be considered. You might like the color of a particular green ink. Is it readable? Does it suit your content? If there is a photo of ground beef, for example, do you want it to be green? Use common sense. If the printed piece is going to be mailed, then be sure that the ink color you choose is readable by postage scanning equipment.

Photos actually reproduce best when using black ink on white paper. The darker the ink and the lighter the paper, the better your grey tones will reproduce. Unless your intention is to be outrageous, you are better off trying to be tasteful.

Summary

To repeat an earlier premise, graphic designers spend years perfecting their skills. The best are formally trained for four or five years and have many years of professional experience. You won't achieve that level from this chapter alone.

The concepts are not hard to understand. Use common sense. Consider your message and your audience. Keep everything simple. Know that the eye is attracted to balance and order. Any visual element needs to be a strong image clearly related to your message.

Though we've concentrated on printed materials for use in a newsletter, the basic principles apply to other designs. A hand-drawn poster requires the same process of thought. A color slide relies on the same concepts to be effective. It's all related to how visual elements can help you communicate.

A great way to learn is to be aware of what works in commercial advertising. The next time you look through a magazine, pay attention to the ads and how they handle space. What visual elements are effective? Try these tactics on your own work. If you're not satisfied with your first effort, don't worry. You learn more with each effort.

Exhibit Design And Production

Exhibits can be a cost-effective method of communicating messages to large audiences. There are transportation, setup, and staffing problems that must be faced with each exhibition. But these are outweighed by the potential of cost-effectively presenting messages to large audiences at gatherings such as festivals, fairs, shopping malls, trade shows, meetings, and conferences. If properly designed, they can be easily updated and used again many times.

Exhibits can include many different media: printed copy, illustrations, photographic prints, projected images, live/real materials, television, computers, interactive devices, and others. They can include live presentations such as show-and-tell, demonstrations, acting/role-playing, story-telling, and informative talks. Consider the appropriateness of each of these methods and media for getting your message to your audience. Which do they prefer? Exhibits should be designed to communicate visually and should be fun, or at least interesting to view.

Most communication media have viewers follow a set reading/viewing pattern, A to B to C. Exhibits allow viewers to begin anywhere and spend more time with whatever elements interest them. Part of an exhibit's advantage is that viewers enjoy the freedom of quickly choosing attractive items and bypassing less interesting topics. Information must be condensed for exhibit presentation since most viewers spend only a few seconds to several minutes looking at it. Visual displays often have vivid graphics to guide viewers to points of interest within the display. If viewers scan an exhibit and are not attracted by some interesting item or items, they'll move on to something else.

In this age of electronic media, attention spans are growing shorter. We must compete with many other forms of communication for the viewer's attention. The competition is bigger, brighter, more animated, and more colorful than ever. If an exhibit is to be effective, it must be planned well, visually exciting and attractive, but condensed and direct. Only then can it compete effectively.

Planning your exhibit

Purpose. If an educational exhibit is to be effective, it must convey to the viewers something they didn't know before viewing the exhibit. You may wish to modify their behavior in some way, educate them on a particular topic, or influence their attitudes or beliefs. Decide if you want them to take specific action, change opinions, or just be aware of some new information.

The purpose of an exhibit is usually decided before the methods and media are selected. Decide if the purpose is to teach, show relationships, or promote. If the exhibit is to be an effective communication tool, one must keep in mind the purpose for communicating throughout the planning, design, and production process.

Subject. Select a subject or approach that has personal appeal to a large portion of your audience. With many agricultural topics, for instance, many larger audiences may be more interested in consumer information than production techniques since so few of them are closely associated with actual farm production. Timing is also essential. For example, a vegetable variety exhibit would interest more people before spring planting time than it would in the fall. And if an exhibit is localized, it will draw greater interest. Displaying materials or quoting facts from your local community or county is usually more interesting than using information or materials from a distant part of the country.

Choose a subject that's specific. A broad subject will be harder for you to cover adequately and more difficult for your viewers to comprehend. A simple subject is easier to design and communicate successfully, particularly if you limit the number of main points to three or four. You can't tell all you know in a single exhibit, so focus your message on a point that's particularly valuable to your audience.

Be sure to include only material that provides a real contribution toward your purpose. Look critically at the information as your viewers will see it. Emphasize the main points of your subject and minimize the details. Detailed information can be printed in a handout, or you may provide an address or a telephone number for further information.

Audience. Decide exactly who your audience will be. Many of the decisions involving design will be affected by the age, sex, background, educational level, and lifestyle of your audience. Important questions to ask yourself are: a) What does my audience know about – or b) What's their attitude toward – me, my organization, and my topic?

Change your methods as your audience changes. Consider a different means of presenting information to younger groups than you would to older, more conservative individuals. Bright colors, large graphics, and more hands-on materials may work better for younger audiences. Adults often prefer a more straight forward presentation that shows how your ideas may be applied to daily life. Generally, you can find several people to represent your specified audience and ask them for opinions on message content and design ideas before you go on.

Consider the location(s) where the exhibit will be displayed. What form of exhibit will work well there? What will it take to visually "grab" them? What kinds of people will be there? What are their interests? How familiar will they be with the information covered in your exhibit? What can your exhibit do for them?

Tell the story with visuals. The exhibit on the left has too much copy, not enough visuals.

Visual attractions

Exhibits are intended to be different than newspapers, brochures, and magazines. Messages should be conveyed in a vivid, pictorial manner. Minimize the copy. Viewers will not spend time reading long paragraphs in exhibits. Consider handouts to convey detailed information.

Live or real objects. Because of the convenience of obtaining, mounting, and displaying visual representations, we often overlook the possibility of using real objects. Live animals always attract attention. Plants, equipment, or other real objects are usually superior visuals if you can use them.

Models. Whenever the size or visual limitations of a live or real object are prohibitive, a model may be helpful. A model can provide a miniaturization of a much larger objec, or an enlarged version of a smaller object. A model allows viewers to focus on the important parts by eliminating unnecessary details or visual obstructions. Cut-away views can show "inside information."

Photographs. Photo enlargements can provide a realistic look at an object or a situation. The photos should eliminate distractions and irrelevant details and should zero in on the areas that support the desired message. This medium can condense large objects or enlarge small ones. Often closeup shots are better at focusing on your point than broad shots. Avoid having many small photos; use fewer but larger prints. Use a mix of sizes and formats for added design appeal. Avoid "lining them up" in rigid formation. They'll have a friendlier look if they're clustered in one or more informal groupings.

Projected images. Motion pictures, slides, filmstrips, overhead transparencies, and television can be useful as exhibit visuals. Common sense must keep the designer from expecting the audience to spend much time viewing this type of visual. Just because the pictures are moving or changing, or they are accompanied by sound, doesn't guarantee that viewers will spend much more time watching. Unless they have a strong interest in your subject, you can't expect them to give your exhibit much time.

An important consideration relating to projected images is image size. While it may be desirable to have a large image, you'll find that the larger the image size, the less brilliant it becomes. Since exhibits are usually displayed in well-lighted areas, it's normal for the image on the screen to look weak unless it's kept fairly small (no larger than 24 inches), or unless you provide a canopy to eliminate the ambient light.

Computers. Using computers in an exhibit can add interest. They can be programmed to demonstrate or teach certain parts of your message. Some hands-on programs can solicit yes/no answers or lead viewers through a unit of information or a set of questions. Commercially produced colored pictures and computer "movies" are growing in availability. Computer applications that assist communicators in producing and presenting them are becoming less expensive and more user-friendly.

While computers may attract attention, they also may narrow the audience, since fewer viewers can work on keyboards or respond to touch-screen monitors. Projectors are increasingly used to present computer information to larger audiences on larger-format screens. Again, the larger sizes may be less brilliant and require a canopy to eliminate ambient light.

Illustrations. With illustrations, the creator can eliminate unwanted detail, exaggerate portions to provide emphasis, and communicate a message in its most basic form. While the appearance should be attractive, it's not necessary for the illustration to appear as a beautiful work of art. It may be accompanied by a headline or message statement or stand alone to convey its own message.

Graphics. Charts and graphs can be helpful visuals in showing changes, relationships, and differences. Be sure to choose the appropriate type of graph to communicate your message. Try not to have too many bars in a bar chart or pie slices in a pie chart – keep it simple. A variety of computer applications are available that can provide good assistance with chart and graph making.

Other graphics include large or unusual letters, words, shapes, and design patterns that assist in attracting attention, guiding the viewers' eyes, and communicating a message.

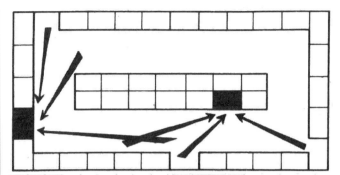

Consider traffic flow and viewing distance. With large lettering and visuals, you can increase legibility and attract attention at a greater distance.

In addition to the unusual visuals, large or unusual letters, words, shapes, and designs can assist in attracting attention and communicating a message.

Exhibit design and construction

An exhibit background or framework organizes the basic shapes formed by the visuals, the copy, and the unused portion of the background (negative space) into an interesting and balanced unit. One definition of design emphasizes that "the elements themselves are subordinated to an overall, unifying plan."

This plan should be pleasing to the eye, yet simple in concept, and should enhance the communication of the message.

All elements should contribute to an overall design that attracts viewers and helps tell the message. Choose straightforward communications and don't allow "artsy" notions to interfere (such as overly-fancy lettering that's difficult to read).

You, as the designer, should have some knowledge about where the exhibit will be located. The theme of the event and the nature of the exhibit location will affect design. The designer should find out about the assigned display space: location, lighting, traffic flow, and viewing distances.

Stage 1: Information gathering

The exhibit-designing process begins by gathering relevant facts and conditions, or limitations about the exhibit: its purpose, the subject, the audience, its location, and the resources you have to work with. Write them down. You usually begin with much more subject matter than a simple, direct design will allow. Organize it into some logical order so viewers can follow easily. Try to focus on an angle that's most interesting to the

audience. This information may then be boiled down into simple phrases or brief statements. Don't hesitate to delete information of lesser importance. Make several attempts at creating a short, catchy title that identifies the topic and gets viewers involved. Use active verbs and vivid words. Be sure the audience can relate to and be invited by the title. The title doesn't have to cover the exhibit topic entirely, only announce its focus.

Stage 2: Organize and visualize

After you've condensed the message into simple phrases or statements, you then must consider the opportunities to support, clarify, or explain them with visuals. Jot these ideas down on paper. Consider a variety of approaches for each visual, but aim for visual ideas that are simple and to the point. Say, for instance, that your exhibit would benefit from a visual that relates to horses. List a number of alternatives: a group of horses, one horse, half a horse, a horse's head, a horse's hoof, a horseshoe, a bridle, a saddle, a riding boot; the list can go on.

Now put yourself in the place of your viewers. Which visual alternative is most appealing? Which best communicates your message? Which is the least complicated? Often the simpler idea is the easier idea to produce and has less chance of being misunderstood.

Stage 3: Sketch a plan

At this point, you begin to imagine how some of these elements interrelate visually. Sketch out your ideas, using pencils and markers. Asymmetrical, or informal, balance is usually more interesting than symmetrical, or formal, balance. Asymmetrical (informal) design avoids "centering the elements," and achieves balance through less-formal means. Informal design gives you or your organization a less rigid, friendlier appearance.

Group your visuals and copy together to make points. Don't try to space them evenly over the entire background. Allow sizable areas of negative space around groupings. A variety of sizes and shapes of negative space adds appeal. Exhibits will look less crowded, and negative space will tend to highlight the visual groupings. As with a printed page, viewers are inclined to read an exhibit from left to right, top to bottom. But design

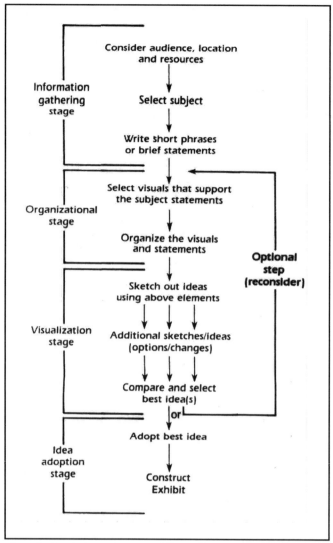

Consider audience, location and resources

↓

Select subject

↓

Write short phrases or brief statements

↓

Select visuals that support the subject statements

↓

Organize the visuals and statements

↓

Sketch out ideas using above elements

↓ ↓ ↓

Additional sketches/ideas (options/changes)

↓ ↓ ↓

Compare and select best idea(s)

or

Adopt best idea

↓

Construct Exhibit

Information gathering stage

Organizational stage

Optional step (reconsider)

Visualization stage

Idea adoption stage

Though the design of every exhibit will vary, this model may be useful during the planning process.

arrangement and visual attractions can overcome that tendency if you wish.

After you've made sketches of a number of ideas, compare and select the sketches you like best, those you think will be most effective with your intended audience. If you reach a point where you've run out of ideas, stop and come back to the project at another time. Ask others for their opinions. It's easier to change at this point than halfway through production.

Stage 4: Ideas become a plan

You may need to allow more time for digestion, and you may have to repeat these steps, or some of them, several times before everything falls into place. When you feel your ideas effectively communicate your message with design elements united into a simple, pleasing, communicative unit - you can move toward final design.

A scale drawing is a common step at this point, followed by the construction of a scale model. Even a quickly-done scale model will provide valuable insight into the visual impact your design will command, as well as production considerations relating to assembly, disassembly and portability. (like how it will fold or how pieces will detach for packing). Then you're ready for the selection of materials and the actual production of the exhibit.

Attention-getters

A good design unites the various elements in such a way that the overall appearance is attractive, inviting, and worthy of attention. If the viewers don't bother to look at it, they won't get your message. A good choice of visuals can be interesting, but coupled with one or more of the following your exhibit can draw considerable attention.

Size. Keep your visuals and lettering large. If your entire exhibit is small, then you must limit your selections in order to keep them as large as possible. If surrounding exhibits have 1/2" lettering, you have a considerable advantage if you use 1" or 2" lettering. This also may require that you use much less copy. Good! Exhibit viewers won't give it much time anyway. And viewers prefer to receive information from visuals rather than words.

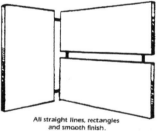

All straight lines, rectangles and smooth finish.

Texture adds interest and the oval draws attention.

Lettering is too small.

Larger letters draw more attention.

Visuals alone are attractive, but size, shape and texture also can increase the attention-getting capacity of an exhibit.

Shape. Many exhibits appear to use only square or rectangular shapes. The use of a round, oval, or other unusual shape can draw immediate attention. A strong vertical shape will contrast with the predominant horizontal lines formed by the lines of lettering, the table, or the top and bottom edges of the exhibit background. Backgrounds need not always have horizontal and vertical lines, even though they are convenient. When the major panel lines are horizontal and vertical, break them up with other lines and shapes.

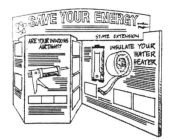 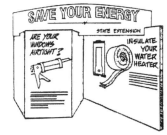

The design should be basically simple, with few elements and much negative space. The exhibit on the left is too crowded.

Using the very large, bold shape of an item that depicts generally gets the exhibit topic generally gets attention. One production technique is to project a small drawing with an overhead projector to make a large graphic that will grab attention.

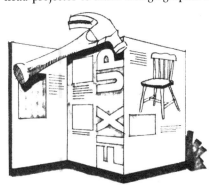

You can design your exhibit so the panels aren't all on one plane. Have some closer and some farther away. And you can use the third dimension in other ways. By mounting a two-dimensional object like a photograph on a thick mat or foam board then placing it on the exhibit surface, your image will appear elevated from the background.

Texture. If much of your exhibit has smooth surfaces, it may be advantageous to add a rough or textured area. This is easily accomplished with rough wood, corrugated paper, burlap fabric, and the like. You can even give this effect by partially painting an area with a sprayer or paint roller, or by striping or mottling with a brush or felt-tip marker.

Color. Be cautious with colors. Extremely bright background colors will detract from the visuals and other exhibit elements. Usually a continuous soft background color and one or two other brighter colors for lettering or visuals are adequate. Bright colors can attract attention or draw interest to certain areas of the exhibit, but be careful how colors are combined and used. Be sure to draw viewers' eyes to where you want them. You can check on your color and other design choices by constructing a scale model for a "sneak preview."

Motion. Many kinds of motors can be used to achieve animation. They can be purchased at an electric supply center or through mail order catalogs. Keep your eyes peeled for small, used motors, such as barbecue grill rotisserie motors or sewing machine motors that are often found at flea markets. They can provide inexpensive animation that's easily usable because they're geared for slow motion. Live animals also provide motion and usually get considerable attention when they are part of an exhibit. And lively demonstrations draw and hold viewers' attention well.

Light. Make sure your exhibit is lit well with about 150 watts per 4 x 4-feet area. While floodlights are used to light broad exhibit areas, intense spotlights can draw attention to specific exhibit areas. Large, professionally-produced exhibits often use quartz floodlights to achieve a well-lit effect.

Moving, flashing, and blinking lights can attract attention, but common sense must dictate their intensity. Incandescent lighting intensity can be controlled by using higher or lower wattage bulbs or by varying the voltage with a rheostat.

Exhibit backgrounds

Exhibits may be constructed from a large variety of materials. Consider the ease of handling, durability, and attractiveness when selecting materials and designing an exhibit. Those made with metal or plastic supports and with lightweight backgrounds can be purchased from a number of exhibit-production companies. Instead of constructing your exhibit, you may want to purchase it, then design and mount your visuals on these panels. Most exhibit companies make lightweight, strong, attractive display backgrounds that fold or disassemble to a manageable size. And they usually come with convenient carrying cases that enhance portability. But for some, the cost can be prohibitive. Contact an office supply store for catalogs and prices.

If you can't purchase a commercial exhibit, construct your own. A wide variety of materials is available for use as exhibit backdrops. Before selecting one, you should answer some basic questions concerning the exhibit:

- What will be the final size of the backdrop?
- Must users fold or disassemble it for a manageable size?
- How small must it be packaged for transport and storage?
- How sturdy and durable must it be?
- How heavy will it be?
- How easily can it be set up?
- How often and how long will it be used?
- Can visuals be mounted/changed easily?
- What colors and textures would be helpful?
- What's the initial cost?
- What'll be the production time?

Some commonly used background/panel materials

Plywood. Available in 1/4, 3/8, and 1/2-inches thick, 4 x 8-feet sheets – strong, but heavy.

Plywood paneling. 3/16 inches thick, 4 x 8-feet sheets – moderate in weight and sturdy.

Masonite. 1/8 and 1/4 inches thick, 4 x 8-feet sheets – strong, but heavy.

Styrene and urethane foam. 1/2, 1, and 2 inches thick, 4 x 8-feet sheets – light, but not strong.

Foam board. 1/4 and 1/2 inches thick, 4 x 8-feet sheets – lightweight with a good paper surface.

Corrugated cardboard. Various sizes – lightweight, but surface must be coated.

Posterboard. 14 and 28 ply, 28 x 44 inches and 30 x 40 inches – light, good surface, needs support.

Plastic sheets. Various sizes and thicknesses – light, durable, may need support.

PVC/composite sheets. Various sizes and thicknesses – light, durable, may need support.

The above list shows commonly-used materials. Other wood, paper, plastic, and cloth materials are available. The design requirements of your exhibit will guide your choice of materials. Limited storage space and smaller auto sizes increase the necessity for designing exhibits that are lightweight and can be squeezed into smaller packages.

Lightweight paper/foam and plastic/foam sheets can be used easily as backgrounds for tabletop displays. They need additional support or framing when used for larger displays. These lightweight sheets usually can be folded to pack into cases or evelopes for easy transport and storage.

Large, free-standing exhibit backgrounds may be constructed with any of the aforementioned materials, provided they are adequately supported. Plywood is sturdy when framed with 1 x 3 inches pine lumber, and sections can be coupled together with bolts through the framing. The reverse side (non-grooved) of plywood paneling makes a good surface. The grain can be filled, or simply sanded and painted with several coats.

Lettering

Lettering brushes can create fine letters if you've developed the skill or can hire a professional. But often the available resources are prohibitive in cost. Tempera poster paints are easier to use and quick drying but they are not waterproof. Poster paints are available that will dry quickly and will withstand some weathering. Sign enamels are weatherproof and durable but have a glossy finish and need 24 hours to dry.

Felt-tipped pens often are used to produce lettering and illustrations for display purposes. The felt-tipped pens containing permanent ink produce a more opaque, longer-lasting product. Metal-tipped pens are more easily mastered than the lettering brush and can be used to create quality lettering. These inexpensive pens work with many kinds of inks, but India ink is the most opaque. Art supply stores and office supply stores offer an assortment of ready-made letters. Dry transfer letters, cut out letters, and stencils are available. Placement and spacing of letters that make words, and words that make lines of copy require a certain amount of skill and time.

Modern microcomputer desktop publishing systems can produce sharp copy from laser or ink-jet printers. Computer applications are available that allow you to print "banners" or large formats. Many copy centers now offer these services. You can print as large as possible on a letter-size sheet of paper and make a photocopy enlargement. Some engineering and graphics firms have extra large photocopy machines that can enlarge up to 400 percent on paper 36 inches wide or more.

Exhibit titles should have letters at least three inches in height and a line thickness roughly one-sixth the height of the letters. Larger sizes are preferable where possible. Try to keep the lettering size of the body text no smaller than one inch tall.

Lettering visibility

Size. Use large, visible lettering.

Line thickness. The boldness of the lines that form the letters should approximate one-sixth the letter height.

Style. Choose a style that is bold, easily read, and not too fancy.

Contrast. The letters shouldn't blend into the background. Use light-colored letters on a dark background and dark-colored letters on a light background.

Mounting and fastening

Quite a few commercial exhibits come with panels covered in loop fabric. This allows the user to attach photos, copy boards, and other graphic materials with Velcro, or Hook 'n Loop fasteners. Even the main panels themselves can be secured this way if they are lightweight.

The most reliable method of mounting photographs to cardboard or plastic materials is with a dry-mount press. This service is often provided by photo and framing shops. Adhesive photo-mount is available from graphics supply stores and catalogs. This material comes in sheets, and you peel a paper layer off to expose the adhesive, which is on both sides of each sheet.

Another very reliable fastener is adhesive transfer tape (Scotch #463). With this material you peel away the tape and only the adhesive remains. It acts much like rubber cement, except it doesn't dry. Temporary fasteners often are made by making a small tape loop with the adhesive on the outside. Cloth or masking tape is often used for this.

White glue, epoxy glue (very strong), and other liquid glues can be useful for fastening items together. And different brands of photo mount spray are on the market, but these tend to hold for awhile, then let go.

Staffing an exhibit

Many public exhibition areas become cluttered with disposable food and drink containers, handout literature, etc. Be sure that someone has the responsibility for keeping your exhibit working and the immediate area neat and clean.

Exhibits need attention in other ways also. Lightweight

There are several reasons for having individuals work an exhibit. Keeping the exhibit working and the surrounding area neat and clean are the minimum requirements.

exhibits can be bumped out of alignment, and display materials that are handled often need to be repositioned. Handout leaflets should be kept in neat stacks and the supply replenished as needed.

Persons who staff an exhibit should be neat and well-groomed, appropriately dressed, and properly introduced with a name tag or other means. They should greet viewers, help them make new friends, and answer their questions. They might give a short talk or demonstration to spark audience interest. This responsibility is demanding, requiring many hours of standing, while looking enthusiastic and fresh. Line up plenty of help so they can take enough breaks to continue looking fresh.

Individuals assigned to work an exhibit should be prepared to answer questions concerning the exhibit subject and to provide other information about the sponsoring organization. It's usually desirable if they're also prepared to give food, drink, and restroom information. It may be appropriate to have reference materials available to assist them in answering the harder or more technical questions. A pencil and pad should be kept handy so requests that can't be filled immediately can be recorded for later attention.

Exhibit design tips

Consider the following suggestions any time you are working your way through the exhibit design process.

Be sure the basic design is simple, with few elements

Because most structured panels are manufactured in rectangular sheets, it is common to see exhibits with horizontal and vertical lines. Any effort to break up this horizontal and vertical effect, as shown on the right panel, should increase audience interest.

and plenty of open space. The most common error of exhibit design is too many elements or too much copy. Such designs can be difficult to comprehend and can give viewers an impression of being cluttered. It'll turn them off. Try to communicate visually.

Make certain that the exhibit "reads" well – usually left to right, top to bottom. The overall design, the title, the visuals, and the copy should have an obvious message that can be quickly grasped. All elements should contribute to communicating that message. Does the exhibit accomplish the purpose that was intended?

Put yourself in the position of one viewer from your specified audience. Imagine the exhibit in its intended location. Is there a strong attention-getter? Does the message come through loud and clear? Is that message positive and worth your time?

Summary

- Remember that most onlookers usually view an exhibit for only a shorttime – from several seconds to several minutes.

- You must have an attention-getter and a quickly understood message to communicate to viewers before they move on.

- Decide first on your purpose, subject, and audience; then design the exhibit with those in mind.

- Do a good editing job, allowing only the most relevant points as part of the message.

- Tell your story visually.

- Leave plenty of space in your exhibit; it shouldn't have that discouraging, crowded look.

- Select appropriate materials for construction. It may be necessary to pack your exhibit in a convenient, transportable package that's lightweight and easy to handle.

- Keep the lettering to a minimum in quantity, and large in size.

- Have the display set up on time. Keep it looking good throughout the exhibition.

- Make sure persons working the exhibit are neat and well-groomed, enthusiastic, and above all, interested and helpful.

Posters

Posters are a commonly-used, inexpensive medium to publicize an item or event. They can be very effective for publicizing meetings, shows, contests, dances, picnics, and yard sales. They might also be used to promote a political candidate or an educational idea or to advertise products or services.

Posters differ from flipcharts and other teaching aids because posters stand alone. No one calls attention to them, identifies their purposes, answers questions, or provides further explanation.

Most people glance at a poster just long enough to identify it. If the poster's graphic treatment is exciting or the subject interests them, they might look further for the complete message.

Posters are normally produced on paper or posterboard but can take other forms such as promotions printed on trucks, billboards, T-shirts, and bumper stickers. The form your poster takes should depend upon the target audience and the most cost-effective way of reaching that audience.

What and who

You should begin by deciding exactly who you wish to reach and what you want to say. Write these ideas on paper and continue to search for the best possible words and images to express your ideas clearly, simply, and precisely.

Consider the message your poster will deliver from the audience's point of view. What is the age, education level, and background of your audience? What do they know and what are their attitudes about your topic, your organization, and you? Is your choice of words and visuals appropriate for this group? Will the poster capture their interest? An understanding of the audience also will help in making design decisions regarding the color, type style, visual approach, and basic layout.

Jot down ideas

Your poster's message will depend on the words and illustration you choose, along with the treatment of them. During the planning stage, jot down words and phrases and make rough sketches that help describe or clarify the message. Begin to visualize and arrange these elements in a logical order.

Select the most important words and pencil them into a rough layout in large letters. This title, with an accompanying visual, may serve as an effective attention-getter. If needed, use smaller-sized lettering (body copy) to explain details of your poster's overall message.

Now rethink what you've done in planning so far. Did you select the key words from the audience's point of view? Do the words and visual interrelate to convey the message? Show your ideas to others that can identify with your audience. They can help you decide.

The visual

The visual (illustration, chart, photograph, etc.) is usually an essential element in the poster. Try to develop a visual idea that will quickly communicate your idea as well as catch the eye of your intended audience. Explore various approaches for the visual, but aim for one that's simple, compelling, and to the point. The visual must reinforce the message, or better yet, carry the message.

If the message you've selected for your poster relates to vegetable gardening, you can list a number of visual approaches: an entire garden, one row of plants, a group of plants, one plant, an array of vegetables, one vegetable, a slice of vegetable, a jar of canned vegetables, a hoe or cultivator, a person holding a vegetable, an expression of satisfaction on a person's face. Your list can go on.

Now put yourself in the place of the viewer. Which idea best communicates the message? Which is most appealing? Which of these ideas can you carry out without risking confusion? Which visual idea has greater potential as an interesting shape (design element) in adding impact and drawing the attention of the audience? Seek a simple solution to these questions. For instance, just one, two, or three vegetables is/are easier for you to draw and less confusing for the viewer than a whole garden or a group of a dozen vegetables.

A basic poster design often uses a single visual (may include a group of several items) that contributes to attracting viewers' eyes and communicating the message. Therefore, the final choice and approach of the visual is critical to the effectiveness of the poster.

Layout and design

Good poster design organizes the basic shapes formed by the title, the illustration, and the body copy into an interesting and balanced unit. The elements themselves should be subordinated to an overall plan. This basic arrangement should enhance the communication of the message, be simple in design, and pleasing to the eye. Designs that are informally balanced (elements not centered) are usually more interesting and provide a less-rigid, friendlier appearance.

One effective approach to poster layout and design is to use a short, catchy title, with large letters, along with a simple illustration. Other necessary details may appear in smaller-sized body copy. The title and illustration grab the viewers' attention and lure them in to study the details more closely. You can avoid a symmetrical beginning by placing the title to the left or right, rather than centering it. You then may place the illustration toward the opposite side to balance the title. It's usually necessary to sketch a variety of layouts to see the interaction of the title, illustration, and body copy.

Design guidelines

Keep the *message* foremost in your mind throughout the project. One to five key words should appear as the title in large type and be legible at a distance. These words should suggest your message and have impact upon the audience.

No single design formula will guarantee your success. Many rules have proven helpful over time, but they may be broken without dooming the design to failure. The key is only to break a rule when you have good reasons and follow most of the rules most of the time.

- The major design elements are the blocks of space occupied by the title, the illustration, and the body copy. It's usually easier to plan a successful design with three elements than it is with many elements, especially for a novice designer. One of the elements, either the title or illustration, should be noticeably larger than the others. This contrast in size catches viewers' eyes.

- Poster *design elements* are more effective when grouped than when spaced over the entire poster area. Therefore, you should try to avoid creating multiple elements. For instance, three words of a title might be printed in a design with the words tightly fitted together and appear as a single element. Another treatment would be to space the three words so they appear as three separate elements. These three elements along with a visual and a block of body copy would total five elements, making the design unnecessarily complicated.

- Leave plenty of *space* between and around most elements, with extra space along the edges of the poster. Avoid the look of crowding. Sometimes elements can touch or overlap at one place without causing a crowding problem. People expect ample space at the edges of the design. They need "elbow room" visually to avoid a "crowded" feeling, similar to being in a crowded elevator.

- Allow for several fairly large areas of unused, open space. A design begins to look crowded when the open space areas fall below 20 percent of the total area. Many successful posters have 30 to 40 percent of the area in open space.

- The *configuration* of the open space has just as important an impact on the basic design as the shapes formed by the lettering and visuals. It's usually desirable to have a variety of sizes and shapes of open space.

- Balance, or the relative "weight" of the visual elements, is an important part of poster design. If a large element appears on one side of a design, two or more smaller elements can be placed on the other side to achieve balance. While it usually is undesirable to scatter the elements evenly over the entire poster area, it usually is ineffective, also, to crowd all elements into one end or one corner of the area.

- Balance is necessary to design, but it's often less effective if achieved by centering all elements on the poster. This is formal balance - where the right side is a mirror image of the left side. Asymmetrical, or informal balance usually is more interesting, more fun to work with, and more challenging (creative) than symmetrical balance. Informal balance is less static and monotonous; it suggests movement. It also presents a friendlier, more flexible, informal appearance.

- In most good poster designs, either the illustration or the lettering dominates, rather than having an equal division between the two. A design with the visual occupying more area than the lettering grabs a lot of attention, but be sure that the visual supports the message. People often resent tricky visuals or misleading words that do not support the overall message.

- Horizontal lettering is normal and easy to read. Vertical lettering is difficult to read and is not recommended. Therefore, most poster elements appear in the horizontal position. Use a vertical illustration or line when you can. It'll attract attention. This is also true of angular lines and shapes that contrast with the vertical and horizontal edges of the usual poster format. It may be effective to place some words on an angular or curving line, but be careful that they can be read easily. After all, you're trying to communicate.

- Lines create direction and flow and cause eye movement. The juncture, real or imagined, of two or more lines easily can become a focal point or center of interest within a design. As you become more adept at using lines and direction, you have increasing control over the viewer's eye movement.

- An effective poster has a strong center of interest at the words and/or illustration that identifies your core message. This reinforces the idea that communicating the message is your main goal. The center of interest usually is more effective if it is placed one-third of the distance up, down, or in from the left or right edges of your poster. Avoid placing it in the geometric center of the poster area, too close to the edge, or cramming it into a corner.

- Designing is easier when the body copy is short and to the point. Edit and present the message details so they appear in a relatively small area. Consider with care the information presented there. Complete sentences aren't necessary – just key words and phrases. You cannot overlook certain necessary facts, such as

time and place, but an excess of body copy requires very small lettering or uses too much space. Editing for conciseness helps keep posters from looking crowded.

- Be certain that the choice of color does not detract from the message and is acceptable to your selected audience. A related color plan, one that uses colors located next to each other on a color wheel, is a conservative, safe approach and seldom jeopardizes a design. Certain designs and specific audiences, of course, might benefit from the addition of a brighter, contrasting color. Older people might prefer a more conservative color plan, while teenagers like bold, contrasting, and even vibrating colors. If you use a bright color, be sure it draws attention where you want it.

Legibility

Your design decisions should support legibility. Messages are unclear when words are difficult to read or a visual is complicated and confusing. An audience seldom bothers to look at a poster that requires much effort to read. In addition to the previously mentioned principles, a number of factors influence legibility.

Size. Lettering and illustrations must be large enough to be easily seen and understood at a reasonable viewing distance. A large poster, 22 x 28 inches, should have the title printed in letters that are 2 to 4 inches high. A smaller format, say 8.5 x 11 inches, should have title letters roughly .75 to 1.5 inches high. Body copy is often printed in letters that are one-fourth to one-third the height of the title.

Contrast. The lightness or darkness of the elements compared to the background they are on affect your ability to see and "read" what's there. Maximum contrast is black on white or white on black. This is tiring on the eyes when used in excess. Minimum contrast, such as pale yellow letters on a white background, is difficult to read. A combination just short of maximum contrast is desirable. This could include black or brown letters on a yellow paper, white or light yellow letters on medium to dark (but not black) colors, or deep red letters on a beige or sand-colored background.

Style. This pertains to the character, fashion, or tone of the graphics. Some lettering styles, such as Helvetica or Times, can be read easily. Ornate or overly fancy styles are hard to read. A visual also can be too detailed, causing confusion for viewers. Try to select styles of lettering and visuals that are simple, easy to read and handsome and that will enhance the message.

Line thickness. Line thickness for letters must be reasonably bold for good legibility. Ideal line thickness is roughly one-sixth the height of the letter. A three inch tall letter with a line thickness of one-sixteenth of an inch is not very visible. A three inch letter with a line thickness of one-half inch (one-sixth of letter height), on the other hand, is legible at 80 to 90 feet. Fairly bold line thickness is also necessary for good visibility of illustrations.

Materials

Many of today's posters are produced on desktop computer systems and printed on laser or ink jet printers. These produce sharp letters. When using a dot-matrix printer, it's often advisable to make a photocopy to swell out the dots for a darker, bolder image before reproduction.

There are many packages of ready-made electronic clip-art available on computer diskettes or compact disks (CD-ROMs), and a number of computer applications can assist you in generating art on the computer. Many designers sort through their collection of electronic clip-art and find an illustration that's close to what they want, then use it as-is or adapt it in some way. Others scan (digitize) images into the computer from other sources such as from clip-art books, pencil sketches, ink drawings, photographs, or from other printed sources. Then they may alter/adapt them with graphics applications on the computer. The more artistically-inclined computer users generate artwork directly on their computer. There are lots of graphics/design applications to assist with these tasks.

If you letter your poster with felt-tipped markers, select those with permanent ink for denser, more stable colors. Other inks, such as India ink, may be applied with a metal tipped pen or a brush. Different kinds of paints are available, but tempera poster paint is easiest to use and cleans up with water.

Select a paper or cardstock that has a smooth, hard finish. This finish is less absorbent and produces sharp, crisp lines. Cardboard suitable for poster production is available under a variety of names: Bristol board, railroad board, show-card, illustration board, and posterboard. They vary in thickness, in overall size, in hardness of finish, and in price. Examine them closely and test them for smoothness and absorbency.

Letters that are commercially available include rub-down transfer letters and pressure-sensitive paper or vinyl letters. They are expensive and time consuming to apply but are very precise, clean letters. Stencil guides may be used to outline the letter shapes on your poster. Be sure to fill in the letters where the centers are attached to the rest of the stencil.

Some individuals prefer the look of precise, machine produced or computer generated letters. But hand-produced lettering can have character that provides a less-formal, friendlier, more humane appearance. And that look could be a plus for you and your organization.

Showing

You've done your best to create a good poster, so how and where you display it should be just as important. Even an excellent poster can be ineffective if displayed at the wrong location or under poor conditions. Think of the places that your target audience might congregate or pass idle time. Some examples: A smart agricultural extension agent places farmer-intended posters at livestock sale barns where farmers wait in line to pay for their purchases. A family living extension agent promotes her nutrition program with posters in doctors' and dentists' waiting rooms. Display your posters where your selected audience frequently goes.

When possible, place posters where they're highly visible and not lost in a confusion of competitive clutter. Attach them securely so they can't fall or droop. Posters are usually seen best at eye level or above, and on a pleasant looking bulletin board, wall, or other backdrop.

Posters should be seen in adequate lighting. Fluorescent lighting will influence the color scheme, and the poster could appear much different than when viewed under incandescent or natural lighting.

One to three weeks is usually adequate lead time for posters to advertise an event – it varies with the audience. A poster advertisement for an agricultural field day might be effective if it were up for a couple of months before the event, if placed in a farm supply store aiming at farmers. The same poster placed in a shopping mall where there is a diverse audience might be

effective for only a week or two prior to the event. Check on the condition of posters several times throughout the display period to assure they remain in top condition and maintain an acceptable appearance.

Summary

People mostly just glance at posters. They'll investigate further only if they quickly catch a message that appeals to their interest. You must carefully select the key words and/or visual to grab their attention and communicate the message.

Good design organizes the elements into an interesting and balanced unit, where the elements are subordinated to an overall plan. Effective posters are not only pleasing to the eye, but present a bold, clear message.

The basic design should be simple. Limit the number of design elements. Leave lots of room at the margins, and some larger areas of open space within the design. The most common mistake in poster design is using too many elements and scattering them over the entire poster area. This gives the viewer the impression that the poster is cluttered and difficult to read.

Always keep the message and the intended audience in mind. Speak their language. You must communicate in order to succeed.

Slide and Slide-Tape Production 11

Slide and slide-tape presentations can combine audio and visual elements to communicate your message quickly, effectively, and inexpensively. They can be useful tools to educate, inform, motivate, and/or entertain your audience. If you have visual information to present and you do not require motion, a slide presentation may fill the bill. Slides are particularly useful for large audiences and large rooms because slides retain their clarity when projected across large spaces.

Playback and production equipment is generally readily available, inexpensive, and easy to use. You also can take your wn equipment with you, if necessary, without too much effort.

A slide-tape presentation is a good way to present the same information in the same way to numerous audiences at different places and times. Slide shows can be revised and updated easily and they are easy to duplicate. Slides and cassette tapes are durable so they can be used over and over.

This chapter will guide you through the planning and production of a slide-tape presentation.

Description

What are you producing when you create a slide show? Before embarking on a new creative journey, you need to know what the result of your efforts will be.

A standard single-projector slide-tape presentation is a six-to-12-minute production with 80 slides and a "sync-pulsed" soundtrack on cassette that advances the slides automatically. Some topics may require less time and fewer slides. Slides also may be used without a soundtrack as visual aids for a speech. Multiple-projector slide shows have fewer limitations, but here we will discuss the standard single-projector show.

Ten minutes is the maximum length for most presentations because attention spans are short and a longer show will drag if you only have 80 slides. 80 slides fit in a carousel tray. Although slide trays that hold 140 slides are available, these are not good for synchronized shows. This is particularly true if you have older equipment. In order to get 140 spaces, the slots are very narrow, which can cause the slides to jam. This means, 80 is the maximum number of slides for most applications.

The screen will be black for one second every time a slide changes, so you will have 79 seconds of dark screen in your show. You will need to remember this when writing your script so you don't require rapid slide changes.

Most slide shows use 55 to 70 photographic images and 10 to 25 graphic slides, depending on the content and purpose of the show. Graphic slides can help the viewer (and the producer) organize the content of the show. They also add emphasis to key points, provide transitions, and help explain difficult concepts. If you intend to use more than 25 or 30 graphic slides, you may want to reconsider your chosen medium. This may mean that your topic is not visual enough or that you don't have the resources to obtain the photos you need. Your audience may be served better with a printed piece of some kind. On the other hand, if you have few or no graphics, you're omitting a technique that can strengthen your presentation.

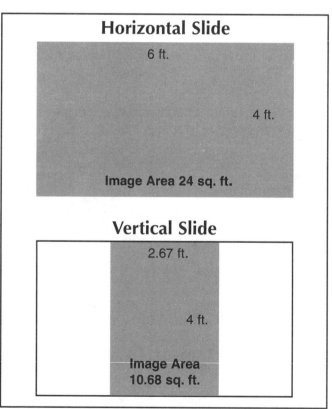

Comparison of projected image size with horizontal and vertical slides.

All slides should be horizontal. This means the longer side is parallel to the floor and ceiling. A mixture of horizontal and vertical slides can distract and confuse the audience. To understand why, realize that most screens have a horizontal format 3-to-2 ratio fairly close to the 3-to-2 ratio of 3mm slides. even if the screen is quare, you normally set up the projector so the horizontal images are as high and as large as possible to give the people in the back of the room a chance to see the show. When vertical slides are projected, up to a third of the image my be lost as portions of the slide show on the ceiling and below the bottom of the screen.

Planning

Most creative projects benefit greatly from advance planning. Slide-tape presentations are no exception. Before you begin, you need to know what you want to say (the message), who you want to say it to (the audience), and what outcome you expect (objectives). In fact, if you continually ask and answer the "who cares?" and "so what?" questions, you will remain focused on the essentials of your project.

What is the message?

What do you want to say? What is this show all about? Do you intend to inform, educate, persuade, entertain? Is this a training presentation? What do you want the audience to know, feel, or do after seeing this show?

Who is the audience?

Who will view this program (age, gender, education, etc.)? How much do they know about this already? Are they motivated to view this program? Will they be receptive to this presentation? Where will they watch this presentation? How many people will watch in total and at one time?

The more you know about the audience, the easier it will be to create a presentation that is relevant to it. You do not need to conduct an extensive and expensive analysis, but you do need to find out enough to get a feel for their point of view with respect to your message.

Components of Audience Analysis

- **Demographics**: Age, gender, education, socio-economic status, ethnic background, religion, family status, geographic factors.
- **Psychographics**: Attitudes and beliefs that affect lifestyle and behavior and distinguish groups of people from others in the same demographic categories.
- **Behavior**: What do they do now (with respect to your topic) and why?

- **Communication habits:** Where do they go for information on this topic? Do they seek information on this topic? Do they actively avoid encountering information on this topic?
- **Topic knowledge:** What do they know? What do they think they know? Are you providing new knowledge or correcting misinformation?
- **Motivation:** Do they want to be exposed to your message? Will they see it on their own or will they be a captive audience? Will they want to remember and use the information?
- **Topic attitude:** How do they feel about the topic: Are they positive? negative? indifferent?
- **Setting:** Where will they watch this show? How many people will be there? What time of day?

What are the objectives?

What is the desired outcome? What will you consider "success"? Will learning take place? If so, what type: cognitive, psychomotor, affective? Is this training? Is this information? Will this program be supplemented by other materials? Will results be measured? How will they be measured?

When you have answered all these questions, you can proceed to prepare a detailed content outline describing exactly what the audience needs to achieve the objectives. Use the content outline to your script.

Content development

Now that you know what you want to accomplish with your slide show, it's time to figure out how to do it. You need to come up with a message strategy or treatment.

Write a treatment

The treatment describes how your will present your message. It should address the type of mood you want to set, the basic audience interests to which you will appeal, and the use of any special audio or visual effects. Try to describe "the look" and "the sound" of the show by describing any recurring elements such as graphics or theme music or photographic subjects. Describe the sequence of the slide show: chronological, topical, problem-solving?

In writing the treatment, you need to keep your audience analysis in mind. For example, if your audience is indifferent to your topic, you should be as slick and creative as you can be in order to grasp and hold their attention. If they are highly motivated to watch your show, a straightforward business-like approach may be most suitable. If you know the show will be viewed in a darkened room after a meal, you'll want to keep it lively to keep your audience awake.

Sample Treatment

Laura's Letter
General Recruiting Presentation

The presentation begins with several shots (long, medium, and then close up) of a young woman in the library sitting at a table, looking out a window In front of her are a small pile of photographs, some textbooks and notebooks, and stationery. Our subject (Laura) is a first semester student. She is writing a letter to her friend Tracy who is a senior at Laura's old high school. Laura is the narrator of the piece, and a student will read the script in the rhythms and cadence of someone writing a letter. Next, there will be a shot of Laura's pen writing (or having written) "Dear Tracy" on the stationery, followed by a shot of Laura thinking. Laura begins: "Hi, Tracy. I told you I'd write you a long letter telling you all about this place, and here it is. First of all: Don't look at the pictures yet. This is going to be nice and orderly–un-like men–so hold on! Well, I'm sitting in the library (Yes, the library. I know you didn't think I'd get caught dead in a library, but here I am alive and well!) It's really a nice place, and I've got my own special window here. Now you can look at the first picture: this is what I can see from my window. This is followed by a shot of the campus as seen from the library. And thus begins the slide show. Laura writes of her experiences and shows photographs of the campus to Tracy. As Laura develops here letter and reviews photos, the audience will see and hear the major messages: the campus is beautiful; although it is large, it has a small-college atmosphere; it's a good value in higher education. By using the Laura character, we can insert bits of humor and comment that will mean more than having an adult lecture on the subject. We will seek input from students on campus to make sure that the phrasing, slang, etc., is as realistic as possible. By using the student's view both figuratively and literally of the campus, the audience will have a personal view and description of the university and its people. This personal aspect can bring out the uniqueness of the university in a way that young people and their parents can relate to.

Assemble information

This is the research component of your slide show production. A detailed content outline should guide you in finding the specific information you will provide to the audience. In fact, you'll probably have more information than you'll be able to use. This is the time to delete what you don't need. Let your audience analysis be your guide.

Organize information

Now you take the assembled information and insert it into your treatment in outline form. A slide show is a linear medium, therefore, the message must proceed in an order that makes sense to the viewer. You already may have determined a sequence of some kind when you wrote the treatment: chronological, topical, or problem-solving. Use that now to create the outline from which you will write your script.

Writing the script

A slide show script, like a video script, contains both aural and visual elements, so you must consider both at the same time.

Some people find it helpful to "storyboard" their productions. You can use pre-printed storyboard pads like the one on this page or you can use index cards.

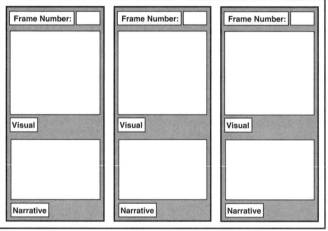

Preprinted "storyboard" pad.]

Sketch or describe the image you want in the "visual" field and then write corresponding copy in the narrative box below. This technique will help you think visually. You need to write with the emphasis on the pictures, using words to enhance the visuals.

The script format shown in the following photo also helps you think of the aural and visual aspects of the show at the same time. Notice that the narrative portion of the script is continuous, so you will be less likely to lose context as you go. You also can see how much narration you are writing for each slide, you either need fewer words or more slides. If you have several slides and only a line or two of narration, you may be fine as long as the slides carry the message alone. If they don't, you'll need more words to help out.

Visuals

Let the pictures tell the story whenever possible. Cover only one main point per visual. To make more than one point,

This script format helps you think visually and verbally at the same time

use more than one picture. Visuals should move from the general to the specific, from the wide shot to the close-up. A close-up can be disconcerting without the context that a wider shot can establish.

Photographic slides of people are usually preferable to artwork or cartoons, depending on the subject, of course. However, simplified artwork may be preferable to photographs to illustrate complex physical processes or the operating principles of machines.

With complex diagrams and bullet list text slides, plan progressive disclosures or "builds." This is a series of slides that start with the smallest element inthe first slides. Each additional slide incorporates one more element. This technique can help the audience focus attention on a specific area of the slide.

Consider using split-image and composite slides in moderation. Split-images can show contrasting conditions at the same time. Three- or four-way composite slides can show a whole range of conditions at once.

Narrative

The narration should support and enhance the visuals. Avoid over-writing or telling the audience what they already know or can see for themselves. In other words, don't give detailed descriptions of your slides.

Use words the audience understands and avoid jargon or technical terms whenever possible.

Write for the ear and not for the eye. Your audience will never read the script, they will only hear it. Write the way people talk. Use an informal, conversational style. Vary sentence

length. Use personal pronouns ("you" and "we") whenever possible. Use good grammar and avoid awkward wording.

Read your script aloud as you write. Minimize modifiers and use active voice whenever possible. Avoid long series and lists. Avoid terms such as "etc." and "i.e" as well as parenthetical phrases. These are very difficult to read aloud.

See the radio and video sections of this handbook for more tips on scriptwriting.

Music and sound effects

Describe any music or sound effects you intend to use. Keep it simple. Take care that they don't detract from your message by calling attention to themselves. Music changes or sound effects can be used to help make smooth transitions from one section of your presentation to another. Many slide shows benefit from music at the beginning and the end of the show only. Don't overproduce yours by using too much music or too many sound effects.

Finding the active voice
Tips for changing passive sentences to active:

- **Relocate the actor**. Turn the sentence around. "The horse was examined by a veterinarian" becomes "A veterinarian examined the horse."

- **Find the missing actor**. Discover who did it and put it in the sentence. "The tractor flipped over into the ditch."

- **Change the verb**. "The sirens were sounded at noon" becomes "The sirens blared at noon."

- **Drop forms of the verb "to be."** Try to avoid using is, am, are, was, were, be, being, been. "The headlights were shining in their eyes" becomes "The headlights shone in their eyes."

Review and revision

Reread the script yourself and make any changes you think would improve it. Then ask one or more of your colleagues to read it. If possible, have some representatives of your audience do the same. If they've had no experience reading scripts, you may want to read the narration to them while explaining the visuals. You'll have to decide. Ask what they think the script says and if they understand it. Revise accordingly.

Quick tips for slide show script writing

- Develop aural and visual aspects at the same time.
- Keep it simple.
- Read copy aloud as you write.
- Write the way people talk.

- Avoid jargon or technical terms the audience won't know or won't care about.
- Use personal pronouns. ("You" is best.)
- Vary sentence length. Minimize adverbs and adjectives.
- Use active voice as much as possible.
- Avoid long series and lists.
- Don't say too much. Don't state the obvious. Your visuals are presenting much of the message.

Production

Now it's time to start putting it all together. If you have professional photographers, graphic artists, narrators, and audio producers available to you, use them. (Remember to remind the photographers and graphic artists that you are producing a slide show and that means you need horizontal slides.)

Photography

Whether you use the services of a professional photographer or plan to shoot the slides yourself, you will benefit from developing a shot list. This is simply a list of the images you need to complete your show arranged by categories that apply to your project. The sample below shows part of a shot list. Note that graphics are listed together, new photography is listed by location, existing slides are listed separately.

Sample Shot List

Shot #	Image Type	Description	Source	Status
1	Document	Cover page of news magazine featuring boitech at main topic	Document	Document
2	Document	Montage of biotech articles from journals and magazines	Document	Document
5	Graphic	Main title: "Florida's Biotechnology initiative"	Graphic	Graphic
28	Graphic	Comparsion of biotech firms: Fla. vs. US	Graphic	Graphic
17	Slide Photo	C-U of microchip	Slide Photo	Slide Photo

If you must shoot your own slides, please read the photography chapter of this book. Plan to shoot a lot of slides, at least four times as many as you need. Keep it simple. When you look through the viewfinder, look at the scene as a picture. If the picture is good, take it. If you see distracting elements in the background or foreground, move before you shoot. If the main point isn't the main element of the picture, move or rearrange elements of the shot.

Whenever possible, shoot from the point of view the audience would have if they were looking at the scene directly. Be sure to use some close-ups. They add impact and clarify what

the audience needs to see. Remember, when you need close-ups, it is less confusing to show a progression from wide to medium to close so the audience knows what they're seeing.

Put people in your photos whenever possible. People like to look at other people, so have your models do something that makes sense in the context of the picture. If there isn't really anything to do, the model should look at whatever the picture is meant to show. Make sure your audience sees people like themselves in the photos" use appropriately diverse models.

Use a little imagination for title slides

Graphics

If you are able to use the services of a graphic artist, you will need to be able to communicate what you want your graphic slides to say. Be sure to remind the artist that you need horizontal slides.

Producing graphics yourself is not difficult if you use a computer. Many computer programs can help you create effective, attractive graphic slides. Effective graphics deliver information without calling attention to themselves.

Try to convey only one main idea on each graphic slide. This also will help you with your script writing. If you want to relate several concepts, consider using separate slides for each one or a "build" approach, adding new material to what the audience has already seen.

Keep each graphic as brief and simple as possible and limit copy to six or eight lines of text. More words means the lettering becomes too small to see and the slide will have to stay on the screen too long.

Keep the color simple. Choose a neutral color for the background. Choose another that contrasts without clashing for the text. Use only one or two more colors for emphasis and follow the same color scheme throughout the presentation.

Somtimes photos can be used as background for superimposed graphics or titles. Just be sure that the text is easy to read.

Use your imagination. Title and graphic slides can often be created in other ways. The "Laura's Letter" slide show used in the treatment example used the letter format (handwritting on stationery) for title slides.

Soundtrack

The finished soundtrack will consist of the narration, music, and any sound effects mixed together onto a cassette.

Select the "talent." If it's important that you be identified as the authoritative source of the information presented, then you probably should narrate. However, if you are at all uncomfortable, don't do it. As a rule, find a professional with training and experience to narrate for you. The narrator should not detract from the message, and the voice should have credibility with the audience. Think about dialects and other regional speech patterns, age, gender, obvious ethnicity, and other voice quality considerations that might influence the audience. The narrator should read naturally, using variations in stress and speed to help the audience follow the material. The narrator must be aware of the visual side of the script to be sure there is enough time for all slides.

The narrator can read the script into a cassette recorder, but it is far better to use a recording studio and audio producer to put together your soundtrack.

When selecting music, you should avoid popular songs. Use "production music" licensed to your institution or other music in the public domain to avoid copyright problems. Also, the audience may start humming or singing along with the song to the neglect of your presentation. Keep the music volume low enough that it doesn't interfere with the narration. Consider the match between the mood of your show, the mood of the music, and the voice qualities of the narrator. If you use music throughout your show, you may wish to use music changes for transitions. You may not need to use music for the entire show, however. For many informational or training presentations, a short piece of music at the beginning and again at the end is sufficient. Some presentations include a short montage of music and pictures with no narration at the beginning or end of the program.

Slide assembly and tape pulsing

Once you have all the components of your show, you need to get your slides in order and put them in the slide tray. Be sure to number the slides so you can put them back in order easily if they should fall out or otherwise leave the slide tray.

Next, you will add synchronized pulses to the cassette soundtrack. For this, you need a cassette machine or a combination slide projector/cassette machine that generates and records standard 1000Hz pulses.

If the operating instructions are available for the machine you'll be using, read and follow them. Otherwise, to pulse your tape, simply play the soundtrack with the machine in the "pulse record" mode and push the "slide advance" button each time you want a slide change. This will be easier if you mark the script to show exactly where the slides should change. Remember, the screen will be blank for one second between slides. If you make a mistake, go back and try again. Many machines allow you to rewind past the mistake, reset the slides, and begin pulsing again. If not, just start over.

After pulsing the tape, play the show back to be sure it works the way you want it to. If it looks and sounds right...Congratulations!

Designing Visuals for Presentations

Make your presentations more memorable by using visuals that have impact and increase the amount of information your audience will remember. This chapter explains how to plan, prepare and present educational projected visuals (slides, overheads, and computer presentations) that are easy to read and understand and that help clarify your speech.

Why use visuals?

Can't people, especially adults, just hear what you have to say, understand, and remember? Research indicates they can't very well. One test showed that when the same material was taught with and without visuals, adults remembered more from the visual presentations, especially over a period of time:

Adults remember more with visuals

Percent Remembered	with Visuals	no Visuals
3 hrs later	85%	70%
10 days later	65%	10%

Researchers estimate that of all the information we know,
- 6 percent comes through touch, taste, and smell
- 11 percent comes through hearing
- 83 percent comes through sight.

Visual elements should not replace verbal, but the two complement each other and achieve results that neither could achieve alone.

Good visuals can accomplish several things simultaneously. They can:

- **avoid misconceptions** by illustrating, clarifying, and supporting your verbal material
- **focus attention** on what you are saying and away from distractions
- **save time** because concepts are presented faster and understood more quickly
- **show concepts**, places, and new experiences not easily explained
- **help the talk progress** in a logical order and let the audience see where it is leading
- **make learning easier** and more enjoyable.

Where do you begin?

As always, know about your audience. Define characteristics that could affect your presentation: age, education, gender, economic level, or occupation. Consider problems such as low literacy, poor eyesight, etc. Have a good idea how large and diverse the expected audience will be.

Be able to describe the outcomes you hope to achieve. Define your objectives and how you will evaluate them.

Find out what the facilities will be like: room size and seating arrangement; if the room can be darkened; or if there are visibility problems. Ask if audio-visual or computer equipment will be available or if you need to bring your own.

Check on resources that may be available in your preparation and presentation: people? equipment? services? (The last section of this chapter describes in more detail facility preparations to make in the planning stages.)

Once you have a clear understanding of your audience, outcomes, facilities, and resources, you can make decisions about how to present the material, what kinds of learning experiences may be possible, whether to use visuals, and what kinds to use.

Choosing the most appropriate options

Using a variety of teaching methods reaches more learners with different learning styles. Hands-on, purposeful experiences can be the most effective way to learn. Observation (through demonstrations, field trips, exhibits, models, videos, audio tape, or photos) is the next level of effectiveness, followed by learning by symbolizing (visual and verbal symbols). The more active the educational experience, the more impact it will have.

Some options may be eliminated based on your planning. For example, the audience may be too large to make a hands-on approach practical. Or the room may be impossible to darken, eliminating most projected visuals. Other limitations such as budget, facilities, or time, may eliminate other teaching methods. Don't overlook some low-tech old stand-bys like the chalkboard and flip chart, but use the same visibility rules described later for projected visuals.

Projected Visuals

If you decide to use visuals, look for variety. Include maps, charts, graphs, photos, illustrations, or cartoons in your presentation. Most presentations consist mostly of word visuals, but images are more motivating, persuasive, and memorable. The kinds of images you want to use may influence the media.

> ## Projected Visuals
> - ● Overheads
> - ● Slides
> - ● Computer Presentations

Projected visuals have several advantages:

- If enlarged enough for clear viewing by everyone, they are practical with large audiences.
- They are easy and inexpensive to produce.
- Although they require projection equipment, it is usually portable, or available at the site.

- The visuals themselves are small.

Overheads have several unique features:

- The speaker can face the audience.
- Some lights may be left on for easy note taking.
- Overlays permit the speaker to build on a concept or add to an illustration.
- Covering and revealing one part at a time allows the speaker to focus attention.
- Markers can be used to emphasize points or add information on prepared overheads.
- Blank overheads and felt markers can be used as a chalkboard substitute.
- Overheads can be re-arranged to suit a particular audience, even during the presentation.
- They're practical for charts, graphs, and simplified diagrams.

The most common weakness of overheads is type that is too small even when projected. Typewriter or text type (10 - 12 points) is inadequate and must be at least twice as large on the overhead. Also, realism is difficult to achieve because since photographs can be expensive to convert to quality overheads. Color transparencies output to a color printer or made on a color copier provide good color for emphasis, variety and aesthetics, but may not match well enough when color accuracy is important.

Slides are extremely versatile and have many advantages:

- Tables, charts, graphs, diagrams, models, or art can be captured and presented in sharp detail.
- Slides shot on location integrate realism into your presentation.
- Text slides are easy to produce and can unify the above variety.
- Color – in an infinite pallet and complete accuracy – is the rule, not the exception.
- Slides are relatively inexpensive and easy to produce, especially with presentation software.
- Slides can be culled, re-arranged, or added for a specific audience.
- With proper close-up photo equipment, the original can be as small as an insect or typewritten words.
- Slides are very portable, either with or without the projector.

Slides are extremely flexible for presentations, whether supporting a speech or combined with other teaching methods. An automated slide show, synchronized with taped narration and musical background, can be a stand-alone package, at an exhibit for example.

The major disadvantage of slides is the need for a completely darkened room to be most effective. This limits the locations for use and restricts the audience's ability to take notes. Also, slides need to be carefully selected and edited because viewing too many for too long produces sleep, not stimulation.

Computer shows are produced using presentation graphics software that also edits, arranges, and projects directly from the computer. They have many similarities to slides and overheads, and, depending on the software, some unique advantages:

- Production is instantaneous: no film, processing, printing, etc.
- Revisions or additions can be made minutes before the presentation.
- Pre-designed templates make developing well-designed, unified presentation easy.
- Color is integrated and costs no more (with color projection hardware).
- Computerized "slide shows" can be programmed to run unattended.
- Word-processing text, spreadsheet tables or charts, computer graphics, scanned images, and even digitized photos can be integrated into one versatile presentation.
- Full-size or reduced printouts can be made easily for hand-outs, scripts, or storyboards.

The biggest disadvantages relate to the technology: incompatibility between software, computers or projection devices, or the inability to incorporate everything you want into the digital format. Unfortunately, if something can go wrong, it will, in front of your largest or most important audience. Even computer people bring back-up overheads or slides as insurance.

Planning your visual support

The following guidelines apply to all projected visuals:

- **Visuals should complement and support the verbal message**, not replace it. Normally, visuals should not be expected to stand alone. An effective speaker balances brief but explicit words with visuals that emphasize key points and illustrate or clarify complex concepts.

- **Don't repeat the obvious**. "This is a picture of...." Your audience can see that. Take the image a step or two further by giving more information than is seen readily. Don't read the visual's text to the audience. It should be large enough to be read and the speaker should flesh out the information.

- **One idea per visual**. Several simple visuals are easier to understand than one complex one. AV materials are fleeting images controlled by the speaker and should not contain more information than described by the speaker, or more than the audience can comprehend in the brief viewing time.

- **Simplify the information** and, if necessary, put the complex version of a chart or illustration in the handout, proceedings or abstract. If you can't simplify, you may be trying to cover too much material.

- **Provide handouts** of your visuals or supporting print materials, which can be studied more thoroughly and referred to later to help the audience remember your message. Presentation software often has a script or notes format that allows you to print small versions of your visuals for handouts or note taking.

- **Keep a balance of verbal and visual**. Words and pictures should support each other and what is being said. Usually a title or heading is needed to identify the visual or coordinate it with the talk. Add color for variety and emphasis but don't overuse it to the extent that it bogs down the message.

- **Sequence materials** logically but not always chronologically. Move from simple to complex, familiar to unfamiliar, or concrete to abstract.

- **Pace the visuals** throughout the talk or that portion requiring them. Develop a rhythm. Visuals lose impact if shown for too long and distract people when the speaker has moved on to the next topic.

- **Test your presentation** on a few people representative of your audience. Revise anything that was unclear to them. This important step can make the critical difference in the understanding of your material. When you know the subject so well yourself, it takes someone less familiar with it to spot the gaps.

Wording

Wording on visuals should be brief and concise. Just use key words, rather than complete sentences. Visuals should support the speaker who will fill in the details.

For example, the 27 words in the above paragraph can be reduced to eight words in the visua on the next page:

- **Make type large** enough to be seen easily by everyone in the room. Follow the rule of thumb that projected lettering should be one inch tall for every 25 feet of viewing distance. So if the back row is 75 feet

Wording

- brief
- key words
- incomplete sentences
- speaker support

Type

All decisions about type should be based on ease of reading from a distance. Computers give us many type choices, but few are appropriate for professional-looking, legible visuals.

Choose a simple, yet bold, block type style. Type that is too light is lost in the light from the projector. Condensed or narrow type is less legible than a style in which each letter has a distinct shape. Roman type, while preferable in print, is less

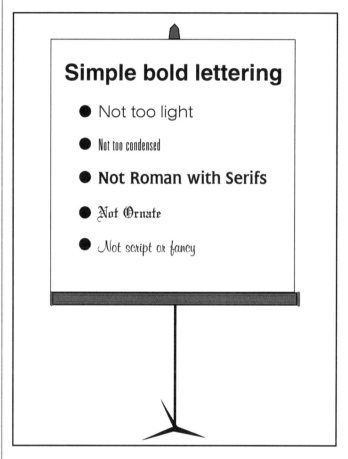

Simple bold lettering

- Not too light
- Not too condensed
- **Not Roman with Serifs**
- Not Ornate
- Not script or fancy

from the screen, letters must be projected three inches tall. (How to achieve optimum type size is discussed later.) This is why you must know audience and room size before producing visuals. The fewer words used, the easier it is to make lettering large enough for everyone to read.

■ **Limit each visual to 15-20 words**. If your presentation has very many visuals with more than 20 words, do more editing or split the content between several visuals. Headings should identify, not duplicate, the material.

■ **Simplify tables** or tabular materials, or convert them to more visual charts. Tables are often too complex to work well as visuals. Reduce each to no more than 15-20 elements, or five rows of three or four columns, for example. If a table is larger, divide it into smaller tables, repeating the headings on each one, or eliminate any elements (an entire column, for example) not covered by the speaker.

Readers should not have to add columns of numbers or percentages; do it for them. Use a horizontal line or more than the usual amount of space between lines to help group information and so that the eye can easily follow across several columns.

successful for visuals. The characteristics of Roman type are thin and thick strokes with serifs, the little feet at the ends of the strokes. Roman types, when projected or viewed from a distance, lose their thin strokes and the serifs, making them difficult to read. Ornate, script, or fancy type styles are inappropriate for visuals and too hard to read.

Good type styles for visuals are Universe, Helvetica, Helios, News Gothic, or similar styles in bold or demi-bold weight. Standardize with one style so your visuals are consistent. Letters within a word should be spaced close, but not touching. Headings can be a larger size, bolder style, or different color.

Use lower case letters (a, b, c) because they are more legible than capitals (A, B, C). Use caps only for the first letter of

WORDS IN ALL CAPS
ARE HARD TO READ
because they lack the
unique shapes of words
in lower case type.

Color
● saturated colors
● limit to two or three
● bright color for emphasis
● same color scheme throughout
● type contrast with background

titles or proper nouns. We read by recognizing word shapes as well as individual letters. Some lower case letters have ascenders or are taller (b, d, f, h, k, l, t); others have decenders or go below the base line (g, j, p, q); and others are in between (a, c, e, i, etc.). This variety gives lower case words easily recognizable shapes. Capitals are all the same size and have the same rectangular word shapes.

Capitals are often used and incorrectly assumed to be more legible because they are larger:

LOWER CASE IS MORE LEGIBLE THAN ALL CAPITALS.

However, it's better to enlarge the lower case lettering than to rely on capitals:

Lower case is more legible than all capitals.

Color

Color can help attract or focus attention, set a mood, or snap up the presentation. When misused, it can be over-done, detract from the message, or confuse the audience. Saturated colors project best; pastels look faded and don't provide enough contrast for readable type. Limit yourself to two or three colors plus black and repeat them throughout your presentation. Select one bright color to highlight an important point and consistently use it for emphasis. Use the same color scheme throughout your presentation. Make sure type contrasts with the background for best visibility.

Never alternate colors from one letter or word to the next. Color should serve a purpose that is always clear to the audience. For example, if yellow is used to highlight the most important point, it should do so consistently throughout the presentation. Don't use colors that clash or otherwise detract from readability.

Color also can give the presentation an aesthetically pleasing look. Computer visual templates often provide a good use of color as background or border designs. It's important to carefully select the one that goes best with your presentation.

Graphics

Art, illustrations, diagrams, photos, charts, and graphs are the picture part of a well-balanced presentation. Like words, the picture needs to be simple, clear, and concise. Edit any unneeded elements or details that may confuse or detract from the visual's message or distract from what the speaker is saying.

- **Art** can be used to show what a photo cannot – insides, enlargements, simplified details, abstractions, exaggeration, humor, etc.

- **Photos** are more appropriate for realism, accuracy, and technical detail.

- **Art and photography** can be combined effectively in the same presentation to show both sides of the subject – abstract concepts or difficult-to-picture items, and the actual subject or process.

- **Text**: titles, tables, and other type-only visuals round out the presentation.

Art, just as type, should be consistent throughout the presentation. Use the same art style, technique, graph format, and color scheme on all illustrated visuals. Published graphics usually are too detailed for direct conversion to visuals. They should be redrawn, simplified, color added, lines darkened, and type enlarged:

Art for Publication

Soil mound created at time to retain cane moisture until buds break - later removed

Mounded area to create watering well

Soil level

Amended soil

Shank

Cultivar

Bud union (graft) 2 to 4 inches below surface

Rootstock

Art redrawn for Visual

Soil mound

Mounded area

Soil level

Amended soil

Shank

Cultivar

Bud union

Rootstock

Charts and graphs

Well done charts and graphs convey statistics faster and more efficiently than a written or spoken description or a table of data. Data that are visually presented shows comparisons that prove your point without burying your audience in the numbers. If the data behind the charts is important, include the details in the handouts or proceedings rather than the visuals, which are on the screen only briefly.

Some general principles apply to all types of charts and graphs:

- **Simplify** charts to essential elements, especially for a non-technical audience.

- **Emphasize** the data.
- **Clarify**; do not create charts that deceive.
- **Redo** charts to have bolder lines and type; do not use print graphs on a visual.
- **Label** the bars, lines, and pie pieces right on the graph; do not use a key.
- **Show numbers** (if critical) on the chart; do not expect viewers to tell from the axes.
- **Convey** one clear idea with each chart; do not try to say too much.
- **Eliminate** footnotes and complex titles.
- **Set horizontal type**; vertical type is too hard to read.
- **Minimize** grids, tick marks, axis labels, etc.

Graphs that have axes should start at zero or indicate clearly that a section is missing so as not to mislead the viewer. The vertical axis should have no more than four to six sections (e.g., 0 to 100 could be labeled 20, 40, 60, 80, and 100). Similar graphs in a series should use the same axes for ease in comparison.

Bar graphs

- show comparisons at different times, locations, conditions, etc. – interval data
- can group bars to compare different data sets
- are easy to understand
- can be either vertical or horizontal.

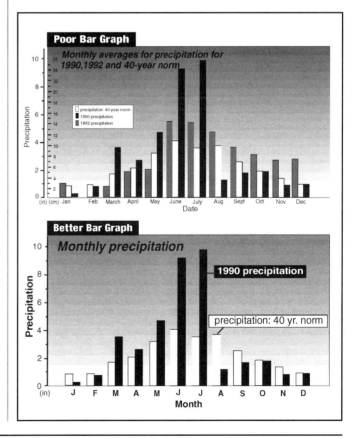

Avoid software's three-dimensional bar charts option because the results are rarely easy to understand and the bars are harder to compare than a two-dimensional version. Limit the number of elements in the chart, including title, labels, axes, and a maximum of 25 bars. Horizontal bars work best when you need to place the label directly on the bar.

Line graphs

- display trends, frequencies, overall patterns best – continuous data
- should have no more than four or five lines, or the comparison can become confusing
- best distinguish lines with color or line thickness, not symbols or dashed lines
- can show current data with solid lines and future data with broken lines.

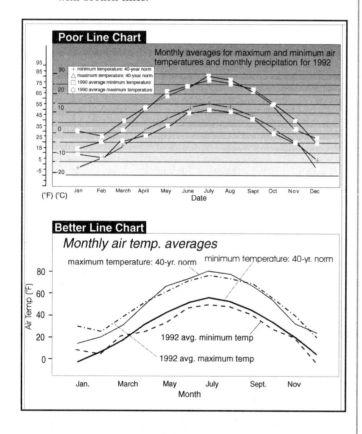

Lines necessary to convey content (such as a bell curve) should be two or three times as thick as the structural lines of the graph and should clearly dominate. Avoid using grid lines because they interfere with the data lines. Use color on the data lines if possible and be sure that each color is equally visible.

Pie charts

- are best at showing what parts make up the whole and comparing relative sizes of the parts

- show proportions better than actual figures or the percentage
- are most effective with six or fewer sections
- should eliminate very small segments (less than 10%) by grouping them together (e.g., "other")
- are clearer if segments have solid colors rather than patterns or hatch marks.

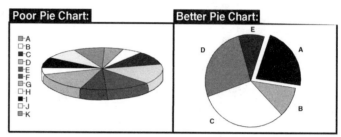

Each slice in the pie chart should have its own color. Don't repeat the title color in a segment unless the title refers to that piece. Another way to emphasize a section is to explode it out from the rest of the pie. Three dimensional pies are often difficult to interpret because the tilt distorts relative size. (Two sections of equal proportions could be different shapes if one is on the top and one on the side.)

Organizational charts

- explain structure, chain of command, and relationships
- show equal elements at the same level
- should be limited to 10-15 boxes, combining similar elements into one box if necessary.

Flow charts

- present sequences of events or show a step-by-step procedure
- should try to visually simplify a complex process
- normally read from left to right or top to bottom.

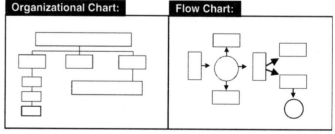

Rules of thumb for projected visuals

One advantage of projected visuals is that projection allows enlargement. Then, why have you found yourself in an audience trying in vain to read the screen? Are your audiences straining to see your visuals?

Successful projected visuals require coordination among:

- type size on the visual
- size of image on the screen
- screen size
- room size.
- It's not as complicated as it sounds.

Create visuals that are readable at a distance of six times the width of the visual.

Artwork (meaning any master from which a visual will be made: (art, type, charts, etc.) can be checked for visibility by using 6-to-1 ratio the same 6-to-1 ratio before making the final visual. For example, if a graph is five inches wide, look at it 30 inches away and the type will be about as easy to read as from the last row of the audience.

- **Slides**: You should be able to read it held up to the light six to eight inches from your face.
- **Overheads**: Put it on the floor at your feet and read it from a standing position.
- **Computer**: Read the monitor six feet away.

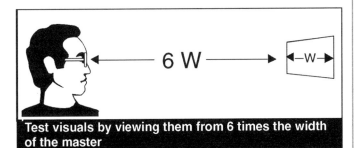

Test visuals by viewing them from 6 times the width of the master

Always place the projector so your visuals fill the full width of the screen.

Even well-designed visuals cannot be seen if they don't take full advantage of projected enlargement. A common problem is for the slide, overhead, or computer projector to be too close to the screen, making the projected image too small. Test the equipment ahead of time and move it to maximize image size on the screen, even if it means rearranging the room.

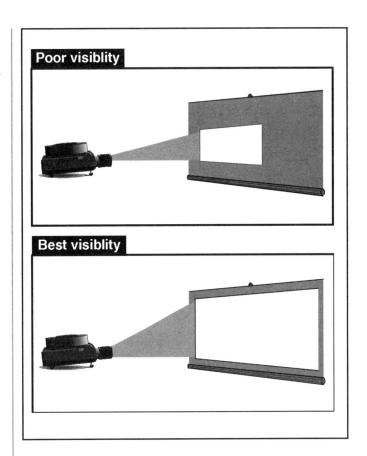

Poor visiblity

Best visiblity

Six times the width of the screen should be the distance to the last row of the audience.

In other words, if the screen is seven feet wide and the image on the screen is seven feet wide, no on should be viewing it from more than 42 feet away (6 x 7 feet = 42 feet). Most classrooms, meeting rooms, and lecture halls with permanent screens follow this screen width-to-view distance ratio, but it never hurts to double check. If your visual follows this rule and it fills up the width of the screen, it will be visible.

Make all visuals horizontal to maximize their size on a horizontal screen.

If you must use a horizontal screen (e.g., eight feet wide by six feet tall), and horizontal images are projected eight feet wide, the last row can be 48 feet away from the screen (6 x 8 feet = 48 feet). However, vertical images will fall off the screen a foot at the top and a foot at the bottom. To keep the vertical images on the screen, you must reduce their projected size to six feet, which also reduces the horizontal image to six feet wide, and the distance viewed to only 36 feet (6 x 6 feet = 36 feet). Chances are that a room with an 8 feet x 6 feet screen will have seating 48 feet back, and audience members in the rows in the last 12 feet will not be able to see the visuals well.

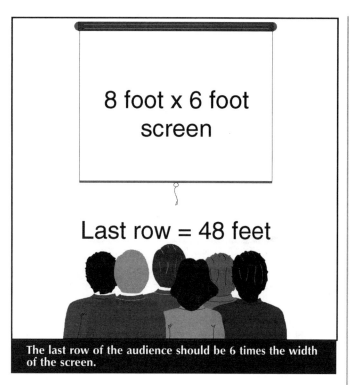

8 foot x 6 foot screen

Last row = 48 feet

The last row of the audience should be 6 times the width of the screen.

Some program organizers require all speakers to use only horizontal visuals to guarantee maximum visibility and so that projectors won't have to be moved between each presentation. If a square screen is used, both horizontal and vertical visuals fill the screen equally well and viewing distance remains unchanged, but often you don't know the size or shape of the screen or cannot control it. Horizontal visuals are safest. Computer-generated visuals tend to be horizontal by default since the monitor is horizontal.

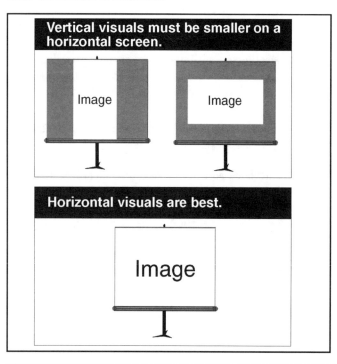

Vertical visuals must be smaller on a horizontal screen.

Image

Image

Horizontal visuals are best.

Image

Design visuals to be the correct proportions to maximize visibility.

- **Slides** are 3 x 2 inches proportions.
- **Overheads** are 4 x 3 inches proportions.
- **Computer** screens are about 10 x 7 inches proportions.

Make the graphics and type as large as possible to fill up the frame of the visual.

Text does not match the proportion of the slide

Minimum Letter Sizes for Various Viewing Distances			
viewing distance in feet			
12½'	25'	50'	75'
letter sizes in inches			
½"	1"	2"	3"

Text is proportional

Minimum Letter Sizes for Various Viewing Distances			
viewing distance in feet			
12½'	25'	50'	75'
letter sizes in inches			
½"	1"	2"	3"

Type should be as large as possible. Fewer words permit larger type.

Type size is measured in points. Below are some common type sizes used in preparing art for projected visuals.

Type sizes 10point, 12point, 18pt., 24pt., 30pt., 36pt., 42pt.

Ten point type is about the same as elite typewriter type and 12 point type is approximately pica typewriter size. Typewriter type can only be used for slide masters if the type style is bold, the original is no larger than 30 x 20 inches, and a special close-up lens is used. Typewriter type is never large enough for overheads unless it is enlarged on a copier about 300 percent. Below are guidelines showing acceptable type sizes for the width of the visual or master.

Width of master	Headlines	Copy/subheads	Smallest type
2 inches*	12 pt. (pica)	10 pt. (elite)	10 pt. (elite)
3 inches*	18 pt.	12 pt. (pica)	10 pt. (elite)
4 inches	24 pt.	18 pt.	12 pt. (pica)
6 inches	30 pt.	24 pt.	18 pt.
8 inches	36 pt.	30 pt.	24 pt.
10 inches	42 pt.	36 pt.	30 pt.
* requires special close-up photography equipment			

The higher the resolution of computer output, the higher quality the visual.

Computer word processing and presentation graphics programs make it easy to produce type large enough for visuals. However the resolution of the output, or the number of dots per inch, (dpi) affects the quality of the visual when it's projected. For example, your laser printer probably prints at 300 to 600 dpi (high end printers are 1,000 dpi or higher), which will project as very clean type and graphics.

However, dot matrix printers that only print at 75 to 150 dpi produce poor quality output for projection. Some software can increase the resolution of the printed master on a dot matrix printer, but only by viewing it projected can you tell if the quality is acceptable. Usually, however, resolution less than 300 dpi looks unprofessional when projected.

The best resolution is achieved by saving the visual to disk and sending it (on disk or via modem) to a service bureau to create the slides or overheads electronically. This service also can add special backgrounds and colors or do artwork, all at a cost.

A liquid crystal display (LCD) panel or a video projector connects to your computer and permits you to project your visuals right from the computer, without making overheads or slides. Most LCD models are projected from an ordinary overhead projector, and others have their own projection capability built in. Computer projection devices' resolution usually matches the computer screen resolution, but enlarges the pixels.

What LCDs and video projectors lack in resolution is made up for in flexibility. While showing visuals from your computer,

you quickly can switch to another application, a spread sheet, or even the Internet, for example, and project data or a demonstration. You will need to adjust the type size in these other applications to meet the proportions rule and assure visibility for everyone in the audience.

Checking facilities

When planning your presentation, find out what the facilities will be like. More specifically, you must know:

- room size, screen size (if one is available), and if it fits the rule for proper proportions.
- what audio-visual or computer equipment will be available, if you need to reserve it, or if you need to bring your own (Don't assume equipment will be available, even something as simple as a chalkboard or screen. Check.)
- if you will be setting up and/or running equipment, or if an AV or computer technician (to whom you will need to supply a well-marked script) will take care of those details
- how much time you will have before the presentation to set up and make sure everything is running satisfactorily.

Test your visuals. Ideally you should request the opportunity to try the presentation room and the actual equipment. Asking questions over the phone may not surface a problem, especially in a room not usually used for teaching. Some things to check for potential problems:

- if the room is too long for the size of the visual on the screen – will the furthest viewer be no more than six times the width of the screen?
- if the room is so wide that people sitting on either side will have trouble seeing the visuals
- if the ceiling is too low relative to the size of the room (e.g., you determine you need a 9 x 9 feetscreen because the last row is 54 feet back; however, the room only has 9 feet ceilings so the screen cannot be raised above the heads of the audience.)
- if there are other visual problems, such as pillars, glare from windows, etc. Try to correct them by rearranging the room if possible.
- if the room can be darkened–if not, projected visuals, except overheads, cannot be used
- if the projector is permanently installed where it does not project an image maximizing the screen size, or proportional to the room size (this is sometimes the case with a rear-projection screen)
- if acoustics are adequate for the room size, or if you will need a microphone.

Allow time to check everything again when setting up for the actual presentation. Something could have changed since your preliminary check.

If using overheads, adjust the screen to eliminate keystoning, which distorts the image and occurs when the projector projects up to a screen. It can be corrected by tilting the screen so that the bottom is farther from the projector than the top. In other words, the light should hit the screen at a 90 degree angle to prevent keystoning.

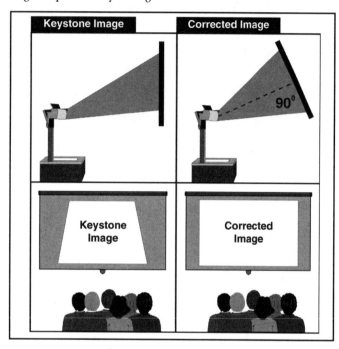

During the presentation

How you present yourself and your visuals is as important as the design of the visuals themselves.

- Look at the audience, not the visual.
- Don't repeat what the visual shows; add to it.
- Give the audience a chance to look and absorb each visual before talking about it. It is hard to read one thing and hear other verbal messages at the same time.
- Pace your visuals: don't go through them so fast they can't be comprehended, and don't leave one visual up so long that it begins to distract.
- If the same visual is referred to more than once, have duplicates inserted where needed rather than backing up or flipping through the previous visuals to find the one you want.
- When showing overheads, overlap them only for a split second, not removing one visual until after the next one is in place. This eliminates the annoying bright-

flash between each overhead.
- Don't blind the audience with the projector light shining on a blank screen. Know which is the last visual, and while it's still on the screen, shut off the projector. One easy way to cue yourself is to add a visual that simply says, "Questions", at the end of the presentation or each subsection. This lets you and the audience know it's the last visual and time to entertain questions.

Humor and humorous visuals have their place in a presentation. They attract attention, add life to dry material, and can provide a waker-upper or change of pace. Humor in the form of exaggeration (often accomplished through artwork) can emphasize a point and etch it in the memory.

Don't overdo it, however. The audience can lose track of your point if it is buried in jokes. Too much humor also can damage your credibility. Humor that is degrading to an ethnic group, race, gender, or religion has no place in a professional presentation. Be alert to your audience and avoid topics about which they may be especially sensitive.

Evaluation

If you or the program coordinators evaluate your presentation, be sure to include a question about your visuals or the method of presentation, as well as the content. If your visuals were prepared by AV specialists, pass this feedback on to them. You will learn if your early analysis of the audience and your content were accurate and if your choice of methods, including visuals, was appropriate.

With this feedback, revise in any way necessary to improve the next presentation. Rarely will you use those same visuals again exactly as used the first time. Determine their appropriateness for each new situation or audience. This constant review and revision makes the difference between a speaker with lively, up-to-date, appropriate visuals and one who tries to make do with the same old material, no matter how inappropriate, for every audience and situation.

If you do this constant review, your audience will appreciate it, remember what you had to say, and remember you as an outstanding presenter.

Effective Meetings

Why have a meeting?

As more and more communication takes place when people are separated in time and space, opportunities for people to meet face-to-face should be special times. "High-tech," people crave "high-touch," and meetings can provide the opportunity to share ideas and generate enthusiasm.

An essential component of a successful meeting is lots of space for human interaction. One of the findings from a study of 4-H club meetings was that the more the 4-H'ers talked during the meeting, the more they rated the meeting as successful. The 28 percent who said nothing beyond "yes" to the roll call were the least likely to consider their meetings successful (Tai, 1968).

It's a rare person who enjoys meetings, and some meetings trigger stomachaches and headaches among those attending. Yet meetings can be a source of comfort, synergism and creative energy if they are carefully planned, executed, and evaluated. Running a meeting, whether it's a large conference or a small group around a table, can be successfully accomplished by following some guidelines. Here are some general guidelines that apply to every meeting, no matter what its size or intent.

Meeting guidelines

- Consider the participants. Consider their time schedules, other responsibilities, preferences for food and drink, and needs for breaks, as well as their interest in the meeting's content.

- Give participants choices for their involvement in the meeting. Make sure everyone has the opportunity to participate actively. This means a chance to talk, if not to the whole group, at least to one other person.

- Ensure that everyone has timely access to all the information, that they can see, hear, and understand. Make arrangements for late comers and early leavers.

- Entertain, as well as educate and/or inform. Feed the soul as well as the mind.

Standing committees, boards, task forces

Every standing committee board of directors or task force needs a leader–someone who can organize efforts and maintain efficiency of the group. Leadership of this type is not for everyone. Being able to direct a meeting properly is a skill most good leaders have learned through experience.

Choosing the leader

If you're in a position to elect or select a person to serve as chair, what criteria will you use for choosing the right person? Will you make your choice simply by the person's knowledge of the issue(s) or perhaps the person's length of service on the committee or board? Often, a leader is selected by these criteria, but that person may not have the skills needed to be an effective meeting leader.

Better criteria for choosing a chair include organizational skills, knowledge of the organization or task, dedication, decisiveness and communication ability. For example:

- The chair should have demonstrated ability to organize and meet deadlines.

- The chair understands how your organization works, understands who reports to whom and knows the rules that govern the organizations and its committees.

- It's very important to have leaders who focus meetings on the mission or task and not on side issues or themselves.

- A chair must be able to make sensible decisions at the meeting, sometimes without the advice of other committee members. Also, the chair must be able to accomplish tasks between meetings.

- To be a good chair, the person must be able to communicate clearly. For example, some issues involve preparation of the committee members. And, some issues involve people outside the committee. As a matter of courtesy, those people should be informed of the actions being considered. A thoughtful chair must do that.

Why must a meeting be efficient?

No one likes to be in a meeting that gets bogged down in pointless discussion, does not accomplish or complete its agenda or runs past the time for adjournment.

A person's time is valuable, especially today. If you expect people to attend your meeting, make it worth the time they invest. By respecting your colleagues – and the time they invest in your meeting – they will become partners in the task before you. They will look forward to your meetings because they know you care enough about them to use their time properly and because you meet the goals your meeting is designed to accomplish.

In general, an effective meeting is one in which all parties have input into the discussion, the agenda is completed and the group is adjourned on time or before. A chair who accomplishes this in most meetings will earn the respect of the committee members and the organization served.

Before the meeting

- Consider the purpose. What will be accomplished in a face-to-face meeting? Is a meeting the best way to accomplish the purpose? Would e-mail messages, telephone calls, letters and/or one-on-one visits do a better job?

- Decide whom to invite (or whom to encourage to attend!). Many meetings have a prescribed set of attendees. For others, you may have discretion over who should attend. The purpose should determine the attendance. Maybe not everyone needs to come to every meeting. Or perhaps the whole group can meet first and a smaller group before or after. If you give people the choice of coming to all or part of the meeting, you will increase their feelings of control over their lives and thereby make them happier.

- Arrange for a date, time and place. Set this up well ahead of time (usually one to two weeks before) so people who have other obligations can make arrange-

ments. You may need to send out schedules with several possible dates and ask people to check their preferences and return their schedules to you. Avoid using valuable meeting time trying to find a date that suits everyone. Invariably, people don't have their calendars or discover a conflict afterward. Some groups will have regular meetings. If so, consider canceling meetings if there is no business to conduct.

- Prepare the agenda. As chair, you should prepare and announce the meeting agenda in advance. It depends on the nature of the meeting, but generally a meeting that involves a lot of people should be announced with an agenda no less than one week before the meeting occurs. The same is true for "electronic" meetings, by audio teleconference or by computer. When you share the agenda in advance, you "share the power" with others. Also, you give those who will be attending a chance to think about the items and to be ready to contribute ideas.

- Contact committee chairs and guest speakers. If it's a task force, ask the person who defined the task to come to the first meeting and describe the task for all to hear. If your meeting is part of a larger organization, study the organization's constitution or governing documents carefully. Make arrangements for someone to record the minutes.

- Notify people of the meeting, title of the meeting, date, day of week, place, starting time, and duration. Recheck the information to be sure it's correct. Have you indicated whether it is a.m. or p.m.? Does the day of the week match the calendar date? If you need a reply, have you left a spot for the name and included an address to send it to? Put yourself in their shoes and think about what participants need. Do they need more specific directions, perhaps? Signs up on the doors? Someone to direct them to the right spot?

- Arrange the meeting room. (Arrive early to do this.) Set up tables and enough chairs (but not too many!) and place them far enough apart to be comfortable. Try the lights and adjust the thermostat and the windows. Make sure everyone will be able to see and hear.

Find chalk, flip charts, pens, equipment as needed. Try it out. Arrange for coffee, soft drinks and snacks, if desired. Put out nametags, if needed.

Place those inclined to dominate next to yourself and the shyer participants directly opposite (Krueger, 1994). This enables you to use sustained eye contact to encourage others to participate and to avoid looking directly at the talkative person.

Agenda format

The written agenda for a meeting is important, and the order in which things appear on the agenda should have a logical sequence. In what order should things appear on the agenda? Generally, you should follow this format.

- call to order
- approval of previous meeting's minutes
- reports of officers or standing committees
- reports of special committees
- old or unfinished business from previous meeting(s)
- new business
- special program or announcements
- next meeting date
- adjournment

It helps to place easier items at the beginning and end of a meeting and to place more difficult items in the middle.

Do any items on your agenda require some explanation? If so, explain with a short paragraph at the bottom of the page, on the back, or on a separate sheet of paper. For example, if your agenda surprises people with an item that says something like, "Consideration of $1 billion contract for services," you will have some explaining to do. A paragraph that explains the proposal or some supporting document(s) supplied ahead of time to help explain what you mean will help prepare committee members for the discussion. And, it will calm many anxieties!

Directors or subcommittee leaders may come to your meeting prepared with recommendations for your group to consider. In general, it's best to require that recommendations with explanations be submitted to you in advance of the meeting. Those reports should be distributed with the agenda for two reasons.

First, valuable meeting time should not be wasted by members who must read reports just handed to them. Second, by giving committee members a chance to read reports in advance, they can be prepared when the report is discussed.

Another reason for preparation and advance distribution of the agenda is what can happen at the last minute! If you wait until the night before, something may happen (an accident or illness, for example) that will prevent you from preparing the agenda. Doing it early means you are well-prepared and so are the members of your committee. Your meeting will benefit. And, you can always identify the chair of the committee who is not prepared for the meeting!

The meeting itself

When you've done your homework to prepare for a meeting and you've properly informed the members, begin your meeting on time. If you say you will convene your meeting at 9 a.m.,

start at 9, not 9:20. A good way to irritate your committee is to announce you will "wait until all members are present" or you'll "wait until more people get here." This is not a good way to start your meeting, especially for those who arrived on time.

Of course, if a quorum is required, you cannot transact any official business until enough people are present.

Parliamentary procedure may be needed for your meeting, particularly when official business is considered. It's helpful if the chair understands the basic rules of parliamentary procedure. Sometimes, a member of the committee understands the rules better, and you may want to appoint this person as parliamentarian to help you conduct the meeting.

What can parliamentary procedure do for you? There are three things it can accomplish: it helps you conduct business with speed and efficiency; it protects the rights of each individual who wants to be recognized and to speak on issues being considered; and it preserves a spirit of harmony within the group (Overstreet, 1995).

Many books and pamphlets contain basic rules of parliamentary procedure. Henry Robert's *Rules of Order and Parliamentary Practice* is a commonly cited source. There are many editions.

Have you made arrangements for someone to record the minutes of your meeting? Generally, the chair should not take the minutes of a meeting. The chair should appoint someone to take and prepare the minutes of the meeting. (Do it before the meeting date, not when members arrive.) In some cases, a secretary with this responsibility is elected for a standing committee or board.

Once the minutes are prepared, consider how you will distribute them. Minutes should be prepared immediately after the meeting concludes and forwarded to the chair (or someone designated by the chair) for distribution to the members. This is very important, because it's generally the only official record you have of your meeting. If there is a problem with how the information is reported, members will spot the error quickly, and it can be corrected immediately. If you wait too long, members may forget what transpired, and a critical error may not get corrected. Correct minutes are important, especially if you need to refer to them later.

At the meeting, there are a few rules a chair should observe.

- Do not influence members to vote one way or the other. The chair fosters discussion among the members but generally doesn't offer opinions unless a tie is to be broken with the chair's vote.

- Stick to the agenda. Don't allow unannounced issues to distract the discussion. You announced an agenda, and it should be the guide for your committee's work at the meeting.

- Be sure questions or needs for additional information are followed up with a deadline. Don't leave questions open-ended. If you need more information to act on an issue for the next meeting, assign someone to investigate the matter and set a deadline for receiving the information. And, distribute the details so everyone has the answer before the next session.

- Use common sense when managing discussion. If you follow parliamentary procedure, a proposal for a vote must include a motion and be seconded before the discussion begins. That puts the matter officially on the table. If you sense most views on a particular subject have been heard, ask the members: "Is there further discussion?" or "Are you ready to vote?" If no one speaks, then vote and move on. Discussions should be thorough, not unnecessarily long and repeated.

Group stages

Anytime a group is involved in a series of meetings, it tends to go through a series of stages. This is true of new groups and also of established groups as they take on new projects or responsibilities. If you, as a leader, recognize these steps as normal progressions, you can be prepared to guide group members through the rough times. Tuchman and Jensen (1977) described the natural ebb and flow in catchy words: forming, storming, norming, performing and adjourning. Wells (1988) called the last stage transforming and stated that it could be regrouping or reverting as well as adjourning. The tension during the storming stage ranges from polite disagreement to noisy shouting matches, but it is an essential stage, full of energy and creative ideas. A knowledgeable leader can help the group achieve the most in each stage.

If things really get sticky during the storming stage, some conflict resolution may be in order. The model by Fisher and Ury (1981) has these principles:

- Separate people from the process.
- Focus on interests, not positions.
- Invent options for mutual gain.
- Use objective criteria for evaluating solutions.

Large conferences

Working with a big conference? Don't worry. Most large conferences are planned by small committees. Many of the suggestions for small groups are useful for large ones, such as know your audience and know your purpose before you start your plan. Nadler and Nadler's (1987) book is a comprehensive guide with checklists and detailed instructions for who does what in planning a large conference. Here are some added suggestions:

- Look at previous conference schedules and read through the evaluation comments to repeat past successes and correct past errors.

- Consider having a reaction panel after a speaker or breakout groups for discussion.

- If introducing a speaker, have a question ready yourself to ask or have one planted in the audience. Wait 20 seconds to give people a chance to think of questions.

- Organize a panel of participants to provide feedback as the conference is proceeding and be ready to make changes as needed in the schedule.

- Most people like to have a choice – of where to stay, what to eat, which session to attend.

- The younger the audience, the more it needs frequent breaks.

- The older the audience, the more important that everything be convenient and easy to find.

- People get sleepy after lunch. This is a good time for discussions or tours and a bad time to schedule speakers with slide presentations.

Be sure the meeting facility is accessible and your program accommodates people with disabilities. Meeting announcements should include a request that people with special needs (sign language interpreter, audio enhancement, enlarged type, wheelchair access) contact the meeting host/chair in advance so preparations can be made.

Meeting rooms should allow space for wheelchairs. Places without chairs mixed in with the group tables may need to be raised slightly. Supplemental materials may need to be produced in alternative formats for participants with visual or hearing impairments.

After the meeting

Send newsworthy items to appropriate media. Make personal contacts with those who have missed the meetings and get ready for the next one. Do calling early for arrangements. Give other people plenty of time and save the last-minute things for yourself.

Send thank-you notes to speakers and guests. A brief, timely thank-you is appreciated more than a longer, delayed one. A nice touch is to include a copy of the thank-you to the speaker's supervisor.

Resources

Fisher, R. & Ury, W. (1981). *Getting to Yes: Negotiating Agreement Without Giving In*. New York, N.Y.: Penguin Books.

Krueger, R. (1994). *Focus Groups*. Newbury Park, CA: Sage.

Nadler, L. & Nader., Z. (1987). *The comprehensive guide to successful conferences and meetings*. San Francisco: Jossey-Bass.

Overstreet, K. (1995) *Parliamentary Procedure Quick Notes*, Louisiana Cooperative Extension Service, LSU Agricultural Center, publication 2577.

Roberts, Henry, M. *Rules of Order and Paliamentary Practice*. Numerous editions.

Tai, S. W. (1968). *Participation during meetings of 4-H clubs in four Washington counties*. Unpublished master's thesis, Washington State University, Pullman.

Tuckman, B.W. & Jensen, M.A. (1977). "Stages of small groups revisited." *Groups and Organizations Studies*, 2. 419-427.

Wells, B. (1988). "Work with groups and organizations." (Module 5) In E. J. Boone (Ed.), *Working with our Publics*. Raleigh: North Carolina Agricultural Extension Service, North Carolina State University.

Public Speaking 14

Effective speaking

Upon completing this chapter, the reader will be able to describe audience characteristics, clearly state the purpose of the speech, develop a speech that is relevant to the targeted audience, and deliver the speech.

Imagine that you have been asked to make a formal presentation to the board of directors next week. The presentation is to be a report about last year's activities as well as a request for funding. You observed last year's presentation but have never presented such a report before. What can you do to make a positive impact on the board? The following tips should prove useful to you as you prepare and deliver this or other types of speeches.

This chapter will review the following:

- analyzing the audience
- determining the purpose
- developing the speech
- delivering the speech
- evaluating the speech

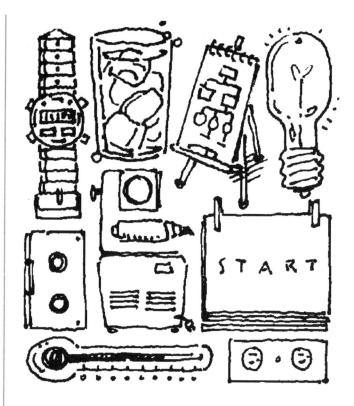

Analyze the audience

The first step in preparing and delivering an effective presentation is to ask questions about the audience you will be addressing. This, in effect, gives you necessary background for meeting the expectations of the target group. Whom do you ask? Start with the person who has issued the invitation. Then, if you know any of the potential audience members, talk to one or more of them.

Questions to ask (directly or indirectly):

- Why have I been invited to speak?
- What is the topic, and why does this group want to know about it?
- How long have most of the members been with this group?

- What groups do they represent (school teachers, bank officers, doctors, lawyers, neighborhoods)?
- Who are they (gender, age, ethnic group, education)?
- Where will I be speaking?
- What does the room look like (auditorium, conference room, cafeteria)?
- What control do I have over the room (lights, temperature, noise)?
- Will everyone be able to see projected or displayed materials (videotape, slides, flipchart)?
- When will I be speaking (time of day, position on the agenda)?
- How long am I expected to speak?

Determine the purpose

Your next step is to define the purpose of your presentation and determine how you can address audience expectations based on this goal. Presentations can be classified under one of four general types. Each type has a primary purpose.

Inform (explain or teach)

This type of presentation helps the listener know or understand more about a topic. You may be sharing goals, strategies, key events, good or bad news. Or you may be showing or demonstrating how to do something. People of any age will learn more readily when they are involved

> - progress reports
> - how to...
> - expansion or restructuring plans

with information or ideas, rather than just listening. If you hope the group will learn something, get them involved in discussion or an activity.

Persuade (convince)

The listener is encouraged to accept a challenge, change an attitude, or take action as a result of this presentation. Your presentation flows logically: (1) problem, (2) criteria, (3) possible solutions, (4) best solution, (5) action.

> **Request the audience to**
> - **buy**
> - **participate**
> - **vote**
> - **support**
> - **provide funding**

Inspire

This presentation should have emotional impact on listeners. The topic, examples, and delivery contribute to an inspirational presentation.

> - **dedications**
> - **gift presentations**
> - **memorials**

Entertain

This presentation helps the audience enjoy a specific occasion. It may involve additional speaker-audience interaction.

> - **Secretary's Day**
> - **birthday**
> - **holiday dinners**

Your presentation may incorporate more than one of these purposes. Effective presentations usually include features of each type, but the main purpose is based on what the audience is expected to know, do, or believe at the end of the session. Complete the following to help you determine your primary goal:

"After my session, the audience will_____."

Now that you know who is in your audience and what you want them to do following the presentation, you can begin to outline the components of the speech.

What are the three most important points you wish to make? Yes, you know a lot more than just three points, but remember your time limit, the audience, and your final goal. Limiting yourself to three key points will help you keep the presentation focused.

Develop the speech

You've defined your audience; you've gathered all the parts and pieces; now you are ready to put it all together. When you begin to assemble it, a speech or presentation is much like a paper: it should have an opening, a body, and a closing.

O P E N I N G

The **opening** should grab the audience's attention. You can:

· ask questions.
· quote well-known people.
· make a provocative statement.
· set up a problem.
· tell a (short) story.
· use a visual aid.

The opening also should include a brief overview. In other words, tell them what you will tell them.

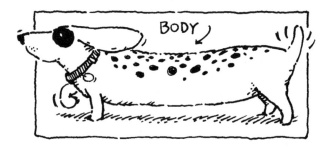

The **body** of your speech will be based on your key points. The points should be discussed in terms that are familiar to the audience. Include examples and stories audience members can relate to. Refer to your audience analysis for insights about what will appeal to them. Consider using support materials to reinforce your message and to keep the audience more actively involved in the presentation.

Reflect on how you will use the support materials. Make sure displayed items are large enough to be seen by the entire group. When you create transparencies and slides, use key words or phrases, white space, and pertinent graphics. Don't include so much information that no one can make sense of

them. Decide where to stand so that you don't block anyone's view of the transparency, slide, or flip chart.

Support materials:

· **handouts**   · **slides**
· **transparencies**   · **audio tapes**
· **flipcharts**   · **physical objects**
· **videotapes**

As you assemble the content and materials, list potential questions. Review the narrative. Have you addressed the questions on your list? If you haven't already included answers to the questions, determine how you will address them when they arise.

Use transitions to move your audience from point to point. Transitions create a logical flow to the presentation. They can help build momentum for your final point and dynamic close.

In the **closing** you tell them what you have told them. It should include a brief recap of the points you've covered. Remember that once you have indicated you are coming to the end of your presentation, you should end it shortly thereafter. Don't continue for another 20 minutes. The closing should include some type of charge to the audience. Refer to your presentation's goal to determine how to charge them. For example, the purpose of the presentation to the board of directors referred to at the beginning of this chapter was to persuade the board to fund your organization. The closing charge might be:

"As you can see, we have had tremendous success this year, thanks to your past support. We want to maintain the momentum, but we can do this **only** if we have your continuing financial support. "

I N   C L O S I N G...

Deliver

The speech is together, all your support materials are prepared, and you're ready to deliver your speech. But nervousness is setting in. Where did it come from?

Stage fright has struck. We tend to get nervous about making presentations because we want people to accept what we say. Most of us are concerned about what the audience thinks of us. We want to make sure that we have covered everything and are always afraid we'll forget something. Finally, most of us have an internal picture of the perfect presentation that we can never match. The combination of these elements leads to sweaty palms, shortness of breath, and blank minds. There are several things you can do to lower your anxiety level.

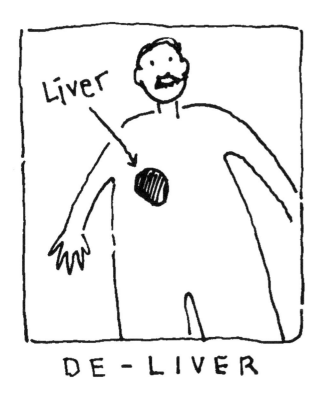

General actions

- Take a course in public speaking.
- Imagine yourself as a good speaker. It will be a self-fulfilling prophecy.
- Identify your fears, categorize them as controllable or uncontrollable, and confront them.
- Accept some fears as being good.

Before the presentation

- Check the facilities and the AV equipment.

- Obtain information about the group (audience analysis).
- Know your material well. Ensure that you are the expert.
- Practice your presentation. Ask friends or relatives to critique the presentation. Talk to yourself in the mirror. Videotape yourself, and review the tape.
- Practice responses to tough questions or situations.
- Anticipate potential problems and prepare probable responses.
- Rest up so that you are physically and mentally alert.

Prior to and during the presentation

- Convince yourself to relax; breathe deeply; meditate; give yourself a pep talk; think affirmatively.

- Identify advocates in the audience.

- Introduce yourself to the group in advance. Meet and greet them as they arrive.

- Create an informal setting.

- Provide an overview of the presentation.

- Provide for and encourage audience participation.

- Learn audience members' names and use them.

- Establish your credibility early. Know the topic; display confidence and professionalism.

- Use eye contact to establish rapport. However, if you are talking to a group from a different culture, make sure eye contact is appropriate.

- Prepare an outline and follow it.

- Use your own style. Don't imitate someone else.

- Use your own words. Don't read, unless you want to share a direct quotation with your audience.

- Dress comfortably and appropriately.

- Put yourself in your audience's shoes. They're asking, "What's in it for me?"

- Assume the audience is on your side. They aren't necessarily hostile.

DELIVERY BOY

Your **stage presence**, how you look and sound when you deliver your message, is very important. Your message is actually delivered through three channels: visual, verbal, and vocal.

The most effective presentations are those in which all three channels reinforce the message.

Visual Channel. At least 50 percent of your message is sent visually. What does your appearance say about you and the message you intend to send? When you think about what to wear the day of the presentation, think about the audience and where you will be making that presentation. A suit is nice but not quite appropriate if you are talking to a group in the horse barn. On the other hand, jeans are not appropriate in an office or other formal setting. Check with the person who invited you about appropriate dress. What is customary attire for the meeting? A word of caution: if the customary attire is something that you would not normally wear, choose something that is close but comfortable. For example, if the customary attire is jeans, but you don't own a pair, wear slacks and a shirt or sweater. (A tie would probably not be appropriate.) If your clothes or accessories detract (or distract) from your intended message, they are inappropriate.

Most of us don't like to talk about it, but personal grooming

FREE DELIVERY
FREE DELIVERY

plays a big role in the visual message we send, too. If the clothes are right but the hair is dirty, needs cutting, or is the first thing the audience notices about you, they will be paying more attention to that than to the intended message. Don't let your personal hygiene detract from your message.

The visual message is also conveyed by your demeanor. Body language – how we hold our arms and hands, how we stand, our facial expressions – speaks volumes about us. The next time you are in an audience, observe the speaker's body language. Where is the speaker standing – behind a podium or table or close to the audience? Is she turned toward or away from the audience? Is he making eye contact with members of the audience? What is her facial expression – solemn, happy/animated, sad, frowning, no expression? Where are his hands – in his pockets, behind his back, gripping the podium, waving around?

Standing behind a podium, table, or piece of equipment puts a barrier between the speaker and the audience. Sometimes it may be necessary to do that, but consider moving from behind that barrier and closer to the audience to create a more informal, intimate environment. If you need a microphone, request a wireless or hand-held microphone so that you can get closer to the audience.

Don't write out the entire presentation and read from those notes; just use an outline and your own words. You can refer to the outline from time to time to ensure you are still on course.

Look at the audience; make eye contact. Eye contact gives the impression of talking directly to individual members of the audience. Of course, you should not talk to the same individual for the duration; instead, look at people throughout the room. Include the entire group in the "conversation." Making eye contact with just one side of the room can make the other side feel ignored and left out of the conversation.

If there are questions or comments from audience members, be sure to look directly at the person speaking. Looking at your notes or another part of the room may give the impression (correctly or not) that you are not interested in what he or she has to say.

S P E C I A L   D E L I V E R Y

What are your hands doing while you're talking? Many people don't know what to do with their hands, so they have a death grip on the podium, rattle loose change and keys in their pockets, or play with a pen or pencil. These are habits that can drive an audience crazy. Instead of stuffing your hands in your pockets, develop gestures that provide emphasis (no rude ones, please) for the points you are making.

Facial expressions also provide clues to the audience about your feelings. Raised eyebrows can indicate surprise, shock, alarm, or that you have a question. Lowered eyebrows may give the impression that you are unhappy, angry, or disapproving. A smile, frown, tightly closed lips – what do these expressions convey to the audience?

The audience is reading your body language and you should be reading theirs too. What are they thinking about? As you look around the room, note what their actions are: looking at you, reading, staring into space, fidgeting. This body language can tell you pretty quickly whether or not your audience is still with you. Are they slumped back in their chairs, avoiding your eye contact, or are they sitting straight up and toward you, perhaps even on the edge of their seats?

Ask yourself if they are leaning back and avoiding eye contact because they disagree with what you are saying. Are their arms crossed and bodies turned away from you? This could mean that they disagree with what you are saying, or it could mean the room is too cold. Are their faces puzzled?

Perhaps you need to explain in more detail or rephrase a point. Read their body language and respond as appropriate.

> - **Choose attire that contributes to perception you want to create; make sure it does not distract from your message.**
> - **Be subtle when referring to notes.**
> - **Make eye contact with audience.**
> - **Use appropriate gestures and movements to add meaning.**
> - **Be conscious of your head movements. (Do they convey affirmation, denial, curiosity, uncertainty, confidence?)**

Verbal Channel. A second channel your message is delivered through is one that most of us think about first. That is the verbal channel. What words will we use to deliver the message? It is crucial to refer to the audience analysis when you think about what you will say. The most effective presentations are those that use clear, straightforward language the audience can relate to.

Jargon is specialized or technical talk of a specific group. Unless your audience is part of that group and familiar with the jargon, avoid it. Polysyllabic words are usually unnecessary and may cause some audience members to quit listening to you. Use emotive words to build the audience's emotions so that they will complete the charge you leave with them at the end of your presentation.

> - **Use simple, straightforward words.**
> - **Use language that will move the audience to act.**
> - **Choose words and phrases carefully.**
> - **Repeat key points.**

Vocal Channel. How does your voice sound? Do you speak in a monotone or do you change your tone to match the words you are speaking? A monotonous voice will put your audience to sleep. Changing the tone adds interest and variety to the spoken words. How loudly do you speak? Can everyone hear you or does your voice go no further than the first row? A softly spoken word used at just the right time can create drama and keep the audience on the edge of their chairs, but if the entire presentation is spoken very softly, you may appear to be timid.

Most of us tend to be very uncomfortable with silence, especially when we are the focus of attention. When we don't know what to say, fillers like "um," and "aah" get sprinkled into the void.

Silence is not bad and can actually be used to your advantage. It can provide a brief rest and mental review for your audience as well as an opportunity for you to re-focus. Like any other new habit, you must practice deliberately using pauses before they seem comfortable to you.

> - **Vary tone of voice appropriately.**
> - **Vary speed.**
> - **Use pauses.**
> - **Avoid fillers (um, aah, er).**

Fielding questions should be an integral part of your presentation. The audience has listened to you, and now it is your turn to listen to them as they ask questions or make comments. Courteous attention from you is always appropriate. Listen to the question or comment, determine the nature of the question as well as the actual intent, and then respond. Demonstrate that you are listening by turning toward the speaker and looking at him or her.

Make sure that the rest of the audience has heard the question. If they did not, repeat it, checking with the questioner to ensure you have repeated accurately. Include the audience by looking at them once you have acknowledged the questioner.

Give yourself time to think about your response before you open your mouth. Remember that it is better to say you don't have an answer to a question than to try to bluff your way through it. The response should be as short as possible without being abrupt so that you will have time for other questions.

What is the intent of the question asked? Sometimes you will need to address the emotion behind a question rather than the surface question you hear. Perhaps it's reassurance the questioner needs rather than a direct answer to the spoken question.

What if an audience member doesn't agree with you and wants to argue? There are a few options for dealing with these folks. Unless this is a debate, you probably don't want to argue with the person. Instead, note that you appreciate his point of view but you don't hold the same one. Or, you may want to say that it is a good point, but in the interest of time, one that should be explored on another occasion. You might offer to discuss the point after the session is over. By remaining calm and courteous, you can maintain control.

Steps to remember:

- Listen.
- Determine nature and intent of question.
- Respond (keep it short and simple).

Evaluate

For most of us, evaluation is the least appealing part of any project. Evaluating how you did as a presenter/facilitator/speaker can be very productive, however.

Questions to ask:

- Could everyone hear?
- Did I use an effective tone of voice?
- Did I avoid fillers and distracting gestures?
- Did I have an appearance of confidence?
- Did I use terms and language the audience knew and understood?
- Did I personalize the content for the audience?
- Did the materials support the content?
- Was the content appropriate for the audience?
- Were visuals legible and accurate?
- Were the visuals necessary?
- Was there too much/too little content for allotted time?

Taking the time to review and evaluate the presentation will help you the next time you are asked to speak. Request feedback from the audience and from your sponsor. Also review what you did yourself. When you review, you might want to jot down or note what you liked about the presentation and what you learned before you think about what you disliked. Then you will be ready for the next time!

Media Relations

An organization's success is dependent upon how effectively it deals with the media on a regular basis. In the case of a publicly funded entity, the payoff is in citizen support for programs and in accountability. It's critical that the media-relations practitioner and anyone else dealing with media keep service in mind. It's one thing to remember the basic tenants of truthfulness and prompt response. But a full-service approach to media relations will go a long way toward solidifying your position with the media and your publics. This chapter offers a few basic tips for both the public-information practitioner and the individual serving as a media source for information. We've also included some hints for those interviewed and their media-relations consultants.

Dealing with the media

Reporters basically want the same thing from you they've wanted for years: a reliable, credible and available source. If you can't fill that need, don't expect calls or cooperation in the future. And how you go about filling those needs is more than a reflection on you. It's the image your organization will hold with some very important image makers – the media.

Anyone dealing with media must remember the following:

- You can't fool a reporter and have no business trying.

- Response time is paramount in today's high-speed media environment. Deadlines are tighter than ever. Reporters remember how fast you respond.

- Perception is too often reality. Don't add to negative perceptions by not cooperating with media. This is especially true for those who work in public agencies – public accountability and responsiveness to citizens (media) is a hot issue.

- You're expected to understand the media's role in public accountability and how reporters do their jobs.

Reporters get paid to dig, to ask uncomfortable questions. There's no use getting upset over it.

- "Never pick a fight with someone who buys ink by the barrel or owns the nightly news." Your relationships with reporters who cover your "beat" are what makes you a successful media-relations practitioner or media source. Those relationships are often the toughest part of the job. You're not "one of them" even though you may wish reporters to view you that way.

Some interview basics (or what to think about when "they" call)

Call reporters back. Even if you're not the expert and don't have one on staff, a returned call proves your organization is cooperative. You may want to recommend an expert on the topic from elsewhere. This somewhat controversial practice among media relations-practitioners – some view it as "helping the enemy" – is a sure way of establishing your credibility with media.

Accept the media for what it is. The media is a conduit for public understanding. It's a way to get your message out and educate people. But the media is also a business interested in subscriptions or viewers.

Don't fight over simplification. Face the fact that media audiences don't know what you know about your expertise. You have an obligation to help reporters bring things down to public levels – to speak the "common" language. Help the reporter understand any technical concepts you introduce. If you can't do this, don't agree to the interview. If you develop a reputation for being too technical or unwilling to simplify, reporters won't be back. A good media relations practitioner shouldn't set interviews for this kind of source.

Thou shalt not lie. Say no more.

Honor the power of the press. Being interviewed as an expert source is an honor and involves a lot of responsibility. You're the voice of not just your organization, but often your profession. Take that seriously and be ready for the interview.

Don't be a "Crusader Rabbit." Disclose any agendas up front. A good reporter is going to see them anyway. Be frank but don't put on the obvious hard sell for your point.

Be prepared at all places and all times. If you're the expert on a topic that's "hot," be prepared to answer the call from reporters. If you have facts that you want to refer to in doing an interview, carry them with you. A good reporter will find you.

A checklist for the actual interview

- What are you wearing? Be conservative. You want people to pay attention to what you say, not what you look like. Match your attire to the topic, location and your position. This is particularly critical for TV interviews.

- Where does the interview take place? Think carefully. The interviewee must be comfortable with the setting. Depending on the topic, you may want the reporter to be comfortable too. If it's a TV interview, the backdrop should be appropriate to the topic (e.g. a story about milk shot in a milking parlor or in front of a grocer's milk case). A rule of thumb: it's rarely advisable to do the interview on the reporter's "turf." The exception would be a talk show you really want to appear on.

- Physical presentation. There's a science to the image you present. Good media-relations practitioners know their sources strengths and weaknesses and act accordingly. Consider the topic: do you want to create some authority and status? Do the interview from behind a desk. Consider the individual: Is the person being interviewed a big man who could be viewed as intimidating? Position him near a desk or large outdoor structure and make sure he smiles – casual attire might also help. If it's a TV interview, be sure the source is at eye level with the interviewer or camera. The appearance of looking down on an audience or looking up at one can have distracting subconscious effects on the audience.

- Set a time limit. It's one thing to be helpful. It's another to spend too much time. Having a reasonable time limit says your source is cooperative but busy.

- Learn something about the reporter – the kind of stories she typically covers, reputation, agendas.

- Define the kind of image you want to portray. What points or examples will help you set this?

- Prepare your points. It's common advice to prepare several points that you absolutely want to make during the interview. Practice these. Make sure they pertain to your

expertise. It helps when you have a unique angle on the topic. Play that up. Avoid the temptation to robotically repeat your "talk points." But also avoid the temptation to wander too far from them ... and your expertise.

- Can you demonstrate or illustrate? This is particularly useful when complicated scientific principles or techniques are involved. And critical to a TV interview.

- Recordkeeping. Be ready to keep track of the interview. Tape record the session. (It may be less awkward if you say you want to evaluate how clearly the person interviewed answers questions so they can be a better source.) Or at least jot down the questions and the gist of the answer.

- Profile sheets. It's a good idea to give this to the reporter ahead of time if possible. Include the name of the person interviewed, title, address, a follow-up phone number, educational background, significant publications/accomplishments related to the topic, other areas of expertise that may be of interest, and your name and number as the media contact.

- Be aware of habits the person interviewed or distracting speech patterns. Coach them ahead of time.

- Ask ahead of time for the interview topic and any particular areas the reporter might want your interpretation of. Don't expect to get a list of questions in advance.

During the interview

- Relax. A good interview is a fun exchange between two well-prepared professionals – even if the topic's difficult.

- Talk naturally. Concentrate on simple, short phrases at all times. Pretend you've just finished running a race and have to take short breaths. It forces you to be succinct. It also makes it easier for a print reporter to get the quote right and the electronic media reporter to get a sound bite that says what you want it to say.

- Maintain comfortable eye contact. It shows you take an interest in the questions and aren't being evasive.

- If you don't know, say so. And offer to help find the answer later.

- Never say "No comment." It's antagonistic and makes you look like you're hiding something. Practice softer versions of that response: "Sorry, I don't have anything to say about that right now." "Now John, you know I can't talk about those issues yet!" Keep it relaxed.

- Make your point and stop talking. Some reporters will pause to try to encourage you to talk more and possibly reveal something you hadn't intended to.

- If you don't understand the question, ask for clarification. Some reporters don't ask clear questions – it may be intentional to confuse you and lead you in a direction you didn't intend to go. Or it might just be an unclear question.

- Identify your main point quickly. Saying something like "The critical part of the debate as it relates to my research is...." emphasizes your position and expertise.

- Make sure you've covered all your points before ending the interview.

- Related stories. You and your media-relations expert may want to prepare a couple of related story ideas that are favorable to your organization or rely on some of your colleagues' expertise. Casually dropping those ideas at the end of the interview may be a good way of solidifying a relationship. But don't be pushy.

- Off the record. You're never "off the record" – no matter how well you know the reporter. That includes after you think the interview's over. The tape may still be rolling.

Media-relations work is a service industry. And those reporters you serve have some of the longest memories you'll ever meet. It's a game of relationships. You must play for the long term. A media contact that you do well with today can make a career. And last as long as a career. Make that lasting impression favorable.

Media relations: technology to serve

Media- relations work in the 1990s is an even greater challenge than during the 1970s and 1980s when we were swamped with investigative reporter "wannabes" following the lead of Woodward and Bernstein. Competition was great in print then, but media outlets and access to information were more finite than today.

What brought about this dramatic change? Electronic-communications technology, tighter bottom-lines in media organizations, and a greater variety of media outlets mean it's no longer just newspaper, general magazines, radio, and television. Today we're dealing with all those and a massive influx of specialty magazines, newsletters, and syndicated broadcast programs. Network news is giving way to local news – 24 hours a day. New computer networks give reporters and the general public access to more information – information about your business – than ever before.

All this represents opportunities for you as a media-relations practitioner trying to place your experts and their stories in this quickly broadening world of media.

Welcome to cyberspace

The "**Information Superhighway**" is the fastest lane in this new media environment. The trick is avoiding the speed bumps. Here are a few quick things you must know to survive the media- relations business beyond 1996:

E-mail. Without an address you're way behind. A rapidly growing number of reporters use e-mail to search for story ideas and sources or to receive background material and personalized analysis of an issue. Some even may want to interview your experts by e-mail.

Here's what you do:

- Get that e-mail account and put the address on your business card, letterhead – any place a reporter might see it.

- In your dealings with reporters, ask if they have an e-mail address and the kinds of things you may send them that way. Remember that a lot of reporters still pay for their accounts out of their own pockets and may not want to run up charges with your unsolicited "helpful" information.

- Database e-mail addresses the same way you do addresses, phone, and fax numbers. And guard that information closely – junk e-mail is worse than junk faxes.

- Use that e-mail address to keep in touch. Periodically drop a story tip, an appropriate backgrounder or even a compliment. (Warning: don't patronize.)

- Keep track of the placements you get using this technology as a way of convincing your boss it works.

- Those placements also should be ammunition to network your entire organization – reporters may want to contact sources directly. You'll want to place e-mail addresses in your media directory for your top sources who are online.

Backgrounding. Reporters aren't the only ones who can use computer networks to background stories. If you're running an educational news service, you may need information that your experts don't have readily available. It's time to jump on the information superhighway.

Learn to use data bases and to run gopher. Use the powerful search engines of the World Wide Web. If you're not familiar with these yet, check your local network support person or check out a good book on the Internet. The power here is your new ability to locate government statistics, traditional library resources which are now text searchable, information on individuals at academic institutions, background on various subjects, or technical documents on thousands of subjects.

You even might want to offer backgrounding as a service to media who aren't on the networks yet. And knowing how to search on-line databases can allow you to check placements of stories in major publications or on national television news.

News groups. Most Internet connection services offer some form of USENET NEWS. These are essentially thousands of specialized "chat" groups. You may have access to commercial news services in this way – good for following issues and breaking stories. Most are informal gatherings of people interested in a particular subject. If you're stuck without a source, this may be a good place to ask. News groups are probably the last bastion of truly free speech, and you don't have to be an "expert" to sound like one in this environment. Keep that in mind as you use this resource.

Specific media relations tools. ProfNet is a commercial service that allows reporters to contact hundreds of academic institutions and government agencies at once with requests for sources or background on a specific topic. Membership is reasonable. The service has been wildly successful in giving universities and colleges wider reach for their experts with minimal effort. For more information, send e-mail to: PNinfo@aol.com. Likewise ACEMEDIA offers similar service as well as shares educational information for media relations practitioners in food, farm family, youth, and natural resource/environmental news. If your organization works in these areas, someone in your office should be part of this list server. Contact sernst@ndsuext.nodak.edu for more information. On the business side there's BizNet. And other organizations such as the National Association of Science Writers and the Scientists' Institute for Public Information run finder services for media and those working with media.

World Wide Web. The interactivity and linkage capabilities of the Web offer lots to media-relations practitioners. Several options to consider in building your site on the web:

- Interactive expert lists. They're loved by some, hated by others. You really need to have more than the basic bios or contact information your contact sheets and source directories typically contain. Establish direct e-mail links from your web site. Link to some of the source's best papers. Consider a video or audio interview segment on a hot topic to catch reporters' interest and give an idea how good a source they are.

- Establish links to major resources and search engines in your field.

- Link to resource sites for media such as journalism journals, ProfNet, newsstands, etc.

- Build question sites – an "ask the experts" forum on your web site may benefit others as well as media.

- Build in feedback mechanisms. Asking questions gives you a chance to find out more about the media visiting your site and what they're interested in. Consider asking them to "register" but remember that may chase some away.

"Old" technologies for media-relations practitioners to reconsider

- **Phone conferences**. Great for briefings and impromptu press conferences – especially if there's a key issue at hand or if a key player is out of town. Not good for TV, but print gets the information it needs, and radio can get decent audio.

- **Electronic news systems**. Special computer-and satellite-delivered news and information services exist for primarily agricultural and financial industries. Work with these firms to make your organizations expertise available. Such services may end up delivering through the Internet or direct-broadcast satellite in the future. Will your Web development help them in that transition?

- **Satellite TV news feeds**. If the issue is hot enough and so is your expert, consider feeding live "press conference" format to TV news outlets. Tell them when you're on what satellite and give the opportunity to call in questions. The draw: they don't have to send a reporter and camera to your location to get a "personal" interview. You can do this for a group of stations at once or set up individualized feeds.

- **Cable systems**. The expanding cable television and radio industry is bringing with it a host of opportunities for your experts to reach highly involved audiences. Programs are targeted to specific interests, and local news is expanding. It's your job to know what opportunities exist in your markets and to make the most of them.

What's the future for media-relations practitioners?

More and more, you will become categorized as either information brokers or public-relations "flacks." Brokers will be seen by media as useful places to go for help in tracking down a story. The "flacks" out there will probably be tolerated, but always will be viewed cautiously because of their obvious agenda. (That's not to say that information brokers don't have agendas!)

Media want to know the brokers because it helps them do their jobs better. To achieve "broker" status, you must:

- Show a true interest in helping reporters do their job well

- Not come across as merely trying to sell your organization or source – it may not be a bad idea for you to present a source from a competing organization;

- Stay on top of the technology that helps you find the information necessary to be an information broker

- Know today's issues and have a sense of emerging issues

- Always, always be straightforward with the media you deal with. If you work honestly and hard for them, you'll gain a reputation that will buy your organization more positive "public relations" than any strict promotional approach ever can.

Technology, new and old will play a major role in your future. But it doesn't replace basic concepts of service and news savvy. You need to think of the concepts discussed here as tools and use them to enhance your overall program. Let your goals direct these tools, and put media service as the top objective of every new undertaking. That approach will keep you in this business for the long run and possibly keep your business in business.

Campaign Communications: Public-Information Campaigns

Floods in Missouri, a new apple variety in Minnesota, gardening in Oregon, agricultural disasters in Georgia. What do they all have in common? They make fine topics for public-information campaigns.

So what's a public-information campaign? It almost defines itself: It's an effort to disseminate information to the public during a specific time. Its versatility comes in its creative and effective ways to deliver that message.

You may launch a public-information campaign strictly through mass media, even narrowing your scope to one form. Or you could target your audience with direct-mail pieces. You may decide a multi-media campaign is the answer, right up to news conferences and down to refrigerator magnets.

Depending somewhat on your background and training, you may see a public-information campaign disseminated solely through mass media to reach the public quickly, effectively and inexpensively. A spot on the evening news reaches thousands and costs you pennies; a headline in the right daily newspaper alerts a broad audience and establishes you or your organization as a credible source of information; a radio station broadcast into homes, cars and businesses can spread the word almost instantly.

Mass media. You just can't beat it for blanket coverage.

Another approach to public-information campaigns employs marketing strategies. This technique looks to the target audience(s) first and chooses the communication tools based on the audiences' needs and the desired response. The arsenal of tools includes mass media, of course, but it also can involve direct media such as flyers and newsletters; personal contacts; paid advertising; and creative contacts ranging from billboards to bumper stickers to those ubiquitous refrigerator magnets. The narrowly defined target audience dictates the medium.

And the winner is ...

What topic qualifies for a public-information campaign? Like any good news story, it has to be important, timely, directly and interesting and it has to affect the target audience. But a heavy rain in a hot, dry summer would meet those qualifications. What else does a topic need to qualify?

Joe Marks, news director for the University of Missouri, says a topic has to meet two criteria: importance and policy.

"Is the topic something our clientele really should know about? Is it something that will help them ... be safe, feel better, earn more money, etc.?

"Is it the policy of the Extension Service, for example, to promote safety or good health or fitness? Well, if it is, those are things worthy of multimedia campaigns," Marks says.

And don't forget the real world of business and public awareness.

"Major campaigns are often developed at the request of administration," says Emery Tschetter, Agricultural Communications department head at South Dakota State University. "For most campaigns, the goal is to not only share information, but to position South Dakota State University as the best source of information in South Dakota."

Larry Etkin, Experiment Station editor/communicator in Minnesota, takes a distinctly marketing approach to choosing topics. He refers to an award-winning campaign to introduce a new apple variety, the Honeycrisp Apple.

"We are talking marketing as the major component of determining information worthiness," Etkin says. "Promotional campaign efforts from our unit are dictated by several factors." The main factors in the Honeycrisp Apple instance, he says, were a request by the specialists who developed the variety and also the money to finance the campaign.

Laying the groundwork

Once the decision has been made to prepare a public-information campaign – by administration, marketing leader, product manager, communications leader or whomever – the work begins.

Every campaign requires a team to carry out the plan. It may be as small as two: a writer and an expert.

Carol Savonen, an Oregon State University science communicator, conducts an award-winning mass media campaign with just herself and her information sources: She writes three articles a week for home gardeners, checking her copy with extension specialists.

To respond to the Mississippi River floods, members of the Missouri Communications staff became part of the Extension

Flood Response Task Force. The task force identified the key issues, and the media staff pumped out the information.

"As good as our news team was, we would have missed three or four issues without interacting with the task force," Joe Marks says. "The other reason for such a committee is a matter of expertise, knowledge, and subject-matter background. We expand our base by getting a variety of people together."

Sometimes the best system involves a media team with a liaison with administration. Emery Tschetter says that's how it works in South Dakota.

"While the committee will vary according to the project, Tschetter says it always includes Ag Communications specialists in print news, broadcast news, publications, and occasionally educational design. The committee is chaired by an Ag Communications staff member and works closely with subject-matter specialists. This structure allows communications specialists to develop plans and actually lead the process. The campaign-committee chair works with administrators to identify goals and audiences and maintains two-way communication during the process."

Larry Etkin, who worked on the Minnesota apple variety campaign, said the project started with a simple request for a "release sheet" but quickly mushroomed.

Soon two specialists, two photographers, a contact person from the funding group and Etkin each were working in various pairs on the project. As it grew, he became the logical person to "assume the hub role of maintaining communication with each of the other parties."

Now they have devised a more systematic approach for pulling together the right team for each campaign. Their unit has established a process that entails more formal conversations between specialists, product managers (design and production team leaders), the unit's marketing leader when appropriate, and/or the communications-technology leader, who would function as a kind of "account rep."

"Our account reps have 'bigger picture' contacts with departments and colleges that provide information that could influence product decisions," Etkin says.

So who should be involved in a public-information campaign? Only those who need to be – no more, no less.

The logical leader of the team should be a communications person rather than a subject-matter specialist. He or she can speaks for the team in explaining the campaign, can understand timetables and deadlines, and can alert the team to changes in the situation.

Targeting the audience

So who is the audience for this campaign? Too often, we dismiss the question with an off-hand answer: the general public. There may be a General Mills, a General Electric and a General Eisenhower, but there is no general public. At least not in public-information campaigns.

If you don't know who you're talking to, how do you know what to say? Few messages are so general that they apply to every living, breathing soul. Target your audience so you can target your message.

Look at how the audience-message dichotomy can work. Say your target audience is flood victims. You could generate mass-media material for that audience easily enough. But you could be more specific if you knew whether they were flood victims last month or last night, whether they are without a home or without a farm, whether they need help or want to help. Each level conjures up different story angles and different media outlets.

Use the planning stage to brainstorm who your potential audiences are, the responses you want from them, the messages that will trigger that response and the methods to reach them.

Do a little research at this point. Don't assume you know all about the potential audience just by digging out the weekly newspaper mailing list. Try to be as specific as possible with each potential audience, looking at demographics if necessary. If you can name them, you can reach them.

Donna Southard, of Purdue University, put together an educational-materials marketing catalog and built a public-information campaign around it. She identified her audience as traditional and nontraditional. Their campus and county staff, past users, commodity groups and legislators were their traditional audience. The nontraditional were visitors to the Indiana State Fair, Ag Day shoppers at a popular discount store, the Purdue Visitors Information Center, county fairs, and campus promotional outlets.

Once you've identified key audiences, search for ways to reach them. Do they have a common interest that would put them on a mailing list? Do they listen to similar radio stations? Can you reach them through schools or businesses, ministers, or garden centers? If you offer an opportunity, will your target audience identify itself?

Identifying and reaching target audiences is crucial to the success of your public-information campaign. If necessary and financially possible, consider contracting with a direct mail company to help you.

Making plans

With the team in place, the first order of business is establishing goals and setting timetables. As the old saying goes, you'll never get there if you don't know where you're going.

Southard's goals for the educational-materials marketing catalog were "to more effectively advertise the educational materials produced by Purdue's specialists and market the Cooperative Extension Service to both traditional and nontraditional audiences."

The marketing model calls for targeting the audiences, determining the desired response and deciding how to reach them. With those decisions made, you can work backwards.

If you want apple growers to buy a new variety to plant, time your message for when they are making those decisions.

Two publications reach this audience, so lay the groundwork for running an ad or an article in these publications. Learn the deadlines and allow production time to meet them. You have a timetable.

Get your plans down in writing. In the heat of a campaign, tangents can look logical and inviting at the time. Keep your eye on the goals and stay out of back alleys.

Your plan should include goals, target audiences, desired responses, each method/medium to deliver each message to each target audience (the media mix), deadlines, responsibilities, estimated costs and evaluation.

Share the plan with the appropriate leaders, managers and administrators to generate both financial and administrative support. Keep key people informed about major projects – they don't like surprises.

The plan will show you've done your homework. It will help you see the big picture and catch any omissions. For a large team, a working plan will help everyone focus and understand the strategies.

Build in evaluation tools along the way. You can't measure success if you don't have a yardstick in hand. The project goals determine success, but measurement is up to you.

This is a stage too often overlooked. But dissemination of information cannot be a goal in itself. It must serve a purpose. So build in reasonable, measurable goals. If you're introducing a new apple variety, success could be measured in the number of apple growers reached, the number of inquiries about the new variety and the actual count of sales.

If your goal is to reach and help flood victims, your success may need to be measured by tracking the media use of your material.

"We carefully traced the impact of our information effort by using a clipping service, a tracking device to record the number of persons who called in to get our radio reports, and personal contacts to determine use of our television news features," says Joe Marks of Missouri's flood campaign. "Besides that, we tried to keep personal records (a little like diaries) of any special media response to our efforts."

Measuring actual instances of lifestyle change or learning is hard, if not impossible in some cases, but don't discount comments passed on from others, thank-you notes scribbled on a post card requesting a publication, and editorials recognizing the effort.

And don't forget spin-offs. One good thing often does lead to another. Your efforts in writing regular gardening releases might prompt several newspapers to compile special gardening sections around your material. They make ad dollars based on the credibility of your material, and more people see the information.

Stick to the message

Now comes the creative part. If you had to put down in one sentence what you want people to learn or do when the campaign is over, what would it be?

"The flood victims of Missouri know they can count on the Extension Service for practical, timely information in an emergency."

"Minnesota apple growers are aware of a new variety from the Experiment Station, and a certain portion will invest in planting it."

"Oregon gardeners and newspaper editors look for gardening material from the Extension Service that answers current gardening questions."

The beauty of a public-information campaign is its focus. The more well-defined the goal, the easier to target audiences and prepare materials.

Advertisers prove every day that slogans work. People remember a catchy name or jingle or a memorable spokesperson. On an election year or during a crisis, the local television station usually develops a logo that defines every story related to that topic.

To unite your campaign, define it with a slogan, a logo, or a name. It may be as simple as a special slug on news copy entitled "From the Extension Flood Response Task Force."

Or it could be a walking, talking animated character that graces television, billboards, balloons, and stuffed toys, spouting the company line: "Only you can prevent forest fires!" says Smokey the Bear.

Your audience determines how you package the message. If you have the luxury of time and funding, set up a focus group of members from your target audience. What catches their eye? Which slogan or logo appeals to them? How do they interpret the message? What response would they have?

Time and money: do you have enough?

Finances must be a crucial consideration before launching any public-information campaign. Many long-term, multimedia campaigns require extra funding and possibly extra staffing.

Of Minnesota's apple campaign, Etkin says, "The information-gathering phase alone for media buys is time-intensive, even when you know who to call. And follow-up for getting the bills paid properly and cross-charged to appropriate accounts also took time. As for budgets, this could not have happened without the special grant."

Campaigns, particularly those triggered by emergencies or disasters, drain resources from other projects or require more hours and dollars to get the job done.

Of the flood campaign in Missouri, Marks says, "The big extra cost was time. We just shifted our effort from covering usual subjects to devoting full attention to flood issues. We increased our volume of news releases by 50 percent, radio broadcasts by 70 percent and our television news features by 20 percent during the six weeks we were going all out on the flood.

"As for time, we sure could have used more of that. I think most of us worked longer work weeks and shifted responsibilities. We didn't add any extra help. We probably should have."

That's an option you should consider: adding extra help. A public-information campaign is ideal for free-lancers. It's short-term, sometimes specially funded, tightly focused, and well-defined. A good free-lancer can take that kind of assignment and run with it.

Just make sure he doesn't run away with the budget. Any major project should have a detailed budget worked out in advance. Make sure the grant or sponsor covers what you have in mind. Figure in loss of staff members' time on regular work while they shift to the special project. Build a plan both you and the sponsor can live with. You don't want to run out of financial and creative steam halfway through the campaign.

Tools of the trade

A public-information campaign can be as simple as a weekly column or as complex as a multimedia extravaganza. Each can accomplish its goals, as long as the media mix is based on the target audience's needs.

Look at what you can use:

• mass media

• interviews

• press conferences

• direct mail

• promotional tools

Mass media

If you need to reach a broad audience, plan to work with mass media. Keep in mind that mass media works well to inform, build awareness, and respond quickly. If you have a narrow target audience and you want that audience to respond with commitment or action, look beyond mass media. It can deliver your message quickly and widely but is not the best motivational tool.

Elsewhere in this handbook, you'll see how to prepare news releases for print and broadcast. For a public-information campaign, work closely with key media to give them what they want, when they want it.

Prepare your materials to meet their needs as well as present the information. If the newspaper wants it delivered electronically, find out how to arrange it. If the TV news director wants an interview in an hour, be there. If the radio station manager just wants an index card with the pertinent information so he can grab it and read it, find an index card.

Mass media can deliver your message into every home if you can convince the gatekeepers this is one message that needs to get through.

Ever wonder why you can't get media to run your stuff? Maybe they don't know what they're doing. Or maybe you need to understand how they approach a story.

Think like a reporter. Stay current on what makes news.

Read, listen to, and watch all the news you can. Notice the angles they take. What you think is the most important thing about a story may not be what the media will notice.

Notice the difference in coverage between print and broadcast. The newspapers cover more of the story, while television looks for the visual angle and radio wants timeliness and brevity.

Media like to personalize a story. That's why they interview people the news directly affects, not just experts. Take advantage of that approach when you design your campaign.

Reporters aren't educators. They aren't passing judgment on what's right or wrong; they're reporting opinions. The clearest way to show the differences in opinion is to find the greatest extremes. But they don't want wild-eyed radicals on either end of the scale: they want the ones just to the left and right of center who are logical, well-spoken, and willing to take a stand.

Follow trends. Sense what the public wants, what people are concerned about, how opinions change. Use them in your campaign.

Keep up with the events that affect your campaign. If something breaks, be ready with background information and be able to explain clearly what it means.

Be available to your media people. Give them your business card with work and home phone numbers. (Being a media source can be a 24-hour-a-day job in a crisis.) List the subjects you can address.

If they call for information, get it to them quickly and courteously. **Understand deadlines**.

Be a story source. If you see a good story or know an interesting person, tell them about it. Once they see you as a story source, they'll call you for ideas.

To devise a media strategy for a campaign, consider several possibilities: news releases for print and broadcast, news tapes (audio and video), public-service announcements for print and broadcast, guest editorials, fact sheets, briefings, tips, letters to the editor, and many more.

You can prepare a complete packet that contains all the information, slow-release it on a schedule, or respond as the need dictates. Just be sure each item, no matter when it's released, is tied visually to the campaign through a logo, slogan, or slug.

Another media option is paid advertising. You certainly control the message and the medium; however, check on legal or professional repercussions before you pursue this option. Your institution should have a clear policy and guidelines on when to buy ads and when to ask mass media to donate air time or space for public service announcements.

Developing an advertisement for print or broadcast requires research, testing and evaluation as well as skills in copywriting and design. Work closely with the publication or broadcaster involved to make the ad deliver what you want. Unless someone on the staff has some advertising experience or training, you may want to subcontract this assignment.

Media interviews

You're almost guaranteed coverage when the media come to you for an interview. You can insure a productive session by making some preparations and by developing interview skills.

Here are a few tips to help you get your message out:

Call reporters back. Always respond to reporters as quickly as possible. Remember, they work on deadlines and appreciate a prompt response.

Set the guidelines. You can set the time limit of an interview, making it as long or as short as you like.

Before an interview, find out its subject and scope. But don't ask for a list of questions. Reporters want your spontaneous reaction, not a rehearsed response.

Do your homework. Study the subject thoroughly, checking the latest facts and figures. Try to anticipate questions.

Practice brief answers, especially for broadcast. Your subject may be complicated, but broadcasters will expect you to keep your answer within 20 seconds.

Decide on one or two key points and emphasize them. Know what you want to say and keep pulling back to that message. At the conclusion of the interview, summarize your points with, "The main point is ..."

Don't wait for them to ask the right questions. You certainly know more about your program than they do, so have your own agenda of what needs to be covered. If they don't ask the right questions to get to the heart of the story, volunteer it.

Don't offer your opinion as fact. Stick to the facts and let the audience draw its own conclusions.

Clarify. Try to make sure the reporter understands what you've said. You can usually tell by the questions if they are missing the point. Keep it simple.

Stop talking when you've made your point. Many people say things they didn't mean to say after they've answered the question. Don't worry if there is a silent, awkward pause. A reporter will often use this pause as a technique to get you to volunteer information.

There is no such thing as "off the record." And don't say "no comment." It implies guilt.

The interview is never over until you or the reporter leaves. A microphone and tape recorder may still be running and a reporter may jot down a few more notes after he leaves.

Never lie to a reporter. If you don't know the answer or don't want to answer the question, say so.

Press conferences

Once you enter the media arena, you take up the debate about the value of press conferences. Done correctly, a press conference can make a major media splash by kicking off your campaign in several outlets simultaneously.

However, press conferences are becoming restricted to politicians and sports figures. The reason is simple: unless you've got a real barn-burner of a topic or getting the reporter to the location is critical to the story, media people just won't show up.

Broadcast media and many print outlets prefer an exclusive interview, not a rehearsed presentation. They don't want to get the same material their competitors are getting. And if your timing is off, you allow the broadcast media to scoop the print media – a mistake you don't want to make.

As Etkin bluntly states, in planning the apple campaign, "There was nothing sufficiently dramatic or imperative to suggest any kind of media conference. It was never a consideration."

Even in the flood-information campaign, media conferences didn't work, Marks says: "We could get the information to the media so fast and already had developed a thorough list of who these people were, that getting them to an actual spot for a media conference was a waste of time."

So why is it even an option? Because in certain situations with certain media, it works. If you have a major event, and the media people are already covering it, they'll appreciate a briefing.

At the Sunbelt Agricultural Exposition in Georgia, the media people are invited to come the day before the event opens so they can preview the show. They hear the expo director give a summary of the event; then he stays around for individual interviews. They also enjoy a sponsored lunch. (Media people like to eat, too.)

The criteria to justify a media conference are:

- **Topic**. It better be important, timely, and interesting.

- **Location**. Media people won't commit to traveling far from the station or news room. It helps if the location is crucial to the story.

- **Timing**. Set it up before the evening news and before the copy deadline. Early afternoon is a good bet.

- **Spokesperson**. Whoever presides should be ready to give each speaker's name (spell it), title, and a few facts explaining why this person is speaking. The speaker should be quotable, comfortable before cameras and well-briefed to answer questions. He or she should have a prepared statement.

- **Background material**. Give the reporters facts, photos,and other background material in a well-written packet.

- **Telephone lines**. Many reporters carry their own computers and file stories by phone. Have several lines available and be ready to absorb the cost if possible.

- **Follow up on any requests for further information, interviews, or photos**. Respect their deadlines.

- If **appropriate, put on a pot of coffee, set out some donuts, or even provide a sponsored meal**.

Direct mail

Mass media isn't the only way to reach an audience. Targeted media – also called direct mail – can place your material right in your target audience's hands. It includes newsletters, publications, letters, flyers, post cards, meeting announcements and brochures.

With direct mail, you control the message and the distribution – a crucial advantage over mass media when you have a well-defined target audience. Mass media is ideal for building awareness, but if you want your readers to take action, direct mail is the one to use.

Personal contact is one of the most effective ways to get people to try or adopt an idea. And direct mail is really a form of personal contact – it's the next best thing to a visit or phone call. Direct mail is to public-education campaigns what personal letters are to friendships: They bring people together.

Take full advantage of the control you have over the message and the distribution (both time of distribution and the mailing list). Direct mail works best when you recognize that the reader's interests and needs always come first. Show your readers a benefit, and they will serve your needs too.

One way to ensure that you reach the right audience is to buy and evaluate mailing lists. If you develop your own list, work continuously to update it. If you buy one from a mailing-list broker, be practical. Lists can be expensive.

Direct-mail advertisers have associations for education and exchange. Monthly magazines such as *Direct Marketing and Target Marketing* provide many ideas and references.

A simple way to check your mailing list for dead wood is to send a questionnaire or card to each person on your list. Ask if he or she wants to keep getting your direct mail pieces; include a few questions to help gear your future efforts even better to readers' needs. Do this once a year.

Your post office will pass along removals and corrections. Use returned envelopes to purge and correct your mailing lists. Ask about the U.S. Postal Service is centralized-data-base National-Change-of-Address program if you use direct mail often.

You can save money by keeping up on the new laws and rates. The easiest way to do this is to check with the local postmaster while your mailing piece is in the planning stage. The postmaster can tell you if your proposed direct mail piece will conform to bulk mailing regulations and can advise you on the most economical way to mail it. Don't wait until it's ready to mail. Check with the postmaster as you plan it.

If you're building a new mailing list, here are some ideas:

Check your office letter files. The best place for names is often your own office letter files, which has names and addresses of people already interested in your products and organization. Check local stores selling items to people you want to reach. The local library has state and national directories listing names of people active in businesses and organizations.

Keep names of people who request publications. Keep track of their areas of interest.

Include media. If you want to use direct mail as part of your educational program, make sure names of radio and TV stations, daily and weekly editors, magazine editors and other media outlets are on your list.

Think "users." Depending on the purpose of the list, you may need names of local dealers, leaders, and cooperators. Contact these people for names of customers, neighbors, and friends who might be added to your lists. Check membership roles of service clubs; business groups; farm, home, and youth organizations. Ask county clerks about lists from tax records, birth registrations, marriage licenses, building records, etc.

Use a giveaway. Many businesses use giveaways just to collect these names for their promotional mailing lists.

Check the telephone directory. A rundown of the Yellow Pages will remind you of business people you should add to your lists.

As you gather names and feed them into your computer data base, **set up a system to retrieve them in various ways**. Categorize names by location, business, age, interests, gender or any other category that will help you target an audience. When you can identify your audiences, you can reach them with the message they want and need.

When writing for direct mail, remember its distinct benefit: direct contact with a target audience. Put yourself in your readers' shoes and keep the readers in mind throughout the message. Whether you are writing a letter, a flyer, a newsletter or a publication, always sell them benefits, from the first paragraph to the last. If you will save them time, trouble, or money, help their families, or solve their problems, tell them.

The opening sentence is vital. It carries 90 percent of the weight of the piece. After all, if your reader doesn't get past the first sentence, it doesn't matter how eloquent the rest of the sentences are.

Come to the point quickly. Don't waste the reader's time; make every word count. Anticipate that your direct-mail piece has reached your reader at the worst possible time – the children are fussing, the dog is in the flower bed, guests are coming, it's been a bad day at work. Can you break through and sell your message on the walk from the mail box to the house?

Understand what your copy says to the reader. Let your writing cool, then reread it. Pretest it with a sample audience. Rewrite it until you're sure it will answer your audience's questions.

If you want action from your readers, give them a reason to respond quickly. Explain why that action is important and make it easy to do.

Check in other sections of this handbook on the specifics of how to produce certain types of direct mail, such as newsletters and publications. Also note the section on graphic design. These writing and layout techniques apply to all forms of printed direct mail.

Direct mail can involve so many communication forms that it's hard to generalize the subject.

However, every successful direct mail piece has several points in common:

Set goals. Know exactly what you want your mailing to do. Then handle one goal at a time with each mailing. If you want your audience to do several things, use a series of messages. Sell them one idea at a time.

Write "benefits." Let your audience know what your idea will do for them. Appeal to the things they are interested in. Give them all the information they need to take action.

As a direct-mail specialist in a lawn-seed company so succinctly put it, "In our copy, we must never forget for an instant that people are interested in their lawns, not in our seed."

Let layout enhance your message. Make the layout and format of your mailing tie in with your overall plan and objective. Weigh the quality and expense against the type of image and message you want to convey.

Mail it to the right person. Your first job is to compile a complete, accurate mailing list, with names spelled correctly. Then keep the list up-to-date.

Help the reader. Make it easy to take action. Take all the guesswork out of the mailing.

Tell your story again. Few salespeople make a sale on their first call. It isn't reasonable to expect one mailing to produce a large return. If your objective is sound and your mailing list is good, you'll get more results from a planned series of mailings than from a single attempt.

Appearances count. Avoid misspelled words, poor grammar, incorrect punctuation, trite expressions, substandard usage, and slang or jargon.

Research your direct mail. Is it reaching the right people? Does it contain ideas they need or can use? Are your messages being read, understood, and acted on? Plan a follow-up evaluation.

Promotional tools

Sometimes the best way to reach your target audience is with creative promotional tools. Let the audience, message, and budget guide your decision to include such tools as billboards, balloons, stickers, magnets, key chains, folders, notepads, notebooks, hats, caps, pens, pencils, signs, cups, banners, pins, posters, displays, free samples, bags, coupons, T-shirts, and other promotional and novelty techniques.

You'll find a wealth of novelty-item ideas when you contact local suppliers. Ask for ideas and estimates from several suppliers – it's a competitive and creative field.

Each item carries a message – and each carries a price tag. So make sure each is chosen for its ability to reach the right audience with the right message.

For instance, if the local emergency services are introducing the 911 switchboard to a community, they may choose to supplement media stories and public service advertisements with billboards, balloons, stickers, magnets, pins, banners, and T-shirts. They want to reach the most people quickly with a simple message: Need help? Call 911!

A year later, the same emergency services are having trouble with crank calls and nonemergency use. They want to educate the public on the proper use of the 911 service, so they supplement media contacts with displays, posters, and information packets.

It's easy to get caught up in the gadgets and flashy images of these tools. So make selections based on the best possible way to reach your audience with your message for the least amount of money.

Case study:
after disaster — the first call

Subject: The University of Georgia Extension Service plans to educate farmers, producers, and families about management techniques to help them cope with and overcome problems caused by natural disasters such as drought, flood, snow and ice storms, hurricanes, tornadoes, etc.

Production team leader: video producer

Production team: one radio/TV news producer, three writers

Secondary team: one artist, specialists in agricultural economics, and other subjects as needed

Target audience: farm producers and their families in disaster areas

Secondary audiences: other agencies involved in emergencies, agricultural-commodity groups, agribusiness leaders, decision makers such as legislators and county commissioners

Goals

1. To prompt a 25 percent increase in the number of requests for information from the target audience to the local Extension Service during or following a natural disaster.

2. To establish the Extension Service as a credible, reliable source of agricultural information, measured with local image surveys conducted among the target audience, and unsolicited personal testimonials (letters, comments, editorials, etc.).

3. To increase visibility for the Extension Service's work in the agricultural community, particularly among farmers and among decision makers, measured by media use of materials, number of publications distributed, and volume of participants in programs.

Message: Farm Family's Help on the Line – The County Extension Service

Media mix

- five- to six-minute educational video short

- public service announcement (PSA) series for radio, TV and print media

- packet of news releases, columns, newsletter articles supplied to county Extension agents, ready to release when disaster strikes

- media campaign: three television news stories, eight newspaper stories for statewide release, five magazine stories for targeted agricultural publications

- 800 number (restricted to disaster area, designed to ring in caller's county Extension office, not a central state office)

- disaster management handbook for agents (completed by specialists prior to public-information campaign)

- Promotional items (billboards and magnets with 800 number, folders for emergency programs, displays, posters).

Deadlines

December: All materials completed and distributed

November 1: Print packet written, delivered to printer; make arrangements for 800 number; prepare television news stories and newspaper stories

October 1: Make print packet assignments to writers

September 1: Tape Public Service Announcements, collect bids on promotional items

August 1: Scripts complete for PSAs, video; design promotional items, including displays, magnets, folders and posters write magazine stories and arrange for publication.

Estimated costs

Video:	7,500
PSA series:	12,500
Media support:	1,000
Travel for team:	2,000
TOTAL	$23,000

Funding source: Congressional disaster management grant

Summary

A public-information campaign is just a fancy name for a planned educational effort. A good one requires a strong and important message, a well-defined audience and a plan to get these two elements together.

A poorly planned campaign will splash the message out to a fuzzy audience who let the information dribble away. It will drain your staff and your resources and leave you wondering why you went to all that trouble.

So plan wisely. Take time to define your audience and discuss what you want them to do with the message. Put together a media mix that reaches the target audiences; know where your time, money and resources are going; do your homework with budgets and, sponsors; and build in some form of evaluation. Then you're ready to put words and graphics to paper and visuals to film.

A solid public-information campaign is hard work, no doubt about it. But when it works, it almost looks easy.

The United States has a rich volunteer history. Colonist volunteers organized the Boston Tea Party. Women sewed uniforms for Civil War soldiers. Soup kitchens and volunteer bartering efforts helped Americans survive the Great Depression. More recently, volunteers in the United States and abroad have attacked illiteracy, hunger, and AIDS.

People still will volunteer for worthwhile projects, even though most are busier than ever. Entire families plus working parents, single parents, youth, and retirees are working with Boy Scouts, 4-H, food banks, hospitals, churches, and Habitat for Humanity. Many times you only need to ask them.

Volunteering is not only alive and well, but some people even predict long-term, world-wide growth in volunteer activity as we approach the end of the 20th century. Although overall volunteering in the United States is down (from 54 percent in 1989 to 48 percent in 1993), most of the decline came in the form of informal volunteering, such as baby-sitting for free or baking cookies for a school fair. But in the Midwest, volunteering increased during the same period – from 58 percent in 1989 to 64 percent in 1993 (Gallup Survey, analyzed and published by the Independent Sector).

Volunteerism is changing and poised for renewal more than it's declining.

The most significant increases in volunteering have been among senior citizens, ages 75 and older (36 percent volunteered, up from 27 percent in 1990) and among divorced, separated, and widowed people (40 percent volunteered, up from 36 percent in 1990).

Other national trends in volunteerism

- More than one of four volunteers (27 percent) volunteered five hours per week or more. It's estimated that 23.6 million American adults volunteered five hours or more per week in 1993.

- When asked personally, people are more than four times as likely to volunteer than when they're informed by other means of the need for volunteers. Among the 45 percent who reported they were asked, 82 percent volunteered. Respondents least likely to be asked were African-Americans and Hispanics; families with household incomes below $20,000; those who are single, divorced, widowed, or separated; and persons who are not employed. But when asked, these people volunteer at a similar or even higher rate than the national average!

- Young people whose parents volunteered were nearly twice as likely to volunteer as adults when compared with those whose parents had not volunteered. Among the 44 percent of respondents reporting that one or both of their parents had volunteered, six out of 10 volunteered as adults.

- Memberships in a wide range of associations are associated with very high levels of giving and volunteering: religious organizations, voluntary organizations, civic associations, fraternities and sororities, alumni organizations, service clubs, business and professional societies, and political organizations.

- Experience in a youth group and volunteering when young lead to higher rates of volunteering as adults. Among the 56 percent reporting they'd belonged to a youth group or something similar, 61 percent volunteered.

• Nearly three-quarters of respondents (73 percent) agreed that charitable organizations play a major role in making our communities better places to live.

So how do you develop a volunteer program? The following 7-step I-S-O-T-U-R-E process was originally developed by Robert Dolan at North Carolina State University:

I-S-O-T-U-R-E...
A volunteer development process

1. **I**dentify people who have the competencies and attitudes for specific volunteer responsibilities.

2. **S**elect volunteers. Study the background of potential volunteers; motivate them to fill selected positions.

3. **O**rient volunteers so they know what to expect.

4. **T**rain volunteers to improve their performance.

5. **U**tilize volunteers to make the best use of their skills and abilities.

6. **R**ecognize and reward volunteer performance.

7. **E**valuate the results of volunteer performance.

Family volunteering is the hot new trend of the 90s. If you're familiar with 4-H clubs and families, which provide a successful 75-year model, you'll note many similarities. The 4-H club is led by volunteers – many of them parents. Older youth or junior leaders also work with younger members.

It's this same togetherness and sense of helping others that families seek when they volunteer at nursing homes or food banks. If you're recruiting families, here are some guidelines.

Family volunteer expectations

• Have clear job descriptions so the volunteers know what's expected.

• Get organized! Volunteers will sense good or bad management quickly.

• Present a realistic time commitment. Some "this won't take long," projects can go on and on.

• Give feedback. Volunteering families want to know how things are going.

• Make sure projects have value. Busy families aren't interested in busy work.

• Treat family members as equals.

• Involve children and teens in planning. They have some great ideas.

• Make the projects enjoyable – fun.

• Help families do their best. They want to make a difference.

Many companies encourage employees to include family members as part of their community volunteer efforts. An example is Target Stores of Minneapolis, Minnesota, which has a long history of active community service.

Consider the developmental stages of children if you're working with children, youth, or families.

Six-to eight-year-olds are influenced by adults. They like their activities to yield products (baking cookies for a senior center, collecting cans of food for the needy, collecting empty beverge cans). They're better suited to short term projects. Fundamental skills such as reading and math may be limited and may vary widely. That means you want to keep their activities product-oriented, with a limited number of steps to complete the project. The activities should show immediate success.

Phot by Don Breneman

A Master Gardener volunteer mentors young people through a school program.

Nine-to 12-year-olds have a short attention span, which means directions must be simple and short. They like to be part of an organized group and to ask questions. It's important to vary the pace and number of activities and praise them as individuals.

Twelve-to 14-year-olds may have great personal skills (such as working with computers) that can be put to good use. They want adult guidance, but reject being dominated by an adult. They also resent criticism and have a wide range of experiences and vocabulary. They want to be together. Emphasize the positives and show care and concern.

Fifteen-to 19-year-olds like to make their own personal decisions. They need adult guidance (but won't seek it). Their interest span is similar to adults, and they're good at applying information to problem solving. Make good use of their personal skills and talents and help satisfy their desire to help others.

Photo by Don Breneman

Volunteers are the key to many conservation programs.

In summary, when you're working with youth volunteers, remember they:

- have lots of energy
- like to be with friends
- like to have fun
- need reflection time to talk about what they've learned
- should work with a coach
- appreciate adults who can speak and understand their language
- are results-oriented
- require flexible scheduling.

Working with adults

Adults as potential volunteers can be grouped into four age categories:

- **Seniors**, born in 1926 and earlier
- **Builders**, born from 1927 to 1945
- **Boomers**, born from 1946 to 1964
- **Busters**, born from 1965 to 1983.

Each group offers unique characteristics you need to be aware of.

Builders and seniors

- value the volunteering concept
- desire "peak" personal health
- value church and related organizations
- like short-term commitments
- may live on fixed incomes, savings, and have income considerations
- are concerned about safety (lighted parking, safe neighborhoods)
- value the radio as a communication channel
- desire results vs. personal relationships.

Boomers

- are risk takers
- apt to be workaholics
- like to network
- are very goal-oriented
- have a strong sense of self worth from the volunteer job
- like to operate from a position of power
- value rules and traditions
- may be subject to emotional and physical fatigue.

Busters

- many emphasize personal benefits
- often challenge existing rules; seek reasons for "why" something is being done
- life meaning may be derived from personal interests; not through work
- many have frequent job and career changes
- may want others to entertain them (movies, television).

The recruiting challenge

Target and plan your recruiting efforts before you start asking people. Asking these 10 key questions can help. You'll note most follow the 5Ws and an H format: who, what, where, when, why and how.

1. What job do you need done?

2. What type of people are qualified to do it?

3. Who would want to do the job?

4. Why might they want to do it? Or, what motivated them

5. How can you match their needs and desires to the job? Consider flexible scheduling, personal satisfaction, learning new skills, different experiences.

6. Where can you find them?

7. What will you say to them? Tell them what needs to be done, how they can help, how they can benefit. Address their fears or concerns.

8. When should you ask them? Plan ahead – people are busy. Many seniors travel.

9. Who will do it? Not a minor detail. Don't neglect it.

10. Ask them – close the deal.

At the beginning of this chapter we said seniors are volunteering in record numbers. Here are some tips for recruiting seniors.

Senior recruitment

- Senior centers are great places to recruit.
- Word of mouth is effective. Many seniors meet regularly in groups.

Phot by Dave Hansen

Senoir volunteers offer food and nutrition information to young families.

- Use articles and ads in senior newspapers. Study the newspapers for ideas.
- Many will be seasonal – northern "snow birds" go south in winter.
- Recruiting through a spouse or significant other can be effective.
- Retirement classes are good possibilities.
- Corporate retirement programs. Many corporations have active retiree chapters. They may be looking for your good cause!

This is only a start. You'll find lots of information out there to help you. Volunteer management is a young but growing professional discipline. Volunteer management newsletters, books, and tapes are available.

Resource

The Association for Volunteer Administration (AV – in Boulder, CO., has about 3,500 members and publishes the *Journal of Volunteer Administration*.

Radio

Radio is the medium of the mind. With visual stimulation supplied by your mind's eye, you can unlock a world larger than life, brighter than brilliant,and more intense than anything our physical world can deliver.

Radio is effective. Even more, it's efficient. Compared to other methods of direct mass communication, it can be one of the most cost-effective. With a modest investment in a cassette recorder and some concentrated effort on your part, you can make contact with a part of your audience that is increasingly mobile and distracted by other messages.

The challenge in radio is to understand what it can do for you. Then use innovation and creativity to make it work for you.

This chapter will cover eight basic areas of using radio as a communication tool:

- reasons for using radio
- methods of using radio
- the three basics of radio
- writing for radio
- reading for radio
- interviewing for radio
- working tools of radio
- promoting yourself and radio

Reasons for using radio

Radio works

But why? Dr. Elizabeth Loftus, University of Washington psychologist, quoted in an article in the March 14, 1983 issue of *Advertising Age* that a person will react faster to a sound than a picture. According to Loftus, people respond to light in 180 milliseconds (ms), but respond to sound in an average of 140ms.

You may be satisfied if your program is within the allotted minutes and seconds provided, let alone milliseconds. But those 40ms may be more important than you think. According to the article's authors, Al Ries and Jack Trout, psychologists speculate the brain translates visual information into sound-like information the mind can comprehend to account for the 40ms delay in comprehending pictures.

Not only do we hear faster than we see, but this same study showed that our hearing lasts longer than our seeing. A visual image fades in one second unless our minds do something to file the idea away. A heard idea lasts four or five times as long.

That's why some of us easily lose our train of thought when we read printed words. We end up backtracking to review the message. Because sound lasts longer in our minds, spoken words, songs, and jingles are easier to follow and remember.

Based on this, Ries and Trout spend a lot of time convincing their clients that a picture is not worth a thousand words, as Confucius supposedly said 2,500 years ago. The agency owners point out how ironic it is that Confucius is remembered not for what he looked like, but for what he said.

Radio as a communication tool

Social scientists believe people go through a multi-step process when making up their minds about something. These steps include: awareness, interest, evaluation, trial, and adoption.

Radio and other mass media are most effective during the first two steps: the awareness stage, when people first learn of an idea, and the interest stage, when they get more information about it.

At the evaluation, trial, and adoption stages the most important influences are friends, neighbors, and personal experiences. But the process is highly interactive. People are often influenced by previous mass media exposure. Radio interviews, news stories, public service announcements, and personal testimonies of success will affect this process beyond just the awareness and interest stages.

Radio is local

Local stations thrive on local names, local events, and local situations – the exact information you have to supply. Listeners find out what local and regional events are taking place, and they like information about the people in their community.

Radio is popular: Arbitron, a radio rating service, says 96 percent of all people 12 and older listen to a radio station at least once a week. And two out of three listeners tune into FM stations, according to an article in *American Demographics* (February 1986) magazine.

Radio can't do everything

Radio, however, cannot be everything to everybody. Because a listener can't fold up a radio program and file it away for future reference, radio works best when notifying, reminding, or telling uncomplicated stories that are easily remembered. Radio is most effective when messages are simple and to-the-point. Today in radio there is a growing emphasis on shorter, fragmented, information programs and more music and entertainment programs. That has become a major challenge for people who use radio to disseminate information.

Methods of using radio

Marketing

The fact that virtually everyone has a radio makes it a powerful marketing tool. But the key to success is also marketing. How well can you sell the idea that what you have to say is important enough to increase the audience's willingness to listen to the station? Successful marketing requires an understanding of the priorities of radio station operation.

Station staff

The process of getting your information to your audience is one that includes many potential barriers or gates. Although you are always aiming to satisfy the information needs of your audience, you must pay attention as well to the people who control the gates. In radio, it's those gatekeepers who decide whether your information deserves to be broadcast. Your goal should be to package your basic information in a style and format acceptable to the gatekeepers.

To begin to understand radio-station operation, let's first look at the management structure. Although staff organizations will be slightly different from station to station, there are some basics.

Station manager. This person is in charge of all operations. At smaller stations, the station manager is often also the owner, the program director, and the chief engineer all wrapped into one. At larger stations, the station manager may be higher in the organization than you need to contact. It could be that the manager of the larger station may not be closely enough involved in the everyday programming of the station to be able to help you.

Remember, station managers have multiple interests. They are responsible for everything at the station, not the least of which is sales. Make sure your discussion takes into account how you feel the information you are offering will affect the audience's overall perception of the station.

Program director. This person could be your initial contact at a station. Program directors are responsible for the combination of music, news, and information you hear on the station. With the program director, too, you must concentrate on what your information will do to enhance the listener's image of the station.

News director. This person may be your most frequent contact at a station. After having sold the idea that you generate useful information on a regular basis, you will end up providing much of it to the news director in the form of news stories, news tips, and calendar information. Job turnover can be relatively high for news directors, especially at small stations. You may need to build new relationships regularly.

Networks

Radio networks are an important piece in the puzzle of what we call radio today. There have always been radio networks, back to the original proliferation of radio around the United States. But recently, specialized radio networks have been growing on a regional basis, especially in rural areas. Local and regional networks can provide quality information to a station too small to develop unique and specialized news stories on its own.

This is one more question you need to consider when reviewing which stations do what in your community. One key observation on your part might be hearing the same or similar sounding stories on stations in neighboring communities. That would be a strong indication the stations are sharing stories via a network.

If and when you identify a network source of information serving your area, you should consider the possibility of wider impact of your information. Is your information useful to people in the larger area of your region? Are you discussing issues that affect people statewide as much as they do the people in your community? If so, perhaps you should make contact with the network directly. However, in many cases the radio station in your community serves as a network source. Discussing with the program director whether your story might be of broader interest could get it sent to the network for you.

As mentioned before, it is important to understand the needs of your local radio station. If you have something the network will find interesting, then it may be to the advantage of your local station to be the source. In many cases, stations are rewarded for providing information to the network.

Identifying your audiences

Remember "Rule Number One." Know who you want to talk to and why.

Think about natural groupings of your clients: groupings by age, political interest, geographic location, family income, gender, lifestyle, and many other segregating factors. Think of each group and combination of groups as a target. How can you reach the target?

Take older adults as an example to get you thinking about grouping and targets. Many older people tend to be home a lot. Radio brings the outside world to them and literally keeps them company. To reach them with information about an upcoming workshop on housing alternatives, you could send a public-service announcement to an all-talk station.

Think carefully about who will use the information you have to offer best. Then, compare that group or groups with the various listener groups that are attracted to individual stations in your area. Be specific. Target your audience carefully. This is the same targeting process an advertiser uses to deliver a sales message to a specific audience. Take the time to really listen to the radio, especially the commercials. Take a cue from the way advertisers get their message across. Notice how they get your attention. Then apply that knowledge to the information you deliver.

After you have identified your target audience, go to the radio station and talk with the program director or station manager. Do they agree on your mutual target audiences? If so, you can be of mutual benefit to each other.

Radio's strength is in its ability to reach target audiences. Take advantage of this by learning the listening habits of your clients and working directly with the stations that reach them.

There are three basic formats available for your use: news, public service announcements, and radio programs. Each is effective with various target audiences. Each will require varying levels of involvement on your part. Yet each is a unique vehicle for your information.

News

News is the easiest way to start using radio because it's fueled by your basic product – information.

Radio news stories are becoming shorter and more to-the-point. A typical story is less than 30 seconds long and tells one piece of information clearly. Stories work best when someone involved tells how they feel about what is happening.

What is news?

News can be defined as any piece of information that will affect your head, heart, or pocketbook. In other words, news is information that will stimulate someone's curiosity or intellectual interest; information that will create an emotional response; or information that is of economic importance to individuals or groups.

Another important dimension of news is time. The information must be timely. Did it just happen? Will it still be interesting tomorrow? Will it continue to be an interesting topic? Or in the case of long-term work, such as scientific resarch, will the information be released soon at a national scientific meeting? That is, is it timely?

Review your information and make a list

As you think about the information available from your organization each day, list the types of information and their sources. Head, heart, or pocketbook. Then sort that list according to timeliness and interest. Soon this type of sorting will become second nature.

Review the stations and make a list

Remember the part about knowing your audience? It's very important here. Your first audience includes station gatekeepers; your second is the target group of listeners.

Listen to the stations in your area. Decide which ones emphasize news directed to your target. How many hours or minutes of news do they present? How many voices do you hear? Do they run newscasts on the hour and half-hour? Do they only supply network news with no local news? Do they spread their local news through certain parts of the day? Start making a written list of the traits you identify with each station. Soon a pattern will emerge, and you'll be able to tell one from another.

Why not just go to the station and ask what its news department needs? In this age, information is power, and time is a salable commodity. If you want to be effective with a radio news department, assume that everybody will be in a hurry, whether they look like it or not. Don't use some of your precious time allotment for an explanation of already available information. Do your homework before you talk. You'll be able to accomplish more.

What goes into a story

Your local radio station is primarily interested in local news. These are news stories that easily lend themselves to localization:

- major events
- the week's activities
- timely problems and solutions
- experiences of local people
- weather information
- market information
- local information about national news stories
- timely information from your area of expertise

Delivering the news

In mid-size to smaller markets, you may arrange to deliver radio news quotes, known as actualities, to each station. This will allow each station either to run or edit them to fit its style.

Most stories should run 60 seconds or less. Begin with a lead for the station announcer to read. Then, write a brief but specific introduction to the story. Use one or two short recorded actualities from the main source of information. Close with a conclusive remark and a generic sign-off.

Soybean growers should consider forward pricing (:42)

Announcer: Corn and soybean crops in Louisiana are progressing well this summer. Earlier this year, prices were at profitable levels for each, but prices have fallen since planting. An Extension Service economist says occasionally, prices will rally, and that's a good time to consider pricing a portion of the crop. Otherwise, prices likely will trend down toward harvest:

Actuality: "As a matter of fact, USDA is predicting soybean prices to get as low as $5.50 and corn back to as low as $2.25. This is considerably lower than prices right now." (:10)

Announcer: Doctor Daniel Robertson of the L-S-U Agricultural center says pricing can involve forward contracts, put options and the futures market. This is John Brooks with the L-S-U Agricultural Center.

Louisiana peach crop (:47)

Announcer: Louisiana's peach harvest is in full swing, and for most growers, they'll continue to pick through July – some into August, with later varieties. An Extension Service horticulturist says this year's crop is excellent, and growers were not affected by untimely freezes:

Actuality: "This is something we haven't been fortunate with in the last 10 years. We've had several back-to-back freezes in the late '80s that discouraged a lot of additional acreage." (:10)

Announcer: Doctor Earl Puls of the L-S-U Agricultural Center says in recent years, the Ag Center has released several varieties that will mature later in the summer. Puls also says in the fruit production business, it's best to diversify and produce a wide range of fruit crops. This is John Brooks with the L-S-U Agricultural Center.

Southeast Louisiana bell-pepper crop comes to market (:51)

Announcer: Bell-pepper growers in Southeast Louisiana are bringing their crops to market this month and they're pleased with a larger-than-usual crop. Since they planted in mid-March, the weather conditions have been good. Tanipahoa Parish Extension Agent Annie Coco says the harvest is in full swing:

Actuality: "They like to start picking around the end of May and go through the first week or so of July. Hopefully it will last that long this year." (:09)

Announcer: Anton Liuzza's farm in Independence has 75 acres planted with peppers. He says this year he expects to harvest more than 700 bushels per acre.

Actuality: "It looks like one of the best yields in production we've had in the last five to six years." (:08)

Announcer: LSU Ag Center horticulturists say producers also have been getting a fair price for their product. This is John Brooks with the L-S-U Agricultural Center.

Some stations will run a story just as it is. Others will take your script and actualities and have an announcer read it. Still others will take only a single actuality and shorten the story to fit their needs.

Major market news

In large media markets, it's becoming more difficult to place radio news. Because competition is strong, many stations stylize their newscasts to stand out on the crowded dial. They simply refuse to run anything their competition also might have received. In most large markets, it's best simply to become a news source. Provide information in a regular and timely fashion. Develop a relationship with the station news staff that allows them to trust and call on you when they identify a story. In return, this allows you to call them when you feel you have newsworthy information.

Wild sound

Sound is what makes radio effective and unique, no matter what the market size. For you to be effective, think of sounds the station can use to sound unique.

The Associated Press advises its news reporters to pay close attention to background sound. Also known as wild sound, background sound can enrich and enliven your report. Sound carries the atmosphere and mood of the story. Artfully used, it will help bring your listener into the story.

Wild sound, however, should never dominate your story. You should write the story so that it can stand alone without wild sound. Then, be able to add it appropriately so it will enhance your effort to communicate.

Again, pay close attention to the style a particular station uses. If you are supplying information to a station that uses a lot of wild sound, deliver additional taped wild sounds and ambiance from the scene for them to use. If nothing else, it's more likely your story will be used because the station knows it will be able to create a story a little different from its competition down the street.

Public service announcements

Public service announcements, known as PSAs, are short spot announcements, usually between 10 and 60 seconds long, that provide important information to the listener. Primarily, these spots contain what is known as mobilizing information – information that will help the listener do something. For example, a PSA can be about an upcoming meeting, with the site, time, and topic. Or it could be gardening information that helps people choose seeds or provides tips on planting. Or it could cover the subject matter of one of your publications with a final line on how and where to get a copy.

At one time, radio stations were required to run PSAs free as a public service. But those regulations were abandoned in the early 1980s. Now the radio station marketplace is the controlling factor. Many people felt this wold mean the end of PSAs. But, to the contrary, PSAs are alive and well.

Most stations realize that information is part of the reason people listen to the radio. And if the station can provide the kind of information that helps people do things they want to do, the stations will build and maintain a loyal audience. This provides outside information sources, such as your organization, a key to understanding what information should be provided to a station in PSA form.

Oregon's Agricultural Progress radio PSA

(00:30) Drought

Rain – or the lack of it – has been on most people's minds throughout this year. For statewide agricultural research, the drought has answered a few questions but posed many more: What did we learn? and What happens now? Check the latest edition of *Oregon's Agricultural Progress*, the magazine that lets you know how science is helping Oregon grow.

Get a free copy at your county extension office or write:

Editor
Agricultural Experiment Station
OSU
Corvallis   (30 sec.)

"Your money matters" radio spot(:30) kill: (last date to use)

When you're spending more than you're bringing in, when your credit card owns you, instead of the other way around, when a "savings account" is just a fantasy – sounds like you could use some money management skills. If you're a single parent or married, eighteen to thirty-four, you can learn more about budgeting, about spending, and about saving. And you can do it without cost. Call your local office of the Oregon State University Extension Service. Ask about the new home study series, "Your Money Matters."   (30 sec.)

Returning again to the concept of knowing your audience, spend some time and effort deciding who a station's audience is. Then, help the station help you by providing information that audience can use.

The best use of PSAs

Because of their length, PSAs are difficult to use as teaching tools. They are used best to attract attention and then explain where listeners can get additional in-depth information. The 30-second PSAs shown in this chapter are typical. The first two-thirds of the copy attracts attention. The last section hooks the listener with the mobilizing information. What, where, and how to get it.

PSAs are excellent tools for reminding people about your organization and its services. Even when people do not write for the information, they still are pleased to know that you are offering this service. PSAs are important to public institutions because they help satisfy the public's right to know abut where its tax dollars are being spent. PSAs are an excellent method of telling people what you are doing as you help meet their needs.

Ask radio stations how they prefer their PSA information. Some stations have 3 x 5 inch - card boxes next to the on-air announcer so she or he may read announcements when needed.

If this is the case at your station, try providing a brightly colored 3 x 5 inch - card that will slip easily into the station operation.

Radio programs

A third way to use radio to distribute your information is to write and possibly record your own two-to 30-minute radio program.

Longer-format radio programs typically have been used by many educational and informational organizations in the past. As radio stations compete for a significant slice of the audience pie, it can become more difficult to justify the greater amount of time needed. But it is not impossible. Careful attention must be paid to the type and style of program proposed. It truly must satisfy the needs of the audience. If it does, anything is possible.

Situations that may work for longer - format radio programs include how-to programs, call-in programs that answer questions directly, daily market - information programs, and consumer-oriented programs that supply timely information about saving money, conserving resources, and making informed decisions.

Remember, radio is the immediate medium. It can reach people with timely information well before newspapers and television can. Use that to your advantage by being the first source of that useful piece of information.

Radio program construction

Let's start at the beginning and look at some of the parts of an effective longer-format radio program. An opening to a radio program serves as bait to grab listener attention. Billboarding – telling what topics you'll cover – is a good technique to catch and hold attention.

You can use the same technique at the end of the show to promote the next program. For example, if you have a program coming up the next day, you might say, "Tomorrow we'll talk about a new method of garden tilling...a simple and easy way to fertilize shade trees...Join us again on 'Extension Reports' at noon tomorrow."

Local events offer a double-barrelled opportunity. Prmote them before they take place, and then provide follow-up coverage. Interviews or reports recorded at the events give your broadcast that needed change of pace. Localize out-of-town events by telling how they affect listeners in your local area.

Timely information related to local issues makes good radio listening. And no story beats the successful experiences of local people.

Good ideas for radio programs

Your week's activities provide a never - ending source of ideas for radio talks. Who wrote to you? Who stopped by the office? What were their problems? Whom did you visit? What observations did you make?

A question-and-answer program is a good example of a radio program that will fit into the style of radio today. It satisfies your need to deliver information to a broad spectrum of people and to keep a record of the broad-based and interesting questions that come into your office during the week. Once a week, answer them on your radio program. The format is universal and well-tried. Audience interest is high because the questions are generated by the members of the audience themselves. As a bonus, your office reinforces its reputation as a credible source for solving problems.

From the radio station's point of view, this is a true radio-style program, not just an educational program crammed into a radio format. A professional question-and-answer program such as this makes the station look good by providing a valid public service.

....or try this one:

Take a look at the organization of the radio script shown. It has a simple structure you can use for any radio program.

- open/intro
- teaser/headline
- body/substance/advice
- billboard
- close/identification

Start by identifying yourself. It tells your target audience who you are and what qualifies you to be handing out advice. Then open with a sentence that both grabs interest and sets up the topic. Continue with your advice, arranged simply and logically, with each step in the correct order.

Remember this is radio – you get one chance to be understood.

You may wish to end the body or advice portion by indicating other sources of information, promoting a publication or an upcoming workshop. Then, promote your next program and close with appropriate identification for you and your organization.

A few final don'ts

Getting and staying on the air means pleasing the gatekeepers. But......

- Don't beg, plead, or threaten to maintain free air time. A good program will stand on its own merits. If you are having trouble, find out why and fix it.
- Don't use free air time to promote a project or an idea for which you would buy newspaper space. If your project has an advertising budget, alot some to radio. Legally, broadcast media that use the physically limited public airwaves are considered different from newspapers where, in theory, space is limited only by economics. But don't abuse the difference. Remember, radio stations no longer are required to provide free time.

Sample radio script
Hi, I'm _____, with the _____County office of the Oregon State University Extension Service. Today I'm going to tell you how to dig and store your potatoes for the best possible quality.
To enjoy the great taste of new potatoes, dig them right out of the garden, wash them off, and pop them in the oven. There's nothing like it! Remember though, new potatoes will keep for only a few days, so don't harvest more than you can eat.

Now if you want to store most of your crop to enjoy later in the year, don't dig any potatoes until the vines have been dead for two weeks. You can wait for them to die on their own, or you can cut them off when the potatoes reach ideal size. Let the potatoes lie in the ground the full two weeks to toughen the skins, so they'll be more resistant to cuts and bruises. When the time has come and the soil is dry, dig up your potatoes and put them directly in bins or ventilated containers. Don't' wash them first and don't put them into plastic bags. Store in a room that stays pretty consistently at 45 degrees. That will keep them from sprouting, shriveling, or rotting.
Tomorrow I'll tell you when to harvest garlic.
I'm_____from the _____County office of the Oregon State University Extension Service.

- Don't promote anything related to games of chance.
- Don't promote commercial products if you are a non-profit organization. Always be even-handed and use generic product names if possible.

Writing for radio

Visual imagery is the key to writing for radio. Make your listeners "see" what you are saying. Help them visualize themselves taking action in a situation you are describing.

Researchers have found that audience recognition and recall are much higher when you use imagery-eliciting words and phrases in your copy.

Writing PSAs is an example of radio writing at its toughest. PSAs are short and to-the-point. On the other hand, their shortness may allow them to be lost in the cacophony of the radio station's combination of music, news, and information. When writing for radio, imagine yourself riding in a car with the window rolled down and the car noise and traffic distracting you. How will you be able to grab and maintain the listener's attention?

Be careful. Commercial producers sometimes use cheap tricks to grab people's attention. A little of that goes a long way in this business. Instead, think of word pictures and alliterations that will subtly attract attention.

Visual radio writing

Here's an example of imagery from a study reported in a recent issue of the *Journal of Broadcasting*.

Straight announcement copy:
"Acme Puncture-Proof won't leave you stranded on a dark and deserted highway...."

Imagery-eliciting copy:
"There you sit on a dark and deserted highway. It's midnight, and every second brings a strange sound. You have a flat tire. You wouldn't be in this situation if you had purchased Acme Puncture-Proof..."

Notice the first style does have some visual words in it. But the second style actually puts you into the situation described.

When writing copy or scripts or just putting an outline together for a radio show, always remember what radio does best. Help your listener imagine the scene you're depicting.

Know why you're using radio

Before you write one line of copy or say a word on the air, decide exactly what you want your listeners to know, feel, and do. How do you want them to behave, react, or change? List specific message objectives. Decide on one basic, timely idea for each program. It may be part of a larger idea. Collect and orga-

nize logically all related information, facts, data, and substantiating evidence that will make your message believable and acceptable to those who hear it.

Get your listener's attention

Use a visual fact, an interesting idea, a thought-provoking question, or a challenging statement. Arouse interest, curiosity. Your lead must catch the attention of even the most casual listener. The first two sentences of your story or spot are the most important. If you don't get the listener's interest in the first seven seconds or so, chances are you won't get it at all.

Try reading this:

"Feeding immediately following the flowering period of many shrubs is becoming a common and recommended practice."

Pretty confusing! But use the same content for this kind of attention-getting lead:

"Do your flowers and shrubs look hungry right now? Well, that's only natural. Flowers and shrubs need a little snack, especially right after blooming. For many, that's now."

This line has visual and timely appeal. Your mind's eye sees the hungry plants needing food right this minute.

Use mass-audience appeal

Never exclude anyone who may be a listener. Present your information in such a way that it will be of interest to many listeners. Which of these two versions has the broader audience?

"Poultry producers : egg production is highest and profits are greatest when layers receive 14 hours of light per day."
Or:
"Hens don't lay eggs in the dark! They need 14 hours of light each day for top production. This pays off in two ways: higher profits for the poultry producers...and lower egg prices for us all."

The nature of your information may dictate that you tailor your message to a select audience. Always remember, whatever your subject, there are people who will hear you who do not know what you are talking about. This advice applies to any subject, whether it's agriculture, building construction, or economics.

Always figure your audience has a generous portion of the "general public" in it. Instead of talking "to" your audience, talk "about" them. Tell what they do and why, and how this is important to those who aren't familiar with your subject. Anyone should be considered a member of the general public when you are talking about specific subjects, outside his or her professional interests. Berry growers are part of the general public if you are talking about some other aspect of agriculture, such as growing corn.

Identify your sources

Give the source of your information logically, naturally. Listeners are more likely to believe what you say if it is credited to an authoritative source. If the source is you, then try to indicate the basis of your information. Other sources should be identified, but don't belabored this. Handle attribution as if you were "telling" the information to a friend. In radio, attribution generally precedes the statement, whereas newspaper style usually has the source following the statement.

For instance, say:
"Science may have caught the bug. Fred Stormshak, Oregon State University animal scientist, says he thinks he's found the bacterium causing the recent outbreak of intestinal dairy disorder."

Instead of:
"The bacterium causing the recent outbreak of dairy intestinal disorder has been tentatively identified by Oregon State University animal scientist Fred Stormshak."

Easy listening

Make your program or story easy for your listeners to follow. Remember, radio is the "hearing" medium. Each idea must logically fall into place so your listeners can get your message easily and accurately. Your script must have a liquid or flowing quality. Words like *however, but, on the other hand, or, and, furthermore, therefore, so, well, then, and likewise* act as steering wheels to guide your listener's thinking. Use them to start sentences.

If you are writing a radio program or script, try to bring some conversational quality to it. Write for the ear. That means using phrases and words you'd hear in casual conversation. Use as few technical words for terms as possible. Find the simplest word that will carry meaning.

In each of the following instances, the second word is better than the first:

utilize-use	contribute-give
purchase-buy	facilitate-help
procure-get	option-choice
accomplish-do	however-but
eradicate-wipe out	

If you use a new or unfamiliar word, explain briefly what it means.

Write for reading

To make script reading easier, break hard-to-pronounce or often-mispronounced names and words into syllables. For example: "dacron" (DAY-KRON), "debris" (DAY-BREE).

Write short. Use short, easily read, easily understood sentences. Keep a period at your fingertips. If you use a long sentence, follow it with a short one. This will permit you to catch your breath. Strive for a comfortable rhythm. Remember, your listeners have to understand instantly.

Write words and symbols so they are easy to read and understand. For instance, use pounds rather than "lbs." and percent rather than "%."

Numbers in radio present a special problem. According to most broadcast style manuals, it's hard for people to understand numbers read quickly. To avoid this problem:

- Try not to use long lists of numbers.
- Avoid starting a sentence with an exact number.
- Round off large and detailed numbers.

Repeat. Don't hesitate to repeat or re-emphasize any part of your message that your listeners easily might have missed. This can be done as a summary or as mobilizing information that may include addresses, amounts, dates, titles of publications, sources of additional information, or key points that need stressing again.

Read aloud. Test your writing by reading it aloud. This is the best way to catch poor phrasing and tongue twisters. If you can read your copy easily and smoothly, chances are others can too. Check for readability and listenability while you are writing and after completing the story.

Paint word pictures

Use simple, direct visual language. Use examples and comparisons with which the listener is familiar. Paint word pictures, such as "icing so smooth you hate to put a knife into it," or "mold that looks like a light coat of flour on the leaves."

Use action verbs and a minimum of adjectives. Don't judge the information for your listeners. Present the facts. Descriptive detail allows your listeners to decide for themselves whether the information is useful. Let your audience decide for themselves if an event is "big" or "exciting." How big is "big"? What is "exciting"? Good word pictures speak for themselves.

Use contractions

Your copy will read more easily and sound better if you use contractions. For example, use "don't" instead of "do not". But beware of contractions such as "could've" and "would've". They sound like could of and would of, which are improper grammar. At times, for emphasis, you won't want to use the contracted form, such as "For safety's sake, do not leave chemicals within reach of children."

Punctuation

Some style experts feel punctuation must be unlearned when writing for radio. It is clear that when writing for radio, the fewer extraneous marks the better. The most useful punctuation marks are a comma and a period. A hyphen or a dash can be used to indicate a pause slightly longer than one called for by a comma.

Never use quotation marks. Instead, indicate direct quotes by the context of the sentence. "He said that..." is the same as using quotation marks around what was actually said, and it is much easier to read aloud. You also can insert an indication that the remarks have ended by closing with a phrase like "... and that concluded his remarks."

Many people who read radio copy for a living suggest you eliminate the word "that" as often as possible from your copy. We don't use it much when we talk conversationally to friends, and some consider it a harsh word to hear. Your probably should use it only for clarity.

Timing

A timely radio presentation means more than just timely subject matter.

Radio time literally equals money. Time is sold or time is given away. You should recognize the importance of having your spots and programs exactly the correct length.

Practice writing to exact times. As a rule of thumb, figure 60 words equal approximately 30 seconds to time. Practice writing for yourself, as if you are the person delivering the information you have compiled. Or, if you are writing for someone else, check your script with the person who will read it. Then begin to write for the speed that person reads.

If you are doing a structured but unwritten program, always have useful information available to fill time. Outline your presentation in short enough segments so that if you run long you can cut the last segment in two without appearing to have left something out.

Mechanical helps

Type your copy clearly in the usual manner (not in all capitals), double-or triple-spaced so it's easy to read. Avoid splitting sentences at the end of pages and words at the end of the lines. Write words out – don't abbreviate.

Use 8 1/2-inch x 11-inch mimeograph or other soft-fiber paper. Never use onion skin or bond paper; it rattles. Use a separate sheet for each story.

Number all pages. Underline words you wish to emphasize. Mark places where you wish to pause. Note pronunciation trouble spots. Leave pages loose – don't clip or staple them together.

For answers to specific questions about details of writing for radio or television, refer to style manuals such as the *Associated Press Broadcast Style Manual.*

Reading for radio

The first myth of radio is that you must have an exceptional voice to be believed.

Especially for radio news, you need not have an exceptional voice. Authority and credibility come from rehearsing your copy, being familiar with all the words, and pacing to avoid breathlessness. Associated Press management advises reporters to convince their audience they are the ultimate authority on the story covered – without sounding pompous.

For better delivery

Radio is an intimate medium. It's just you and your listener in a kind of one-sided conversation. And conversation is the key word.

Think of a recent discussion with a close friend or a loved one. Spontaneously, you explain, you soothe, you convey how you feel. Now, read aloud from a book. Unless you have practiced, your voice will probably sound stiff, cold, and distant. The difference comes from conversational writing and conversational delivery.

Your attitude or psychological state greatly affects your radio delivery. A national survey indicates that the biggest faults in educational or informational programs are lack of enthusiasm coupled with poor voice characteristics.

Reading and recording often occur in closed studios with the engineer separate from the program participants.

Enunciation and pronunication

Do you enunciate each part of a word clearly? Or do you slur certain syllables? Problem words include?

- temp-a-ture for temp-er-a-ture
- prob-ly for prob-ab-ly
- git for get
- jest for just

Don't drop the final "g" in sewing, cooking, and other words ending in "ing." And often is pronounced "of'n." The "t" is not sounded. It takes practice and conscious effort to perfect the art of radio speaking.

Rules of radio delivery

Think the thought. Regardless of the topic or idea, think about it, see it, feel it. Project your personality. Sell your listeners on the points you're making. Be persuasive. Enthusiasm and sincerity will help convince them you believe what you're saying. Visualize the insect pest you are describing. Taste that suggested low-calorie dessert. Be impressed by that new research finding.

Think the thought through to the end. Read or speak by phrases. Know how the sentence will come out before you start it. Keep half an eye on the end of the sentence while you are reading the first part. This will add smoothness to delivery and will help you interpret the meaning of the phrases as part of the whole idea.

Talk at a natural speed, but change occasionally to avoid monotony. Vary the pitch and volume of your voice to get variety, emphasis, and attention. Control your breathing to take breaths between units of thought; otherwise, you'll sound choppy. Avoid dropping your voice when it sounds unnatural to do so.

Gesturing and smiling, even to an empty studio, adds personality and vitality to your broadcasts.

Use your body. A relaxed body helps produce a relaxed-sounding voice. Do a few exercises just before going on the air. A little physical activity reduces tension. (Just don't be out of breath.) Sitting up straight as you read helps your breathing too. Also, try some voice exercises. An easy one is to whisper the alphabet as loud as possible. It sounds a little strange but it does wonders to loosen vocal cords and throat muscles.

Talk to an individual, not a crowd or a microphone. Speak clearly in your normal, conversational, friendly tone. Your aim should be to talk to your listeners, not to read to them. Talk to the individual you've pictured in your mind as if they've never before heard what you're saying and they never may hear it again. You must get your meaning across the first time.

Your voice reflects your state of mind and body. During humorous lines, smile – your audience will "hear" the smile in your voice. To emphasize a point, use your hands. Frown, shake your head in disbelief, count off on your fingers – all these mannerisms help you "feel" the material and help your audience get the message.

Practice. Never give up practicing speech and delivery techniques. This is an area that needs constant attention. Try reading the newspaper aloud once or twice a week. It's a good way to remind yourself to practice.

Always listen to the final product, whether it's a recording of you on the air or someone else reading what you have written. Listen to how it sounds to the audience. Listen to what you did as if you were an individual in the target audience. Did it work the way you thought it would? If not, why not?

Three Bs of delivery

- Be yourself.
- Be at ease.
- Be enthusiastic.

Interviewing for radio

According to Ken Metzler, author of *Creative Interviewing – The Writer's Guide to Gathering Information by Asking Questions*, many people are inherently uncomfortable in an interview situation. Although they are quite capable of carrying on a pleasant conversation, when it comes to doing a formal interview they become tense and unnatural. This is a problem all of us face even when interviewing someone we've known for a long time.

It doesn't have to be that way if we take some time to create the needed quiet-conversation conditions and to relax ourselves. Things like prepared notes and excessive thoughts about the next question all contribute to an uptight interview. Relax, and the person you are interviwing will relax. Don't pretend you are Phil Donahue or Ted Koppel. Just be you, talking to an interesting person.

Some tips

Metzler and others offer some general interviewing tips:

Let your guests know why you are interviewing them. This will help you get the answers you want and will help put them at ease because they know what you want.

Always prepare well in advance. Many trial lawyers suggest never asking a question that you don't already know the answer to. That's a little extreme for most situations you'll be in, but hardly bad advice. Know what to expect. Know what you want. Be flexible enough to respond to specific information you didn't already know. But have a good idea what you want to accomplish. This will save time for both you and your guest.

Ask "Why?" and "What do you mean?" to gather more and clearer detail.

Never allow your guest to give you vague answers. Remember you may know what she or he means, but the radio station's listening audience does not.

Avoid asking convoluted questions. This often happens when you are well prepared but not-so-well rehearsed. Ask simple straightforward questions without much qualification. Then carefully listen to the answer. And don't ask two questions at the same time.

Don't talk too much yourself. A good nod of the head or an under-the-breath uttered "uh-huh" will give your guest the cue that you're listening without butting in. Remember you want this to appear to be a conversation between two people although the guest will do all the talking. Say only as much as needed to accomplish that feat.

Know your focus. Before the interview, as you meet and initially start talking with your guest, discuss your subject's information in general, but also focus on a specific area, emphasizing two or three main points. List the points in their natural sequence. Suggest how long each section should take.

Prepare your guest. As you visit with your guest, list "lead" questions that you can ask, if necessary, to move the interview along smoothly and on schedule. If you have time, make brief notes about the information your subject will provide when answering the lead questions. These will help you if she or he should forget some of the important points when you actually turn on the microphone.

Encourage you guest to talk freely. Use questions or comments to draw the person out or to clarify a point.

Open the interview with a direct question. Make sure it is one that requires your guest to take the lead in the discussion. Begin your questions with who, what, when, where, why, or how – relying heavily on how, what, and why. The purpose is to frame a question in such a way that your guest can't answer it with a "yes" or a "no". If you begin a question with "Do...?," "Did...?", "Are you...?" "Is it...?," "Were you...?," or "Have you...?," you automatically invite a "yes" or "no" reply. This

forces you to do most of the talking. Another and even more troublesome way of getting into the "yes" or "no" reply, is to give the information yourself, and then ask, "Isn't that true?" After a few statement-questions you'll be interviewing yourself.

Stress the pronouns "you" and "your" in your questions. Ask you guest to talk in terms of I, my, and mine. Make a special effort to show that you're genuinely interested in what your guest has to say. Maintain eye contact and a warm, close feeling; nod, smile, and give positive, supportive feedback. This will demonstrate your interest and boost your guest's confidence. In addition, your audience can "hear" your interest in the discussion.

Be interested in your guest as a person. Be knowledgeable and enthusiastic about the message. Your audience and the gatekeepers surely will know if you aren't.

Working tools of radio

When you want to provide a radio station with information requiring little or no editing, your basic tools are a good quality cassette recorder and a good quality microphone. When you actually assemble, edit, and produce your own story or spot announcement, you will need a more sophisticated set up, including reel-to-reel tape recorders and tape editing capabilities.

Tape and tape recorders

There are two tape formats currently available. They are cassette tape and 1/4 inch reel-to-reel tape. The increasing quality of cassette tape and cassette recorders, along with the diminishing size of the recorders, has made cassette tape the preferred medium for gathering information for use on radio. After you have gathered the information, the possibility of using reel-to-reel tape comes into play.

Cassette tape

Audio tape consists of a very thin layer of iron oxide emulsion cemented to an acetate or mylar base. The recorder generates magnetic signals that arrange the iron particles on the recording tape into "sound patterns."

A radio producer at Oregon State University once said buying cassette tape was like buying tires. The temptation is to go for the medium value at the lowest price. But, if you're after quality, whether for a weekly radio show or for delivering raw news and information to radio stations, you should buy a reliable product that suits your needs.

The first rule is to stay away from generic or non-brand-name, three-for-a-dollar tapes. They are not worth the money and could waste your recording effort. Choose recognized brand-name tapes. When you record speech, choose a Type 1 tape. The package will tell you it's a ferric oxide (Fe_2O_3) normal- bias (or normal position) tape. Most recorders are designed

Professional quality is available in multi-channel decks and in battery-powered cassette and reel recorders.

for this type of tape. These will work perfectly for your radio show and your news story. If your cassette recorder and microphone are high enough quality, and you are going to record the higher dynamic range of music, you should buy the highest quality Type 1 tape you can find.

Some newer portable cassette recorders and most home cassette decks allow you the option of using Type II "chrome" (CrO_2) high-bias tape. This is good for music recording or split production where you will be using a music background.

Cassette-tape recorders

Knowing which cassette recorder to choose for your office will depend on how much money you feel you can spend and what you plan to do with the equipment you buy. However, there are several general points to keep in mind.

Make sure it has a tape counter. As simple as this sounds, some recorders are made without them. You need a counter when you are recording an interview so you can note a point on the tape at which something important has been said and find that point later.

Choose your options. You'll be offered the choice of a stereo or monoaural recorder. Although stereo might seem more sophisticated and therefore more desirable, for the purpose of information gathering and distribution, stereo is of litle help. And in a portable recorder, you are probably better off spending your money on something else essential to your task.

That could be having the option of manual or automatic recording-level control. Many modern cassette recorders have some kind of automatic-level control. However, you'll find it helpful to be able to switch from one to the other as needed.

Generally, recordings are of higher quality if you watch the recording levels and adjust them manually and subtly. The word "subtle" is important. An automatic level control is designed to search for available sound and almost instantly bring it to a constant level. This is not subtle. A person standing 10 feet away from you should sound different than the person standing six inches away. With the choice between automatic and manual

level control, you have the option of allowing them to sound different.

Consider weight and size of the recorder. Don't skimp on size and lose quality, but don't get something so large and cumbersome that you tend not to take it with you at a moment's notice, either. Some of the best recordings you'll make will be the ones you get just because you grabbed your recorder and microphone as you were going out the door. Recorders come in all shapes and sizes. Find one that gives you adequate quality but still is small enough to fit your working style.

Choose a plug-in recorder. Be sure your recorder will let you plug in a microphone so you're not forced to use an inferior built-in microphone. While checking for a place to plug in a microphone, known as an input, check for auxiliary inputs for another recorder or the telephone.

Get good headphones. Finally, consider a good set of headphones, instead of the typically-supplied earplug. This will help you hear the true quality of your recording and help you work unobtrusively in a busy office.

Digital

Digital Audio Technology, commonly called DAT, offers a higher quality option with some unique additional benefits.

Digital audio recorders – most that are available for the consumer market are cassette recorders – place a digital signal on the tape, rather than an analog signal. Although there are many technical differences, the primary benefit to the user is in sound-reproduction quality. You can record a digital signal over and over without losing quality as you do with repeated recording of an analog signal.

This is especially important when it comes to electronic editing. One of the primary concerns about tape-to-tape electronic editing is that every time you record from one recorder to another you lose signal quality. If you make enough copies from one tape to another without returning to the original, the tape will be almost useless.

To many people DAT audio recorders look similar to analog cassette recorders. But to your audience, there will be a significant improvement in your sound quality.

Microphones

The microphone is the front line of your radio efforts. It takes the most abuse and is arguably the most important link in the chain.

Microphones are devices that change acoustical energy into electrical pulses. Although the microphone principle of sound reproduction hasn't changed in years, new developments and refinements have been incorporated in microphone construction.

Each microphone has its own pick-up pattern, output impedance (high or low), frequency response, and output level. These

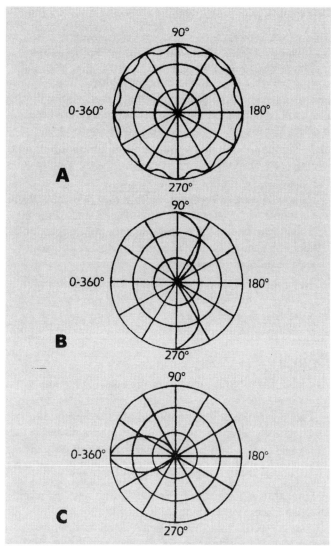

A microphone's response pattern (sound pickup designation) should correspond with the mike's application. The most common response patterns, Illustrated by thick lines are (A) omnidirectional, (B) cardioid, and (C) unidirectional.

characteristics determine the type of microphone best suited to your recorder and need. Be sure to buy your recorder and your microphone as a set or take your recorder with you when you buy your microphone.

Basic types of microphones include:

- **Condenser**: excellent frequency response, low distortion, expensive, crisper-sounding, more sensitive to faint signals.

- **Dynamic**: sturdy, unaffected by atmosphere, good frequency response, medium-priced, will handle loud sounds with minimum distortion, requires no batteries, your "best bet".

Another important aspect of microphones is the pick-up pattern. Some are unidirectional, meaning they will pick up sound primarily from one direction. Others are omnidirectional, meaning they will pick up sound from all directions. Some are cardioid, meaning they will pick up sound in a heart-shaped pattern favoring one side. And there are hypercardioid or shotgun microphones designed to pick up sounds from a limited area over long distances.

Most often, an omnidirectional microphone will be the most useful to you. In some cases, however, you may have a special need for a unidirectional or even a shotgun microphone.

Common sense is important with microphones. Get one that works well with your recorder, and take care of it like the fragile tool it is.

Some experts say too much emphasis is placed on the kinds of microphones available. In fact, the most critical factor in determining whether the microphone works for you is how well you use it. Skill and technique come from practice. Learn to use the tools you have to their full capability.

Tape editing

The magnetic sound patterns on recording tape are similar to the printed word. Just as words, sentences, and paragraphs on a printed page can be edited, deleted, or rearranged, so can words, sentences, and paragraphs on tape. With practice you can become quite adept at building the tape content to fit your particular needs.

The irrelevant, the unwanted, the distracting have no place in any radio presentation. Remove them by editing. Often it is necessary to shorten a program or a quote. Do this by editng out the weaker parts, keeping only the portion which makes the point you want. Experienced tape editors have perfected their art to the point that they can make singular words out of plurals by eliminating the "s" sound.

There are two editing methods: recording from one recorder to another, called electronic editing (also known as dubbing), and cutting and splicing the original tape. This method is usually used only on reel-to-reel tape.

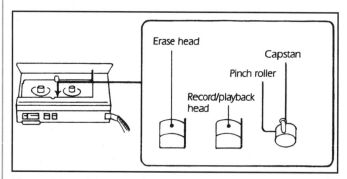

The position of the recorder's components can be seen easily in this diagram.

Electronic editing

This requires two cassette recorders connected by audio cables from the auxiliary output of one to the auxiliary input of the other. Electronic editing is particularly useful for inserting interviews and other previously recorded material into a program or spot that you're assembling. Use one recorder to play your selected actuality and the other to record it. It's important that your recorders are equipped with pause switches. Using the pause or edit switches, cue or position both tapes to the proper location, and then start them simultaneously. It's that simple.

It usually helps to locate and identify the closing phrase so the tape can be stopped before reaching unwanted audio. After the last sound of the phrase passes the playback head, push the pause switch on the record machine or quickly turn down the record volume. Practice a little and you'll have no trouble.

Cutting and splicing

The combination of cutting and splicing is by far the most accurate method of editing. And, it's the reason you use a reel-to-reel recorder.

The first step is to remove the head cover on your machine and locate the playback head. Identify where the recording takes place in the middle of the head. Next, listen to the tape carefully, perhaps two or three times, before you do any cutting.

Decide what you want to take out and how you want the finished tape to sound. Use a grease pencil on the shiny back side of the tape to mark the starting and ending points of the part to be cut out. Place the marks in the short, silent spaces between words you want to keep and words you want to take out.

With a single-edge razor blade or scissors, cut to the inside of the marks on the portion you wish to remove, known as the outtake. Lay the outtake aside; don't discard it until the finished product is to your satisfaction.

Your editing job is made much easier and faster if you use a grooved splicing block. The block allows you to make precise cuts with a razor blade.

Then splicing tape is used to rejoin the two cut segments of the tape. It is a little narrower than the recording tape and is placed over the cut so it doesn't extend beyond the edges of the recording tape. If used carefully, no trimming is needed.

Better recording techniques

Proper recording and microphone techniques become especially important with the low-cost, non-professional equipment in wide use today. Noisy recording areas and poor acoustics, commonplace in most offices, increase your chances of making poor-quality recordings.

Here are some tips to help you cope with or overcome any environmental problems you may encounter.

Always start with a clean tape. This means using a new tape, or one that has been erased. Bulk tape erasers, also called

Tape erasers (demagnetizers) remove previously recorded signals and should be used prior to recording.

degausers, are available at most electronic equipment stores. A poorer-quality alternative is to run the tape through with your recorder in the record mode with the record volume turned all the way down.

Cleaning your recorder

If the sounds from your recorder are muddy or muffled, the problem may be caused by dirt. Avoid this quality loss by regularly cleaning the recorder heads, the capstan, which is the shaft that actually drives the tape, and the rubber pressure roller. Use a cotton swab dipped in denatured alcohol and gently clean these main functioning parts.

Begin with the heads – both playback and record. Then move to the capstan, the vertical metal spindle that spins. And then clean the pinch roller, the rubber wheel that pushes the tape against the capstan when the recorder is playing.

You're actually cleaning away metal oxide that rubs off the tape. If you use high quality tapes. You'll have fewer problems than if you use bargain tape.

If you are working with a reel-to-reel recorder or one of the larger cassette recorders, the heads and other parts will be easy to get to. Smaller portable cassette recorders with doors that hold or enclose the tape make cleaning more difficult. Try pushing the PLAY button to move the heads out in the open.

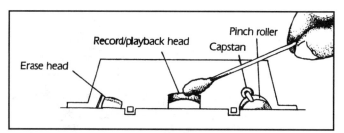

A cotton swab can be used to gently clean main functioning parts of a recorder.

Additional recording hints

Always turn the monitor speaker off when you are recording with a microphone. That's a primary cause of squealing feedback.

Record at the highest volume at which no distortion occurs. The higher volume on the recorded track helps cover up any noise that might be inherent in the tape or the recorder.

If your recorder has a VU meter, adjust the volume upward to the point where the needle just touches the red on the loudest parts. The sound should be clear, strong, and undistorted when played back on your machine. Do a few test runs.

Always observe the recorder manufacturer's recommended

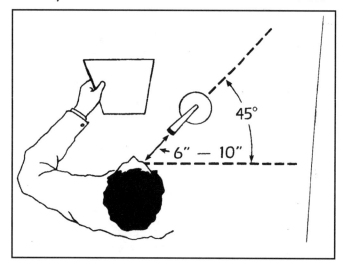

Proper microphone technique showing proper distance and angle.

operation and maintenance procedures by reading and fllowing the manual's instructions. Remember, your recorder is a sophisricated electronic instrument; it take s a lot o practice to operate it correctly. The more you use it, the better your final product will be. And don't bang it around. Underneath that rugged shell are delicate operating parts. Do not haul your recorder inthe trunk of your car, either. If possible, place it on the seat, on a cushion, or on a piece of foam rubber.

Always allow your recorder to warm up before you use it. Run the tape for a couple of minutes before starting to record. This is especially critical in the winter when the recorder has been in a cold car for several hours. If possible, bring it inot a warm building several hours before recording time.

Proper microphone technique

Hold the microphone six to 10 inches from your mouth and at a 45^0 angle to the direct line of speech. This will help prevent "blasting" and distortion of explosive letters "P" and "B" and the sibilant letter "S". Also this will diminsh the effects of poor room acoustics. The optimum distance and position will vary with different microphones. Experiment! In all cases, sit or stand in a comfortable position. When holding a microphone, remove rings or other jewelry to avoid striking it.

Place the microphone as far from the recorder as possible. A sensitive microphone will pick up the recorder's motor and tape transport noise. If you use a microphone stand, try to avoid placing the recorder on the same table as the microphone.

In the beginning

When you start recording, be prepared to keep at it. Stopping and starting usually results in distracting noises and varied recording levels and voice quality. You can edit out silent pauses later.

Don't speak for 10 seconds, at the beginning or end of your recording. This gives the tape a clean, silent leader and close.

When you do begin, it helps if you use a standard reference opening that includes the date, the place, your subject's name, and your name. Later you will find this valuable information as you sort through a dozen tapes looking for a specific piece of information.

You also may want to count down, "five, four, three, two, one. ..." This allows your voice an opportunity to stabilize as you start.

When you begin, speak in your normal conversational tone and volume. Don't whisper and don't shout. When talking, always maintain the same distance form the microphone.

If you clear your throat or cough, be sure to turn away from the microphone.

Remove all paper clips and staples from your copy before starting the broadcast or recording. It's too much of a temptation for everyone to start fiddling with them when nervous. Keep your notes still.

Avoid tapping your pencil or clicking your ballpoint pen. Also be careful that the person you are interviewing isn't doing so.

Tape storage

Store reels of tape in boxes or cans. The original box protects a tape from dust and physical damage to its edges. For periods of long storage, metal cans sealed with adhesive tape are best. If the tape came in a sealed plastic envelope, leave it there until you're ready to use it. Wind reels of tape loosely. Store upright on edge, not flat. Avoid stacking. The weight may warp the plastic reels or damage the edges of the tape. Also, because of the possibility of the magnetic signal transferring from one layer of tape to the next, it's best to store all your tapes' tails out, meaning the end of the recording should be at the outside of the reel.

Store away from radiators, heating vents, hot water pipes, and windows. Do not leave tapes on a car seat or on the ledge behind the back seat, exposed to the sun's damaging rays. Store away from even slight magnetic fields, such as those created by electric motors, magnetic tools, TV sets, or computers.

Store at an ideal temperature (72°F) with an ideal humidity (50 percent), if possible.

If the tape is exposed to extreme temperatures, such as in mailing, allow several hours for it to return to room temperature before using.

Promoting your efforts

Word of mouth

This is one way to spread the message that radio stations in your area are helping distribute your information. There is nothing wrong with plugging your broadcasts at meetings, during office visits, on farm and home visits, in telephone conversations, and elsewhere.

Posters

Simple posters you make yourself can be very effective. For wider distribution, you might want to use more refined printed posters. Display them at meetings, in store windows, at grain elevators or anywhere members of your target group will see them.

Brochures

If you have a regular radio or television program or time slot, brochures might be helpful. In some states, producers make extensive use of brochures to promote radio and televison series and spots. Brochures are particularly useful in providing your audience with dates, air times, topics, and talent listings.

Newsletters

These are ready-made for promoting your broadcasts. People on mailing lists are familiar with what you do and will make up the nucleus of any audience for your information.

Displays and exhibits

Fairs, field days, shows, store windows, bulletin boards, conferences, meetings, conventions, and festivals all offer opportunities for displays or exhibits. These are great places to promote your radio and television programs.

Invitations

As a good-will gesture, invite station personnel to your organization's functions as guests. Remember they are part of the public you are trying to reach. Be especially watchful for things that could benefit them as individuals as well as media professionals. Once you have a station representative coming to your functions because he or she wants to, you have a friend who will be much easier to work with in the future.

Conclusion

Radio can be a useful, cost-effective, and creative outlet for your information. To make radio work for you, remember these basic ideas:

Know your audience. The more you know, the better you will be able to prepare information that actually reaches the target and has a positive effect.

Use your creativity. Explore the many interesting ways to use radio to distribute your information.

Know what news is and practice finding it. Sound news judgements can accentuate the power of radio.

Regularly review your radio work. Self-criticism can be tough but it is one of the best ways to improve your presentation.

Work at the level of production in which you are most comfortable. Once you overcome the technical aspects of radio, you can judge your potential and increase your proficiency as needed.

Be yourself. Practice until you are comfortable. Then you'll be able to concentrate on getting the information correct rather than worrying about how or what to do.

Television News

The accuracy of television

Telling an audience about a news event in print is one thing, but showing them that same event in words, natural sounds, and moving video can be much more powerful and memorable. The same story that you just finished typing for release to newspapers may have a much larger impact on videotape.

The key to making the decision whether or not to produce a television news report lies in how visual your story could be. What shots could you get to draw a viewer's interest?

Nearly 20 years ago, *The Camera Never Blinks* was a famous book by Dan Rather of CBS about the network television news business. The title suggests that television news is the proven, and often unforgiving, medium in delivering the most accurate, "lawsuit-proof" coverage of events.

Because the camera never blinks, communicators must realize that, along with their intended message, any cracks or wrinkles of an organization or program will appear on videotape as well. Therefore, utmost care must be taken in the planning of a television news production.

This chapter will cover the following areas of television news:
- reasons for using the television medium
- TV news marketing/self-promotion
- television script writing
- reading for television
- television interviewing techniques

Reasons for using the television medium

Let's face it, most Americans spend more time watching television than listening to the radio or reading a newspaper. It's become America's choice for information and entertainment. You can take advantage of this medium by producing ready-to-use news reports for your television network affiliates to plug into local newscasts.

It's much more convenient at the end of a day for a person to pick up the remote control and turn on the local news for a rundown of the day's top stories than it is to thumb through the newspaper to search for those same stories sprinkled among advertisements.

In just 90 seconds, a report on a new after-school extension youth program, for example, can tell a sizeable audience how well their tax dollars are being spent. Many television news reports last only 30 seconds, but because they also offer pictures to accompany the anchor's narration or a source's soundbite, the information is disseminated faster.

Television news marketing

Getting your story told can be very challenging, particularly in larger television markets. No matter how good your story is, you can't get airplay without an effective marketing plan. Because time is limited, many news organizations are extremely selective about the types of stories they air. Some simply prefer to do their own story, negating the need for you to run out and lease or buy a room full of expensive video gear.

Visualize the story

Regardless of who has the equipment, a news director or assignment editor will want to visualize the story you want told. Plan for this before calling a station with a story idea. Imagine how that story will be shot – what kinds of non-talking shots, or "B-roll," are available to illustrate your points?

For example, instead of simply lining up an indoor studio interview with a cotton-pest researcher, find a nearby cotton field to serve as a frame around the researcher as he or she talks. Locate samples of the pest in your story for closeup shots. If you have a map, circle the infested counties for the viewers to see the size of the problem.

By putting yourself in the shoes of a TV-news field producer, you can save a lot of time for the camera crew. By anticipating what shots they'll need and lining those shots up in advance, you'll earn the crew's eternal gratitude and increase the likelihood that they will visit your organization again for another story. These details should be communicated with the station's assignments editor to show them that a story is "doable." Having your source, in this case a pest researcher, available with a flexible schedule also will help build a strong working relationship with local media

A resource guide

An additional help to an assignment editor is a resource guide from your organization. Listing subject matters in alphabetical order with subject matter experts and their phone numbers can save a TV-news producer a lot of time in setting up an interview. This is of particular importance when a station wants a local reaction to a national story. For example, if the

surgeon general suddenly came out with news conference on the harmful effects on milk on teenagers, your local TV stations could quickly refer to your Resource Guide to contact an in-house dairy expert for a response.

Produce it yourself

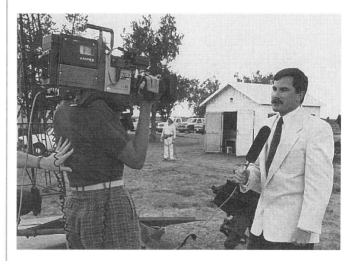

Perhaps you have a commercial television news background or training and are quite comfortable producing your own TV reports for distribution. Check the details of video production techniques in Chapter 20 for guidance on producing your own video reports.

Start by calling ahead to individual stations in your viewing area. Each station may have its own "ideal story length," so make note of that length in your initial call.

If they do accept reports from freelancers or organizations, find out exactly how a station would like the "close" or ending to a report. For example, a station may want all reports to end as, "...for Action 7 News, I'm (your name) reporting from (your location)." Send a separate videotape to each station with their custom audio close on it. That way, the station feels more of a sense of ownership with the report and the reporter. This technique also gives the TV-news department the look of having a larger staff without the financial burden of hiring more reporters.

Before you start making duplicate tapes to send out, determine what format of video tape particular stations use. These could range from 3/4 inch to Beta SP.

Variety increases airtime

Agricultural stories often end up in the early morning news programs during network "break in," or may be played on noontime programs. By offering a variety of reports, such as one on an extension nutrition education for low-income families and one on garden pests, you can break the "time-slot barrier" and get the story run during the prime time news. Relate the narrow focus of your organization to the larger needs and concerns of the public. For example, if your work relates to agriculture, show that your story is not just for farmers and ranchers, but that agriculture is all-encompassing—from the food we eat to the clothes we wear. Seemingly "narrow-focused" stories such as these, however, require a little extra push (a quick phone call) to the TV-news assignment editor or news producer in order to get the attention you thinkl they deserve.

Expand distribution

Once you are comfortable with the daily or weekly production and distribution of your TV reports, consider expansion beyond your immediate area to such national networks as "Ag Day." This network, for example, broadcasts reports from organizations like yours to more than 135 stations across the country six days a week. That means great exposure for your organization.

Television script writing

Putting together a television script is similar to building a radio script, but the writer, field reporter, or correspondent goes one more step in separating the visuals from the sound. Read the guides to radio scripting in Chapter 18 for even more detail about writing for the ear.

On the left side of the script is a column designated for which shots will be inserted by a video editor. On the right side is a column for the reporter's voice and those of his or her sources, also known as "soundbites." As with a radio news script, the writer must remember the importance of brevity, while still managing to include the "five Ws": who, what, when, where and why.

Any time a soundbite is used, note the "in" cue, the first two or three words and the "out" cue, the final few words. Then include the total running time of the soundbite in seconds. Provide a suggested introduction for the news anchor to read. Always spell out numbers (not years) and hyphenate initials.

When a source appears with a soundbite on a script, it's important to include that person's name and title, along with the time period for the production director at a station to superimpose that character generation. Do not superimpose text on the video. Leave character generation to the individual stations because many prefer to use their own fonts and logos. If an unusual word is used in a script, use a phonetic spelling to make the anchor or narrator's job easier. Study this example of a script which uses these techniques.

Alcalde center funding

Suggested anchor intro: Smaller growers of eleven North-Central New Mexico counties have been getting some help in the form of agricultural expertise from New Mexico State Univerity's Sustainable Agricultural Science Center at Alcalde, just north of Espanola. (Reporter's name) reports on the need to expand services there.

RUNS: 1:45

Video	Audio
B-roll of Alcalde...	The Rural Agricultural Improvement and Public Affairs Project, or RAIPAP, based at Alcalde, has been helping small growers of North Central New Mexico since 1991 in such areas as sustainable agriculture, marketing, and financial planning. RAIPAP Director Edmund Gomez of New Mexico State University's Cooperative Extension Service says the project must expand to better serve limited-resource clientele in eleven counties.
BITE... Insert: (:29-:35) Edmund Gomez RAIPAP Director	IN: "We've been running... OUT: ...within the area." RUNS: :18

AUDIO BRIDGE...	The project was started through a grant from the W-K- Kellogg Foundation. Gomez says N-M-S-U will request additional funding from the state legislature in January to hire specialists in fruit crops, vegetables, biocontrols and sustainable systems.
BITE...	IN: "Most of the... OUT: ...future generations." RUNS: :29.
AUDIO CLOSE...	Successful funding will allow the center to continue serving small farmers when Kellogg funding expires. From N-M-S-U's College of Agriculture and Home Economics, I'm (reporter's name).

When your story gets airtime, don't be surprised if the station has edited it down to a 30-second "voice-over," where the anchor reads a condensed script. News producers make the tough decision to edit or completely eliminate some reports in every newscast. A certain amount of airtime has been sold to advertisers, and breaking reports or "live shots" may eat into time alloted earlier for your particular report. When that happens, don't get mad. Just keep submitting material in the format that station desires, and, chances are, they'll continue trying to run it.

Follow-up surveys

You can keep track of how useful your reports are by sending out a survey every few months to every station in your network of distribution. Ask questions about the frequency of use

for your submitted reports, the feedback they may have received from their audience, any trends in the time of day your reports air, how often your reports are edited, and any particular subjects they would like to see covered more.

When you survey your network, try to find out their opinions on the quality of writing, shooting and editing. You may think you're doing a good job, but without answers you may be operating in a vacuum and wasting everyone's time.

Attention getters

Keep in mind that a story with a gimmick is more likely to run than others. For example, let's look at a story about forest management. Instead of opening with the reporter's voice, try opening with the sounds and sights of a chain saw getting pull-started and slicing through a dying tree, felling it with a thunderous crash. Then start with your narration leading to a soundbite with a forest management specialist. The strong visual and sound will pull viewers into this story, and the news director will welcome the freshness of the opening.

Reading for television

The technique used to read television news, called the "delivery," can make or break a story. Pregnant pauses, stuttering or the inclusion of "um" between words will make a well-written report sound amateurish and could ruin your organization's reputation for story quality.

Gone are the days when an announcer had to be without a detectable, regional accent. No one's asking you to sound like Walter Cronkite, Leonard Nimoy or some other recognizable narrator. You simply need to be well rehearsed and confident before the tape is rolling.

Long sentences can make you sound like you've just climbed 20 flights of stairs. Break down those behemoths so that they are manageable with your natural reading pace.

Common Mistakes

A pitfall among young broadcast journalists is the "sing-song" delivery The narrator's voice drops in tone, then climbs in tone, then drops in tone – well, you get the picture. It's a great cure for insomnia, but your audience will miss your message while they sleep. Think of yourself as telling your story to someone else in the room. It may help actually having someone in your studio while you record your voice, just to get that conversational sound. If you're recording a "standup" on location, do several takes beyond what you felt was acceptable. There could be a problem beyond your control (a wrinkle on the video tape or a person waving in the background where your one good take was recorded), so cover yourself with extra takes.

Believe in what you're saying, and the viewers will too. When you've finished recording your voice, play it back for another person to hear. A little feedback can prevent embarrassment later, particularly if you've left out or mispronounced a word.

Television interview techniques

A feeling of trust must be cultivated between a reporter and a person being interviewed before that source can come across with confidence on tape. You can build that trust by presenting

your source with a list of possible questions before the interview is recorded. Give the person being interviewed a chance to collect some thoughts about the response.

Occasionally, a surprise question spawned from the response to a prediscussed question can add some excitement or human emotion to an interview. It makes the source appear much more natural and unrehearsed as if speaking from the heart and not from a script.

Caution the person being interviewed beforehand not to respond to questions by leading off with your name. Remember that the reporter is not the story and should not be promoted with constant reference.

Knowing something about the subject matter before the interview will make both the interviewer and the source more comfortable. It helps to avoid asking basic questions, such as definitions, when the narrator can look up that information just as easily. Beware of daydreaming during lengthy responses on camera. By staying alert, you'll avoid asking a question that may have just been answered.

As the tape rolls, your camera operator should be wearing headphones and will let you know if a question and response need to be repeated due to unexpected background noise, such as an airplane or motorcycle passing by. During your interview, maintain eye contact with your sources as much as possible.

As you prepare your questions, write them in such as way that the person being interviewed cannot respond simply with a "yes" or "no" answer. Construct questions that will draw details from your source. Those same "five Ws" (who, what, when, where, why) can come in handy when the microphone is on and the tape is rolling. Be sure not to ask two questions at once, or you may lose a valuable response as your source focuses on only one question.

A word of caution

In the book, *Television News: Anatomy and Process*, author Maury Green views television news interviews as a form of verbal fencing, where the reporter plans an attack to extract closely guarded information from the source. A relentless barrage of argumentative questioning can uncover some interesting and controversial responses from a source. This technique may work well for "Hard Copy" or "60 Minutes", but it could burn a bridge between you and sources within your organization.

In a cooperative interview, you can still get the sound bites you need through gentle persistence, persuading the source to state his or her point of view. Remember to treat your source like gold because you'll probably have to interview that person again someday for another story.

Video Productions

In this Information Age, television and video permeate every aspect of life. From Channel One in the classroom to CNN news around the world, from home shopping to home movies on demand, from giant-screen Monday night football, to tiny video clips on the World Wide Web. Video technology is a dominant force in entertainment, news, elections, and the development of a national culture. Unfortunately, it has not reached its full potential in education.

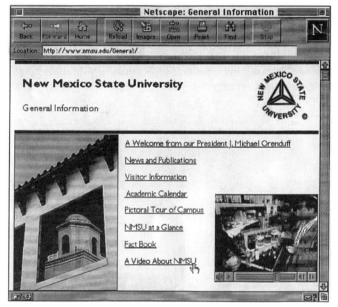

Video is a daily source of information, from traditional TV shows to Web pages. New technology has put video production within the reach of most educators.

As society continues to move from institutional control of the media to "democratization" of the media, television, videotapes, and video clips on computer networks can be an educator's forum to speak to millions of people where they live, study, work, and play. The possibility of producing a customized, effective videotape is within the grasp of any educator who will work to understand both the mechanics and the creative process of video productions.

This chapter is written primarily for educators without television production degrees who are working in an office, a classroom, a public agency, or a small educational video unit. It will cover the entire videotape production process, from planning, scripting, and taping, to editing, graphics, duplication, and distribution. Details about television news and working with TV stations are covered in Chapter 19.

Chapter overview

Planning:	Message, Audience, Medium
Pre-production:	Scripting, Site survey, and Talent preparation
Production:	Field equipment, Set-up, and Technique
Post-production:	Graphics, Linear editing and Nonlinear editing
Publication:	Duplication, Distribution, and Presentation

Planning

Video program design

If your program is viewed on a television monitor, your audience will subconsciously compare it to programs seen nightly on network television. While locally-produced educational programs may never look the same as high budget, commercial

The type of video shot you need is determined by your message and the needs of your target audience. In this video, for example, the crew tapes a large number of close-ups because of the audience's interest in scientific details.

productions, they don't have to look like home movies either. You can increase the professionalism and effectiveness of your productions by carefully planning your message. Start with a clear understanding of both your message and your audience. As you move through the processes of taping, editing, and distribution, the decisions made in the initial design and planning stage will complement (or hinder) every step.

What is your message?

Crafting an exact message to be conveyed is perhaps the most overlooked and critical step in video production. Without a precise, one-sentence message statement, all your production and editing efforts could be wasted time and money. Unfortunately, many video producers never clarify their intended message, so they never know when their programs have succeeded. Vague missions, such as, "I want to make a tape about Extension programs,... about plant disease, ... about improving 4-H meetings," lack focus and excitement. Instead, bring the message into sharp focus.:

- "Extension is worth our taxpayer's investment."

- "Tomato diseases can be identified and treated."

- "Communication skills will improve 4-H meetings."

Once your message is clearly defined, every production decision should be checked constantly against this message:

- "Which activity best shows a return on the taxpayers' investment?"

- "Can the problems of this plant disease best be explained with a live plant or with a diagram?"

- "Would role-playing be better than a lecture to teach effective communication skills?"

It is important that you keep the objectives of your program to a minimum. Too often, videotapes try to achieve too much at once, and, as a result, accomplish nothing. It is far better to make several short, single-concept videos than one long, involved program.

Who is your audience?

Before the first cable is connected to the video camera, you should ask yourself some questions: "Who will want to watch this tape?" "Why should they care?" "What difference will this tape really make?"

Segment your audience. Saying you want to reach "everyone" or "the general public" is generally a warning sign that

Focus groups are an important tool in understanding the audience's needs and attitudes. Listen for important cues about how to make your audience care and understand your message.

you need to give more thought to your mission and target audience. Even if the video will be viewed on commercial television or in a public setting, you should be aiming it at a specific segment of the public who has specific needs and interests related to your goal.

Focus group. As you shape your message, consider the preconceived notions, the values, and the needs of your audience. Don't simply guess what your audience wants or needs to know. Ask them. Ideally, you will have a scientific survey of their knowledge and attitudes. But many producers find focus groups can be equally or even more effective than statistical data.

Assemble a group of representative members of your target group (not just people who are easy to find or your friends). Ask open-ended questions about your intended message. Assess not only current knowledge, but also the overall interest in the subject. Listen for ways to help them to "care" about your message. Learn what effect your message will have on their lives. Look for trigger points, the "outrage factor," and catch phrases. Ask what they liked and disliked about similar tapes they have seen. In short, this is a time to listen, not educate. Don't argue or explain. Instead, absorb and evaluate key insights about ways to reach your audience.

At the conclusion of your focus group, you should know how much your audience already knows about the subject and the importance placed on it. If they already feel the subject is extremely important and have a good grasp on the terminology and concepts, move quickly to the core point of your message. Long introductions to a knowledgeable audience give the impression that no new information will be presented.

By contrast, if the information is fairly new to the viewers, or if they don't understand yet why your main message is even important to them, establish the background and context first. Without this foundation, the videotape could appear complex and confusing.

What is your target setting?

Consider where and when the video will be viewed. Videos designed for use in noisy public settings, such as at a state fair or grocery store, should have only one simple main point, be highly visual, and be extremely short. Videos for public meetings, especially if they are only part of the agenda, should rarely be longer than 10 to 12 minutes and should be carefully edited to make every second count. Tapes designed for home study use, especially those containing step-by-step processes or covering numerous aspects of one topic, such as home gardening techniques for the Southwest, should include numerous close-ups, text on the screen to underscore major points, possibly review segments, and contain a clear outline of the lessons on the tape box.

What is your target medium?

Video is not the best tool for every situation. Producing and editing a video is expensive and time consuming, so a video should only be chosen when the message is truly visual, emotional, or action-oriented. If the presentation is simply a lecture (a talking head), is it really important that the audience see the speaker? Would an easy, inexpensive audiotape be just as effective?

If you are presenting technical or detailed information, would a printed publication be less expensive and more effective? If the information is likely to change or will be shown to a wide variety of audiences, would a slide series be easier to modify and adapt for the viewers? If you are responsible for showing the videotape at a large conference, will you have the video projection equipment needed to show it to 300 people at once?

Maybe a combination of print and video is best. In this case, your video can focus on motivating and demonstrating, while the printed material will contain the details. Invest your time and money to produce videotapes only on projects for which they are appropriate and practical.

Are other tapes available?

Before producing an educational tape, you should know that it is almost always cheaper to buy an educational tape from another source than to make your own. Never undertake a video production project until after you know what tapes are available on the subject. If nothing else, reviewing similar tapes can give you ideas for your own production.

Phases in video creation

In general, there are four phases of a video creation process:

1) **Pre-production:**　　outline, treatment, script, story board, site survey

2) **Production:**　　videotape on location, direct talent

3) **Post-production:**　　log tapes, create graphics, narrate, edit

4) **Distribution:**　　Duplicate, package, copyright, evaluate, promote

Pre-production

If, after examining your message and target audience, you determine a video program will meet your needs, you are ready to start the process with the pre-production phase. The decisions you made in initially planning the project should be formalized here and will guide you throughout the process. Careful pre-production can save time and money in field production and editing.

Resources

Evaluate the equipment, talent, crew, time, and production budget available. Be aware of your constraints and plan to take full advantage of your strengths.

This is the time to touch base with everyone related to the project: subject-matter specialists, members of your target audience, people providing financial support, administrators, and on-screen talent.

Treatment

In brief, your treatment will be a chronological description of the entire program, from start to finish. You should include it with a brief overview of the entire project.

Start with a brief statement of your goal and purpose. Also include your one-sentence message statement, target audience, key elements, production elements, budget, and time line. This treatment is the framework for all work to follow and will help you gain cooperation from administrators, subject-matter specialists, and collaborators.

The treatment for a video can range from a simple one-page overview of the entire program to a small booklet. In any case, the treatment should include a brief statement of goals, purpose, audience, and the message.

The actual treatment will include the overall approach you will use to convey your message along with a section-by-section description of the entire program. Will your program be a studio shoot (such as an interview or a panel discussion), a field demonstration (such as a specialist demonstrating horse shoeing), a documentary or event presentation (such as a review of a crop year), a dramatization (such as actors modelling family communication skills), or an animated illustration (such as visualization of environmental changes on rangelands)?

Editing options

Determine the editing system you will use because it will make a difference in the way you pre-produce and shoot your footage. If you do not have access to editing facilities and the raw video will be viewed exactly the way it is shot, then titles, introductions, and narration must be shot in sequential order, and camera starts and stops must be carefully coordinated with the talent or subject-matter specialist During pre-production, organize events not necessarily in the easiest way, but according to the way they will appear on the final tape.

However, **if you are going to edit** (and can rearrange events and insert close-ups later) your pre-production will aim for maximum efficiency. If you know you can add text over your video later, the script for the talent can be concise with details inserted later by the character generator.

If your editing style will use a smooth story-telling approach (continuity editing), you will need to pay special attention to continuity and cut-aways when you tape. If your editing style will use a fast-moving collection of impressions (montage editing), you will need to tape numerous dynamic images, including extreme close-ups and beautiful shots that may not fit a story line immediately, but that help convey the emotion you want.

Study commercial videos

Once you think you know the treatment you want to use, study TV shows or commercial tapes using a similar treatment. You might want to tape your "example program" for detailed analysis by your co-workers on the project. Start by turning off the sound and counting every time the camera angles change and shift. Notice how many different shots are used. You will need to plan enough time in the field for several different camera angles, especially if you are using only one camera.

While analyzing commercial programs with the sound off, take time to study the lighting, the framing, and the way the talent reacts to the camera. Watch the camera movements, focus, depth of field, and the use of titles and credits. Ask yourself why they made the decisions they did. This will give you insight about good video techniques and will get you thinking like a video producer.

As you begin to plan your own program, remember that time is one of the most valuable commodities in the hectic video world. If your educational video will be only 12 minutes long, you have to plan each shot carefully. Keep the action moving, make every shot as effective as possible, and plan lots of close-ups to give each viewer a front row seat.

Scripts and story boards

Shooting scripts. If you will have control over most of the action seen during your video, such as a demonstration, drama, or animation, write a fairly detailed script *before* the video is shot. Editing the video first and narrating it later usually makes it sound like a home movie and rarely meets your audience's needs or your goals.

If you are documenting a public event or a process that can't be repeated, you have to shoot the action as it is happening. This is called a "verité" style. You can't script this program in detail before the event, but you *can* make a detailed outline of the points you expect to occur and the scenes you anticipate along with any words or catch phrases you want to illustrate.

Interviews also should be left unscripted so your talent doesn't try to memorize answers and lose the spontaneity. However, a detailed outline, prepared questions, and a shot sheet are still critical.

When scripting narration for video, write for the eye as well as the ear. Know what your visuals are and allow them to speak for themselves; don't describe in words what your audience can see clearly.

For example, instead of saying, "You start the machine by pushing this red button located in the lower left hand corner.", try saying, "Start the machine like this." Let the visuals do the talking.

Use an informal, conversational style that is grammatically correct, yet pleasant to hear. Even if the tape eventually may be

---

College of Agriculture and Home Economics
Recruitment Video
4/28/95

<u>Video</u>	<u>Audio</u>
Barbara in front of pond near Gerald Thomas Hall on a beautiful spring day.	**Barbara:** Here you are thinking about college. There are so many questions: Is it a good school? Will it train you for the future? How much will it cost?
	Barbara: No, wait. That's your parents. They think about those things.
Cut to: Two students are in dorm room studying and talking. Pan to Barbara; camera widens so we see entire room while she talks.	**Barbara:** You have other stuff on your mind. Where are your friends going? What are the dorms like? Where do you get quarters for the laundry? Is it true you don't get a locker?

A two-column script format allows presentation of both the audio and the visuals. It becomes the master guide for the entire video production.

viewed by thousands, you are really talking to only one person at a time. Unlike formal scientific writing, it is perfectly acceptable to use "you" when scripting a videotape. Be direct.

Make every word count. Write in the active, instead of passive, voice. Keep sentences direct and uncomplicated and be sure that they are appropriate to the visual. Make the transitions smooth and logical.

Read your script aloud often as you work. If it sounds too formal and stuffy, change it. Then listen to someone else read it, preferably the actual narrator you will use. Listen for long, difficult, or unfamiliar phrases or words. Allow the narrator to change words or phrases if it does not affect the meaning. Smooth out rough sections and formal passages. (For more ideas about writing, see the sections on writing in Chapter 18, "Radio" and Chapter 2, "The Art of Good Writing.")

Script Layout. Prepare the script in two columns, one for visual information and one for audio. Use script-writing software or a word processor that supports columns to allow independent editing of the columns.

Be alert for places where the video can provide the entire message without words. Carefully note all video needed to enhance and emphasize the educational message. Describe close-ups, special angles, and transitions.

VIDEO STORYBOARD

Project: *Recruiting Video*
Date: *April 1, 1996*   Page *1* of *40*

Video: *Barbara Copeland by pond in Spring time.*

Audio: *Is it a good school? How much will it cost?*

Video: *Barbara in dorm studying*

Audio: *Where are your friends going? What are the dorms like?*

Video: *Barbara in front of Gerald Thomas Hall as graduate*

Audio: *College of Agriculture and Economics and Financial Aid are good.*

Video: *Barbara in high tech. computer lab.*

Audio: *Does it have the latest equipment and technology?*

For more complex video productions, especially those involving a large production crew or many locations, consider a story board. Simple sketches can help everyone envision the final product.

Site Survey Checklist

Site logistics:
- ✓ Do you have clear directions to your location? ✓ Maps?
- ✓ Can you drive a vehicle near the location to unload equipment?
- ✓ Can you park nearby?
- ✓ Do you have permission from the location owners, managers, and users?
- ✓ Do you need security clearances?
- ✓ Is there a cart available for easy transporting of the equipment?
- ✓ Are there security problems related to the video equipment?
- ✓ Are bathroom and refreshment/meal facilities available nearby?
- **OPTIONAL:** ✓ Can you carry a cellular phone to call for extra help without leaving your equipment?

Space:
- ✓ Is there enough room for you to use the video equipment?
- ✓ Can people pass through the area without interrupting a shot?
- ✓ Can the camera be placed the correct distance from the talent?
- ✓ Can you separate the talent from the back wall enough to eliminate cast shadows?

Power:
- ✓ Is electricity available?
- ✓ Will you need long extension cords?
- ✓ Will you need three-prong adapters?
- ✓ Will you need a fused power strip?
- ✓ Will you need to tape the extension cord to the floor to prevent people from tripping?
- ✓ How many batteries will you need?
- ✓ Do you know the location of the fuse box?
- ✓ What is the amperage of the circuits?

Sound: (Close your eyes at each location and just listen.)
- ✓ Is there traffic noise?
- ✓ Do airplanes, trains or bells interrupt regularly?
- ✓ Is there a hum from central air-conditioning or heating?
- ✓ Is there equipment nearby thatl creates an electric hum?

Lighting:
- ✓ What is the natural lighting in the room/location?
- ✓ Is it a mixture of several types of light?
- ✓ Will windows interfere with the shot?
- ✓ Do you need to bring extra lights, reflector curtains, or light-correcting window film?

Talent and crew accommodations:
- ✓ Have you made arrangements to include necessary "extras" from the location, such as farm workers or audience members?

Carefully go through the sight survey several days before the actual videotaping date.

Story boards. More complex programs may require storyboarding to help everyone involved visualize the shots needed. Put each scene on a card to allow easy rearrangement of the scenes. The visuals from the story board can be transferred to the field shooting script to help guide camera operators, talent, and production assistants.

Take the time to sketch the details. If you don't note that you need an extreme close-up of a farm tractor gauge, for example, you can't assume it will be shot in the field, even if *you* are operating the camera!

As you complete the script, review the program's purpose and message. Does your one-sentence message come through loud and clear? Think about your answers to the original questions about the audience: Who are they? Why should they care? and what difference will this tape make to them? With those answers in mind, ask yourself whether your script is appropriate and effective. If it is not, or if it could be made better, you need to rewrite it. Write specifically for your target audience, using their vocabulary and comprehension level.

Site survey of locations

For many educational programs, the "set" is a real location – kitchens, classrooms, barns, homes, and gardens. While this is less expensive and sometimes more convenient than a studio, it also can have its own built-in problems. Therefore, *always conduct a site survey before the production day* (see Site Survey Checklist on previous page).

Make a simple sketch of the area. Mark the electrical outlets, windows, doorways, and major pieces of furniture. As your planning is finalized, you should sketch in the location of the talent, camera, lights, and microphone. If you need close-ups or wide shots, mark the locations of these camera movements or positions.

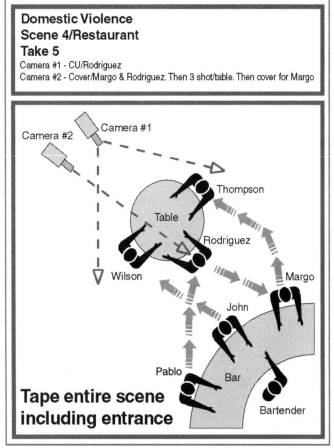

The location sketch should show the movement of all talent, placement of props, and camera angles.

From your site sketch, you can tell if you need to work with the owner to move furniture, plants, paintings, or room decorations. You may have to bring in extra electricity and add lights. As you consider the placement of furniture, allow for plenty of

room between the background and the talent to avoid "cast shadows" (harsh shadows created by the artificial lights). This extra space allows you to aim separate lights on the background and the talent, therefore creating better depth-of-field and a more 3-D look.

Locate rest rooms in public areas for the talent and crew. Find the best place to park for easy loading and access to elevators. Locate phones where you can call out at any time.

Carefully evaluate the results of your site survey to solve problems long before production day. After the site survey, develop a complete list of props, equipment, and arrangements needed. Organize people to help, finalize the scripts, prepare a shot sheet, make a time line, and prepare to work with the talent.

Shot sheets and time lines

Shot sheet. The script is a road map for the entire tape. Once it is completed, you are ready to make a shot sheet – the road map for the individual field taping sessions. By now, you should know if you are going to show the raw tape just as it is shot in the camera or if you will edit afterwards. If you will *not* edit, every shot must be planned to fall in sequential order just as it is on the script. Try to plan so carefully that you do not have to turn the camera off between scenes. Instead, only use the pause control so there will be no break in the tape.

If you can edit later, organize scenes from each location together, even if they appear in different parts of the program. Organize similar shots, such as close-ups of people or props, so they can all be shot at the same time.

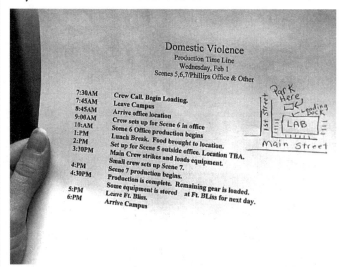

The shot sheet and time line outline each field-production day. Note that the scenes may be shot out of order for edited productions. Special notes, such as parking or contact names, should be written boldly.

Carefully note each shot and location for all on-camera talent, and what props or pieces of equipment must be taken to each location.

When you actually tape, use the shot sheet as a checklist for your day. Cross off each shot as it is completed. This will give you a quick, visual update of how much work is left and ensure that nothing is forgotten.

Time Line. As you work, a time line will begin to emerge. Plan your taping dates with the talent in mind. It may be most efficient, for example, to cluster all on-camera narrator shots on one day. On the other hand, if you are working with children or other talent who tire quickly, you may want to schedule several shorter sessions or do those sessions early in the day, while the talent is fresh.

Also consider the probable weather conditions during your taping days. If the wind usually increases in the afternoon, tape outdoor shots early and then move inside during the windy or hot part of the day.

Work through your shot sheets several times, comparing them to the original script to be sure you have included every shot and location. For each location, doublecheck the equipment, talent, and extra help you will need. Oversights here can ruin an entire shoot! It's better to under-schedule than over-schedule. This allows for unavoidable contingencies.

For more complex programs, make sketches of the camera angles and talent locations. Remember to consider the movement of the sun and shifting shadows as you plan the production day.

Talent selection and preparation

When selecting the person who will appear on camera, remember that the message is all-important. This means the talent must be able to communicate technical information in a clear and direct way.

Many educational and industrial programs call for the use of subject-matter specialists who have little or no video experience. Any preparation you can give these speakers will go a long way toward making your final production more effective. If they continue to freeze up before a camera, even with practice, limit the time they are seen on camera and ask them to read their section for use in a voice-over narration.

"Screen test" your potential talent with a three-to-five minute demonstration or interview before you make a long-term commitment. Give them some room to grow; many subject-matter specialists can improve their television appearance through practice. On the other hand, some highly knowledgeable specialists have distracting or even irritating mannerisms that cannot be suppressed. It is best to discover these problems early.

If you decide to work with non-professional actors, start the taping session by explaining that they may need to repeat some sections many times. Tell them *before you start* that requests to repeat the presentations do not necessarily mean they have made mistakes. Explain that the use of different camera angles, changes in audio set-up, and backup shots are important in

video production. If you do not explain this ahead of time, your actors will begin to feel they are doing something wrong and will appear impatient, nervous, uptight, and uncomfortable.

As a general rule, do not have a television monitor in the talent's view during the recording session. An inexperienced actor cannot avoid watching and being distracted by a monitor during the performance.

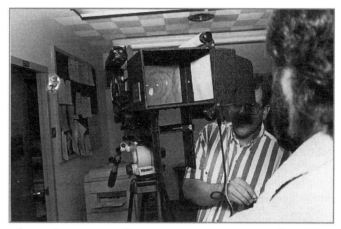

If you plan to use a teleprompter, encourage your talent to practice *before* taping day. It takes experience to look relaxed and natural while reading from a teleprompter. The teleprompter operator and the talent also need time to adjust to each other. Homemade cards will *not* substitute. Actors reading cards look unnatural and "shifty-eyed."

Use only a professional teleprompter with non-professionals. Do not use script cards. Untrained actors clearly will appear to be reading, and the overall performance will be stilted and insincere. Instead, if the talent needs notes, allow them to be held in plain view. In many cases, the talent may actually be more comfortable holding note cards (even if they rarely look at them) or just "ad libbing" the presentation segment-by-segment so that it could be edited into one smooth production later. (Just remember to alter your camera angle enough between segments to allow a smooth edit between them.)

Basic video production equipment

Equipment quality

In the video world, there are basically three different quality levels of equipment, each with their relative price and output-quality standards: consumer, prosumer (formerly called industrial), and professional.

With new technology innovations, the lines between these levels get blurred at times. What was "broadcast standard" yesterday is "sub-consumer" quality today. Chip-based cameras, recorders, and edit systems that were consumer quality when first marketed have been beefed up and expanded (at an increased price tag) to set new professional standards today.

But over the long haul, there is a reason why "prosumer" equipment costs twice as much as "consumer" and only a fraction of "professional" equipment. The extra value may be in durability, extra capability, the ability to interact with computers or other equipment, or outstanding quality output, which may not be apparent until the raw tape is edited and copied through three generations.

What is good Enough?

The key question is: What will be "good enough" for you, your goals, your message, your delivery environment, your audience, and your budget? If you are taping 4-Hers practicing demonstrations so they can review them and improve, your home video equipment will perform great. On the other hand, if "The Today Show" has asked you for a video clip, you should get the camera team from the TV station to run a few minutes of tape on their professional equipment.

This chapter assumes that most of your work will somewhere between these two extremes. If you are an experienced video producer working with professional equipment, you probably already have the instructions and training you need. Therefore, this information is aimed at the Extension agent, teacher, one-person PR team, or young video professional who wants to make a training tape or simple documentary, and probably will be using consumer or prosumer systems.

Tape format

Each quality level of video equipment generally includes several tape-format options. However, you don't necessarily have to edit on the same format you shoot on. It is common to use lightweight, easy-to-operate equipment, such as Hi-8 or S-VHS in the field, and then transfer, or "bump-up," to higher quality final formats, such as Betacam SP tape format for editing. Some of these formats are analog. (Visual information is captured and stored as a continuously variable waveform.) Betacam Digital, D2, and other new small cameras are digital. (Visual information is converted to a stream of 1's and 0's for easy and accurate storage and processing.)

Consumer formats. These formats generally include VHS, 8mm, VideoMovie, new digital cameras, specialty cameras for surveillance, and miniature cameral for sports applications. In general, they are great for simple documentation of an event when you plan to show the raw tape to your final audience. Editing is possible, but quality will drop off fast with each "generation," or "copy of a copy." If you need many copies, consider "bumping-up" to a better format. If you are using nonlinear editing, expect to see a degraded image on the computer unless you start with a digital format.

Prosumer formats. These formats include S-VHS, 3/4 SP, and Hi-8. They are generally the "minimum" you should use for serious nonlinear editing or complex editing projects.

Common camera formats include the Beta and BetaSP (top), VHS and S-VHS (middle), and Hi-8 (bottom).

Today's Hi-8 chip cameras often produce a better image than yesteryear's "broadcast" 3/4 inch tube units, but Hi-8 tape is prone to dropouts, so minimize shuttling in editing or "bump-up" immediately. The SP version of 3/4 inch is an improvement on the old format but still is considered mostly for industrial and training use. While S-VHS is considered by some to be slightly below Hi-8 quality, both formats separate out the luminance (brightness) signal from the chrominance (color) signal – which is important during editing.

Professional format. In the rapidly exploding world of video digital applications, Betacam SP is the only analog format widely used today in the professional world. Digital formats emerged in the early 1990s, but high costs and the lack of an industry standard slowed their acceptance. Now digital cameras are also a good choice!

Beta SP composite analog is a popular professional format. Its video signal combines brightness (luminance) with all colors (chrominance) onto one cable.

Component analog Beta SP is the next step up in video quality. It carries the signal on three cables: red, green/luminance, & blue (RGB).

Digital Component Beta provides the best video quality. While the tape looks like a typical Betacam tape, it records the RGB information as a digital stream (0's and 1's) rather than as an analog waveform. If you intend to produce a top quality, highly distributed program, opt for at least Betacam SP, and digital if possible.

If you intend to edit with a nonlinear system, professional video formats give the best results, with the digital formats, naturally, being the best.

Basic field equipment

Once you have selected the best format to meet your goals and reach your audience, select your video equipment. If you are just starting in video production, or only have occasional needs, don't overlook the rent/contract option, which often includes camera operators.

You can do bare-bones field production with only a camcorder (with microphone, or mic), a videotape, and a tripod, but your quality and flexibility instantly improves by adding lights, batteries, external mics, headphones, and a portable color monitor. Important extras include reflectors, extension cords, power strips, gaffer's tape, daylight gels, an equipment cart, a wireless mic, and mic windscreens.

Camera

Features you want. Most cameras today have built-in record decks (camcorders) and, therefore, are often identified with the format of the tape used. No single camera is right for every situation, but there are a few features you probably will want, regardless of the format you select: a zoom lens (at least 8:1), a manual/automatic iris option, one-button white balance, macro focus options, and a built-in mic.

Chip, or tubeless, and digital cameras are fairly standard. They produce excellent color, even in low light, and don't leave a light trail when crossing bright spots, such as jewelry, chrome, or the sun.

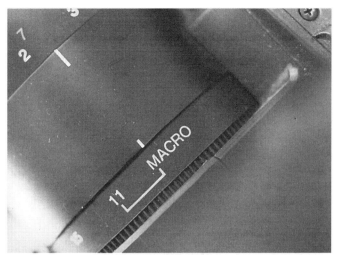

Different camera features meet various needs. Macro focus lenses (top) are helpful, while autofocus (bottom) can cause problems.

Desirable features include: external mic jacks (2-4 jacks are ideal), audio meters, battery-level readout, neutral density filter (for use in bright sun), adjustable shutter speed (ideal for slow-motion playback editing), fast lens (opens lens very wide for low light situations), gain control (boosts video brightness for low light), and sun shade. Some cameras also will accept high quality 35mm still camera lenses.

Features to avoid. Some features on consumer cameras are more gimmicks than real quality improvements. Instead of in-camera titling or fade to black, opt for better resolution or a faster lens.

Automatic focus may seem logical but it often produces distracting video. Because it focuses on the closest object, anything passing in front of the lens (a blowing leaf or a passing person) will trigger the focus control and leave your main subject out of focus. If you buy this feature, be sure you can override it.

Extremely small, hand-sized cameras create a problem with camera movement. The lighter the camera, the more likely it is to produce "earthquake" video. "Palm" cameras, which don't

All videotape formats have some form of record guard to protect previously recorded material from being erased.

A Steady Bag (a bag filled with beans or styrofoam balls) allows the camera person to produce a steady shot at unusual angles, without a tripod.

rest on the shoulder, are the worst offenders. Likewise, color viewfinders seem ideal but are harder to focus and don't reproduce true color anyway. Professional cameras have black-and-white viewfinders.

Videotape

Tape quality. Never economize on tape quality in your camcorder. The image will never be better than the quality of the tape you use in the field. Spending a few extra cents in professional quality is a small investment compared to the time and energy required for field production.

Don't use slow speeds (extra long play) or old tapes when recording raw field footage. Videotape takes a real pounding during recording because the sharp video heads contact it 30 times per second. Slow speed recording or "extended play" decreases quality and some edit playback units rejects it. Also, avoid extended-play (eight hour VHS) tapes because they are much thinner and will not stand up to the shuttling and pauses required during editing. Instead, use short field tapes, 15 to 30 minute tapes, if possible.

Tape labels and guards. It's surprising how many people spend hours recording a tape and then get too busy to label it. An unmarked tape is generally a lost or rerecorded tape. Get in the habit of labeling your tapes *before* you start recording. When you finish recording, break the record tab out of the back of the tape case to protect it from being rerecorded.

Tripods

A tripod is one of the easiest ways to improve your video quality. It stabilizes your picture and decreases your fatigue. Buy a tripod with a maximum weight capacity well above the weight of your camera. Pushing the top of the weight capacity chart wears your tripod prematurely, probably produces jerky camera movements, and endangers your camera if it collapses under the weight.

Look for quick camera attachment and easy-tilt (up and down) and pan (side to side) controls. A fluid head makes the smoothest camera moves and will pay off in the long run. Friction heads may seem smooth at first, but will get more jerky as dirt and sand enter the head and parts wear down. Leg extensions should adjust and lock easily. (Cranking camera elevators should only be used on the smallest of cameras.)

Once you've purchased a quality tripod, use it! Even though it takes longer to set up than a hand-held shot, it will give your production a stable, professional look. (Before moving your tripod, take a look around and see if there are any additional shots you can get from this location. Look for tiny details that will make interesting close-ups and cut-aways.)

If possible, add options, such as a bubble balance, leg spreaders, and a carrying strap. You also can purchase lightweight camera pillows, or "steady bags," for quick or specialty shots; place the steady bag on a car, a desk, or a fencepost, and then settle the camera into the bag so it will not move much.

Lights

There are basically five common sources of light: the sun, fluorescent, incandescent, tungsten, and halogen. Each of these

Type	Common Use	Color	Color Temp.
Incandescent	Household Light	Red/Yellow	~2,800 K
Halogen	Video Light	Yellow	~3,200 K
Fluorescent	Household Light	Greenish	~4,500 K
Sunlight	Outdoor Light	Bluish	~6,500 K

Light types and color temperature

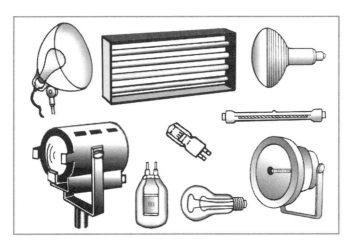

Most video productions are improved by the use of professional or special video lights.

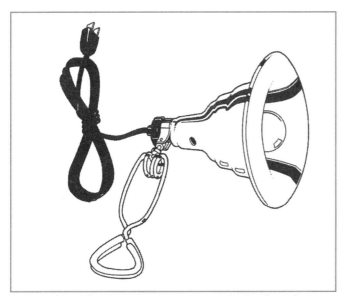

Inexpensive Light. You can use an extremely simple and inexpensive light if you buy a special videolight bulb — ANSI# EST, 500 watt — available from a photography-supply store. Use a simple clamp-anywhere socket from the hardware store.

light sources has a different "color temperature" and different uses (see "Lighting techniques" in *Field production*).

Incandescent and fluorescent lighting is usually "free" because in the form of a common household and office lights. They are usually not considered "video lighting" but can be used as "available light" for simple projects. (Be sure to adjust or white balance the camera for these light sources and don't mix them with any other types of light.)

Tungsten-halogen lights are extremely powerful and highly efficient lights that maintain a steady, bright light source that is ideal for video production. These lights can get extremely hot and must be handled with care. Video lights come in several different styles and price ranges.

Hard lights are the most typical. They use a bare bulb, and are available in flood and spot styles. These lights can quickly

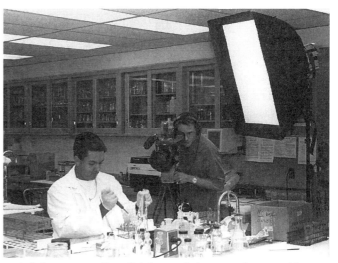

Soft lights are excellent lighting tools because they provide even illumination without casting harsh shadows.

help light an area but can create harsh shadows and an unnatural look.

Soft-light units, in contrast, usually cover the bulbs with some sort of diffusion material and produce fewer shadows. They are more comfortable for the talent and better for general

Video field equipment often includes special light holders, called grips. These tools can hold lights on dropped ceilings, walls, bars, and light stands. Sand bags hanging from light stands can stabilize lights.

use. However, they are more expensive than hard lights and illuminate a smaller area.

A lighting kit should include several key items for support, diffusion, color correction, and reflection. Light stands are the most common type of support. However, simple support items, such as a putty knife with a spud or a butterfly, or C-clamp, are lightweight and will aid in hanging lights quickly. Sandbags can increase stand stability by adding weight to the bottom of a stand.

You can change the characteristics of a light by using a colored gel to correct color temperature or add accent colors, a diffuser (such as spun glass or a glass filter) to soften the light, or a scrim (a piece of wire mesh) to decrease the overall light intensity.

Batteries

There are three kinds of batteries: lead-acid, Ni-Cd, and lithium. They vary widely in cost, charge capacity, weight, and the amount of care required.

Lead-acid gel batteries, for example, should be recharged immediately after each use and should never be allowed to completely run down. In contrast, Ni-Cd batteries should not be stored charged, and should always be drained completely before they are recharged.

Recharging undrained batteries can decrease the amount of power available. Some battery chargers automatically drain the battery before charging.

Ni-Cd batteries can build up a memory quickly of the last use. This means that if you recharge it after only 10 minutes of use for a time or two, do not be surprised if, just when you need a 30-minute battery, you get only 10 minutes. To correct this problem, drain repeatedly and recharge.

Lithium batteries are expensive, non-rechargeable, but ideal for harsh, remote environments. They are not affected by heat or cold and have a longer shelf life than other batteries.

Microphones

Unfortunately, sound is usually an afterthought in video productions. After the camera person has spent so much time with the video equipment, it is sad how often tapes are virtually unusable because of poor sound. *Always carry headphones in the field and constantly monitor the sound.*

There are two kinds of microphones – omnidirectional and unidirectional – each with its own uses.

Omnidirectional microphones picks up sounds from all directions at all times. It is usually the type built into video recorders and used in lavalier mics. While it is great for group discussions, it also can pick up a lot of undesirable, distracting

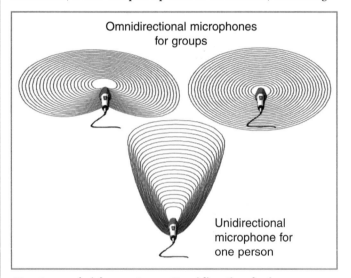

Two types of pickup patterns: Omnidirectional mics are great for groups, while unidirectional mics work best for one person.

It takes only a few seconds to hide a mic cord under clothes, and makes a big difference in the professional look of your video program.

afford. Cheap wireless mics record irritating, metallic sound and are more exposed to interferences.

Equipment care

Ordinary dust, brute force, and simple neglect are probably the three worst enemies of the video camera, recorder, and tapes. Video equipment is designed to operate smoothly and reliably when cared for in a reasonable way.

Dust. Protect the equipment from dust by transporting it in bags and storing the bags in cabinets. The video camera should be sealed, preferably in a foam-lined case. Use a haze or a UV filter to protect the lens from dust and possible scratches from the lens-cleaning process. Instead, clean the filter often by first blowing away all dust, then wiping with a clean, lintless cloth. Never use facial tissue or paper designed to clean eyeglasses; both can scratch. Photographic lens cleaner will work fine.

Even a tiny particle of dust can cause big problems inside your recorder. Cigarette smoke is especially bad, and the damage caused by a spilled drink onto a tape deck could end your production. Therefore, be a stickler for a clean environment for your recorder.

Follow the instruction booklet when cleaning and maintaining the recorder. Head cleaning tapes work by means of a mildly abrasive material. Therefore, it is unadvisable to use a cleaning tape in day-to-day machine use.

Keep all video equipment away from excessive heat or cold during transportation, operation, and storage. Never let the equipment get wet. If it does get wet, have it checked by a repairman before attempting to use it again.

Tape. After all the time invested in field recording, your raw tapes are like "gold on a reel." Protect your investment. Store the videocassettes standing on end in its case with the rewound section down. Storing the tapes flat can damage the edge of the tapes.

Avoid humid or excessively cold storage areas. The plastic cassette will warp at 130 F, and tape becomes unstable at 160 F. Unfortunately, these temperatures are not uncommon inside a parked car on a hot summer day. Cold temperatures cause the tape to contract at different rates on the hub. In addition, extremely cold tapes can pick up moisture when brought into a warm room and sweat much like a glass of iced tea.

When a tape has been in a questionable storage area, allow it to return to room temperature before using it in any machine. Also, be sure to store tapes away from any strong magnetic fields, including large audio speakers.

Mics. Mics should be stored and transported in padded cases. Be extremely careful with the mic cord to prevent kinks and breaks. Wrap the cords in a loose coil and keep them clean.

Always make a test run with your microphone, especially if it requires batteries. If the last user left the microphone switch on, you will probably need new batteries. If the microphone sounds weak or cracks, you may have a broken cable, damaged

Common microphone styles include (Clockwise, starting at top) shotgun, lav, hand-held, camera mikes.

noise from traffic, motors, and unrelated conversations.

A unidirectional microphone, on the other hand, picks up sound only within a very narrow range and must be pointed directly at the speaker. It also rejects other sounds if not pointed in their direction. This can work to your advantage in noisy locations. Most hand-held mics are unidirectional mics, which work well for individual speakers who can stand close to the microphone.

Regardless of the mic you select, *Always get it as close as possible to the talent.* Lav mics should be neatly placed about one hand's stretch from the talent's mouth. Hide the mic only if you are sure you don't hear fabric rub. Otherwise, place it neatly on the tie or collar and dress (hide) the cable.

You can improve your audio quality with a wind screen to cut out wind noise outdoors. If you need to deaden a "live" room (sounds seem to bounce off near-by hard surfaces), use sound baffles or even light reflectors on stands.

A "fish pole" allows a "hand-held" mic to be moved extremely close to the talent (just outside the video frame) without the noise or distraction of hand holding. If your talent needs to move freely, invest in the best quality wireless mic you can microphone, or a microphone with the wrong impedance. Do not start the shooting session until you correct the problem.

Special problems. Extreme heat, cold, humidity, and static electricity also hurt video quality. When taping outdoors in direct sun, shade your equipment. Static electricity, whether from a storm cloud passing overhead or from a nearby coiled electrical cord, can also temporarily cause equipment malfunction or audio interference.

Field production

If you are a crew of one, you will do all of the jobs yourself and have the advantage of knowing they are done exactly the way you want them done. As you go through the production, you can continuously ask yourself, "Is this technique, viewpoint, or camera angle the best I can use to communicate with my audience?" You can see the picture yourself in the viewfinder to be sure that there is nothing to distract the viewer's eye. Last-minute changes will not upset the production crew because *you* are the crew!

If you are leading a crew of two or more into the field for video taping, planning becomes increasingly important. Every minute you waste fixing problems is multiplied by the number of the people serving as crew and talent. Read this section carefully.

Work with equipment in your office to become familiar with it *before* you go into the field. An hour of testing in your office can save days of work in the field.

Preparing for field production. The heart of video production is the equipment. If it doesn't work, you have no "final video production." Therefore, the cardinal rule is to make sure all the video equipment is working *before* you go out in the field. Don't assume things will work! Don't trust that cable or hope the mic batteries are working. Test them.

Drop the batteries in, connect the mic and recorder, fire up the lights, walk around in front of the camera and sing a silly song, recite a poem, or practice your lines. Then watch the tape

back on a color monitor. The five minutes invested in a test can save you hours in the field and a lifetime of embarrassment.

When you arrive. You should arrive at the location in plenty of time to set up your equipment, including lights, sound, and props, and do a run through. Remember, one advantage of videotape is that you do not have to wait for film processing to see the results. Therefore, always use a video monitor on location to help set up your lights and test camera angles before you roll any tape.

The key to good location production is to *control your environment.* Take as much control as possible of the light, noise, and traffic patterns around your location. When you arrive, stake out plenty of area for your equipment and start with the set-up you planned during your site survey.

Lighting technique

Lighting is one of the most important factors in the overall quality of your production. Although many manufacturers claim their equipment can make acceptable video in low-light situations, "acceptable" may not be always "good enough."

Even when your camera says you have "enough light," it is evaluating the overall scene, not your subject. If the talent is standing in front of a bright wall or window, the camera will say you have enough light, but your main subject could be too dark to see.

Even if the "available light" (light naturally occurring in a location) is bright enough to light a scene, it may not be always the type of light you want. Although overhead fluorescent lights are an inexpensive way to illuminate an office, they are not an attractive way to light faces. Locations often have a mixture of types of lights, such as incandescent, halogen, or fluorescent, and are impossible to color balance. In most cases, take enough lighting gear to light a scene without relying on any room lights.

Indoor lighting

While you can use reflected sunlight to illuminate an indoor location, indoor lighting often will involve artificial lights. Most artificial lights are a different "color temperature" than daylight

By using a reflector, outdoor light from a window can be reflected onto the dark side of the speaker's face, providing smooth daylight lighting for the entire scene.

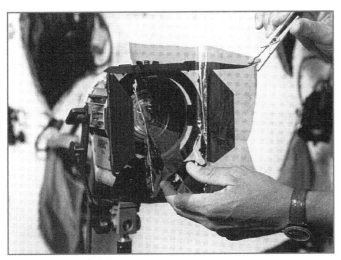

Cover lights with a blue gel when mixing them with daylight.

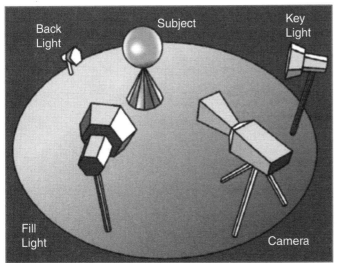

The key light, located on one side, casts the most light. The fill, located on the other side, softens harsh shadows. The back light points at the back of the head and separates the subject from the background.

and will give the subject a different color hue. (See color temperature chart in Equipment section.) If you *do* have to mix artificial lights with daylight, use daylight-correcting blue gels to make the light match the daylight.

It is often best to totally block out the daylight so you can have complete control of the lighting. Close curtains, shades, or blinds.

Basic lighting usually consists of at least three lights, arranged to give good, general illumination. The "key" light is the brightest light and is located to one side of the camera, facing the subject. The "fill" light cuts the shadows created by the first light and evens out the illumination on the face. While these two lights provide good lighting to the subject's face, the picture will look rather flat without a "back" light to separate the subject from the background. This third light also softens the shadows created by the first two lights.

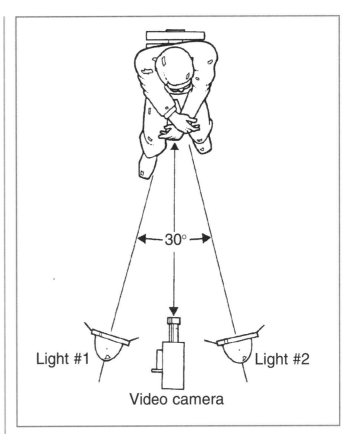

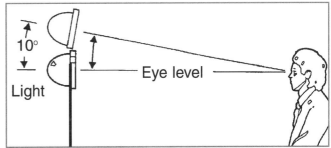

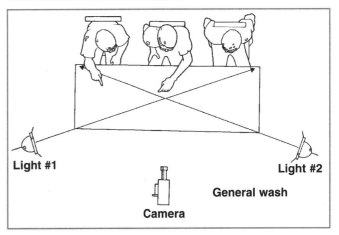

While a great deal of lighting creativity is possible, standard lighting procedures call for lights to be at least 30 degrees apart (top) and at least 10 degrees above eye level (middle). Simple lighting for large groups would involve a general "washing" of the entire scene by bright lights (bottom).

Since video is immediate, you can look at the results of your lighting during set-up and make changes until it is right. Set up the camera and analyze the scene carefully in the viewfinder or a monitor. Don't trust your eye to determine what looks good on the screen. Your camera will "see" the same scene differently, especially in terms of color temperature and therefore color hue.

A shiny object in the camera's view will distract from your subject, so move it or cover it with non-reflective tape. If you get a reflection from the glass on a picture, prop either the top or bottom of the picture away from the wall with a balled piece of newspaper. The new angle of the glass should show no glare yet look normal on the television.

Remember that lighting always involves both light and shadows. As you light your production, look at the shadows, especially on faces. Remember that shadows work like a seesaw: raising the light source moves the shadow downward and moving the light to one side causes the shadow to move in the opposite direction.

As a general guideline, the shadow at the side of the nose should not touch the cheekbone, and shadows around the eyes should never obscure the eyes. Shadows under the chin should not fall on the collar. If there is a shadow of the body on the background, the body and the shadow always should overlap.

Outdoor lighting

If you are shooting outdoors, you will have unique lighting problems there as well. One of the easiest lighting conditions for outdoor shooting is a bright but hazy, or overcast, day because there are few shadows and your talent will not squint.

In contrast, bright sun will give you brighter and more vivid colors, but you will have shadows to contend with. In this case, position the talent so the sun falls on one side of the face as a strong fill light. This will, of course, cause strong shadows on the non-sun side of the face. You can fill in these shadows with reflectors.

Without a reflector (top), shadows on the face can be harsh and distracting. By adding a reflector (bottom), the shadow is deminished yet still present, providing a natural appearance.

In bright sunlight, a reflector should be used to soften shadows on the face, especially if the speaker is wearing a hat.

You can make a reflector out of a wide variety of materials, but foam core is probably the best. This material, available from art-supply stores, is lightweight foam with white paper covering both sides. You also can use commercial flexible reflectors or flexfills with pebbled surfaces to soften the reflected light. Use an assistant or a reflector stand to position the reflector in front of the talent, usually low enough to reflect light into the face.

Most reflectors have one white side and the other, a highly reflective, pebbled silver or gold. The silver provides the brightest reflected light to fill in harsh shadows but can make talent so uncomfortable they may squint. The gold reflector is ideal for brightening faces of talent with dark skin tones. Minimize the harshness of both metallic reflectors by "feathering" the light onto the face, providing only the minimum acceptable instead of a "full blast!"

If you have a long setup in extremely bright sun or other uncomfortable conditions, keep your talent in the shade and use a "stand-in" for set-up. Only when everything is ready to roll, should you bring the talent onto the set.

General equipment setup

Most small video productions operate with only one camera in the field, taping a program that will be edited in a studio after the location taping. If you plan to show the tape just as it comes out of the camera (with no editing), see the sidebar on in-camera editing techniques. If you plan to use two cameras at once on location, see the sidebar on two camera productions. For the rest of this discussion, it will be assumed that you are using one camera and will be editing the production late (for details on specific equipment, see the *Basic field equipment* section).

Camera techniques

Because the camera is the viewer's window into the action, the camera operator must know what the viewer will want to see and present it in an interesting way. The camera operator's moves should be smooth and steady to avoid any distracting elements.

Setup in outdoor settings

If possible, place the speaker in an environment related to the topic. If appropriate, move the talent outdoors. An agricultural economist can stand near an empty corral as he talks about low beef prices and hard times. Get on top of a building overlooking a busy street with the community-development specialist as she talks about community growth. Adjust your camera so you can see the busy city in the background and perhaps go to some cutaways of the community in post-production.

In fact, for long talking segments, consider having the speaker *do* something quiet and relaxing while talking. An elderly woman may quilt as she talks about the history of agriculture in her valley A Native American may create a handcraft or a shop owner may stock shelves at they talk. These natural settings often relax the speaker and provide context and visual interest to your scene.

Hints on in-camera editing

If you do not plan to edit, but will use the tape exactly as it comes out of the camera, you should use an "in-camera" editing technique. Try this:

- Practice with your equipment extensively before the production.

- Understand how much the camera backspaces for a pause and what happens when you hit stop instead of record/pause.

- Look for a "record lock" feature to allow you to disconnect power and move the machine without causing a glitch (a visible video interruption) in the tape.

Hints on two-camera productions

Using two cameras on location can drastically reduce the time in the field, especially if you follow these hints:

- Select cameras that are nearly alike and produce a very similar picture.

- Camera One generally is locked on a tripod for the general, or cover, shot. This camera rarely will change camera angles or zoom in for a close-up.

- Camera Two shoots from a slightly different angle and always remains zoomed in for close-ups.

- Each camera records the video. Cameras are stopped and started in sequence.

A good field unit includes a tripod for stability, a field monitor, for scene set-up and instant playback, and batteries for increased mobility.

One common activity is a driving-and-talk scene. Here, the camera person sits sideways or backwards in the seat and tapes the speaker, who is driving. (Follow seat-belt laws and safety considerations.) Because the outdoor background will be so much brighter than the face of the driver, you may want to position the camera so the background is mostly the car. If you have a battery powered "eye light" you also can balance it for daylight and add extra light to the talent's face.

Set-up in indoor settings

If you must use an indoor studio, and your talent will be seated, select the chairs carefully. A narrow, firm armchair will keep the talent from fidgeting or wiggling. The talent never should be placed in a chair that swivels, rolls, or squeaks! In spite of all warnings, the talent soon will begin to turn in the chair and roll on the wheels. Not only is this distracting to the viewer, it also makes it almost impossible to keep the speaker properly composed and in focus.

A high stool which allows the talent to put one foot on a rung of the stool and the other on the floor can be especially attractive for a short or overweight speaker. Using a stool often makes the talent seem more alert, vibrant, and interesting.

In either case, turn the chair or stool slightly to the side so the speaker must turn to face the camera. This angle will be unnoticeable to the audience, but will help the talent look slimmer and more alert.

Props and backgrounds. If possible, place the chair in front of an unpatterned drape with proper back lighting. Use simple but attractive set additions, such as green plants, an attractive lamp, or a few books. Be careful of set distractions. Spray shiny chrome with dulling spray or hair spray.

When possible, add a visually-interesting, three-dimensional prop to your educational program. Use the real thing or a working model for interesting close-ups. Again, simplicity is the secret.

Props make the production scene more interesting, but too many props will cause it to appear cluttered. Because video allows you to review and analyze the scene immediately, always record a sample shot to check for distracting glares.

Also consider a foreground prop. These make especially strong statements, so make sure they are appropriate for the message. On the other hand, they add extra depth to your scene and help create a dynamic visual.

Camera settings and controls

Every video production uses four basic camera settings: color temperature, white balance, focus, and iris opening.

Color Temperature. The human eye usually does not notice subtle changes in colors when viewed in various lighting conditions, but they happen. The video camera does not have a brain to compensate automatically for these changes, so you will have to think for it. This usually involves two controls: color temperature and white balance.

All cameras provide some techniques for changing the "color temperatures" of the light. Consumer cameras often use small images of a sun or a light bulb, while professional equipment uses the actual degree temperature of the light.

The color temperature adjustment is a set of filters dialed into place within the lens. Professional camera settings show the filter number, while consumer cameras usually have only a simple knob with pictures of a light bulb, fluorescent light, and the sun.

White Balance. Once you tell the camera basically what kind of light it is seeing, it is ready for a fine control. To do this, zoom in on a piece of white paper (or anything white). Activate the white balance control, which is usually a button you push for two seconds. Once the camera knows what white looks like under that lighting condition, it knows how to adjust for all the other colors.

Most cameras require a "white balance" before taping begins to ensure the best color hues in the picture.

Remember that the camera must be readjusted for both color temperature and white balance every time you change from one lighting situation to another, such as from outdoors to indoors.

Focus. Many camera operators have difficulty focusing the camera. Too often the picture will look sharp and clear until you zoom into a fuzzy close-up. This is because you did not focus on the close-up before you started.

In order to focus properly, always zoom in as close as you can, regardless of how far you plan to zoom out for your final shot. Focus on this close-up shot, and then zoom out to compose the picture. Remember, if your subject moves closer to the camera after the tape has started to roll, the close-up will no longer be in focus.

Iris Opening. Most cameras have an automatic iris opening to allow the correct amount of light into the lens. Under normal circumstances, this will be adequate. But in backlit or highly contrasting light conditions, you may need to manually adjust the lens opening.

Video cameras have less tolerance for high contrast lighting than either the human eye or photographic film, and therefore the video will not reveal the detail you see under these conditions. (You can estimate a video's tonal range by squinting your eyes to look at a scene.) If you "stop down" by decreasing the aperture, you will provide more detail in bright areas but lose everything in the shadow. If you open up by increasing the aperture, you increase detail in dark areas but overexpose bright areas (and maybe make them too bright for good video editing). Therefore, it's best simply to move your subject, when possible, to more even light.

Camera Moves

A stationary camera can make three basic in-camera moves: zoom, pan, and tilt. A moving camera (called tracking shots) involves three basic shots: walking, dolly, and crane.

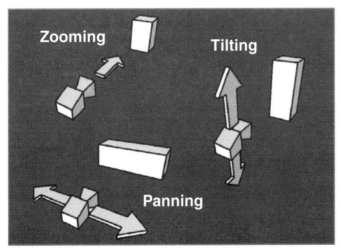

Samples of camera moves

Zooming. A sure sign of an amateur is lots of camera zooms. Zooms can be a powerful tool if used correctly, but too much is just too much! Do not zoom unless you have a very good reason. Simply think of the zoom control as a smooth way

to set up your initial shot.

If you need a close-up, try to plan a pause in the tape and set up while the tape is not recording, then take the camera off pause and cue your talent to resume the demonstration. Never attempt a close-up without a tripod.

Tilting. This move involves the tripod head which tips the camera up or down. It helps bring action to a static shot and fit tall objects, such as buildings, into the shot. Use it to call attention to your subject or to follow the scene's movement.

Panning. This tripod head movement is from side to side and is used in many situations. Most frequently, it allows coverage of a wide scene, such as a mountain expanse or a room full of people. It allows the viewer to see a wide area in full detail ,by revealing a little at a time.

Walking. For extra impact, try a "wheelchair shot," where the camera person and a relaxed, confident guest, but can add real variety to your program. In the walk-and-talk, the camera person walks backwards as the guest walks forward slowly, talking directly into the camera lens. (It is also effective with two people walking together and talking.) Position another person behind the camera person to guide and protect the camera person, who is walking backwards. To add extra smoothness to your shot, consider using a wheelchair for the camera person or a pickup truck's tailgate, while the talent walks down a driveway.

A "wheel chair shot" or "walk-and-talk", requires an experienced camera person and a relaxed, confident guest but can add real variety to your program.

Dolly. If you put the camera and operator on a moving platform the shot becomes a "dolly" shot. Professionals often use large moving wagons called doorway dollys pushed or pulled by a camera assistant (called a grip). Instead of renting an expensive dolly, however, borrow a wheelchair. The arm rests will help stabilize the camera and the cushioned tires will make the movement smooth.

Crane or Pedestal. When the entire camera moves up and down, not just a head tilt, the move is called a crane or a pedestal. These shots add impact to otherwise static shots, such as shots of buildings, orchards, and landscapes.

Renting a crane is expensive, but if you plan carefully, you can get a "lift" in a cherry picker from the university physical plant department or the electric or telephone company. You also can rent a camera-only crane that allows the operator to watch the scene by television and operate the controls remotely.

A shot from a helicopter, a hot-air balloon, or an airplane is another type of crane shot. Camera movement and vibrations are a real problem under these circumstances, however, so select a high shutter speed and edit with slow motion to minimize the distraction.

Composition

Good video producers also will provide a variety of scenes. Often you will want to start with an *"establishing,"* or *cover shot*. These help "place" the viewer, and give a general understanding of the setting where the action is taking place.

As the program developer, use a combination of several different angles and points of view. One of the strengths of video is that each viewer can have a front row seat. Therefore, make regular use of close-ups.

Subject placement. Visuals are the heart of video. There is little that will have a greater impact on the final appearance of your tape than the composition or arrangement of the subjects within the screen. The basics of composition used in still photography apply to television as well. (Refer to the composition section of "Photography," Chapter 7, for an in-depth discussion of composition.)

When composing the overall scene, remember the viewer's eye naturally moves toward the biggest, brightest, or most colorful object on the screen. Consider this as you "paint" your video picture and compose elements to support your message. Minor players or props in your video will become distractions if

Composition "Rule of Thirds"

they are dressed more colorfully, lit more brightly, or have a larger image size in the screen than the main subject.

Classic rules of photography composition advocate the "Rule of Thirds," which divides the screen into thirds both horizontally and vertically. The main subject then is placed on one of the intersections of these lines. (This is simply a rough beginning point for composition and not an absolute rule.)

Traditionally, this means leaving space above people's heads in normal close-ups, medium, and long shots. In most cases, don't have the subject's head touching or cut off by the top of the screen.

For television shots, remember that what you see is *not* what you get. Video systems enlarge the image slightly to be sure the television screen is filled, and therefore, they cut off the edges of the image. Leave a "safe zone" around the edge of your picture.

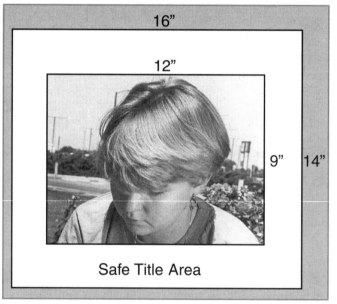

Video safe zone on slides

Special placement. Of course, rules are made to be broken, and showing only parts of a person's face or an object can create extremely strong images if cut correctly. The secret is to avoid cutting the face on a natural cut-off line such as the eyes, mouth, chin, waist, hemline, or knees. Instead, try to cut the close-up of your subject either inside or outside of this imaginary natural cut-off line.

The placement of your subject and the camera angle can convey powerful messages to your audience. For example, to convey a sense of authority for a dean or subject-matter specialist, use a camera angle that places the subject slightly above the horizon, looking slightly down on the camera. On the other hand, use caution when the background for your subject is an overcast sky. Often skies are so brightly lit that the camera's iris opening is so small the face becomes too dark to see. Therefore, move the authority figure to a location in the shade, in a building, or near landscaping, where the sky is not in the shot.

The distant shot (called the cover shot) sets the scene. The medium shot shows most of the action. The close-up shot gives the audience all the details.

Image movement. Video images usually move. It is important to place the dynamic subject in the screen to give room for action or movement. This means that talent should usually be looking into the picture. Movement should go toward the center instead of away from the center. As the subject moves, the camera usually anticipates the action and gives the subject plenty of room to move into the screen. The viewer wants to know where the subject is going, not where it has been. Also remember to consider the direction of movement when you are moving the camera around a static subject.

Shot variety. Plan for a strong mix of long, medium, and close-up shots. Look for unusual camera angles to tell your story. Extremely low or extremely high camera angles can produce an unusual and striking scene. Experiment with wide shots of the entire room, medium shots which include two people, close-ups, which usually take in only the head and shoulders, and extreme close-ups, which show only part of the face for dramatic impact.

While the zoom can provide additional motion, do not overuse the technique. Zooms to an extreme close-up should

never be attempted with a hand-held camera. In general, a tripod improves the shot. If you hand-hold, try to keep the camera lens zoomed all the way out (using the wide angle part of the lens).

Zooms need to be motivated. A zoom-in should reveal something of importance that is small and doesn't have the needed significance in a wider shot. In contrast, a zoom-out should reveal something of importance that could not be seen in the screen's existing frame. A cut to a close-up (CU) or wide shot can be substituted for a zoom, but its effect is more immediate. A zoom allows you to manipulate the pacing of the video.

Depth of the scene. Because television is a two-dimensional medium, it is important to work to create the illusion of depth by including elements in both the foreground and background of the scene. Include tree branches, fences, or furniture in front of the subject to give the scene depth.

Brightly lit subjects in strong colors seem closer to the viewer than dimly lit, less saturated colors. Also remember that zooming in, or using the narrow angle portion of the lens, reduces the illusion of a three-dimensional scene. Zooming out, using a wide-angle portion of the lens, seems to exaggerate depth.

Hints to the talent

Clothing. In general, the talent should wear comfortable clothing. Television has a tendency to add a few extra pounds to the talent, so aim for slim-fitting clothes instead of a heavy, horizontally-striped suit. Avoid clothing with sharp contrasts, such as a dark suit with a bright background. Lighten a dark suit with a pastel shirt. Stay away from bright plaids, busy flower patterns, or herringbone fabrics. These will create a "buzzing" or moray pattern at times.

At all times, your clothing should look appropriate for the subject you are discussing or demonstrating. You will look very uncomfortable and unbelievable if you try to plant a garden or spray cattle in a suit.

In general, it is best not to wear solid white, black, or navy, which sometimes appears as black on the screen. Instead, wear medium blue, charcoal gray, and greens. Reds can stand out too much and be badly distorted. On the other hand, pinks, oranges, yellows, and other warm tones have a more calming effect and are good for video work.

For a formal presentation, men may select a blue or gray suit with a conservative pattern in the tie. In general, avoid vests because they make you look too formal.

Women who dress conservatively should be careful not to appear stuffy. Wear pearls, a simple necklace, or a gold chain. Avoid long, dangling earrings which could distract. Excessive jewelry reflects the light into the camera. This includes shiny wristwatches, earrings, tie clasps, or bright buttons. While dulling spray can tone down flashy jewelry, the talent may object.

Men may need a touch of face powder to eliminate shiny spots on the face or head. Makeup also can help cover a "five o'clock shadow," which often looks blueish on TV.

Make-up. Although better cameras and lighting conditions have done away with much of the need for makeup on the television set, it still can be helpful to men and women alike. Simple face powder can eliminate distracting shiny spots on a face or balding head.

Men should shave immediately before a television appearance. A blade instead of an electric shaver is preferable. The television camera has the tendency to accentuate any hint of a five o'clock shadow and gives the beard a blueish tint. Men with heavy beards may want to use a very light powder or make-up base to overcome this blueish cast.

A woman's normal make-up probably will be acceptable on television. However, dark reds or maroons have a tendency to turn blue-red and look harsh in a television camera. If you have a light complexion or have blonde eyebrows, you may wish to use a slightly darker make-up and darken the eyebrows.

Well-groomed hands are especially important for television work because the camera often will focus extremely close on the hands. Be sure your nails are clipped to a medium length and there are no chips in the polish. If needed, use make-up on your hands as well to give them a smooth appearance.

Glasses and hats. Anything that hides the face or causes distractions is a problem. Glasses almost always reflect lights

and perhaps even a view of the camera! If simply removing the glasses is not an option, reposition the lights and camera to remove reflections, or ask the talent to lift the ear pieces above the ears and tilt the glasses downward. While this may feel strange, it can look normal and will remove most of the reflections. Avoid sunglasses or light-sensitive dark glasses.

Hats that cannot be removed should be pushed back enough to move shadows above the eyes. You also might try an eye light or reflected light directly onto the talent's face to knock out shadows.

Posture. Research has shown that 60 percent of the audience's perception of the talent comes from non-verbal body lang-uage. Because television is such a close-up media, any non-verbal cues will be exaggerated greatly. Casually reclining in a chair, for example, could be interpreted as laziness and disinterest in the subject. Therefore, always lean slightly forward in your chair to show involvement and interest.

Make a conscious effort to keep eye-to-eye contact with the interviewer. If you are speaking directly to the television audience, look directly into the camera and avoid shifting your eyes from side to side. Your eyes give the real cue to the audience as to whether you are trustworthy, enthusiastic, and self-assured. No physical gesture is more powerful than the way you use your eyes.

In an interview situation, always be aware that the camera could come on you at any time, so always look involved and interested. Keep your eyes from roaming. Especially beware of glancing at side-view cameras or monitors out of the corner of your eye.

Television performance mindset

Initially, performing on television may be one of the most difficult and, at times, discouraging of all public presentations. The smallest distracting mannerism is accentuated, and because there is no immediate feedback from the audience, it is difficult to be enthusiastic.

Research has shown that the talent's attitude toward the opportunity to communicate by television will make the major difference in the way he or she is perceived by the audience. Confident, flexible, and apparently-relaxed speakers communicate much more effectively on television than self-conscious, timid, and rigid talent.

The best way to improve television appearance is for the talent to critically analyze a practice videotape for body language, eye contact, sound of voice, and gestures.

Field production technique
Overview

Shortly after you arrive on location and before you start setting up too much of your equipment, assemble everyone involved for a general overview of the production. If *you* are the only "crew member," still go through these steps to give yourself and the talent an overview of the day.

Review the shot sheet, the lighting and camera layout you created during pre-production. Also be sure you have the complete script and the props list. With a crew, review job assignments and encourage the talent to practice lines and arrange props while the lights and camera are set up according to the master plan.

Walk through

When most of the equipment and props are in place, get everyone's attention for a "walk through." This means your talent briefly will zip through the action of the scene. No details of the words are reviewed now, just the major motions, the props used, and talent entrances and exits.

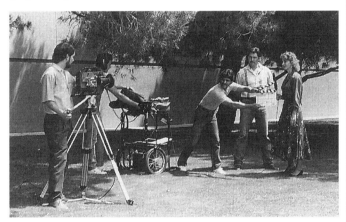

Walk throughs and run throughs help the talent and crew relax and understand what is needed — producing a more professional finished product.

Watch the action in the monitor to spot potential problems. This walk through gives everyone the overall idea so lights, cameras, and props can be placed correctly. Missing props can be noticed now and adjustments made.

Now make final adjustments to your equipment, practice camera moves, finalize the composition, and remind the talent how many times the scene will be taped, and when the action will need to stop for close-ups or to change camera angles.

Run through

Once everything is in place, you are ready for a "run through." This is another review of the action, but this time with much more detail. While the script still can be abbreviated, every action should be pantomimed with real props, if possible. The cameras follow the action, and you can check the shots on the field monitor.

Mic Check. The run through just before the taping starts is the best time to check mic levels. Ask the talent to speak in the

same tone and volume that will be used during the taping. Camera operators generally set the tape audio levels and wear headphones to listen for any background noise. If audio distractions start part way through the taping session, the production will have to be stopped to correct the problem.

Final review. Before you start the recorder, take a final, careful look at the field monitor for any possible distracting glares or video equipment accidentally left visible in the screen. Is the microphone operating properly? Is the picture carefully composed? Are the lights adjusted correctly?

If you are conducting a one-camera production, this is the time for a final review of each stop you will make in the production to go in for a close-up. Make a final review with the talent.

Roll tape

When you are ready, start the recorder but *do not* cue or signal the talent yet. Let some tape roll so you will have some "leader" to use in editing. If your camera records color bars, do it now. This will be critical later during editing. If possible, slate your production according to your field-shot sheet.

Set up a standard routine for cuing your camera and talent (see cuing routine sidebar below).

Allow the tape to roll 10 seconds before the talent starts each sequence and keep the tape rolling another 10 seconds after the talent or action has ended.

Cuing routine

Director: "Ready?" (Asking cameras/talent if they are prepared to roll.)

Camera: "Set!" (Replying that shot is set and tripod is locked or ready to move. Talent often indicate "ready" with a simple nod.)

Director: "Roll tape." (Telling cameras to start recording.)

Camera: "Tape rolling!" (Reply only after confirming that tape is moving smoothly.)

The director checks the shot in monitor, listens for background noise, looks around quickly for potential distractions. If all is ready, wait five seconds for the leader tape needed in the edit room to roll and then give the command:

Director: "Action!"

The talent begins speaking and the presentation begins.

Hint. When an interview begins, ask your talent to state his or her complete name, spelled correctly, and the job title you will need for the on-screen ID when editing. This can save hours of frustration later and will allow for one last-minute audio check before the real presentation starts.

During taping. Once you cue the talent, do not move away from your set location. In fact, everyone in the talent's view (especially if the talent is inexperienced) should stand still during the actual taping session. This usually means no spectators in the area.

Stand immediately beside or behind the tripod and make direct eye contact with the talent. Nod and give an encouraging smile (but don't say anything) to brighten the talent's delivery. It is difficult to talk into an empty lens, so the camera operator or director needs to help humanize the camera for inexperienced talent.

Working with talent. When you reach a predetermined stopping point or when a mistake occurs that cannot be corrected in editing, allow the tape to run about 10 seconds past the stopping point. If you stopped because of a talent mistake, it is especially important that you remain calm. The more tense you become each time the talent makes a mistake, the greater the likelihood that the mistakes will proliferate.

If the talent seems to stumble at the same point, stop the production, talk to the talent, offer a drink of water, and try to relax. Work to change the trouble spot by rewording or reorganizing a statement. Appearing to be relaxed and in control will actually save you production time in the long run.

The talent will be understandably curious about the results. However, unless viewing the tape will help correct the problem, do not show the talent a replay of the videotape until the scene is correct. Show the talent segments that look smooth and professional, and the chances are good that the rest of the production also will look smooth and professional.

Check list. As the day progresses, keep a careful eye on the script and shot lists. Make notes of shots you need to get at another location. From time-to-time, you also might want to rewind and review a bit of the tape to be sure the equipment, especially the microphones, all are working. One of the most important factors to consider is maintaining a smooth flow of the program during editing. This process is called continuity.

Continuity

If you break to change the camera angle, especially for a close-up, review the last camera shot before you begin recording. You want to be sure that the edit will be smooth from the long shot to the close-up. Continuity ensures similarity and harmony between takes and gives the viewer of the edited program the illusion that all the tape was shot at once without any break in the action.

If the homemaker was holding a knife in her right hand on the long shot, be sure she is holding the knife the same way on

the close-up. If you do not make a conscious effort to check continuity, you will discover too late that the knife that was in her hand in the close-up scene suddenly appeared in the rack on the long shot and that the two onions that were in the long shot magically disappeared in the close-up. Such breaks in the action jolt the viewer and break up the smoothness of the program.

Playback equipment in the field will help the continuity process. Any time you are in doubt, take the time to rewind and review the continuity.

Check to see that people are standing in the same place, wearing the same clothes, looking the same way, and holding the same items before you begin recording again. This is especially important if you tape again after several days. Be sure your talent is wearing the same clothes, hair style, and jewelry.

Line of interest. You also can have continuity problems simply by changing the location of your camera too much during a scene. Within a scene, no matter how you zoom, tilt, pan, or crane, all the subjects should stay in the same relative position to each other, going from left to right, so that the viewer is not distracted by the variety of shots.

Draw an imaginary line through the center of your scene, perpendicular to the camera's initial line of sight. This is called the "line of interest" or the "center axis," or the "180 degree rule." The problem arises when you tape from the opposite side

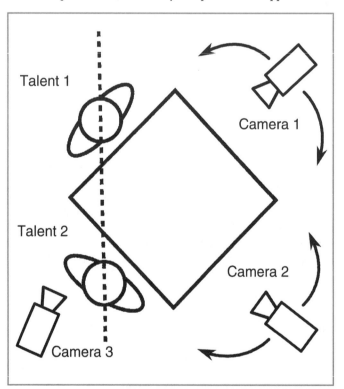

Cameras #1 and #2 can have great freedom of motion because their movements keep both people in the same relative position. However, camera #3 has crossed the "line of interest" and will record a picture with the two people flipped (left and right) from the other two cameras. This confuses the viewer.

of the scene, in which case the position of all subjects appear to flip, left to right. This is called "crossing the line of interest," and can greatly confuse the viewer. It is possible to "cross the line," but in order to do it, you need to plan carefully. Take several extra neutral shots, such as extreme close-ups of faces, or neutral shots, such as an overhead view, to break the viewer's preconceptions of how the subjects "should" be.

Plan to cut to a neutral shot during editing each time you "cross the line."

Special shots during field production

Close-ups. Television is a small-screen medium. Therefore, the more powerful shots are those that "fill the screen." They will affect your audience the most.

Close-ups need to be shot much longer than they actually will be seen in the final product. (Hopefully, if you plan to edit the tape, you have spent time watching a tape-editing session *before* your field production to understand what kind of raw footage you will need. Nothing will improve your field video quite as much as your first editing session.)

Reaction shots and cutaways. Once you have shot the overall scene and the close-ups, you may want to get some additional interesting shots to add variety to the production. These shots are called "cutaways" and "reaction shots." They include the reactions of people in the audience laughing, nodding in agreement, or listening intensely. When taping a presentation, it is especially important to get a series of "reaction shots," showing people reacting to what is said or done.

Cutaways include plaques and mementos in an office, decorations and conversation pieces in a home, animals playing, or plants growing on a farm. These shots could be extremely valuable in the editing session.

For example, if you are taping a father talking about what it is like to be a single parent, you probably will not stop an emotional section to ask him to hurry up! Yet, when you edit the program, you may find that the middle five minutes of his interview is unrelated to the theme of your program and you want to cut it out.

If you simply remove that section, it will be obvious to the viewer that you made an edit because the position of his body and head suddenly will jump or shift. This is call a "jump cut" and always should be avoided in the final edited program because it is distracting to the viewers and clearly signals that you have left something out. If you have taken cutaways in the room—perhaps a shot of toys, pictures, or the child playing—you will be able to edit the tape so the audio flows. Then you can cover the audio edit point with a video cutaway.

Wild sound. Keep the mic on for all shots, even outdoor shots of scenery. These sounds are called "wild" or "nat" (natural) sounds. They are free, so always record sound even if you do not plan to use the audio as the primary sound of the tape. The wild sound might be used as background sound during editing as an audio introduction to the subject, or to smooth out breaks in the narration. Because wild sound can be such an important part of videotape, it deserves the same attention to good fidelity, volume, and freedom from distortion.

Sometimes it helps to record ambient sound of the room or environment in which you are taping (no talking or obvious noises). A one minute, continuous track of this ambient sound can help smooth out variations in your audio when you record dialogue at different times.

For example, if you are in a room where the building's cooling system turns off and on, you may have a big variation in your sound track. By adding the ambient sound track in post-production, you can give the sound consistency.

Note: digital-audio work-stations will allow you to remove distracting sounds and "sweeten" the soundtrack.

Special types of presentations

The talking head. Talking head programs are exactly what the name implies: a shot of a person talking with little or no extra video to illustrate, demonstrate, or animate the message. These programs are common for interview and lecture programs.

While some subjects and speakers may be interesting enough to hold a viewer's attention simply by opening their mouths and speaking, most speakers communicate better if you add other visuals. If visuals will not enhance the message, then why not use only an audiotape?

Sometimes there is no choice but to do a "talking head" program. Maybe time is truly short, and you must record and distribute emergency information. Maybe you are dealing with an administrator or busy talent who only has time for one take. To make the best of your situation, start with an attractive set and maximize the basics of good quality – good sound, lighting, and camera work.

Direct camera address. If the lecturer plans to talk directly to the viewer, stress the importance of looking directly into the camera during the entire production. If the talent must look away, looking down as if scanning notes is probably best. With most talking heads, you can pull into a fairly tight close-up. If the talent continuously looks to the side of the camera, perhaps at other crew members in the room, he or she will appear shifty and untrustworthy in the close-up shot. Therefore, it is common to have the talent look slightly off camera for most of the presentation, perhaps toward another possibly invisible interviewer. This technique often is used for sound bites in news and documentaries.

Interviews. In many cases, especially with a guest who has absolutely no experience with video, an interview situation is the best. Hopefully the interviewer has had experience with the video camera and can help guide the inexperienced guest.

One advantage of the interview situation is that it gives you several options in post-production. If the answers were com-

Because video can be replayed immediately after it is shot, always take time to review the footage before the specialists, actors, or props leave the area. Check the script to be sure you have all close-ups and reaction shots and good continuity.

plete without viewers needing to hear the question, the presentation can often be edited to exclude the questions. If you do this, however, it is vital to have plenty of interesting cutaway shots of things in the room, graphics, or the reaction of the audience. These shots will assist with smooth transitions between edits. (Read Chapter 18, "Radio," for more suggestions on interviewing techniques.)

One-person presentations. If you are taping a one person presentation, position the camera slightly on a side angle of the speaker, but as close as possible to the axis of conversation between the interviewer and the subject. This will be the most engaging angle and will still allow good contact and emotion to pass between the interviewer and the subject.

Once you are ready to shoot a scene that is mostly talking, especially if it is a one-person presentation, it is best to allow the talent to present and record the entire speech from beginning to end with no cuts. Record mistakes, bobbles, and hesitations. Sometimes the first presentation is the most spontaneous, and you may be able to correct any problems in editing. In addition, once the talent knows the entire presentation is safely recorded onto video tape, retakes may be much more relaxed and smoother.

Before the talent leaves

Once you have shot the presentation to your technical satisfaction, ask the client or subject-matter specialist (who is sometimes the talent as well) to review the tape on a field monitor. Before the talent leaves, be sure there are no extra shots you need to redo.

Make a checklist of every error that needs editing. This not only will be valuable to you later, but it also will give the client and talent confidence that you will not allow the errors to appear on the final videotape.

As you review the raw footage, ask the subject-matter specialist which visuals could be added at each point. Make

arrangements to get maps, charts, and other props to add to the tape. If you have access to a character generator, make note of all titles, words, and phrases to be used, and the shots in which they are to appear.

Killer details

This is also the time to check little details, which, if left unchecked, can grow into massive problems. Is every mistake in the dialogue clearly noted and followed by a plan for correcting the problem? Have arrangements been made to collect data slides or data information?

Are all the names in the program spelled correctly? Is each followed by a correct title? Collect business cards and/or tape signs or name plates to document correct spelling and titles. This is also the time to check the spelling and pronunciation of any special technical terms, town names, or techniques. If possible, simply have the talent pronounce and spell the words directly into the camera at the end of the interview to ensure the editor has all the information when needed.

Personal Release Form

For the $_____ consideration received, I give

_____ Productions, its successors and assigns, my unrestricted permission to distribute and sell all still photographs, motion-picture film, video recordings and sound recordings taken of me for the screen production tentatively titled_____ .

_____

Signed_____
Name (please print)_____
Address_____
_____
Date_____
Signature of parent or guardian_____
Witnessed by_____
Date_____

While many educational organizations remove all reference to dollar amounts, it is wise to receive release forms from all models in the video production.

Model releases are critical for every person with any significant role in the production, especially a speaking part. While some universities do not require signed permission slips from employees, everyone else should sign a form for each production. These forms are filed permanently in your main office. You *must* get additional permission signatures from parents of minors.

Common mistakes

As you plan your field production, review these common mistakes made when taping. Use this as a final check of your tape before you "strike the set" (pack video equipment and send the talent home).

Poor quality shot – Bad focus, lighting, color balance.

Poor camera movement – Jerky or inappropriate zooms and moves.

Not enough cutaways – Too few close-ups or shots of people working or walking without talking.

Shots that are too short – Camera didn't hold still long enough to cover the narration. (If you think you need five seconds, record 10 or 15 seconds.)

Starting too soon – Talent starts talking too soon after the tape is rolling, allowing too little leader of the tape for a good edit. (Count to five slowly after tape is rolling before cuing talent.)

"Walking" on the sound – This occurs when the interviewer talks at the same time as the subject, or visa versa. Not only is it considered rude, it is also difficult to edit, especially if you plan to never show the interviewer. Be careful of "uh-huh" and "yes, yes" spoken off camera during a presentation.

Post-production

Everything that is done to the tape after it leaves the camera/recorder is called post-production. It is generally the process of "fabricating reality" – creating an artificial world which captures time, space, thoughts, and emotions to be revisited again and again. The more realistic the fabricated reality, the less conscious viewers are that they are watching a scene in which huge gaps of time and space have been removed. And if you can get the audience to forget that what they are watching is not reality, then you have a strong video production.

In general there are four stages in this process:

- Graphics production
- Logging and screening video tapes
- Video tape editing
- Sweetening the sound track

Graphics for video

As mentioned earlier, video should be prepared for both the ear and the eye. This means that graphics can play a major role in giving your production a professional look. Graphics do not need to be complicated or expensive.

As you are preparing your outline and script, make notes in the margins for any graphics, words, titles, props, or charts that add to the message. Start early to prepare and gather these visual items. Graphics and props are especially important when you are dealing with a program that will be mostly talking heads.

Aspect ratio. Because the television screen is one fixed proportion (3 X 4), the shape of any graphic or artwork becomes critically important. The relationship of the height to the width of the screen is called the aspect ratio. In television, this ratio is three to four. Visuals for video, then, should be prepared specifically with this aspect ratio in mind (see video Safe Zone illustration in *Composition*).

Non-computer production techniques

Today, many graphics are electronically produced. However, graphics on poster board can be easy and inexpensive to produce. Some speakers even prefer to use their own graphics on camera so they can point out special items. These graphic cards also can be shot on a separate tape and added to the final tape during editing.

When designing a graphic for television (if it is not going to be computer-generated), it is usually best to prepare it on poster board cut to 14 x 16 inches. Use light blue or tan poster board instead of white. Outline a 12 x 9 inch rectangle in the center of the board. This will be the correct size and ratio for television use.

You also may find that press-on letters offer the easiest solution to a titling problem. In general, these commercially prepared letters appear far more acceptable than hand-drawn work. The letters are available in a wide variety of sizes and character styles. (For more information on typeface, refer to Chapter 8, "Graphic Design.")

Once the graphics are prepared, the talent can choose to refer to them on camera or they can be added later using insert editing, described below. When producing these charts, try to have five or fewer lines of lettering per card. In most cases, there should be 15 letters or less per line.

Slides

Slides can be transferred to video, but only the sharpest, clearest slides should be used. Video only has a contrast range of 20:1, while film has a range of 100:1. This means that you lose a great deal of detail in each slide transferred to video.

In addition, many educators are surprised to learn that the aspect ratio of 35mm slides is drastically different from the aspect ratio of television. Only about two-thirds of a 35mm slide can be seen on television. This means that slides with important information around the edge of the picture are unacceptable. It should go without saying that vertical slides are totally unacceptable unless used with a film chain which allows the close-up camera to zoom into a small area of the slide.

Computer-generated graphics

Today's personal computers allow you to add great looking, inexpensive animation and graphics to your video that once would have cost a fortune. While this chapter will not attempt

Aspect ratio of television and slides are different, forcing the video producer either to lose part of the slide around the edges or to show a black screen on top and bottom of the slide.

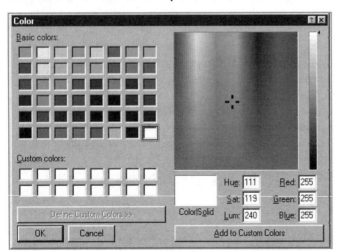

When designing graphics for video, select a color palette that has muted tones.

to cover all the details of computer-generated graphics (see the Graphics and Multimedia chapters for extensive details), there are a few special considerations needed to output quality computer graphics to tape.

Color palette. One of the easiest-to-correct problems is changing the color palette from the typical computer graphics palette (choice of colors) to a video color palette. The color range for NTSC (the TV format used in the USA) is limited. Highly saturated or bright colors that look great on your computer screen will be too "hot" for television and will appear to "bloom," "dance," or be shadowed on the TV screen.

Most professional computer-graphics programs will offer an NTSC palette. These colors will appear much duller and less exciting than the millions of colors you use on the computer, but don't waste your time with any other palette. If your graphics software does not have an NTSC palette, you can purchase additional software, that can, after the fact, go through and convert your graphic into an NTSC-safe image. Generally, however, it is better to design using acceptable colors than to try to filter out bad colors at a later time. Some computers can support more than one monitor, in which case you can preview your graphics on an NTSC TV monitor during creation.

Even when using an NTSC palette, avoid using high contrast colors, such as blue and yellow, right next to each other. Often, dull colors on the computer monitor will come alive on a video monitor.

Equipment set-up. If possible, set an NTSC (TV) monitor beside your computer as you design and check your graphic as you develop. You usually will need a video card to enable you to use a second monitor, in addition to the computer monitor. This will allow you to design with the actual NTSC palette and to make sure that there will be no surprise colors in the final graphic.

Scan conversion. The scan rate for computer images is different from the scan rate used by a video monitor. Because of this difference, images that look fine on a computer monitor often will appear "jittery" on the television screen unless you make some special scan conversions.

This means you will need a scan-conversion box between your computer and your video recorder, or a special video card installed in your computer. The cost can range from a few hundred dollars for a low end, amateur system, to several thousand dollars for broadcast quality. *There is a difference*. If you are producing for broadcast or Betacam productions, you probably are investing days in producing quality graphics. Trying to save $1,000 on a one-time investment of a scan-conversion box only will shortchange your artist and your viewers and is a false economy.

Interlace problems. In reality, the television signal only sends out half of the 525 horizontal lines that make up a television picture at a time. Each second of video contains 30 frames, and each frame comprises two half-frames called "fields." Each field presents only every other line of the visual information. The odd field activates the pixels in the odd numbered horizontal lines, and the even field activates the pixels in the even numbered horizontal lines.

Normally, your eye and the decay rate of the activated pixel in the television tube make this frame change transparent to the typical viewer. However, with computer-generated graphics, this becomes a critical issue.

If you create a horizontal line that is three pixels thick, for example, half of the time there will be only a one pixel line displayed on the video monitor, while the other half of the time, there will be a two pixel line. The result is a single, jittery line. The problem gets even worse when there is a one-pixel line: half the time there is a line and half the time, there is no line at all, making the line flash.

To ensure that your images don't jitter, use horizontal lines with only an even number of pixels or more than six pixels. (Vertical lines can be of any width.)

Two screens showing interlace video

Interlace also can cause problems with animations. If you just put out whole frames of your animations on tape, your animation actually will play back at 30 fields doubled (to create 30 frames) per second, instead of 60 unique fields. This is because

the video monitor is putting out the same image twice in a row (the odd field and the even field are the same image). The result is a much "rougher" animation; the frames per second is cut in half, so the motion will appear jerky. To fix this, you will need to "field render" your animations. In effect, the computer will take a 60-frame-per-second animation and create a new 30 frame-per-second animation, where each frame has the odd lines from odd-numbered frames of the original animation and even lines from even-numbered frames. Although it looks strange on the computer monitor, or even as a still on the tape, it will look twice as smooth when it is played back.

Text. If you have access to a video-character generator and will be editing your graphics into your video program, the best policy is to avoid creating text, especially small text as an element of your computer graphic. Computer text is often difficult to read after the tape is duplicated. Text created on the computer should be no smaller than 18 pt and always should be anti-aliased. This anti-aliasing will "blur" the stair-step edges to letters and soften possible jittery lines, but it also will blur the entire letter if your font is small.

Depending on the font, it may be better to use sans serif

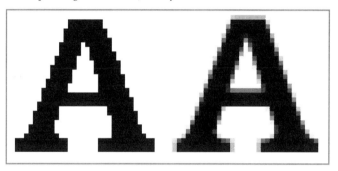

Alias vs. anti-aliased text

fonts (fonts with no tails or feet). The tails on serif fonts may only be one pixel wide, resulting in the jitters.

Overscan. Finally, remember to design for overscan, that area around the outer ten percent of the monitor that can be lost in a video monitor. Keep text and the main action of animations away from the edges of your screen. If you don't, it is possible part of your graphic won't be seen by your final audience.

Tape machine control. For amateur or low-end graphics, you often can record the computer graphic in "real time." (Thus, a 10-second animation would take about 10 seconds to record.) However, for animations that cannot be played back at real time (or for high quality graphics), you might consider a frame-by-frame output to tape. This, again, will take special software and/or hardware, and a tape machine that will accept computer control. Look for software that will lay down multiple frames per pass so that an animation with, for example, 300 frames will require only 50 passes on the tape instead of 300.

Once these graphics are recorded on tape or a digital disc recorder (DDR), they are ready for the program-editing process.

Editing the final program

The editing process is basically piecing together only the video which best relates your message to your audience and removing all the mistakes and distracting blunder. Elements that support your story, such as narration, graphics, sound effects, music, animations, and special effects should be added only to the extent that they increase the effectiveness of your original message.

There are two basic editing processes used to produce the final program:

1) traditional linear editing using standard videotape machines and usually an analog video signal

2) computerized nonlinear editing using desktop video soft-ware to arrange and rearrange randomly-accesse digitized video clips.

Both techniques will be discussed here, but the basic concepts and preparation for an editing session are the same and will be covered first.

Preparing for the edit session

Return to goals and treatment

The time and effort it takes to prepare for an edit session depends on the time and care you took in your initial planning and pre-production, as well as the quality of your raw tape. Generally, editing can be fast and fun if you have done your job well up to this point. This is the time to return to your treatment page and review your message, intended audience, and program style. It is possible for the same script and field footage to yield two (or more) different programs, with the selection of different visuals and sound bits, the pace of the edits, and the choice of music. Without this review of the treatment, it is possible to create a technically flawless video program which totally fails to meet your goals!

The paper edit

Log tapes. After reviewing the treatment, take your script and a pencil to start the paper edit. Review all the raw field tape. Find the segments that best fit the script and purpose of the program, and note them on your script using the counter number on the playback machine (or the time code, if you are using professional equipment).

If you are editing nonlinear with desktop video, or have access to "insert edit" linear video equipment, remember that you can use the sound from one scene and the picture from another. Make notes of interesting close-ups and cutaways (scenes that illustrate or add interest to the straight-action or "talking head" narration).

While selecting the scenes, look at not only the message and performance of the talent, but also at the quality of the field production, such as the lighting, sound, and camera work.

Consider editing style. One of the decisions made when designing the treatment was the basic program style that will direct your editing style. These two editing styles are:

1) continuity editing with a smooth story-telling approach

2) montage editing using a fast-moving collection of impressions often set to music and limited narration.

If you are using the continuity style, all editing decisions and the selection of takes must be concerned primarily with smooth transitions between edits. For example, if pieces are dropped from a long speech, the position of the speaker's body and head will suddenly jump or shift. This is called a "jump cut" and it alerts the viewer that something has been removed, and shatters the "fabricated reality."

Therefore, first select and edit together the video you need to create the desired sound track. Then select cutaways and reaction shots to cover the jump cuts. As you select scenes, open with a general overall scene (called an establishing shot), then select a mix of close-ups, medium shots, and long shots.

If your program is a montage, the shots you select during the paper edit should be especially dynamic images, usually including extreme close-ups and beautiful shots that may not fit immediately into a story line, but that help convey the emotion you want.

This is also the time to locate the music, sound effects, and graphics you want in your program. *Be sure to secure needed copyright clearances.*

Without a script. When trying to organize field footage shot without a script, it is often easier to lay out the important video segments on index cards, color-coded by specific elements you want to include in your program. This allows you to make changes quickly and re-arrange your program before you actually start editing tape. Once you have the elements arranged as you want, create a script and get "sign-off" from all involved in the project before you start to edit.

Finalize script. As you work, it is not uncommon to make minor alterations in the script or narration. Just be sure that you do not stray from the initial message or audience. Once finalized and approved, your script is ready for narration and then the final editing process.

Standard elements of a final edited program

The basic flow of traditional edited programs includes:

1) fade up from black (a black screen with no audio)

2) opening and title

3) program

4) closing and credits

5) fade down to black

The actual editing is some variation on a three-step process:

1) Build the basic flow of the program from start to finish. The flow oftenis built on the audio track (narration or assembled sound bits). The audio can be edited into the program with the video (as with a talking head), or it can stand alone (as with narration), leaving a visual "hole" to be filled later. In some programs, especially a montage, music is added early to "pace" the visual editing, allowing the editor to "cut to the music."

2) Add visuals (video and graphics) and sound to fill the holes. Names and titles often are keyed (superimposed) over speakers, and graphics are added. Transitions and special effects (see Transition sidebar) are included as the visuals are edited into the program. Be sure all jump cuts and breaks in continuity are covered.

3) Add finishing touches, such as wild sound, music, extra reaction shots, opening title, and closing credits.

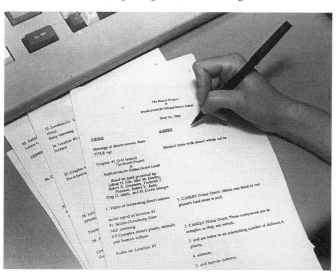

When the script is ready for the editing room, add notes for character generation and music.

Quality first. As you edit, the first priority should be given to the quality of the video and sound. This means you are careful that the audio is not distorted (over-modulated) and is recorded at the same basic level. The video should have the same basic level of brightness and color saturation. If you are editing with professional or some prosumer equipment, this will mean watching wave-form monitors, vector scopes, or at least video-signal dials. If a shot is out-of-focus, plagued with background noise, or the camera movement is poor, don't use the shot. It will distract from the quality of your entire program.

Selecting the best. During the paper edit, you made major decisions about the general shots you wanted for each part of the script. As you select exact "in" and "out" points to record onto your master linear tape or as you trim video clips to insert into a nonlinear project window, you make micro decisions down to the 1/30th of a second. How do you decide exactly where to cut? Professionals use two guidelines – cut for continuity then cut for peak action.

Cut for continuity. In our daily lives, the flow of action is continuous with few abrupt changes. People and things don't suddenly appear and disappear. Positions, places, and motions change in ways we can see in the real world, and they should in video as well. This means if the establishing shot included the farmer looking straight into the lens, then the first frame of his extreme close-up sound bite should be him looking directly into the lens.

Cut on peak action. Good continuity editing removes jarring distractions. Editors often decide to make scene changes (cut to new video) at points motivated in the script or the music (cutting to the beat of the music). Now that you know *where* you want to change the scene, you need to decide *what* scene will be the most exciting.

Do this by selecting the cuts with the most impact – select the river scene at the exact moment the trout jumps, cut to the bull rider at the point he flies off the bull and does a mid-air somersault, dissolve to the extreme close-up of the grandmother's face the moment she breaks into a grin and waves goodbye. If possible, the motion starts with one camera angle (a boy starts to kick a ball) and the motion is completed with a close-up angle (the foot connects with the ball and follows through).

Transitions and special effects. There are numerous ways to change from one scene to another, such as a cut, dissolve, wipe, slide, push, key, and numerous digital effects.

Common transitions and effects

Cut: immediate change in video, most common transition

Dissolve: gradual increase and decrease in opacity between two scenes, second most common transition

Wipe: one fully opaque scene is revealed over another opaque scene by a moving intersection shape

Slide: one fully opaque scene in its entirety slides over a stationary scene

Push: one fully opaque scene, in its entirety pushes another, in its entirety, out of the screen

Key: part of a frame (generally text, a graphic, or boxed video) is superimposed over another

Digital effect: various patterns and techniques for moving one scene into another (can involve twisting, warping, flipping, and turning of the video)

Computers have added complex effects to inexpensive consumer editors. However, just because you can use a complex transition doesn't mean you should use a complex transition. Different transitions convey different messages and should only be used when they enhance the effectiveness of the program. Nothing screams "amateur" quite as much as overuse and inappropriate use of complex transitions.

Audio Track. Audio is often overlooked as a major element of video production. While it may be the visuals which attracts attention, it is the audio track that sets the mood and embellishes the message.

In most cases, narration is recorded in a soundproof room with no background noise. Then editors add music, sound effects, or natural background sound from the video scene (called "nat sound"). If most of the program is edited from on-location dialogue, record the limited remaining amount of narration on location as well so the audio track will blend together.

Music often is used simply as background audio to embellish the visuals and to help set the mood. At other times, especially with the montage technique, it is the driving force of the production. Be sure you have written permission to use any music or sound effect. You can buy CD music especially designed for video and multimedia productions.

Traditional linear editing

The simplest form of traditional linear editing involves two videotape machines connected by cables. More complex levels of editing add tape machine controllers, video processors, and special-effects processors between the play and record machines. Linear editing simply involves copying the video and/or audio portions you want in your final program from the raw tape to the final tape, while avoiding sections of the rawtape you do not wish to keep.

The linear process means that the sections you are keeping must be recorded onto the final tape in the order you want and form you want them to have in your final tape. While you do not have to add every element to the edited master tape in the order it will be seen (after you edit the main motion, you can return to the beginning and add sound effects and video close-ups), you must leave room for additional material. In linear editing you can't slide everything down 20 seconds to make room for an additional sound bite, as you can with non-linear editing.

The simple fact that you are making a copy of the original material means that you will lose some of the video quality. This disadvantage to editing, however, is generally offset by the removal of distracting material and the ability to insert graphics, narration, and music.

In linear editing, however, if you decide you *must* add that 20-second sound bite mentioned above, you must either 1) cut 20seconds near your target spot and adjust nearby cuts to make

room for the new material (a compromise in your script), 2) copy everything to another tape and insert the correction (a compromise on tape quality), or 3) re-edit the entire program from the newly inserted material to the end (a compromise of your editing time). So it's easy to understand why getting "sign off" on the script and the paper edit are so important before you start editing.

Check as you go. As you build your edited program, it's a good idea to review (playback) the last few edits or few minutes (which ever is longer) to check the pace and flow of the program. Without this check, you only edit very short segments together and may miss the subtle nuances that a viewer will receive when the video is played in real time.

Two linear editing techniques

There are two basic linear editing techniques:

- Assemble editing: recording all possible channels of audio, video and control track on a videotape at once, following one video/audio clip immediately with another

- Insert editing: adding or inserting a single video or audio element into an already edited program, such as music to a narrated videotape

To understand these processes, you need to understand a bit about how videotape is recorded. In addition to the one track of video and two to four channels of audio you see and hear on the screen, there is an "invisible" element that holds all the other elements together called the control track. This is the electronic equivalent of sprocket holes on 16mm film.

The final edited master will play back smoothly only if you do not have a single break in this track. The first time you record material onto your edited master tape, you must be in assemble mode (the default on consumer machines). This mode enables you to record control-track information.

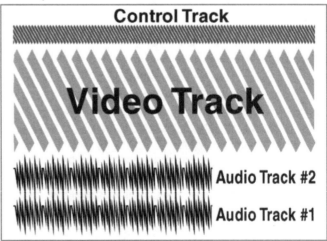

If you could "see" the information on the videotape, it would look something like this.

You can butt one edit up against another from beginning to end on the tape to create this continuous control track. However if you leave even 1/30th of a second unrecorded on this control track, the image will roll or "glitch" each time you view that section and you have to re-edit the entire program. Therefore, most professionals using machines with insert editing capability begin each new editing project by recording black onto their entire edited master tape to ensure a perfect control track (uninterrupted time code in the case of professional equipment). They perform all edits after this point in the program while in insert mode.

Tape organization. Generally, editors will create the basic program using the guidelines described in the basic editing techniques above, with narration and the main audio or narration on channel 1 and music, sound effects, and nat sound on channel 2.

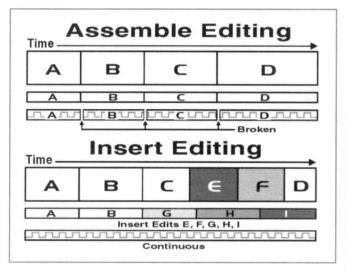

Assemble editing (top) records all of the video, audio and control-track information at once. Insert editing (bottom) builds on a continuous control track adding video and audio independently. This often produces a smoother, more flexible editing session.

Basic linear editing equipment

There are three basic levels of video editing equipment: consumer, prosumer, and professional. Since the instructions for using edit controllers vary slightly from system to system, the only detailed editing instructions given here are for the most basic editing, which does not use any edit control system.

The consumer level of equipment can be two machines connected by simple cables copying the desired scenes from one tape to another. This basic setup uses inexpensive VCRs and costs under $1,000.

More complex consumer systems can add simple fader/editor/titler units, the ability to mix in various audio inputs, and perhaps another television. This system still uses basic consumer VCRs and generally runs under $2,000.

Many simple edit systems are available today that control two tape machines and allow for preview of the edits and smooth edits. For some smaller formats, such as Hi-8, the entire system may be in one unit.

The prosumer level of editing equipment uses a more complex edit controller that is generally either a dedicated video-controller box or a desktop computer using special software. Because the tape machines must be controlled by these units, they usually have RS232 or some similar control cable inputs.

Prosumer systems often differ from consumer systems in the way they process the signal, often using S-video, which carries the signal on two cables (luminance or brightness on one cable and red/blue/green color or chrominance on another).

The features in prosumer equipment vary widely and often include many of the features listed for the professional equipment below. But prosumer systems usually have a lower video resolution and limited control of the signal quality. The cost of these systems ranges from $5,000 to $15,000, depending upon the features.

While it is possible to assemble the components from various manufacturers to create this system, the inexperienced editor would probably save money and headaches in the long run by buying an integrated system from one manufacturer or from a video professional.

The professional level of editing equipment offers extensive control over every element of the signal and is designed with extremely durable high quality components. The costs can range from $30,000 for "one box" solutions (switcher, audio, edit controller-with-bare- bones video machines), to $50,000 to $250,000 for top quality modular systems, depending on the level of signal quality (composite analog is the lowest, then component analog, with component digital being the highest quality of linear editing equipment).

The features which separate professional from prosumer generally include use of video equipment with extremely high video resolution, signal monitors (wave forms and vector controls), video signal processing (often built-in time base correctors), central sync to all machines, slow motion and fast motion

A professional editing system with a dedicated or computer-edit controller offers numerous options for additional equipment.

capability, four tracks of audio, time code instead of control track, and an edit controller with EDL (edit list capabilities) saving and management capability.

Advanced professional systems will include digital effects, multiple machine input (A/B/C roll), options for advanced computer-graphics input, and the ability to interface with a digital disc recorder (DDR).

Linear editing summary

Editing takes time and patience. Because linear editing limits the flexibility you have to make major changes after the master is initially edited, the pre-production and paper editing decisions are extremely important.

It is possible to edit a satisfactory program using only inexpensive, consumer equipment. Although practicing the "brute editing" technique improves smoothness, it will never produce a flawless, high quality tape. For this, you need more control over your machines.

If your goal includes wide distribution to a critical audience, try to gain access to at least prosumer, if not professional, equipment. Contact a professional editor who can edit your final tape, and possibly even "bump up" the quality and add some special effects.

You don't have to be present when the professional editor produces your final edited copy if you make detailed notes on your script during your paper editing.

You might want to make a "rough cut" using the brute editing technique to guide the professional editor. This is especially helpful if your video doesn't have time code. A rough cut will help ensure that the editor selects the shots you want if you cannot be present during the editing session.

Nonlinear desktop video editing

A decade ago, computer technology put the power to create professional-looking publications and graphics in the hands of non-professionals through desktop publishing and desktop-graphics systems. In the same way, emerging video-processing systems on computers are now expanding the capabilities of consumers and educators to produce and edit video programs with graphics and special effects through a desktop system.

The possibility that powerful video-editing capability could someday be available to everyone with a computer has been heralded as the "democratization of video." While desktop video editing is still in its fledgling stage, and has its share of problems as well as advantages, before this book is printed again, many of the problems and concerns will have been answered.

Computers and video processing continuously become faster, and digital storage and hardware cheaper. Nonlinear video editing will become increasingly common and the results more acceptable. Therefore, it is important to understand the basic concepts, the potential, the advantages, and the drawbacks of this burgeoning technology.

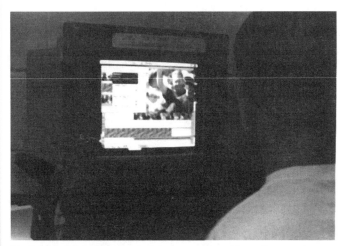

Desk-top video allows you to arrange the video clips you have digitized into "storage bins" onto a construction timeline.

Definition

A nonlinear desktop video editing system has been called a "studio in a box" because it replaces many of the dedicated boxes in the prosumer and professional video systems with software and computer cards generally contained within one computer system.

The process basically involves digitizing video onto a desktop computer, rearranging it, and mixing in sound, graphics, text, animation, and special effects to produce a finished program.

Basic uses of nonlinear editing

Nonlinear desktop editing is basically used for three purposes:

1) Off-line video editing (not editing for a final master tape) to create an edit list (EDL) for later use with traditional linear video-editing systems.

2) Creation of *Quicktime* or *Video for Windows* movies for software, multimedia, and computer-based delivery applications.

3) Complete editing of video programs for final output and presentation on traditional linear video tape.

Off-line. The off-line use is the quickest process since there is no concern about final image quality from the computer. The video is captured in the smallest window, lowest quality, and smallest file size possible. Using the nonlinear system, editors experiment with numerous editing alternatives and generally get the team or client to give final approval of the edit before returning to the original raw tapes for "auto assembly" on a professional linear system. This process combines the best advantages of both linear and nonlinear editing and results in the highest quality video program possible.

Computer movies. The creation of a "movie" for computer-based delivery applications is the second fastest operation. Since the final product is generally a small window of video within a larger computer screen, the rendering time is minimal, and the problems associated with full-frame, full-motion output to videotape are avoided.

Complete desktop editing. The complete nonlinear editing of video for final output to linear video tape is the most complex and time-consuming process of all. It involves the most equipment and the most skill in operating the system. However, as the technology improves, so will the quality of the end product. The details of the process will be explained in depth below.

Steps in nonlinear video editing

In general, nonlinear editing techniques use the same three steps involved in linear editing outlined above but add capturing and outputting steps and offer more flexibility within the editing process. The nonlinear process generally involves five steps:

1) Load elements into the computer by digitizing or capturing video, sound, text, and graphics (often from videotape).

2) Build the basic program by trimming and arranging the clips on a timeline.

3) Review and rearrange the clips

4) Add finishing touches through transitions and special effects.

5) Output from digital storage to linear video tape.

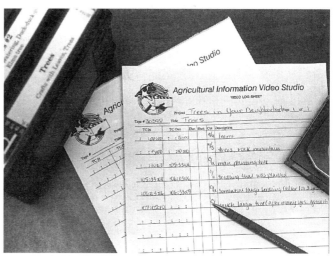

Logging field tapes is important for both linear and nonlinear editing. It is especially important for nonlinear because your first task is to select and digitize the scenes you think you might use. Pre-selection before capture saves you time and computer storage space.

Process details

Up until the editing begins, the video-production process is almost identical for both linear and nonlinear editing methods. Message design and audience identification are identical, pre-production and production are similar, and the start of the paper edit and logging is the same.

Step 1. Because of the time and storage space required to capture and store video clips, it is critical that you carefully screen and select the desired cuts before digitizing starts. The more decisions you can make while previewing your raw field tape (the paper edit), the fewer unneeded clips of video you will digitize, thus saving time, money, and storage space.

Step 2. Once captured, or "digitized," the audio and video, along with any needed scanned stills, computer graphics, and text files, are stored in a "bin" or "visual library", with descriptions of length, name, and file type displayed by a representative picture of the clip. Clips ready for selection can be previewed in the "clip window" or "playback window" before importing them into the actual presentation.

The edited presentation commonly is built on some sort of "time line," "construction window," or "sequencer." This part of the screen often provides input lines for several sources of video, audio, transitions, and superimposed material. Elements, including music and titles, can quickly be dragged over to the time line and viewed in a preview window.

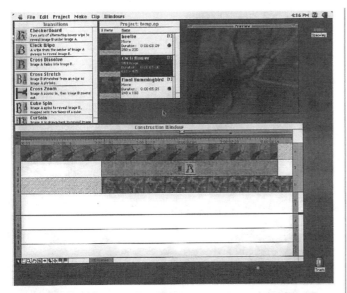

While the actual screen interface may vary, most nonlinear video-editing software offers the use of various transitions (upper left), "bins" for raw elements (top middle), a preview window of the program (top right), and a construction area (bottom). Note how the two video screens of the beetle and the hummingbird are overlapping with a dissolve icon between.

Step 3. Adjustments are relatively easy to make by simply dragging the visual representation of the element along its track. Time and speed of any element can be expanded, and special effects and dissolves can be added. Finally, you can save one version, rearrange everything to create alternate versions, and then compare variations of the edited video.

Video clips can be duplicated and reused an unlimited number of times. Because it's digital, the quality does not suffer if, for example, you duplicate a video clip five times for repeated use in various parts of the program. This is the power of non-linear systems – the ability to change sequences of video or audio without re-editing everything that follows.

Step 4. You can adjust the quality, tint, contrast, and texture of the video or sound by previewing and then applying filters or special effects on one or all of the data files. There is a dedicated track for special effects and transitions on which you can mix and blend video with other video, text, graphics, and sound. All the special effects and transitions in traditional linear video are possible in nonlinear editing, and many more as well. (The same warning against overuse of special effects cited in linear editing applies to nonlinear editing as well.) To date, the use of special effects in nonlinear systems is usually very time-consuming.

It should be noted that while you can "drop" a special effect into a time line, quickly for example, a dissolve between two video clips, if you want to *see* a preview of the effect, the computer needs time to "render," or prepare the desired clip before you can see it. The rendering time varies, depending on the size of the preview window and the complexity of the edit. Dissolves generally take only seconds; previews of complex sec-

tions can take several minutes (or even hours for lengthy sequences) to prepare.

During the editing process, of course, you can save the files and quit the program to use other software. You also can archive and remove the entire system from your hard drive if you need to load another project.

Step 5. Once your video has been approved (by yourself, your team members, or your administrators), you either can compress it for stand-alone viewing on the computer or for use within a multimedia program or you can output to tape. In almost all cases up until this point, the computer has been rendering the special effects and transitions only for a small preview window to speed the editing process. When you are ready to return the program to linear tape, the computer will need to render each programmed edit into full frame, full motion video. This process could be quite time-consuming, depending on your equipment, special computer cards, compression routines, and software. Most professionals plan their edit process so the system can render and output overnight or at least during a lunch hour.

Advantages

While there are many subtle advantages to desktop video editing, those most frequently discussed revolve around flexibility, ease of use, and cost.

There is potential for outstanding video quality *if* the problems with compression can be solved. Quality is maintained because digital video can be reproduced infinitely without degradation of the image and can be stored, transmitted, and downloaded through digital networks, such as the Internet, World Wide Web, and other emerging digital mass-communication systems.

Flexibility. One of a linear-video editor's worst nightmares is to have an administrator or coworker watch a 30 minute, highly edited "masterpiece" and say, "About 12 minutes into this tape you simply "must" add this 90-second quote from our president," or "Although everything else is just great, that theory the scientist demonstrated half way through the program has been proven false and has to come out. Please just snip that one little part out and bring it down to us in the conference room after lunch."

The linear editor has basically only three choices – 1) reedit from the mistake to the end (big time loss), 2) copy to another tape and insert the correction (big quality loss), or 3) negotiate the addition or subtraction of program material to fill the hole created or needed (a big scripting loss). How these "weeping" linear-video editors wish they could magically insert, remove, or rearrange material with only a few clicks of a button!

At other times, the video editors, or producers themselves, are unsure of how to edit a program best. They may long for a way to test different ideas easily without investing too much time in complex linear editing. Once all the video is digitized, nonlinear-video editing systems can allow an editor to quickly try and compare many different options and to make corrections with a few clicks of the mouse.

Ease of use. It is difficult for a beginner to gain access to and learn professional video editing systems. All the buttons, knobs, and dials in a linear-video editing suite can seem overwhelming to the beginner. There are new terms, new machine controllers, and new quality measures to learn. All this makes traditional, linear video editing (beyond the simple system described in this chapter) intimidating and out-of-reach for the average educator.

Nonlinear-video technology, by contrast, can be explored on a computer that already may be in the office. With the addition of just some inexpensive software (free in some cases) and the use of some video clips pulled off the Internet, you can experiment with creating your own motion visuals. The function of the software is similar to other graphics software, and the initial equipment usually operates with a simple and familiar click-and-drag method. Usually after only an hour or so, the user has a short product that is ready for viewing.

Cost. Prices change so quickly that even magazine articles are out of date before they roll off the presses. However, for several more years, users can expect their computer dollar to buy more as prices continue to fall and computer power and software capabilities continue to rise. In contrast, while linear-video equipment costs are also falling, they generally do not start as low nor fall as quickly as nonlinear technologies. Costs will be discussed in more detail later.

Digital quality. The potential for unaltered quality in the digital domain, regardless of how many times the data is duplicated, is outstanding. But in almost all cases, the initial video for the nonlinear demonstration has to be shot on outstanding (and expensive) digital video cameras and be carefully selected and processed to produce an outstanding master.

Is it "good enough" now? The question video editors have to answer is whether the video output from the nonlinear systems within their reach is "acceptable" or "sufficient" for their audiences and intended use.

If the video you will capture and compress into your nonlinear system originated from a consumer camera and is captured realtime through a consumer nonlinear system, then the initial quality of the raw video clips will be significantly degraded from the original. If the final product for the nonlinear video project is a traditional linear videotape, expect the quality to suffer again from the transfer process.

The bottomline is that while digital video has outstanding potential for outstanding quality, at this time, the final VHS product of a simple nonlinear editing operation will be of a lower quality than from a simple traditional linear editing process. It may still, however, be perfectly acceptable for your needs, and the advantages mentioned above could make nonlinear an ideal editing mode for you.

Disadvantages: An overview of the disadvantages includes:

1) massive data storage requirements

2) video quality degradation when capturing and outputting the analog video signal

3) data management within the nonlinear process

4) time required to digitize video, render special effects, and output video to tape

5) technology-imposed limitations on the editing process, which currently could limit editorial creativity or expand the time required for simple editing tasks.

As time moves on, a balance will be found somewhere between the over-enthusiastic salesperson, who says nonlinear editing is an inexpensive, point-and-click affair, and the traditional video purist, who predicts that computerized video will always be poor quality and cumbersome. Whether off-line or on-line, nonlinear video editing will help shape the future of almost all video productions.

Details on special equipment

Typically, new nonlinear editors start with a basic system, then soon begin looking for upgrades, as they discover the speed bottlenecks and quality limitations. The details below will help explain some of these upgrades, which can be added to any of the above systems to improve performance.

Storage and backup. A 500MB drive is a minimum for nonlinear editing, with disk arrays or a series of 1GB drives being the most common. Although no serious computer user should be without a data-backup system, this is especially true of desktop-video editors. The time and money invested in video capture alone is too much to lose in the inevitable hard-drive failure or mistakenly-erased file. In addition, video projects are so massive and require so much "wait-for-approval" time before they can finally be dumped back to tape and erased, that often the files must be removed temporarily to make room for another emergency project.

RAM. Most manufactures recommend at least 64MB of RAM, with 128MB more common.

Digitizing. Video capture boards and the accompanying video compression set is highly varied at this point. Digitizers include simple, low-cost systems (VideoSpigot), midrange systems (RasterOps), and high cost, higher quality systems (Radius ViveoVision, Avid, Video Cube (ImMax), Video F/X and Media 100). Some boards offer digitizing and compression on the same board (Digital Film from SuperMac offers JPEG compression). The details of compression will be discussed later.

Editing software. While simple video editing is possible with *QuickTime* or *Video for Windows*, video destined to return to videotape will probably be edited in an integrated system such as Adobe Premiere.

Encoder. If you want to output high quality video (or animation) back to videotape, you need a way to add the calibration pulses and analog waveform used by televisions. While some cards build this into their digital capture and output cards, the best quality generally comes from a stand-alone encoder.

The encoder does this by first converting the color in each pixel of the digital image (RBG, or red, green, blue) into the TV's NTSC color system (colors represented as hue and saturation). Then the encoder converts the information into an analog waveform and adds the needed calibration pulses so it can be recorded on a standard video recorder.

Two monitors. To make the best editing decisions, it is critical that you have a television monitor beside your computer monitor. While you can edit using a standard, 13 inch or 15 inch computer monitor, there is so much information displayed by the editing software that you will probably want to move to a 21 inch computer monitor.

Tape control. Probably one of the best "extras" you can add is a videotape control system to allow controlled capture and output to videotape, rather than real time capture and output. This will substantially increase your video quality.

Controlled capture also will increase the minimum equipment required in your entire system, including the capability to timecode, computer controlled videotape machines, a faster CPU to process larger files, and larger, faster hard drives. A common software/cable system is the DQ-Animaq from DiaQuest.

Professional nonlinear editors sometimes capture all their time-coded video quickly in realtime, often in less than full frame for off-line editing. As they edit, they usually snip the video to a shorter length or may decide they don't want to use a video clip at all. Then, when the final production is approved and ready, they return to their original tapes to recapture only the exact frames of video they need, saving significant time. Most professional nonlinear-editing software automates this process to allow overnight frame-by-frame capture.

Speed and quality extras. Experienced nonlinear editors almost always add accelerator cards, a PCI or EISA bus instead of a NuBus. More powerful video capture cards, SCSI-2 hard drives, and digital disk recorders (DDR). Removable hard drives, SyQuest tapes, optical storage media, or recordable CD-ROMs help ease the storage and backup problems. These extras will increase the quality, speed, capability, and price of your nonlinear system.

Poor compression candidate. In this sequence, a woman is walking in front of a brick wall. The camera is following her movement, panning along to keep her in the center of the screen. The background will be constantly changing (because the camera is panning), and the woman will be constantly changing (because she is walking), so the entire frame is changing; in any given frame, every pixel will have to be changed from the previous frame. This movie will not compress well, because every pixel is constantly changing.

Moderate compression candidate. In this sequence, the woman walks past a stationary camera. In this case, the background will not change, but the woman moves from one end of the screen to the other. Her image will be constantly changing, and the area she affects will move from the left of the screen to the right. This movie will compress better than the previous one, since the background is static; the computer doesn't have to update any of the background pixels, since they won't be changing. However, a good portion of the screen changes from frame to frame.

Good compression candidate. In this sequence, the woman is sitting on a stool and talking. The background is completely stationary, and the woman doesn't move much. All of the movement is constrained to a smaller section of the screen, and only a small part of that is constantly changing (her face). This movie will compress very well.

Special taping considerations for nonlinear

Compression never improves video quality. The goal is to select codecs and equipment that are set up to make it look the best possible. You can improve the overall look of your video (while reducing the size of your file) by the type of video you shoot.

Compression ideally works by only reducing or eliminating the redundant or repeated information from one frame to the next. However, in reality, most compressors will alter the image slightly to gain a lower compression ratio. Several codecs will give you control over how much it will change your image.

For example, if you shoot a woman sitting on a stool in front of a solid colored wall, probably only her face, hands, and body position will change, and even then, the motion will be constrained to a vertical strip in the middle of the screen. This video should compress very small with relatively good quality because the computer only has to store the portion of the screen that is changing, which is relatively small, in this case.

However, if you have a shot of a woman walking in front of a brick wall, there will be more pixels changing. You will have her entire body moving, as well as her shadow cast upon the wall. In addition, she is moving from one side of the screen to the other. Since much more is changing on the screen, the codec has more information to process, and thus the compression will not be as strong as the first example.

Finally, if you start actually moving the camera angle, such as in a zoom, a tilt, or a pan, just about every pixel on the screen will be changing from one frame to the next, producing a much larger compressed file, since the codec has to update the entire screen many times a second.

In short, for maximum compression, minimize camera movements (zooms, tilts, pans), and constrain the action to a portion of the screen whenever possible. Instead, keep the camera still, and allow the subject to move within the shot. This lack of variety in camera shots often is compensated with extremely close, highly dynamic subjects. (Tropical birds, fish, and flowers are common subjects for nonlinear equipment demonstrations.)

Real-time vs. controlled capture

Most systems allow capture and output of video in *real time*. While the systems are fast, quality may suffer. Try capturing a full-screen, full-frame rate clip to make sure the resulting quality is satisfactory for your purposes before you buy.

Undoubtedly, frame-by-frame *controlled-capture* will be much more accurate and clean than *real-time capture*. Controlled capture gives the computer time to grab only one frame at a time, compress and store it, before capturing the next frame. The amount of information real-time capture can store on each frame is limited by the frame rate and the speed of your recording medium. (It will probably use a lossy compression algorithm to boot.)

However, the time frame-by-frame capture takes may be prohibitive for your needs, especially if you will be digitizing more than 15 or 20 minutes of video. A system that allows you to choose between both methods to digitize may be worth the money.

Audio for nonlinear

Audio is, of course, critical to the final edited nonlinear-video project. But compared to video, digitizing audio is fairly easy and can be completed in real time. Most video capture boards include audio capture, although separate audio digitizers are available.

Distortions. The goal is to have as little distortion, such as clipped or muffled audio, as possible. This generally involves carefully setting the audio level on the output device and the audio resolution on the computer.

Clipped audio. If the volume on your audio output source is too high, it will sound clipped. (Keep output levels near 0db). This also can occur when the volume control is set too high on the digitizing software. If reducing the output volume doesn't work, lower the digitizing volume.

Muffled audio. If the volume is too low, then the audio quality will be muffled. Again, first increase the output volume, and then the digitized volume.

Digital quality. Aside from distortions, audio quality is mainly a function of the bit depth and the sampling rate. While 8-bit audio is acceptable, 16-bit will produce much better quality (and a file twice as big).

The sampling rate tells you how often the signal is cut up to make a digital clip. Thus 8 KHz is sampled 8,000 times a second; 22 KHz, 22,000 times a second, 48 KHz, 48,000 times a second. Higher sample rates create better quality and proportionately larger files. Generally, the minimum you will want to capture is 22 KHz. You should only dip down into 11 KHz if there is no dialogue or other key sounds in the audio clip. The 48 KHz rate is called CD quality. Before using this capture rate, remember that VHS cannot reproduce sound of that quality anyway, so, it would be a waste of precious disk space if your project is destined for VHS tape anyway.

High audio sampling during real-time-video capture can cut the number of video frames captured, thereby hurting the video quality. (Although you always can capture the sound separately and paste it in later!) Controlled capture, by contrast, first captures all the video with no audio, then captures the audio in real time on the last pass.

Publication

Duplication master tape

Your edited master is as precious as gold. Never, never loan your edited master to anyone!! Immediately after you finish a project, make a high quality duplication of the master, or dub master. In most cases, this will be the source for all your duplications.

Many editors mix, or combine, the two channels of audio (one for narration and the other for sound effects and music) onto one or both channels of the dub master to prevent the balance between music and narration from accidently being altered during duplications.

Store your master, all your notes, computer backup tapes, edit lists, and the computerized EDL (if you have one) in a place secure from theft and fire or water damage.

Clearly mark edited masters and duplication master tapes.

Duplication of distribution copies

Duplicate your tape at the highest quality level possible. If you can, use at least prosumer level equipment, which allows you to see the audio levels and check the tracking. Some duplicators offer time-base correction and extra video control as well.

If you need large numbers of duplicates, you might consider a commercial duplication house. It can make hundreds of copies at once, often for less than you can buy the raw videotape. However, the cheapest duplication house is not necessarily the best bargain because it may cut too many corners in the process. Always submit a small order first to test the quality, and be sure you have a money back guarantee on all work.

Labels and tape cases

While it may not be fair to say, "You can judge a videotape by its cover," This is often what your audience will do. Consider carefully your target audience and your distribution mode when deciding how to package and label your tapes.

If your goal is mainly public presentation and the audience will never see the case, a simple title and protective case is

enough. However, the low cost of tape duplications has led many educational groups to distribute hundreds of copies of educational or promotional tapes for home viewing. This makes the tape-case design the first critical interaction with your audience.

One way to get a visually appealing cover is to color copy a photograph made during the production. Again, early planning is needed to ensure you have the right, high-quality shot for the tape case.

Remember to carefully craft the description and the words on the back cover of the sleeve to convey your message even if the tape is never viewed. Use desktop publishing software to lay out an attractive tape cover and make sure there are no typos, Computers have made the use of spot color and four color more economical. If you are going to sell the tape, color is especially important in the cover.

The cover to your videotape is how many people will judge its value. Consider using simple computer graphics to create slip-in labels for videotapes.

Copyright

A word seems in order here about copyright, both on your tapes and on commercially-produced tapes you may buy. If you are a public institution, you need to check with your administrators concerning your policy on copyright. Some institutions feel that nothing produced with public funds can be copyright protected, while others allow it to protect against commercial profit for a private company.

The real copyright concern for educators, however, comes in the possibility that they may violate the copyright of a commercial-production house. Videotape duplication is so simple that many educators duplicate tapes without considering the possibility that they may be violating the copyright law.

While the new copyright act does provide for "fair use," this is not a blanket license to duplicate copyrighted works. In addition, you cannot assume that simply because you are using the tape for nonprofit educational use that you are free from copyright restrictions. While the law does allow for duplicating a portion of work for critique and educational purposes, there are specific disclaimers for films and AV materials. When in doubt, always return to the original producers of the videotape and negotiate duplication rights. In addition to staying within the law, the quality of the duplicates made from the master is always better than a "pirated" copy.

Room set-up and presentation

Videotapes are of no value if your audience is not able to see and hear the presentation. This requires careful attention to the room setup and equipment operation.

Television should never be viewed in total darkness. Normal to dim lighting is not only more comfortable to the eye, it also gives the viewer enough light to refer to educational handouts or take some notes.

Be sure the television is not in front of a window or situated so that harsh light strikes the screen and causes a glare. Walk around the room to check the visibility from all locations.

For public display, you should provide one television set for every 20 to 30 viewers. This may mean that you need to combine television sets with a coupling device. Supplies for splitting and amplifying the signal are available at most consumer electronic stores. If the signal is carried to more than two television sets, it is important to boost the signal as it is split. A power distribution box costs only $10 and is worth the investment.

When showing a videotape to a large group of people, consider a diagonal placement of the chairs to provide better viewing.

instead of VHS, and use professional playback equipment.

Once the televisions are in place, adjust the color to provide the best match possible. If the color adjustment varies widely between various television sets, the audience will be distracted and miss part of the educational message.

Don't forget the sound quality. Separate the speakers and check the quality and volume in various spots of the room. Remember that a room full of people absorbs lots of sound, so the volume will have to be increased from the ideal volume in an empty room.

In general, no one should sit closer than seven feet, or further away than 20 feet, from a 19-inch television. No one should sit more than 45 degrees from the center of the screen nor have to look up more than 30 degrees.

Once the televisions are in place, adjust the volume. It should be loud but not blow over the closest viewers.

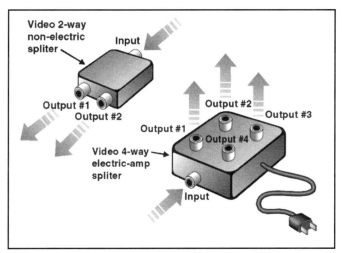

Two types of video splitters: While this simple splitter (top) will operate two TVs, a power splitter (bottom) should be used for three or more.

When presenting a videotape to a large audience, such as a conference or large workshop, remember to tape all cords to the floor. You also might want to consider a large-screen TV or video projector. If it's really an important showing, make a dub of your program of a professional tape format, such as Beta SP

Multimedia

Whether you have found them yet or not, somewhere out there in the multimedia world are powerful tools which could make your work and recreational time more interesting, productive, and exciting. Unfortunately, there are also some big multimedia "black holes" which could consume much of your time and money, giving you little in return.

This chapter is designed to give you a basic road map through the interactive multimedia world, pointing out the quick returns as well as the quicksand. Part I is for potential users and newcomers to multimedia and will explain the basic

concepts, terms, research, hardware, and title selection guides. Part II includes a step-by-step approach for designing multimedia, using the ADOBE model. Part III is a more technical, detailed section on compiling the components of multimedia: text, animation, graphics, sound, video, and programming.

Part I: Multimedia — what is it and how is it used?

On the surface, multimedia may not seem like anything new, because it essentially links traditional types of multiple media into one environment. It is highly possible that the various bits of information grouped together in a multimedia program already exist as text, audiotapes, video, pictures, slides, or charts. But linking them into an interactive multimedia package often makes an educational product or entertaining game more than the sum of the parts.

For example, imagine you wanted to learn or teach about family health. You might want parts of books on first aid and human development; databases on drugs and allergies; pictures of common skin problems and warning signs of diseases; videotapes on fitness exercises for all ages; graphs of life expectancies according to habits; computer software to balance special diets; art and diagrams of internal organs; and maybe even a live link to health experts to answer emergency questions. Finding all these resources could be time consuming and expensive, and sharing information from them before an audience almost impossible.

Now imagine that instead of searching for each of these smaller pieces, you could access most, if not all, of these different types of information from an interactive multimedia CD-ROM on your computer. If you were teaching home health to a group, you could use an overhead computer projector with this single multimedia CD-ROM and easily jump from a chart on the causes of arthritis, to a diagram of joint inflammation, to a digitized movie of helpful exercises to restore motion. You even may be able to respond to questions you had not anticipated, and as a group, to explore new information on the multimedia CD-ROM.

In short, the power of multimedia is its ability to help tame information overload. It can help you find the information you need in one package, without struggling with slide projectors, audio players, VCRs, and a stack of books, journals, and newspaper clippings.

Become a multimedia author

But what if the perfect, all-inclusive CD-ROM or multimedia package doesn't exist on your selected topic? What if you need to manage personal or customized information that only you could ever gather, such as family genealogy or graphical and data information about your local area? What if you want to organize related information you may someday use in an educational presentation, and you need some way to keep track of different types of media?

Today's easy-to-use multimedia software can help you capture, store, link, and manage all the information -- text, graphics, charts, data, and motion video. All your information can be accessible and useful from the start, before you "complete" your project.

Of course, as with any media, the value and quality of the end product is only as good as the quality of the elements you put into the package. If the text is inaccurate, the visuals poorly composed or the data faulty, the resulting multimedia package will be a high tech package of garbage.

Long gone are the days when the "gee-whiz" of getting new visuals by touching a screen or clicking a mouse was enough to engage the users. The novelty of this concept has been replaced with the power and potential of this technology to educate, entertain, and archive. It's this potential power that makes multimedia tools worth the time and dollar investment. But there is one more key element that truly makes multimedia come alive.

Interactivity - multimedia's secret power

Technically, any program combining more than one media (slides and audiotape, for example) could be dubbed multimedia, but purists insist that the concepts of "interactivity" and "user control" are the defining essence of today's multimedia. A videotape is usually a linear way of learning -- viewers start at the beginning and watch to the end -- but a well-designed multimedia system is interactive -- giving the user control and immediate access to all the information in any order -- so each exploration can be customized to the user's needs and interests.

"Welcome to Cornville:" In this interactive educational game, players can choose any of the buildings, ask for help, or exit the game. The player may even click on one of the Cornville residents, or on the cornstalks on the background. It is non-linear, meaning the player can progress through the game in any order.

It was the magic of interactivity which allowed Nintendo's early low-resolution, low-variation games to invade America's homes almost overnight (Kahle, 1991). Linear information arranged on computer screens with pretty pictures and VCR navigational buttons does not qualify as interactive multimedia. That's just electronic page-turning. To qualify as interactive, a program must allow the participant to wonder, to ask, and then to discover (Ankeny, 1993).

Multimedia also can simultaneously engage multiple senses and appeal to a wide variety of learning styles. By using sight, sound, and simulated experience or experimentation, multimedia engages the learner at a level few publications, lectures, or even demonstration projects could ever offer.

Research shows that we retain in short-term memory about 20 percent of what we hear, 40 percent of what we see and hear, and about 75 percent of what we see, hear and do (Newsom, 1993). The military, one of the first and most persistent multimedia users, found it allows students to complete courses in one-third the time of traditional lectures, while reaching competency levels of about 50 percent higher (Feltcher, 1991). Industry training specialists find time and time again that multimedia training is not only faster, it also is more cost effective per student (Donahue & Donahue, 1983).

If the multimedia system is carefully designed, users can move at their own pace, easily access the information and engage in independent discovery learning. In short, multimedia mirrors the multiple channels we use every day to gather data and allows for more "natural" learning by providing sights, sounds, and opportunity for doing, coupled with time for reflection, interpretation, and exploration. It allows users to select their favorite sensory mode of learning and encourages involvement and interaction with the information.

Multimedia computers

The definition of a "multimedia computer" is a moving target, with each new advancement making systems faster, easier to operate, or cheaper. But currently, a multimedia system needs at least a sound card, a graphics card, a mouse, a high resolution color monitor, a CD-ROM drive, and an operating system which will allow a graphical user interface.

The debate over which platform is "best" has raged for years, with IBM-Compatible PCs generally considered more flexible and cheaper, Apple-Compatible Macintoshes and power PC's more complete out of the box and easier to use, and Unix systems providing high-end power and capability. Luckily, current trends are moving towards an end of "platform" rivalries, and cross-platform development will ideally allow a multimedia application to run on two or more of the most common operating systems (DOS, Windows, Macintosh, or Unix).

If you are making a hardware decision, talk to someone other than a computer salesman, and read trade magazines *NOT* targeted towards one specific platform. (*New Media, AV/Video and Presentations* are free to communications professionals. Their addresses, as well as paid subscription options are listed at the end of the chapter.) You may also get guidance from an Internet or on-line Bulletin Board Service, such as the multimedia discussions on America On-Line, CompuServe, or Prodigy.

It is also important to consider the local support you can find for your hardware. Check out service and support departments of local and mail order "stores" as well as your local "user groups." To find your local users group, call the computer company's 1-800 number, the local computer store, or check computer bulletin boards.

Game machines

Once considered only "time-wasters" by parents and teachers alike, the interactive game machines such as Sega, Nintendo, and Multiplayers are moving rapidly into the educational markets. In 1992, Nintendo's after tax profits were more than Microsoft, IBM, Apple, or all the five movie studios combined; and in 1993, Nintendos were owned by one-third of U.S. families who annually spend $160 - $350 for "firmware" (Sheff, 1993).

With the hardware priced at only a few hundred dollars, instead of the thousands required to buy a multimedia computer, these "game" sets offer great potential for education.

Multimedia storage and distribution

The data storage requirements of multimedia are immense by yesterday's standards. The typical size of the multimedia computer's hard drive is at least 500 megabytes with one gigabyte a minimum for development machines. Most serious multimedia developers, especially those working with large video or animation projects, use disk arrays -- several hard drives in par-

allel to increase storage size, speed, and data security. Five gigabytes with capability for expansion is a common starting point.

A data backup system is an absolute must. The question is not *if* your multimedia development hard drive will crash, but *when*. A tape back-up system which can store five Gig or more is popular. Regardless of the system you choose, be scrupulously careful about systematic backups. Carefully date backup tapes and store them off-site -- in another building or a safe deposit box. Buy enough backup tapes and alternate so that at any one time you have at least two backups of each development machine, one from your last backup session and one from the previous one.

Optical media

Currently, optical discs are the most popular media for multimedia distribution. They are an inexpensive way to store, mass distribute, and quickly access hundreds of megabytes of text, numeric data, motion video, stills, animation, or sound. Optical discs are fairly indestructible, and cannot be tampered with or accidentally changed by exploring students or flustered adults. Popular types include CD-ROM, CD-I, Photo CD, and Videodiscs.

CD-ROMs (Compact Disc, Read Only Memory) look similar to an audio CD but require a special player or drive attached to a multimedia computer to come alive. (Most newer model computers have CD-ROM drives built in.) CD-ROMs can hold more

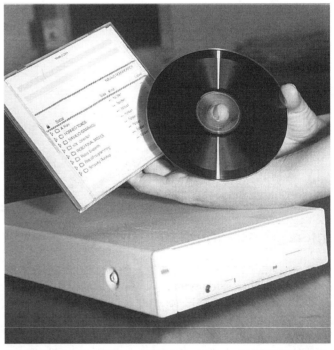

CD-ROM(Compact Disc - Read Only Memory): CD-ROMs look just like audio CDs, but can hold over 600 megabytes of digital computer information. Once something has been written to a CD-ROM, it cannot be erased or written over. Thus, it is called Read Only.

than 600 megabytes of information, or over 400,000 pages of text -- enough to fill 250 large reference books or 10 sets of encyclopedia. A CD-ROM also can hold illustrations, music, software programs, digitized video, animation, and interactive programming. In addition, CD-ROM drives can play audio CDs and single session Photo CDs.

At this writing, CD-ROM drives usually supply information far slower than the same information from the hard drive. Therefore, the speed of your CD-ROM drive is critical. Speed involves the data transfer rate, access speed, and buffer size. The data transfer rate (kilobytes-per-second) tells you how fast large amounts of data can be read off the CD-ROM. The general rule of thumb is the higher the transfer speed, the smoother the data flow. Most recently released CD-ROMs require double, or triple speed models for smoother video and animation playback, and 8X speed models are on the way

Beware of the "super bargain" low cost CD-ROM players which are usually single speed drives (150KB/second transfer rate) and will not play most currently released CD-ROMs.

Also consider the access time (the average time from when a "fetch command" is issued until the data transfer starts). In early 1994, for example, the fastest access time models were rated at 180ms (milliseconds) access time, compared with their 320ms slower competition. Yet, hard drive access time of the same vintage as a rapid 16ms, making even the fastest CD drive seem excruciatingly slow. With access time, the lower the number, the better the CD drive.

The cache or buffer size (a temporary holding area to smooth out the data flow) is another important consideration. In 1994, a 256KB cache was considered minimum for demanding applications, and this "minimum" is sure to grow as applications become more complex and graphics intensive. While there are several interface connections available, SCSI interfaces are the most versatile.

Finally, you should also be sure the CD-ROM drive is compatible with your computer's operating system. Many drives today can interface with DOS, Windows, and Macintosh, as well as OS/2, UNIX and Windows NT.

In summary, when buying a CD-ROM drive, look for a high data transfer rate, a large cache, low access time, and versatile platform connection possibilities. Also be careful of buying any

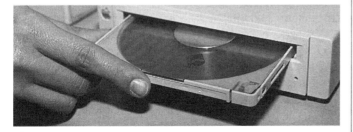

External CD Drives: If you have an older model computer that does not have a CD-ROM drive built in, you can purchase an external CD-ROM drive that 'plugs into' your computer. Before purchasing, check with the manufacturer of the drive to make sure your computer model can support the drive.

hardware during its first quarter of release, before all the bugs have been worked out.

The CD-i looks similar to a CD-ROM but is used without a computer on a special CD-i player with a built-in microprocessor. The CD-i system is highly economical ($400 - $600 instead of $1500+ for multimedia computer systems), will play on a home television, and uses a handheld remote control instead of a keyboard or mouse. With its outstanding graphics, video and information storage capability, CD-i holds great potential. The limitation at this time is an expensive and proprietary authoring system for developers, an extremely small hardware delivery base, and limited variety of titles.

Videodiscs, also called laserdiscs, are one of the oldest interactive visual technologies, yet still play a key role in systems requiring full motion, full screen, high quality video. The traditional multimedia disc (called CAV) holds 30 minutes of full motion video, or 54,000 still photographic frames, along with two or four channels of audio per side. Newer players which can grab and present a still frame from a CLV disc (60 minutes of video per side) offer multimedia developers twice as much visual information for basically the same development cost.

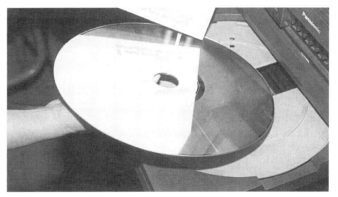

Laserdiscs: Laserdiscs can store and display as much as 30 minutes of full motion video and are sturdier than traditional VHS tape. Laserdiscs can be used by themselves, much like a VCR, or with a computer program.

Multimedia Titles

Regardless of the hardware configuration, it is the multimedia titles and the information, graphics, or educational simulations on the CD-ROM or public information kiosk that makes the multimedia world exciting.

While books can only *tell* you about how Africanized honey bee colonies look and spread, a multimedia CD can provide a movie of how they look, fly, and sound, along with graphical comparisons of domestic bees, charts of their movements, mathematical projections of future movements, and hypermedia links (keyword connections to related material) to other insect outbreaks and control measures.

The old adage, "Just because it's in print doesn't necessarily make it true," applies to multimedia publication as well. So does, "Just because it's in multimedia form doesn't necessarily make it fun, overly useful, or exciting." Unfortunately, at this writing many CD-ROM titles are only abbreviated versions of text-based books with little more than a computerized index and electronic page turner.

For a title to truly be interactive multimedia, it needs to offer many different ways to find the same type of information and present that information in a number of different modes. The interface should be highly visual and attractive, the interaction engaging and the operation of the program intuitive, requiring few instructions.

As with books, newly released CD-ROMs often are reviewed in multimedia, computer and educational journals and magazines (see references at the end of the chapter). With many new CD-ROM titles costing over $50, it is well worth the time to read some reviews before you buy.

Part II: Designing multimedia — a five-step process

With the development of several easy-to-use authoring programs, and lower hardware costs, it is now possible for small groups and individuals to develop their own interactive multimedia systems. From specialized presentations, to CD-ROMs, to public displays, you now have the power to reach a targeted audience and allow your audience to customize the information to fit their personal needs.

However, just as the ability to put printed words on a page does not ensure that you will write the great American novel, so the ability to link visuals, motion, and text into a multimedia program does not insure you will create the great American multimedia program. The genius is in the design, attention to detail, strong teamwork and continuing testing with the target audience to make improvements based on your test results.

Whether you decide to develop a multimedia system yourself or work with an outside design team, a clear understanding of the development process will help clarify each step and enhance planning, communication and evaluation. Although there are a number of design models available to guide the process, the ADOBE model was developed in the Southwest because it reminded the author of the process which binds common elements -- clay, stones, straw, and water -- into an end product far stronger and more beautiful than any of the individual components. In the same way, the ADOBE Multimedia Model sets forth a process for blending traditional and high-tech communication inputs -- animation, computer graphics, digital audio, video, text, databases, computer programming and input and output options -- to create an information medium potentially more responsive to public and user needs than the individual media. In brief, the ADOBE multimedia development model includes the following:

A -- Analyze the audience, goals, resources, and constraints.
D -- Design the conceptual model, interface, and treatment.

O -- Originate the program elements.
B -- Build and debug the computer control programming.
E -- Evaluate the product and process.

Before examining each step of the ADOBE multimedia development process, it is critical to stress that one of the overriding factors that separates success from failure is to focus on the needs and reactions of the target audience. Ultimately, the audience will be the judge of what makes a good multimedia program and what doesn't. Therefore, at every stage in development, target your audience. Is the learning level adequate? Is it relevant to their stage of learning? Is the interface intuitive to the audience? Does it hold their attention? What does your audience consider fun, interesting, and valuable? Will it be worth your time and money?

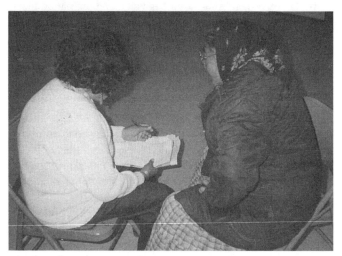

Conduct focus group evaluation: Before developing a multimedia computer program on nutrition for the Navajo Nation, team members conducted focus group testing with members of their target audience. They were able to assess the educational and nutritional needs of their members and evaluate their willingness to accept new technologies, such as computer programs.

One of the most common problems with the development of multimedia systems is that the designers "fall in love" with their own design and continue headstrong with development, failing to test whether or not their intended audience likes, understands, or can easily operate the multimedia system. This can result in a system which is clever, beautiful, creative -- and useless because the audience can't or won't use it.

The solution is to test, test, test. Start with a beta test of the design, the graphics, the interactions, and the graphical user interface. Continue testing during every step of development.

The following sections summarize the major points of most development models. However, before undertaking a full-scale project, you should study each step in more detail, by reading a guidebook to multimedia design, such as the ones listed in the bibliography by Bergman & Moore, Gleason, or Kearsley.

A – Analyze the audience, goals, resources, and constraints

Too many developers pay lip service to the importance of analysis, but then get so excited about the tools and the possibilities, they fail to ask some critical questions which could mean the difference between success and failure.

To ensure success, consider the following questions:

- Analyze your organization's goals and expected outcomes:
  What are your objectives? What are they *really*?
  What will be the bottomline criteria for "success?"

- Analyze the user's needs and characteristics:
  What is the reading level? Visual sophistication?
  What presentation style works best?
  What information is really needed, wanted?
  What delivery equipment is available?

- Analyze the user's needs and characteristics in this delivery site:
  If in public, are users willing to be seen exploring your topic?
  If in public, how long will users stand to read text? Visuals?

- Analyze the delivery site:
  What are surrounding conditions: Is there noise, dust, electrical interference? Is there security for equipment?

- Analyze subject matter:
  Is the audience interested?
  Can the topic be packaged into "information capsules?"

- Analyze resources and restraints:
  Who will be on the team?
  What equipment, software, and multimedia services can you use?
  Who will pay for what?
  What are the biggest roadblocks?

Analysis of audience in the delivery site is critical.
There is a crucial difference in the design approaches needed for development of multimedia programs designed for use in a public kiosk with a touch screen computer, and in the development of a multimedia CD-ROM designed for use on a computer at the home or office. In general, systems designed for public use must be instantly intuitive, effective with only 60 to 180 seconds of use, and logical regardless of where the user starts in the program. Successful designs are effective without users seeing the opening instructions and have information packaged into "information nuggets" which are helpful even if the user sees only one.

Systems designed for non-public settings, such as schools, homes, and the office, should expect that users will spend extensive time using the system, and therefore need to focus on extreme depth and quality of information so the system will be valuable and interesting time after time.

Analysis is doubly important with youth audiences.
First-time designers of multimedia titles for youth audiences often make a critical mistake: they forget to think like kids. They may design an anti-smoking program carefully explaining the long-term health dangers or design a college recruiting program methodically covering each major and departmental option.

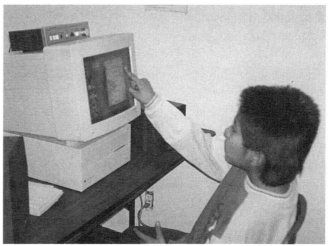

Test your program at every stage of development: While developing a program for Navajo children, development team members tested the program at various stages with the target audience. Make sure that your users will understand your interface, select the information you want them to, and not shy away from using technology.

Analysis of the audience, however, might reveal that kids care little about diseases they might contract when they are 50, or what degree they might earn in four years. Instead, analysis might show that the best anti-smoking multimedia should focus on immediate impacts (bad breath, burnt clothes, or impaired athletic ability), and that teens could best be attracted by your university's proximity to the ski range, the friendliness of the professors, and the type of clubs, concerts, and sports available. A multimedia system that is beautiful and logical to the adult designers and is boring and ho-hum to the targeted teenagers is a failure. *Do not begin design until you analyze the audience.*

D–design the conceptual model, interface, and micro-treatment

Although everyone agrees careful design is important, limited budgets and tight deadlines cause many project teams to abbreviate the process, often leading to expensive delays and revisions later in the project. Anything overlooked during design will haunt the rest of your project. A clearly defined process will make the project construction as efficient and effective as possible.

In general, the steps include:

- Design the team structure.
- Design the evaluation plan.
- Design the macro, or conceptual, model.
- Design the project specifications.
- Design the micro treatment.
- Design the general user interface.
- Design the development strategy -- budgets, timelines, and team tasks.

Encourage teamwork and collaboration: Teamwork encourages creativity. Take advantage of all team members and their ideas. Use a flowchart to make sure all members have a clear understanding of the project and the overall concept.

Design teams are usually best. While new multimedia tools will allow one person locked in a computer room to create a multimedia program alone, most successful programs are based on a team development approach. Teamwork encourages creativity, both in artistic design and in creative problem solving approaches. Brainstorm from the start, and resist the urge to "fall in love" with any idea too early.

Design a wall-sized storyboard or flowchart of your program for display in a team area to be sure all team members have a clear understanding of the program flow and the overall concept of the project. This visible flow chart also is an excellent way to organize and keep track of the development progress of each piece of the non-linear project.

Design the evaluation plan. An emphasis on evaluation should start the moment you begin designing a multimedia project. Formative evaluation will occur throughout the process, and you should know up front what the summative evaluation will include and how it will be conducted.

Design a plan to conduct formative evaluation at each step as well as to evaluate the project's goal and objectives. Get feedback and criticism from your target audience, subject matter specialists, and administrators. This will improve the final product, and it also will help build political support for interactive multimedia development.

Typically, formative evaluation does not involve controlled experimental design with qualitative results or large numbers of subjects. Formative evaluation can involve only a few people and be completed fairly quickly *if* you select genuine members of the target audience avoid using family and friends of team members who soon know what they are *supposed* to say. Learn to use qualitative techniques for extracting as much information as possible from the potential users.

Once the design takes shape, test the graphical user interface with artwork on paper and, later, computer screens. Simply ask potential users what they think will happen when they interact with this screen. Ask open-ended questions and avoid "giving hints." The goal is to learn how users will use the system when left on their own. Later this evaluation will determine whether icons convey the intended messages and whether users intuitively understand the menus and how to navigate through the system.

Developers generally make poor beta test operators because they understand the intended design and want the users to like it as much as they do. Therefore, consider bringing in an outside person to conduct these tests. The development team can gain a great deal from a video or audiotape of these tests. For more discussion about formative and summative evaluation, see Chapter 22.

Design the macro model. The term "macro model" refers to the overall approach or concept of the multimedia project. For example, will it be an encyclopedia? A game? A graphic tour of your state? A locator and quick help service?

Developing the macro design is one of the more exciting parts of the entire project. It's not unusual for these ideas to be sketched out initially on napkins during a lunch brainstorming session or on the back of a conference program after seeing several exciting multimedia exhibits.

This macro model must be creative enough to energize everyone who will have to put many hours into the development, yet simple enough to be completed within the available time and financial resources. If this is your first project, keep your goals and designs simple, elegant and do-able. Simply mastering the development process and the computer tools has enough built-in challenges without tackling an over-ambitious, complex design.

Design specification. This is the time to carefully plan the design specifications, or the "template" your multimedia team will consistently apply throughout the program. Consistency and simplicity are vital to strong design. Without common specifications, each team member may develop creative but inconsistent terminology, operations, and designs. Integrating all the elements into one operating system becomes a nightmare.

Usually, these specifications evolve during the team's development process. They cover such basics as consistent file naming, functions for navigational buttons, methods of acknowledging user input, locations of similar information and user tools, user warnings, timeout processes, writing style, and information presentation techniques. Setting design specifications actually frees team members of these decisions, allowing more time for creativity.

Specifications can cover how the system will operate (i.e., how will users jump to another place, when will the system "time out" and reset to the beginning), how the system will look (i.e., locations and designs of buttons, shape and style of text, and overall layout of screen designs), and how the system's information will be delivered (i.e., how long video or information screens will be displayed, or when animation will be used).

Designing the specifications should also consider the requirements of cross platform programming. Almost all commercial and educational multimedia products of the future will require release on several platforms. Therefore, do some research and ask other cross-platform developers about the pitfalls and safeguards of cross-platform development. For example, Mac designs allow somewhat unrestricted file names, while DOS demands an 8.3 structure. Experienced designers adhere to the 8.3 naming structure, even on a Mac.

Finally, determine your minimums for hardware and

system specifications, such as the smallest screen size (critical on Macs), screen depth (8, 16, 32 bit color -- see *Image* discussion below), and hardware speeds (speed of processor and/or CD-ROM drive). Keep a multimedia computer fitting your minimum requirements in your development area and test all graphics, sound, animation, programming, and overall layout on the lowest common denominator machine. If you don't, you're headed for a multimedia train wreck!

Design the micro treatment. As your plan takes shape, plan the details of the multimedia project or game. This is called the micro design. For example, if the macro design is a theme park full of buildings users can explore, the micro design will include rides, trails, ticket booths, movie theaters, and games.

Designs which entertain as well as educate help maintain user interest. Consider using fantasy, role models, challenging game-like situations, and the element of surprise or curiosity (Arwady & Gayeski, 1989). These techniques may require exciting animation effects, video from exotic locations, interviews with well-known personalities, or action-packed games.

Remember to keep the "multi" in multimedia. The power of this tool is the different media available to present information, so use them.

Don't use text-filled screens that may bore the user when a short paragraph and a video clip may do the trick. Concise

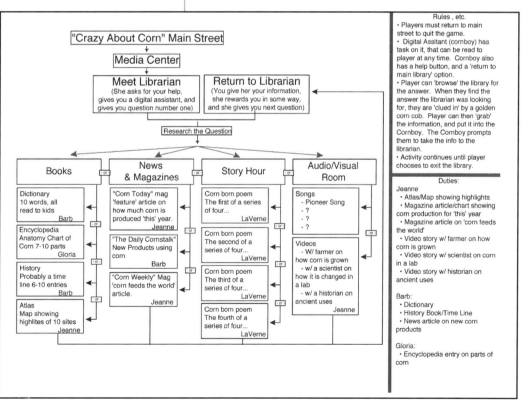

Take advantage of non-linear interactivity. Your user should be able to decide what he or she wants to learn. Give your user several options at every stopping point so that the program is truly interactive.

writing is especially important in public-display programs because users tend to spend less time using them.

Interactivity is the hook of interactive multimedia, and the opportunity to "make just one more selection" is almost irresistible (Ankeny, 1993). Still, many designers deny users full control, creating little more than an expensive linear lesson.

In general, the more opportunity to make choices and the more control users have over the information flow the more attentive and engaged they will be in the multimedia program. Empower users to stop or change action at any point. If there is video, let users stop, rewind, advance, or quit the video. Games should have lots of ways to start and move through the maze or challenge. Design "one button" ways to jump from one screen to another, or return to the main menu from any point in the program. Never "trap" your users or limit interaction to a "next screen" button, if you can avoid it.

Design the user interface. The screen a user sees when making program choices is called the user interface. While flowcharts for the team's use may contain only menu bars of words, the user interface is usually far more graphic and may not even include words at all. Instead, the Graphical User Interface (GUI) is often built around icons or even parts of pictures users click to explore. Symbols often simulate real items, such as building directories to look up names, notebooks to store clues or information, or roadmaps to locate new information.

If your system is for a public place like a mall or museum, remember that two or three minutes is the average user time. Users often walk away without "resetting" the program to the beginning, and a new user will take over, perhaps deep into the program. This means every screen must be intuitive and informative, and must provide a means to immediately go back to the opening menu screen or start of the program. Users should never be forced to "back out" of screen after screen.

Beta testing of your user interface is critical at the earliest stage of design. Icons which seem obvious to the design team could be a real mystery to the users.

Design the master development strategy. Once you have a plan, you can take stock of all the hard work (and creative fun) ahead. It is time to map out your strategy for getting it all done. Attention to detail is the key at this point. Carefully plan naming strategies for text, graphic, audio, and touch pad files (see design specifications), and who will be responsible for each part of the project.

If it is a small project, a simple list of the tasks to be accomplished will do. Bigger projects, however, may require a project room or central place to post records or an overall wall flowchart which can streamline the costly record keeping that can bog down bigger projects.

Speaking of costs, this is the time to make a realistic budget. Along with the obvious costs, plan for contingency funds for backup tools, extra programming consultation, and rush production. While careful planning can minimize emergency costs, contingency funds avoid compromise of the process and final product.

Finally, develop an overall timeline both to keep the process on schedule, to help clarify expectations, and avoid misunderstandings with team members or clients. Again, include contingency time, and be careful not to oversell the team's ability to deliver.

Multimedia applications are so detail-intensive that the smallest error (one misnamed file, one forgotten line of code) often can have enormous consequences. If the system crashes or one obvious interaction is flawed, users may judge the entire project a failure, not realizing that 99 percent of the work was flawless. Allow time for complete debugging and formative evaluation. A simple but effective application is more productive in the long run than a flashy but flawed product.

O – Originate the program elements

The origination step is one of the most exciting in multimedia development. This is the time when all the analysis and design comes to life, producing color, sound, motion, and results. The tools used to produce the elements, – scanners, animation software, desktop video editors, and digital recorders – improve almost monthly. They put more power into the hands of non-specialists while increasing the effectiveness and efficiency of skilled professionals.

The importance of continuing formative evaluation with potential users during the origination and development of program elements cannot be overstated. As screen designs, video clips, and audio helps are developed, they should be tested as soon as possible with potential users to ensure their effectiveness.

In general, this stage of multimedia development should:

- Originate the graphic elements: graphics, illustrations, and screen layouts.

- Originate the motion elements: animation, and video clips.

- Originate the audio elements: audio tracks, the sound effects and the user help.

- Originate the text: bite-sized text blocks, text layouts, and printouts.

More details on the technical elements behind originating the multimedia elements is found in Part III of this chapter.

Beta test each element. The most crucial part of any multimedia development project is beta testing. Without rigorous, impartial testing, it is difficult to be sure an icon is intuitive or he navigation system is understandable to the general public. A video clip that seems about the right length in the design studio may appear too long when the user is surrounded by other interesting things to see and do. A good series of beta tests ensures your program will operate and deliver your message when running without you. If you have to help or give hints to your beta test users, you need to go back to the drawing board.

B -- Build the computer control system to merge program elements

The computer program code is the binding agent that holds the individual elements together and makes the final product more functional and beautiful than the sum of the individual parts. There are a number of relatively easy-to-use multimedia authoring programs which put the power of multimedia within reach of non-programmers.

However, be wary of believing all the promises of any authoring software. Regardless of the authoring system used, the process is still time consuming and requires extreme attention to detail to give the system seamless transitions and quick merging of graphics, text, and video with a high level of user interactivity. In general, the authoring process includes:

- Build the merging process to combine all the elements.

- Build user-centered computer management, such as user control, feedback, and help options.

- Build the desired system controls, such as computer documentation, user tracking and logging, and system maintenance tools.

Program for maximum user control. User control, the magic of all multimedia systems, is made possible by branching options within the computer code. The authoring should always allow the user to interrupt current action, such as motion video, and request direct movement to new information, without backing out of a presentation.

You can speed the authoring process and increase the consistency of the program by creating templates which simply are modified for each new branch.

Program user feedback and system helps. Consistent user feedback should be built into every branch of the authoring system. Feedback can include audio, motion sequences, animation, animated characters, and beeps. In addition, the computer program should provide feedback and response to user non-action. This is especially important for systems designed for public use. For example, when a user walks away from a public kiosk, the system should first ask for input -- "Are you there? Touch the screen." and then reset the program to the attract loop if there is no user input. Without this key "reset" programming, the system will appear stuck or broken.

Ideally, the multimedia presentation is so clear and intuitive that users need no instructions. However, the authoring process must provide a means for supplying simple instructions, if only to confirm the user's assumptions. For example, an audio help file can prompt users to simply "Select a path." Simple on-screen instructions also are effective if they are understood easily and can be read quickly.

More complex help messages should be accessible without leaving the current screen location or should return to the current location when completed. Helps should be as specific as possible to the current screen choices and potential points of confusion. While this requires complex authoring, it greatly improves the overall multimedia system. All help messages should be tested early in development through formative evaluation.

E -- Evaluation of the product and process

If formative evaluation has been used throughout the entire multimedia development process, it is a small step to finish with summative evaluation. For traditional training multimedia systems, evaluation can focus on the user's ability to accomplish tasks, pass a pre/post test, or perform skills.

For public information multimedia systems, however, evaluation should focus of the goals of the system and ask, Did the target audience like the system? Is it installable and usable? Does it meet the organization's goals? (Bergman and Moore, 1990).

Additional points to be evaluated include organizational reaction, effectiveness of the process, and future potential for related development. Evaluators usually employ a variety of techniques, including on-line data gathering, observations, exit interviews, follow-up interviews, focus groups, mail surveys, and testing (For details, see *Usability Testing in the Real World*, Mills, 1987).

In general, this final step will include:

- Evaluate the project's achievement of original objectives.

- Evaluate user reaction to overall presentation.

- Evaluate organizational reactions and the process.

- Evaluate future development opportunities.

User evaluation is central. It is possible for a multimedia project to meet its exact program objectives and still draw a negative reaction from users. Perhaps it presents the desired material but is simply too repetitive, boring, or slow. While these problems are undesirable even in self-study courses for "captive users," they are deadly in the public delivery environment. The user will simply walk away, or, even worse, develop a negative image of your organization.

Evaluation of user reactions to public systems is often best achieved by on-site observations, perhaps coupled with exit interviews. Because these systems are in a public place, the presence of an observer often has little impact on user actions. In fact, users usually are not aware that anyone is watching.

Evaluation of desktop systems also shoul include user observations as well as focus groups. In all cases, determine whether the users liked the application, but what specific features were most and least attractive. Evaluators also may try to separate the users' reactions to the technology ("Wow, this touch screen is great.") from their reactions to this specific multimedia package ("It's so easy to find the exact information I want on these animals.").

Bergman and Moore (1990) offer detailed suggestions for conducting various types of evaluations and are valuable sources of specific suggestions for various situations. They point out that it is almost impossible to find consensus on the desirability of any system because the audience is so widely varied. They encourage developers to be most concerned about users who fall in the midrange of user ability.

Evaluate organizational reactions. If the multimedia system was developed to meet specific organizational goals, evaluate the organization's reaction to the final product. In most organizations, this should include reactions from all levels, from top administrators to the field staff, subject matter experts, to advisory group members. Ideally, representatives of each of these groups were involved in setting the original goals, and inform evaluation during development.

The process of conducting this evaluation updates the organization on the results and listens to reactions. Although preparing reports, showcasing the multimedia presentation, and encouraging feedback may be time consuming, it is also a key step in evaluating the current project while building support for future work (Koritzinsky, 1989).

Complaints about features or subjects not included in the original presentation can provide an opportunity for building understanding and support for expanded projects. This showcase evaluation time can also refocus the organization on the original goals and reinforce the notion that interactive multimedia presentations supplement and expand, but do not replace traditional educational programs.

Evaluate production process. Evaluation also should consider the development process itself. How did the group function? What stages were the most productive, and where did the process hit snags?

Evaluation of the process at the conclusion of the project can be difficult. Time can distort the accuracy of memories, and some early problems may be totally forgotten while recent roadblocks take on disproportionately higher importance.

The goal of this type of evaluation is to bring closure to the process and to improve the process before the next project. Especially productive techniques are documentation of helpful software tools, names of responsive subcontractors and subject matter specialists, and time saving tools and products. Pinpointing unsuccessful techniques equally is important to future projects. While no two development projects will ever be the same, identifying and eliminating as many unproductive and uncertain elements as possible will aid in creating a strong multimedia project.

Evaluate future development opportunities. In addition to looking back on the completed project, the evaluation process should include a look forward toward future development. What other information could be easily or economically delivered in a similar presentation? What additional locations could be included?

Developers also should initiate evaluation of emerging hardware, software, and design techniques which would have made the process more efficient, effective, or creative.

Finally, this is a time to evaluate the possibilities for sharing lessons learned, and even program modules, with other organizations.

Part III: Putting it all together — how to create multimedia elements

The first impression, and often the holding power, of a multimedia product is the visual "look." This makes beta testing and formative evaluation of the graphical look and screen designs critical. The software tools and programming tricks for images and animation are improving every day and vary somewhat among hardware platforms. However, the following discussion presents the basics of multimedia images and provides you with a basis from which to grow. For the latest information, refer to articles in the magazines at the end of the chapter.

Text

Writers for multimedia presentations are idea jugglers who often create screen text, audio scripts, feedback to user responses, and video dialogue. Remember that users always can decide to read, scan, or bypass your text, so write in a clear, modular style. Divide large chunks of information into short, clear modules which can be absorbed in short chunks.

Use lists or bulleted statements instead of paragraphs. Each block should be a self-contained unit. Remember that reading text on a computer screen is generally about 28% slower than from paper (Jones, 1989), so keep the layout clean. Make every word communicate.

Principles of text layout for print do not always apply to multimedia. For example, justified text does not increase readability on a screen (Rubinstein & Hersh, 1984). However, using both upper and lower case letters on the computer screen is faster and easier to read (Marcus, 1984; Tullis, 1983). Decreasing text density with white space, bullets, and spatial design increases reading speed (Jones, 1989).

Scrolling text blocks, common in some computer applications, distract multimedia users and are hard to assimilate. Instead, break the text into separate page presentations for higher comprehension and spatial orientation of the information.

Graphics and still images

Before actually creating your first multimedia image, you need to know the type of graphics your lowest common denominator delivery machine can handle. (Important: See *Design specifications* section in Part II.) Then you can choose the best software and graphic tools to help even non-artists create impressive, effective graphics. This section covers the basics and includes designer's tricks for working with screen depth and color palettes, bitmap (or paint) software, object-based (or draw) software, and designer's tools like scanners, image libraries, computed images, and filters.

Screen depth and color palettes

Computer images are created out of "bit planes," which are basically layers of graphic information. The more bit planes in an image, the more graphic information you must store. In this case, "graphic information" refers to the number of possible colors for each pixel. For example, a black and white image requires only one bit plane, because every pixel is either black or white, a 0 or a 1. (Bits are always just zeros and ones.)

Adding another bit plane doubles the number of colors available. So an image with four colors requires two bit planes, an image with eight colors requires three, sixteen requires four, and so on. For example, the industry "common denominator" in 1994 was 8 bit color. That translates into 256 colors, which is generally sufficient if you are creating images that are drawings or line illustrations.

However, if you want to display high-quality photographs, 8 bit color is probably insufficient. With only 8 bit color (256 colors) the computer "dithers," or mixes, pixels from the 8 bit color palette to approximate the colors not in the palette. This seldom gives a desirable result. The solution, of course, is to add bit planes to the graphic. After 8 bit color, the next standards are 16 bit, 24 bit, and 32 bit. Sixteen bit images give you thousands of colors, and near-photorealistic images, while 24 bit images give you literally millions of colors, giving you full control of all three monitor guns (red, green, blue) and is the most realistic color depth you are likely to find.

The next step, 32 bit color, provides the same number of colors as 24 bit color (millions), but it adds another eight bit planes in order to accommodate an alpha channel, a critically important tool for advanced graphic production. This additional information is another grayscale image connected to the normal image and usually keeps track of where the important parts of the picture are to aid in compositing images together.

For example, say you want to put a three-dimensional rendered sphere on top of a photograph of clouds. Your rendering

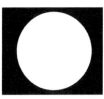

Alpha Channels: Alpha channels create a matte for compositing images. In this example, the computer has selected just the sphere in the first image using the alpha channel, and then placed the sphere into the cloud picture.

software would generate the image of the sphere on a black background, along with an alpha channel telling the computer where in the image the sphere is and isn't. Then you could just lay the sphere image on top of the cloud image, and use the alpha channel to have the clouds show through wherever the sphere isn't. The alpha channel available in 32 bit color is a powerful tool for highly complex, professional graphics.

A designer's trick: So why not use 32 bit color all the time if the images look better and you can save important information in the alpha channel? Simply put, 32 bit color is a real memory hog. Files are big (four times larger than 8 bit), they take longer for the computer to process, and therefore retrieval and screen refresh rates are slow. If you are only working with a single image at a time, perhaps you can "afford" these costs, but animating in 32 bits can cause some computers to crawl (see Animation section, later in this chapter).

There is, however, a trick. Often, you can customize your "palette" of 256 colors (8 bit) to optimally fit any 16 or 24 bit image you hand it. (You won't be able to save an alpha channel in 8 bit, so instead save it to a separate file if it's important.) For example, to create the sphere in the clouds image described above, change your palette to contain only browns, whites and blues, since you won't be using bright reds or bright greens anyway. By doing this, you reduce the number of colors in your image to the best 256 color you can use to represent your image. Sound complicated? It could be a killer without some software help. Luckily, this process is so important and common, software has been developed which automates this task.

Image size

You must know and design for the monitor size on your delivery machine (see *Design Specifications* section). For example, if you try to deliver images developed on a Mac 14 inch monitor on a 9 inch monitor, you will find wide bands of your image sliced from the side and bottom. Set your screen size to the target monitor and then determine the screen layouts and size of all other images within the screen layout.

The smaller the image, the less memory it will take up, and the faster the computer can retrieve and process it. Also, be sure to find out the pixel width and height of the images you can work with before you create them; it varies between monitor sizes and screen resolution. You may have to refer to a user's manual, or make some tests to discover the size of a given screen.

Graphics software

Once you have set a color palette and a screen size, you are ready to create the images. In general, there are three types of graphics software: bitmapped (also called paint programs), object-oriented (also called draw programs) and computed (such as 3-D). Some new programs even combine elements of both approaches, and in the final multimedia product, of course, all images are displayed on the screen as a bitmapped image, regardless of the type of program used to create them. But during this creation phase, experienced designers understand the relative strengths of each type, and probably use each. Here's a quick overview:

Bitmapped, or "paint" graphics. These programs map out the graphics in a series of bits or pixels and store this information in memory related to each pixel (1 bit per pixel for monochrome, 8 bits for gray-scale and 8-bit color, 24 bits per pixel for high end color). Bitmap-based software allows you to paint directly into the image, right down to the pixel level, and use techniques which mimic painting effects, such as spray paint, watercolors, and charcoal. Paint programs are ideal for creating photographic details, subtle shading, and brushlike effects. They are the only choice for working with scanned images.

Resizing shapes and text, however is a real problem in bitmapped graphics, and if you want a larger text font, for example, you have to re-enter it. You also run into difficulties if you try to pull images apart or change the resolution. In addition, image files generated in paint programs can quickly become huge. Some designers use autotrace software to automatically trace a bitmapped image and generate an object-oriented version for further modification and storage.

Object-oriented, or "draw" graphics. For more rigorous, high-resolution graphics, object-oriented software may be ideal. Instead of storing massive data about individual pixels, object-oriented programs store only the instructions on creating the image. For example, for a circle, it would store data about the radius, line thickness, location, and fill pattern. Then if you want to resize, reshape, move, or duplicate the circle, only the instruction data has to change. Objects can be manipulated again and again, joined, separated, and edited separately without affecting the rest of the image. Text can be edited and resized easily without jagged edges.

Object-oriented graphics require far less memory to store the data than comparable paint graphics. Draw software is ideal for technical illustrations, logos, and floor plans. Layering, or keeping key elements separated by the equivalent of electronic clear plastic, is another feature of object-oriented software your

multimedia program may need.

Luckily, even the image-editing bitmap software has released versions which allow you to work in layers, giving you similar power to as object-based illustration. However, object-based illustration still has the advantage of absolute precision of lines, and the ability to resize an image, even nonproportionally, and retain image quality, since the image is computed from abstract objects. In addition, new mixed media software (also known as integrated packages) is combining best features of both paint and draw programs.

Computed and 3-D images. There are several important computer generated graphic tools which offer still more options for multimedia graphics creation. Using 3-D software, the computer can take a simple 2-D image, often created in an object-oriented graphics application, and create images of 3-D models. These 3-D images can be imported into other graphics programs and composited for some stunning results. Text lends itself to this technique and is a good way to start learning about 3-D image creation.

More multimedia graphic development tools

Image processing software. The beauty and power of bitmapped graphics for multimedia is greatly enhanced by the retouching and modification ability of image-processing programs. In addition to adjusting brightness, contrast, and color balance, more sophisticated tools can offer smudging, anti-aliasing, masking, feathering and electronic airbrushes to create entirely new photorealistic and even surrealistic images.

A designer's trick: Image-processing software often offers exciting and time saving filters, mathematical or procedural processes you can apply to any part of the image in adjustable degrees and parameters. For example, some filters can make a photograph look like it is drawn with charcoal, watercolor, poster paint, or even painted by Van Gogh. Others can generate Mandelbrot sets or Julia sets on your images (fractals), or add special gradients, highlights, or embossings to your image. Third-party filters are abundant, and generally are written in a universal format so they can be used by several different image-editing programs. They can turn a simple photo into millions of different, interesting images and are considered important tools to multimedia developers.

Scanners. If you don't consider yourself an artist, try taking photographs of the desired images and scanning them into a graphic file. The cost of color scanners has dropped drastically. They are to quite affordable, and are quite simple to use. On the market currently are flatbed scanners, which scan smaller images on a flat bed, drum scanners, which can scan transparent objects rolled up in a drum, and slide scanners. Each model varies in cost and capabilities, and you should evaluate each for your own needs. Once you have the photo or line art images scanned in, they can be brought into any image-editing software to be modified to your liking, or composited with other images. It is a simple way to make stunning, professional-looking graphics.

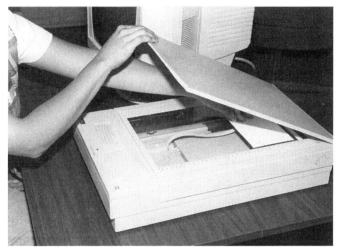

Flatbed Scanners: Through generally not considered the highest quality scanners, flatbed scanners can provide high quality scans and are suitable for low resolution scans used in multimedia development.

Photo CD-ROMs: Photo CDs can be the most efficient way of getting high quality photos, especially if you don't own a scanner. Photo developers can scan your negatives or slides and then store the image on a CD in several different resolutions and sizes at a resonable cost.

Photo CDs offer an easy and affordable way to convert photographic images to digital form, and are an excellent way to store and distribute still images. The photo images can be stored on Photo CDs when the film is developed or digitized from a slide or print and added to an existing Photo CD. At this writing, discs hold about 100 images stored in four resolutions, from thumbnails to high resolution, all ready for direct four-color separations. Images are viewed on a computer screen or a TV.

Graphic tablets. These are ideal companions to paint software and are a popular alternative to illustrating with a mouse. Tablets allow you to actually draw on a flat surface with an electronic pen to generate an image. The tablets often have the ability to sense pressure as well as direction, allowing the graphics package to vary line thickness or amount of color, based on the pressure you apply.

Drawing tablets: Many artists prefer the feel of a pen to the mouse. Graphic tablets plug into the computer just as a mouse would, but often gives the user more control.

Image libraries. Many multimedia developers buy CD-ROMs or floppy diskettes full of images that are royalty-free for their own use. These professionally scanned images come in both small and large sizes, and in low and high resolution. While having your own scanner gives you more freedom to be creative, there is probably a library image that will suit your need. Just be sure your know and follow the copyright restrictions if you plan to distribute your multimedia program -- especially if you plan to sell it.

A designers hint: Ideas for multimedia graphics. Building effective multimedia graphics requires graphic software and tools. It requires a clear understanding of the needs and interests of your target audience in the location they will use the system. Often, multimedia programs simulate the real work, so add excitement and realism by building realistic action into the system -- buttons that depress, knobs that turn, and switches that flip. Instead of visually unexciting menu boxes, create graphics of real world objects which behave like objects familiar to users. Use formative evaluation to be sure your program is intuitive and that control panels or menus are instantly understandable. Test your designs early to be sure your users can tell which areas are 'hot,' responsive to a click of the mouse button. As you design buttons, consider whether your delivery platform will be touch screen, trackball, or mouse. Multimedia programs designed for a touch screen should have buttons large enough for a finger to touch them.

Animation

Animation has become a standard element in most multimedia presentations because it is a powerful and often economical alternative to digital video and a more flashy alternative to text. If carefully planned, it can return big rewards for a relatively small amount of time and drudgery if it is not carefully planned. The seemingly simple animation project can become a "black hole," sucking up immense time and money resources, or looking amateurish and distracting.

The starting point is an analysis of your target audience and your target delivery hardware. Many inexperienced developers funnel massive resources into creating complex animations on their powerful development computers only to discover that on the target machine, the animation takes seemingly forever to load and then is jerky or out of sync with the audio. The bottomline is that slow, poorly executed animations will hurt the value of your entire program. The secret is to keep the design simple and elegant – especially if this is your first animation project – and test it repeatedly with your target hardware. As you run into new problems during development, turn to the multimedia and graphics magazines (see Bibliography), electronic bulletin boards dealing with multimedia and animation, and experienced animators in local user clubs, and in national organizations (such as ACE).

Four types of animation

It is impossible to explain fully all the animation alternatives available on the computer, but here is a simplified look at the four basic techniques.

Color cycling is the simplest form of animation. It involves simply cycling the colors on a part or all of a graphic it is generally used for illustrating flow on otherwise static diagrams or for attract-loops in multimedia applications because it is small enough to run from RAM.

For example, if you want to depict running stream water running towards the right, you could fill it with five different-colored vertical, wavy lines, going from dark blue to light blue. When you cycle those colors, the blues will shift one to the right, and the light blue will replace the dark blue at the left. Repeated cycling will give the illusion of the entire stream moving. If your software supports color cycling, this is a very quick and easy way to animate, and you will only need to create one graphic.

Placement animation. If you need to move an actual item, say a boat on the stream, add placement animation to superimpose and move a tiny bit-map of the boat on the stream, while you continue to use the color cycling to "move" the water. This is particularly easy using the "key frame" interface and the "discrete frame" interfaces described below.

Cell animation. Now suppose that instead of a static boat, you wanted to move a swimmer downstream. You couldn't simply freeze the swimmer in a single position and move her down the stream; she would not look alive. Instead, animate her with several "cells," or drawings, in the various poses. Now, cycle through the poses to give the illusion that the swimmer is moving her arms and kicking her feet.

A designer's hint: Just as hand-drawn cartoon cells often maintain a static background while only smaller foreground items move, the computer's limited memory and load time constraints encourage the same thing in multimedia animation. Spot animation is a popular and powerful designer's trick. It can give the illusion of full-screen animation by only using cell animation on part of the screen in conjunction with placement animation or even color cycling. The computer can animate it faster, since it has less information to change, and it also conserving valuable disk space.

Computational or 3-D animation. Although any mathematically-based series of images can fall into this animation category, it is most commonly used to generate 3-D animations. Since computers can rarely draw satisfactory 3-D images in real time, they must work with things they can draw more quickly, such as wireframe representations, to set up the animation.

Once the wireframe animation is acceptable, using an event-based interface or a key-frame interface described below, the computer renders, or computes, each animation frame. This type of animation can be very time-consuming and can tie up your computer for hours and hours. Thus, plan carefully and work extensively with the wire frames before initiating the rendering phase, or the most you will create is another multimedia black hole!

Animation software and interfaces

Selecting an animation software is generally not an either/or choice. As you combine animation techniques described above, you may also combine products from several different applications in your final multimedia product.

Before you start, test the compatibility of all software, especially in relationship to importing and combining file types. *It is critical to create an entire "test" sample and test it on the target delivery machine before you start the main production.*

This is also the time to calculate the total size of all your animation files and the load times they will require for each branch or subsection of your multimedia program.

Once you have selected the animation technique, select the software. Animation is nothing more than the illusion of movement. How the application achieves this illusion varies greatly, as does the type of interface you are given to "program" the animation.

Single frame interface. This interface, common in presentation software, is most often used to control transitions between one screen or "slide" and another. It includes slides, dissolves, windows and turning slates. It can sometimes perform color cycling.

Key frame interfaces give the illusion of movement by changing the elements and their positions over time. The animation is defined by a process called "in-betweening" or "tweening". You create at least the first and last frame (called key frames) in the animation, telling the computer where all the elements are in the frame. The animation software then computes where all the elements should be in intervening frames.

For example, you might put a ball at the top right of the first frame and at the bottom left of the last frame. Tell the computer how long you want the animation to last. Then the computer creates the needed number of frames, moving the ball slightly downward and towards the left in each frame. While the computer does most of the animation work for you, it doesn't give you control of the "tween" frames. For more control, you must add more key frames.

Event interfaces are similar to key frame interfaces, except instead of the computer tweening movement between key frames, an event interface generates a series of "events," moving the ball in distinct time frames. While the final product looks the same, this approach allows you to place events on a timeline. In the more flexible event interface applications, you have both key frame and event interface power.

Discrete frame interface gives you the most control over your animation but can also be the most time-consuming. Using the discrete frame interface, you tell the computer exactly where everything is and what it looks like on every frame. In most cases, you start with the key frame and tweening process, then you fine-tune each individual frame to your liking. However, this interface may not give you event *control*. That is, you may not be able to say, "Start moving this ball down the screen" three seconds after the overall animation has started without actually putting the ball on the screen where you want it.

Behavioral interfaces are a unique and powerful type of software which focus on the characteristics of the objects, instead of solely a timeline. In addition to setting up the starting positions of the objects, you also designate the type of materials they are made of and how they will act. For example, if you set up a ball flying towards a wall, the computer will animate the action based on the materials. The resulting animation changes if you choose 1) the ball is rubber and the wall is brick, 2) the ball is steel and the wall is glass or 3) the ball is really an egg and the wall is carpet.

You can imagine how powerful and useful (and expensive) this software could be. While it generally requires a bit of programming skill, the results are outstanding.

Storyboarding

Once you have selected your animation software, begin storyboarding, basing it on your application's capability. To get the most from your animations, faithfully complete all tutorials, and search out magazine articles and discussion groups about "undocumented" capabilities. This way, you will know what you can and cannot do.

Sketch out your ideas in a simple storyboard (see TV chapter for details on storyboarding) and brainstorm with the entire multimedia team. Make modifications and *then beta test your storyboard with your audience* before beginning the time-consuming process of animation. Remember that this is a visual medium, and the more concrete your ideas are when you begin, the less time you will spend reworking them later.

Once you have a satisfying storyboard, begin creating the building blocks you will insert into the animation software, such as the backgrounds for spot animations and the three-dimensional wire frames for a 3-D animation. As soon as possible, assemble a complete "test" animation to catch visual flaws early. Take care to correctly name and back up your finished animations products. Animation is too expensive and time-consuming to be lost through careless computer practices. If your graphic files are large enough to require compression, see the discussion under digital video below.

Video

Video in a multimedia system can be a powerful element, whether it comes from a videodisc or digital video file. It adds realism and lifelike demonstrations that animation and stills can never replace. Multimedia video design, planning, and production is the same for both digital and disc video. It involves careful message design, tight scripting, carefully composed and captured field shots, clear sound, and tightly edited video clips.

Because video production is costly, both in terms of production dollars and memory or hardware demands, the design plan should exploit video's ability to capture and convey emotion, action, and the beauty of motion. Do not use it to merely repeat information a still could convey just as effectively. If you are scripting video text, either for actors, narrators, or screen text, remember that the video itself is a message and the script does not have to repeat every message the video is already conveying.

Keep video clips short and meaningful. The hardware and software constraints limiting video clip lengths in multimedia is actually excellent in terms of design. Many older multimedia applications using videodiscs incorporated video clips which were too long. Once multimedia users become "intoxicated" with interactive power, they will rarely sit or stand passively by for minute after minute watching a linear video, or "TV-like," presentation.

About 90 percent of the workforce was raised on TV, and 20 percent on MTV (Johnson, 1994). They expect their video clips to come in bite-sized, fast moving pieces, probably under 10 seconds. In fact, even a 10-second clip can feel like it's playing forever to a user standing in front of a busy mall kiosk when friends and noisy attractions are competing for attention.

The video scripting and production techniques in the field include most of those discussed in the Video Productions chapter. However, if you intend to digitize the video, keep the background static and uncluttered. At almost all costs avoid pans (camera movement side to side) tilts (camera movement up and down), and zooms (camera movement in and out) because these camera actions change every pixel of information in every frame and create huge, difficult to compress video files. Most multimedia videos should probably be set shots (little camera movement) with the action coming from the subject moving within the frame. For talking heads destined for digital compression, set up fairly tight shots before a simple, light colored background.

Videodisc

Common multimedia videodiscs (or laserdiscs) will hold 30 minutes of full motion video, or 54,000 still frames. If full frame, full motion (30 frames/second) video of extremely high quality is what your multimedia application needs, there is still little which can rival the videodisc. In general, a videodisc requires about the same production time as digital video and the quality of video from the disc is not limited by the processor speed or the hard drive space. When creating the master tape for a disc, place a single still frame at the end of each motion video clip to eliminate potential "shuttering" when the disc parks (or freezes) on the last frame. Keep a careful log of all visual resources put on the disc (with a potential of 54,000 stills, creating a log retroactively can be crazy), and run a check disc several times during development to verify that the video and sound levels, video field dominance, and video content are following the design specifications.

Digital video

Computer processing times, software capabilities, video compression techniques, and hard drive capabilities have all finally developed enough to allow video to run directly from the hard drive or CD-ROM. While the motion, size, and image quality are currently inferior to that of a videodisc, digital video eliminates the need for expensive video cards in the delivery machines.

Digital video clips, such as those created with *Video for Windows* or *QuickTime*, usually run in a 1/4 or 1/16 frame window, and often run at frame rates of 12 frames per second,

instead of the 30 frames per second associated with full motion video. Digital video also often looks rather washed out or blotchy because much of the detail is removed in compression. In addition, the color depth, or bit depth, (see discussion above) is normally 8-bit (256 colors), which is a major quality step down from the millions of colors video usually requires. On the positive side, however, these digital video windows usually provide a full control panel to review, fast forward, play in slow motion or skip. Steps for incorporating digital video follow:

Digitizing the video. This is the step when the computer comes into play, and the capability of the hardware makes a major difference between a production that looks amateurish or professional. Because digitizing takes time and valuable hard disk space, script and review the raw footage carefully, and digitize only those sequences you are sure to need.

The computer digitizing the video will require a video capture card (built into the "AV" Quadras and PowerMacs and hardware-accelerated video capture cards for PCs), lots of RAM (16 Meg or more is common), and a fast, fairly large hard drive. The quality will improve drastically by using a bigger, faster hard drive (2GB arrays are common), a professional transcoder (to process the analog signal into video information), and a tape sampling software system (such as DiaQuest) which controls the tape deck for multiple passes allowing the computer to sample every several frames on each pass.

Editing the video. Simple video editing capabilities, such as being able to clip the ends off the video and "glue" segments together, is often available in the capture software. However, if you want to include any sophisticated transitions, adjust the quality of the video, or incorporate text into the video image, you will need more sophisticated editing software.

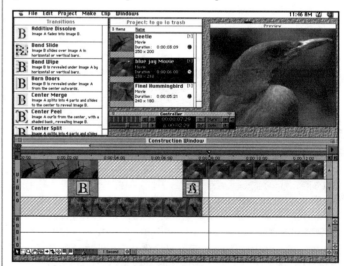

Video editing software: Many powerful video editing software packages now are on the market. Most allow you to store different clips of video, and add transitions, audio, and special effects. Adobe Premiere©, Adobe Systems, shown with permission.

Special effects and transitions can include almost any effect normally seen on TV, including page turns, slow motion, and morphing (slowly transforming one image into another). The overall appearance of each video clip can be altered by applying video filters to darken, brighten, distort, or color correct (similar to filters described in still graphics). This software also allows you to split the screen and play several motion video clips at once or flip and turn the video within the screen. Just remember that *overuse or unnecessary use of special effects* is a telltale sign that an amateur is "playing with some new toys" instead of working to communicate.

Video compression is an important step because it reduces the video file size by removing marginally important data. For example, a screen full of nothing but black video would be described in the initial digitizing process as "The first pixel is black, the second pixel is black, the third pixel is black..." and so on. Video compression would simple say, "Black everywhere," which, of course, takes a lot less memory to store. There are two types of compression: lossless and lossy.

Lossless compression guarantees that the information you uncompress from a lossless compressed file is exactly the same as the information you originally compressed. It is 100 percent accurate, not dropping out any information just to make the file even smaller. This is best used on images that have very precise aspects which are going to be displayed for enough time to look at them, or for object-oriented images, because any lost information will be noticeable.

Lossy compression sacrifices a small amount of the information in order to reap benefits in compression effectiveness or decompression speed. These algorithms mainly are used for sound and video although, depending on how lossy the algorithm is, lossy also can be used to store large, high-resolution still images if space is an issue.

QuickTime™ Technology is a good example of lossy compression. It is an effective way to store video, animations, still images, and sound with stunningly small file sizes. A 640 by 480 pixel, 24 bit color image, normally over 850K in size, can be compressed, using the JPEG (Joint Photographic Expert Group) lossy compressor, down to only about 36K, or less than five percent of its original size. This means you could put about 35 such images on a high-density floppy disc compressed, as opposed to only one uncompressed image. The price you pay, of course, is a degradation of the image. But in busy, photographic images, especially ones which are not going to be displayed for long (such as in video), the benefits of compression can greatly outweighs the drawbacks.

In addition, most lossy compression algorithms are adjustable. For instance, the JPEG algorithm allows you to select anywhere from low quality, which is a decent approximation of the original, to high quality, which is only minutely off. The compression quality you select will depend on how much quality is needed in the image relative to the memory space demands.

Compression algorithms are getting better and better. Your best bet is to make a sample out of each compression algorithm available to you to find out the most effective compressor that retains the quality you require

Sound

Nothing perks up a presentation like adding sound. Most computers you can purchase now either have multi-channel sound capabilities built-in, or can be upgraded to include it. The Macintosh computers come packaged with two or four channel sound, while most PC models need a sound card to take advantage of good sound. Chances are, if you go out to purchase a PC, your retailer will bundle it with a sound card; it's not standard, but it's close.

The sound output on desktop computers has already reached near-CD quality. In fact, you can play audio CDs on them, right from a CD-ROM drive, but the computer allows much more than just CD playback. There are dozens of composition and editing packages that allow you to create, modify, play back, and record original musical scores. Or, you can plug a microphone right into your computer and record your voice. You could also plug the computer into a VCR and capture audio off of a VHS tape. Any kind of sound that can go into a standard tuner can be captured, edited, and returned using the computer.

There are several different ways you can store sound on your computer. Probably the most basic is the AIFF (Audio Interchange File Format) file type. This is simply the wave output of the sound, optimized. It is just about the lowest common denominator of sound files; most audio programs can import and export the AIFF format. Another popular audio technique is use of a MIDI. While AIFF stores the sound in a file, the MIDI "generates" the sound from a stored musical score, using virtual instruments also contained in the file. A MIDI is not particularly appropriate for recording someone who is talking, but it is excellent for musical pieces since you can change the instruments, change the play rate, modify notes, and your MIDI output will reflect the changes. With an AIFF file, you can't do this; you would have to go back and create the file from scratch.

Often, it is convenient to take advantage of the compression technology available in digital video to compress audio as well. It is possible to create a digital video file that has only sound and no picture. This is handy for two reasons. First, sound files can get very large, and any compression is helpful. Second, it is often important to keep track of how much of the sound has been played. Digital video generally has devices that can pass that information to the user, while the AIFF format might not.

Creating sound resources is generally pretty simple. You will probably have an application that will capture or create the sound for you, either by capturing it from an audio port, or by generating a musical score from the notes you have placed in a composition package. But there are still two things you should consider.

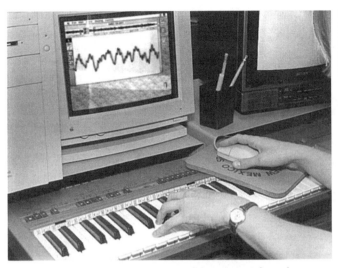

Digital Music: You may choose to edit your sound on the computer and even create your own unique music. Several sound packages are available, and it is now possible to plug a keyboard directly into your computer for composing.

The first is the sheer size of sound files. When you think of how much information has to be passed to the speakers to make them vibrate in the exact manner to produce the sound you want, you will realize that there is a lot of information going out, even in a ten second sound bite. For this reason, it is generally a good idea to find ways to reuse or reduce the amount of sound you will need on a project. Also, the longer the sound, the longer it will take to load. If your application must load the sound before playing it, you will get a long pause before a long sound bite.

The other thing you should consider is the quality of your sound file. Normally, you will want to use the best sound quality possible, but by slightly reducing the sound quality, you can reap benefits in terms of the memory required for the sound. In just about every case, 22 mHz is the standard "sample rate." Standard CD-quality is 48 mHz. This rate simply refers to how often information is sent to the speakers. However, you can often reduce the playback rate to 11 mHz, and still have an acceptable sound, while cutting the memory required in half. There are even slower playback rates, like 7.4 mHz and 5.5 mHz, but these should only be used when memory management is critical, and the sound quality does not need to be good.

Copyright restrictions still apply

The computer's capabilities allow you to easily scan photographs, record audio, capture clips from movies, and digitize text it makes copyrights no less valid than in any other media, however. Copyright infringement, either deliberate or unintentional, should be a very real concern for multimedia developers. Use of copyrighted photographs, music, newscasts, logos, and video is illegal.

To avoid copyright infringement, use care to obtain permission from the owner of the copyright. Many larger companies hire employees specifically to obtain permissions for them. For the smaller developer, royalty-free stock photo CDs and music are a wise investment. But even then, carefully read the fine print, especially if you plan to mass produce or sell your product. Sometimes it is easier and cheaper to simply capture or create your own original material.

In addition to the elements of the program, be careful of copying the look or feel of a program. You only have to consider the Apple Computer vs. Microsoft vs. Hewlett Packard case to be alerted to the dangers of copying the way a program looks, feels, or works, even if you are presenting a different type of material. If in doubt, contact your attorney as well as several up-to-date references.

Last but not least

If all the multimedia hype in the media is to be believed, multimedia will be the technology that will change the way you shop, play, and learn. *Newsweek's* May 31, 1993 cover story proclaimed it the new "Zillion-dollar Industry (maybe)" (Kantrowitz).

It is more likely that multimedia will simply be one more powerful tool available to educate, entertain, and archive valuable information. The real beauty is that new emerging software and hardware have opened the door to the average computer user who takes a little extra time and effort to explore the wonders and pitfalls of Multimedia Land. Regardless of the level of your own involvement, multimedia is sure to influence your life in some way in the years to come.

Bibliography

Ankeny, M. (1993, May/June). "Keeping the What if in interactive." *Computer Pictures*, 11(3), S-22.

Arwady, J., & Gayeski, D. (1989). *Using video: interactive and linear designs.* Englewood Cliffs, JF: Educational Technology Publications.

Bergman, R. E., & Moore, T.V. (1990). *Managing interactive video/multimedia projects.* Englewood Cliffs, NJ: Educational Technology Publications.

Donahue, T., & Donahue, M. (1983, December). "Understanding interactive video." *Training and Deveopment Journal*, 26-29.

Feltcher, J.D., "Effectiveness and cost of interactive videodisc instruction in defense training and education," *Multimedia Review*, Spring 1991, pgs. 33-42.)

Forester, T., & Morrison, P. (1990). *Computer ethics: cautionary tales and ethical dilemmas in computing.* Cambridge, MA: MIT Press.

Gleason, J. (1993). *A Design Plan for Interactive Multimedia Public Informaton Systems.* Self-Published.

Gleason, J., Fedale, S. V., King, D.A., & Miller, M.G. (1987). "Interactive Video: A report from the ACE western regional workshop." *Journal of Applied Communications*, 70(3), 15-22.

Jerram, P. (1994, June). "CD-ROM titles explosion." *New Media*, 4(6), 40-47.

Johnson, D. (1985). *Computer ethics*. Englewood Cliffs, NJ: Prentice-Hall.

Jones, M.K. (1989) *Human-computer interaction: a design guide*. Englewood Cliffs, NJ: Educational Technology Publications.

Kahle, B. (1991, July). "Why Nintendo Games Will Save the World by Encouraging Learning and Growing in Children." (Available from Internet, Brewster@Think.com).

Kantrowitz, B. (1993). "An interactive life." *Newsweek*, May 31, 1993. pp 42-44.

Kearsley, G. & Frost, J. (1985, March). "Design Factors for successful videodisc-based instruction." *2593*, 7-14.

Kearsley, G. (1984) *Training and technology*. Reading, MA: Addison-Wesley.

Koritizinsky, I.H. (1989). "New Ways to Consistent Interfaces." In J. Nielsen (Ed.). *Coordinating user interfaces for consistency*. Boston: Academic Press, Inc.

Marcus, A. (1984, December). "Corporate identity for iconic interface design: the graphic design perspective. *IEEE Computer Graphics and Applications*, 4(12), 24-32.

Mills, C. (1987). "Usability testing in the real world." *SIGCHI Bulletin*, 19(1), 43-46.

Rubenstein, R., & Hersh, H.M. (1984) *The human factor: designing computer systems for people*. New York: Digital Press.

Sheff, D. (1993). *Game Over: How Nintendo zapped an American industry, captured your dollars, and enslaved your children*. New York, NY: Random House.

Tullis, T. S. (1983). "The formatting of alphanumeric displays: a review and analysis." *Human factors*, 25(6), 657-682.

Extra reading and subscription options

Both Macintosh and PC-based environments

New Media
Targets innovative professionals who are serious buyers of multimedia hardware and software.
Published monthly. free to multimedia professionals who qualify.

Presentations: Technology and Techniques for Better Communications
Spans the fields of audiovisual, video, computer graphics, and multimedia. Includes product reviews for the presentations marketplace.
Published monthly. Free to multimedia professionals who qualify.

Computer Graphics World
Designed for high-powered designers, creaters, directors and users of 3-D computer graphics in modeling, animation and multimedia.
Published monthly. Free to graphic artists who qualify.

Multimedia Producer
Creators and developers of interactive multimedia titles and presentations.
Published monthly. Free to multimedia developers who qualify.

CD-ROM Today
Published monthly.

Computer Artist
Published monthly.

Animation Magazine
Published bimonthly.

Macintosh

MacUser
Product reviews on Macintosh products.

Apple
Published monthly.

MacWorld
Dedicated to Macintosh computers, independent of Apple.
Published monthly.
Professional discount for qualifying persons.

Multimedia World
Explores the range of the multimedia-PC market, from titles to multimedia hardware.
Published monthly.

IBM-compatibles

PC World

PC Computing
Magazine for business computing experts using IBM-PC solutions.
Published monthly.

Video, computer graphics, and animation

AV Video

Production and presentation technology.

Designed for professional video producers, includes articles and reviews regarding non-linear editing and computer graphics technology.

Published Monthly. Free to video professionals who qualify.

Digital Video

Focuses on digital video, includes reviews of non-linear editing and computer graphics for all platforms.

Published monthly.

Post Magazine

Focuses entirely on post-production.

Published monthly. Free subscription for video professionals who qualify, by written request.

Presentations: Technology and Techniques for Better Communications

Spans the fields of audiovisual, video, computer graphics, and multimedia. Includes product reviews for the presentations marketplace.

Published monthly.

Instructional Design for Distance Education

Distance education

Distance education provides access to learning when the source of information and the learners are separated by time, distance, or both. Distance education is not tied to a technology. Rather it is the process of designing educational experiences that best suit the learner who may not be in a classroom with an instructor at a specific time.

Distance learning and distance education often are used interchangeably; however, distance learning is the intended outcome of the distance-education process and refers to the learner.

Distance-education trends

While technologies continue to evolve and society continues to change, several trends are emerging which must be considered:

Learners' needs are changing.
People change careers and relocate several times throughout their lives. Learning methods need to become more portable and flexible. Learning is a life-long process.

Learners are consumers.
Distance education provides more freedom for learners and creates more choices than ever before. Technology makes it possible to deliver educational experiences to the home and workplace. Also, universities are in competition for learners with the private sector, non-profit organizations, and other universities.

The role of the educator Is changing.
Education is shifting from a teacher-centered system to a learner centered system. As learner needs change, educators must be flexible and assume different roles. These roles may include facilitator and collaborator. Educators must recognize that learners learn from each other.

These trends point to the need to focus on the learner when designing distance-education programs.

Steps to designing learner-centered distance education

There is a logical process to follow when designing a distance education. Experience in this process is based on instructional-design models that focus on decisions about learners, learner objectives, content, methodology, and delivery.

Although this particular approach identifies steps in a specific order, the process is not totally linear. For example, the instructional designer may be presented with a need and must set goals and define the learner, based on the expressed need.

However, it is not appropriate to define the instructional methodology or delivery method before addressing learner issues.

Goal statement

The first step in designing distance education is to describe the overall objective of your educational effort. This should be expressed in broad terms that are related to an identified concern or needs assessment.

Questions to ask include: What is the need? How specific or how broad is the need?

Defining the learner

The next step is to define the audience (learner) specifically in relation to the identified need. Several questions must be asked, including: Who has this need? Who would benefit from this information? What are the characteristics of these people? What is their environment, culture, socio-economic status, education?

Also consider how they like to get their information: orientation, training, meetings, e-mail, video, etc. What are their time constraints? What do they know about distance learning? What is their past experience with distance education? What do they need to know? What do they know about this topic already? What other information do you know about them?

Be very specific about the audience, choosing one primary audience.

If you are not familiar with the audience, work with someone from the audience or someone who knows the audience.

Learners have unique learning preferences or learning styles. It is important to incorporate as many approaches as possible into the plan to accommodate a wide range of styles.

Writing learner-center objectives

Based on the audience you have defined, the next step is developing learner objectives.

Learner objectives are important when designing all educational experiences because they tell the participants what is expected, what they are to learn, what they are to do, and what the final evaluation will include.

Participants should know the learner objectives for every lesson or module. For the program designer, objectives guide content and its structure. As a rule, they are developed early in the instructional design, checked throughout the process, and revised according to content concerns or audience re-evaluation.

Objectives are derived and written from your audience analysis and goal statement and should be written as action verbs, such as **list**, **describe**, **define**, **verbalize**, **explain**. Words such as **understand** or **learn** are not easily measured because they are not specific as to expected outcome.

One way to develop objectives is the ABCD format:

Audience, Behavior, Conditions, Degree.

(reference: Heinrich, R.M. Molenda, and J.D. Russell. 1989. *Instructional Media and the New Technologies of Learning* (3rd Edition). Macmillan. New York.)

- **Audience** – List the specific characteristics of the audience.
- **Behavior** – Specify the behavior the audience will exhibit if they master the objective.
- **Conditions** - Describe the conditions from which the objective will be accomplished – the restrictions or givens in the situation.
- **Degree** – Define the degree of completion or attainment which participants must achieve for the objective to be labeled successful – what is an acceptable level of performance.

As an example, suppose you are planning a program for faculty in the College of Home Economics. The topic of the program will be designing learner-centered distance education.

A possible set of learner objectives for this audience might include the following:

Upon completing the course, faculty in the College of Home Economics will be able to:

1. List three of five trends in distance education.
2. Define specified technology terms.
3. Outline the steps involved in designing learner-centered objectives, without the aid of reference materials.

Finally, any evaluation of learning should be tied back to these objectives. In designing, consider whether each of the defined objectives can be assessed or measured by some means.

Evaluation

Design the evaluation at the same time the program is being designed. Two types of evaluation used in distance education are called Formative and Summative.

Formative evaluation is done while the program is being developed. A formative evaluation can help you make positive changes to your program while it's taking place or even before it's delivered. It also is used during instruction to see how participants are progressing toward objectives.

Summative evaluation occurs at the end of a program and measures program results, effectiveness, and impact. The summative evaluation can be about the learning, the process, the methodology or any other aspect you wish to measure.

Formative and summative evaluation

Evaluation concern	Formative evaluation	Summative evaluation
Purpose	To make corrections or improvements in a developing or in-process program or participant effort.	To determine if goals of program/instruction were met.
When	During program design.	At the end of program.
What is Evaluated	Program design, content, flow, technical quality. Participant efforts as the program progresses.	The extent to which program goals and objectives were met.
Outcome	Information which improves program or directs instructal efforts.	Final report of program effectiveness and participant achievement.

(Rockwell and King '88)

Developing the content

Using the audience definition, the overall goals and the learner objectives, develop a content outline based on the following:

- What are the key messages to be presented? How do these messages relate to your stated learner objectives?
- What is the order of presentation? (Why was this order selected? How does it relate to the audience need?)
- What examples, metaphors, case studies, or particular details can you use to support the key messages?
- What transitions can be made from one message to the next?

Then, review your list of key messages. Consider the following as you further develop your content outline. How can you narrow the list to focus on the key objectives?

Select the instructional method/strategy

Using the content outline developed, decide on an appropriate method to get the message(s) across. Consider how the audience learns. Some examples include small and large group instruction, self-study, discussion, forums, seminars, problem solving, demonstration, tours, or a combination of any of these methods.

Although many of these methods may seem traditional, these techniques can be used in new ways. For example: a video tour of a facility, an online discussion group, or local site discussion.

Select the delivery method(s)

The final step is to select the delivery or access method. Selecting the primary delivery method must be done while keeping in mind the stated objectives and the instructional method chosen.

A benefit of this process is the opportunity to make decisions about delivery. For some groups, a distance delivery may be inappropriate. If dissemination of information is the primary goal, a news release or media campaign may do the best job.

If a technology is selected as a primary delivery method, first be sure that it is really accessible to learners.

Carefully consider why it was chosen. For example, if there is a need to show a concept, a form of video or still pictures may be appropriate.

Consider how the technology fits the way the audience prefers to get information. If the audience prefers self-instruction, a computer-based tutorial with supporting materials may be most appropriate.

Often, other technologies may be used to support the primary delivery method. For example, an instructional packet with audiotapes and printed materials may supplement a satellite broadcast.

Review the content in light of the planned delivery medium. Can the audience achieve the objectives using this technology? Are some of the examples and key messages inappropriate with this technology?

Decide the level of interaction expected in this project. You may choose an electronic discussion group for large groups who can't get together at one time, or an audioconference for small groups who prefer real-time interaction.

Technologies for distance education

There are a number of technologies available for use in distance education. Most often they are used in combination with each other. There may be one or more primary delivery methods, supplemented by one or more additional technologies. For example, the primary delivery mode may be audio, with print- and computer-based support materials.

The following are delivery and communication modes commonly used in distance education.

Video

This can include distribution of videotape cassettes and live or taped transmission via compressed video, satellite, broadcast, or cable.

Compressed video. Compressed video uses digital technology to compress video images to save transmission-bandwidth. In this way, two-way video conferences can be conducted over telephone lines.

Satellite. Uplink transmitters send a broadcast signal to an orbiting satellite which returns the signal to Earth, for reception by downlink dishes.

Audio

Audio technologies include *telephone*, through the use of conference bridges; *computer*, through the use of audio cards installed in personal computers; *audiotapes* used to augment an instructional package; and *radio*. Audio can be used at a distance as a delivery method or as an interaction tool.

Bridge. An audioconference bridge allows three or more telephone lines to be connected in a single conference. Newer generation bridges allow for polling capabilities among sites with touch-tone phones.

Computer

The computer may be a support tool when self-study software is provided; it becomes an access tool when connected to *Bulletin Board Systems (BBS)* and networks, such as the Internet. The computer allows interaction through electronic mail and the newer collaboration network software.

Electronic mail. *Electronic mail (e-mail)* can be used for communication between and among students and instructors. Lessons can also be delivered to students through an established group list on a preset schedule.

Bulletin board systems. *Bulletin Board Systems (BBS)* provide phone dial-up access to information and discussion through a computer and modem.

Instructors and students are given the opportunity to post information. Various folders (information areas) are established on different topics, and students access those areas to participate in the dialogue.

Internet services. Internet is the global connection of inter-connected computer networks. Gopher is a distributed information system that connects sites worldwide. World Wide Web (WWW) uses hypertext (the ability to "jump" from one subject or idea to a like subject or idea in a different location) to allow students to explore a topic through various multimedia resources including pictures, video, and sound. Internet Relay Chat (IRC) allows participants to join an electronic discussion with other participants at the same time.

Conclusion

This instructional design process is not limited to use in distance education. In fact, one of its many uses is to help the instructional designer determine whether a distance delivery is appropriate, given the audience, objectives, and content. Most important about this process is the emphasis on the learner and the order in which decisions are made.

Satellite videoconference: one form of distance delivery

A popular method of distance delivery is the satellite video-conference featuring one-way video and two-way audio.

This delivery is most appropriate for visual demonstration to large numbers of participants who are geographically dispersed and have some need for real-time interaction.

A delivery of this type requires a fully-equipped television studio or electronic classroom with satellite-uplink capability. On the receiving end, learners must have access to a satellite downlink dish with receiver (television set.)

The key players are the instructional designer, production team leader, content specialist, marketing coordinator, downlink site coordinator, and on-site facilitator. This team must have a close working relationship throughout the instructional design and production process.

In addition, there are several roles and responsibilities to be assigned. The following is a timeline and check-off list that can help keep you organized.

Timelines

Although a four- to six-month lead time enerally is required for program production and marketing, shorter timelines can work if the topic is especially timely or for information-dissemination meetings which don't require much production or downlink site activity. For example, updates on disaster-relief information can be done with very little lead time, provided the information is not available elsewhere.

Initial information about a program, including dates and as much information as possible should go out at least four to six-

months in advance of the program.

Technical information, all materials, and the final agenda should be available one to two months in advance. Keep in mind that many participants don't make final decisions about hosting a downlink site until this information is available.

Pre-production tasks

- Review goals, objectives, target audience

Select content-development team

- Write program-content outline.
- Review instructional methodology and select presentation/training education methods for uplink program and downlink site activities.
- Select programs/projects to showcase.
- Select and secure presenters, panelists.
- Prepare and/or gather handout materials (discussion points, agendas, background materials, bibliographies, information resource guides, exercises)
- Request continuing education credits, if necessary.
- Design formative and summative evaluation.

Select downlink site-coordination team

- Prepare downlink guide. Include all technical information, as well as all handout materials prepared by content team.
- Develop training for downlink sites.
- Respond to requests for information.
- Identify and register downlink sites, coordinators, facilitators.
- Distribute downlink site materials.

Select marketing team

- Create marketing plan including distribution of Downlink Guide, fliers, postcards, news releases.
- Select, prepare and update electronic and surface mailing lists for marketing.

Select production team

- Write draft scripts.
- Select or create supporting visuals, audiovisuals, sets, props.
- Review audience and select appropriate alternative deliveries to comply with the Americans with Disabilities Act.
- Obtain or create presenters' lecture/presentation visuals.
- Create training for panelists.
- Lease satellite time.

- Secure studio-uplink and crew.
- Work with content team to secure program moderator.
- Establish phone or computer-interaction link between downlink sites and studio.
- Create set.
- Prepare scripts for teleprompter.
- Prepare storyboards and character generation.
- Coordinate production requirements with director.
- Conduct rehearsal (technical and programmatic.)
- Preview and modify elements.

Day of broadcast

- Production Team.
- Respond to uplink/downlink technical problems.
- Operate telephones during audience interaction.
- Operate viewer-response system (if interactive tally or other device used).

Post-production tasks

- Hold debriefing meeting with all teams.
- Prepare master tape of videoconference.
- Analyze audience responses/evaluations.
- Write reports.
- Edit, dub, and distribute videotape.
- Prepare and distribute transcripts.
- Review and respond to comments/requests from viewers.

Logistical support

- Invite panelists, speakers.
- Establish and distribute presenters/panelists itinerary.
- Obtain presenters/panelists confirmations.
- Make travel and facilities arrangements (presenters/panelists/moderator, etc.)

Navigating the Internet

What is the Internet?

- Why is it called a superhighway?
- How do I get connected?
- Where is the on-ramp?
- What exit do I take?
- What is the itinerary?
- Will I be able to get off once I'm on?
- What are the rules on the highway?
- Are there any potholes or construction sites?

Are you ready to take a trip inside a world that is not seen, yet is a very active, happening place? This superhighway or infobahn is a high speed digital network connecting people to computers at remote places to retrieve electronic mail messages, data, pictures, video clips, sound, and multimedia documents. Getting on the highway and staying on the road without too many distractions is like sitting at the wheel of your first car.

Ready, set, go – join in with all those who have already traveled into the virtual information world. It is impossible to avoid all the hype in the news which makes it sound like the only place to go for information and communication ventures. The truth is, that it really is a new communication system with great potential.

What is an information highway?

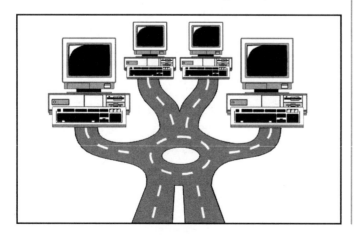

The Internet is often compared to a national highway system similar to the interstate highway system that is found throughout the United States or superhighways in other countries. Some of the similarities are connections to a wide selection of locations as well as easy access to major cities around the country. It is a network of computers at sites all over the world. Every computer on this network has a very specific address so that anyone with the proper connections can access it. Formation of the network structure began as a path for the U.S. Department of Defense to provide access to critical military information. Initial use was limited only to those with high security clearance. Today, the Internet has expanded to become a network globally available to everyone. Since the formation of the network in 1969 with only four host sites, the network has grown to millions of host sites located worldwide. From an extremely limited to a ubiquitous access mode, the Internet has become a very direct connection to everything from neighborhoods to corporate activities. To begin the journey on the Internet, it is necessary to find an "on-ramp" to connect you to information and resources. Before you start your journey, take a few minutes to find out what you need and what you are able to do with the equipment and resources at your site. Indeed, the hype has been strong, but the reality of a very large infrastructure is close to allowing every individual with a computer to gain access. Just like driving a car without any directions, the Internet can be a difficult place to navigate without guidelines and a compass.

Who owns the Internet?

The ownership and management of the Internet is controlled by many sources, but no one specific source has overall responsibility. Transmission Control Protocol/Internet Protocol(TCP/IP) is the language that computers use to communicate on the Internet. A large number of independent organizations agreed to use the same method of transferring data (the TCP/IP protocol) and to connect their networks using this method. A group of networks connected together – any group of networks – is called an "internet". The group of networks that communicates using TCP/IP internationally on a cooperative basis is called the "Internet" (with a capital I).

Each organization owns its own network. Some organizations use common carrier facilities to connect to the Internet. No individual group, organization or government "owns" the Internet. There are policies and requirements to follow and guidelines for appropriate use. The Internet continues to function because it is in each participant's interest to cooperate with the standards. Since failing to cooperate with the standards makes one's network less valuable, these standards have generally been "self enforcing".

A new effort was established to create a network providing broader access and a more organized electronic infrastructure. The National Information Infrastructure (NII) resulted from a bill which seeks to provide access to both resources and people to have connectivity to many educational and research sites. Vice-president, then Senator, Al Gore was the sponsor of the bill, the High Performance Computing Act of 1991, which mandates that federal agencies will serve as information providers, side by side with commercial services, making (for instance) government-created information available to the public over the network. Individuals will have the possibilities to access super computers, computer databases, other research facilities, and libraries.

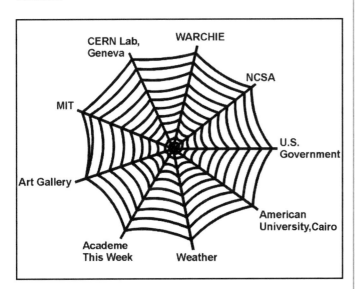

Much of the current network has been established through funding by National Science Foundation Network (NSFNET). This network provides high speed connectivity to the majority of academic and research institutions. The future is unknown, but the Administration has has maintained that the private sector will build, own, and operate the NII, and that the federal investments in pilot projects, R&D, etc., will be a tiny fraction of the private sector investment.

To use the Internet, one needs a computer and a modem or some direct form of connection. Some of the uses of the internet include electronic mail, remote logins to other sites, and file transfers. Those with direct connections to the Internet have additional resources available.

Finding the on-ramp

The toll booth at the entrance to the Internet highway is garrisoned by network service providers. Of course, before you

can pass by you have to pay the tolls which are based on the level of Internet connectivity that you need. Before you get your wallet out, check with the computing center, computer science department, or computer support group at your university or business, to see if they have already paid the tolls. Many companies and schools pay a base fee for their organization's connection and everyone related to those groups is permitted to use it. Many people have access to the Internet and don't realize it. So, make sure you do a very thorough investigation regarding any possible established Internet connections.

All Internet connections are provided by network service providers. Your business or organization pays fees to a regional network service provider for the type of connection, i.e. dedicated, Serial Line Internet Protocol, Point-to-Point Protocol and speed of the connection. There are a number of ways to gain access to Internet. The question is how much do you want to pay for the service.

Types of Internet connections

Direct or dedicated Internet access

The best way to travel the Internet is with your computer directly connected. If you're located at a university you probably have dedicated access to the Internet. Universities and businesses find it economical to lease dedicated telephone lines from service providers that allow them to extend connectivity to any number of people at their site.

If your computer is directly connected to the Internet it will have its own Internet Protocol (IP) address. The advantage of having dedicated access is that your connection is not the limiting factor in being able to run Internet tools, such as Mosaic or NetScape.

Almost dedicated access

The next best thing to dedicated Internet access is through Serial Line Internet Protocol (SLIP) or Point-to-Point Protocol (PPP) software. Using a telephone line and a high speed modem, you can travel the Internet as if you are directly connected. SLIP and PPP are commonly used to connect home computers to Internet either through a service provider or an office network. The advantage of using SLIP or PPP is that they are less expensive than actual dedicated access and your phone line isn't tied to the computer. At this writing, it's fairly complicated to set up your computer to operate using SLIP or PPP but new software is being released to help reduce the confusion. To learn more about SLIP or PPP without getting too technical read "Personal Internet Access Using SLIP or PPP: How You Use It, How It Works," by Frank Hecker (*hecker@access.digex.net*). You can retrieve this document via anonymous FTP from the host ftp.digex.net. The file is in the directory /pub/access/hecker/internet and is called slip-ppp.txt.

Dial-up access to remote host

Another option to access the Internet is through a dial-up connection to a host computer which has dedicated Internet access. With this type of connection your computer is running terminal emulation software and is acting as a terminal connecting to a remote host computer. You can't use all the features available on the network, but it's an affordable option for individual connectivity.

Most computer professionals will tell you to buy the fastest modem you can afford. The recommended minimum speed today will be too slow for the technology of tomorrow. Plan to invest in a faster modem every few years. There are efforts underway to provide more functionality at lower speeds (i.e., compression algorithms) and methods of access (i.e., toll-free 800 numbers). The advantage of connecting to Internet through a remote host is that the start-up costs are low. The disadvantage is you are at the mercy of the service provider and probably only have a few of the Internet services available to you.

Speed of connections to the Internet

Telephone line connections to the Internet vary in both speed and price. The faster your line speed the more it's going to cost. Some of the main lines connecting super computing centers, universities and large businesses are called T3 which can send information at a rate of 45 Mbps or megabits per second. Many refer to the T3 lines as the information superhighway "backbone." It's only a matter of time before the current backbone is replaced by an even faster one. In fact, 1 gigabit per second transmission is being tested. Another connection is

T1 lines move more information at 1.544 mb/sec.

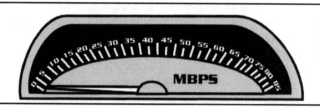

T1 lines move information at 45 Mpbs.

T1 which transmits 1.544 Mbps per second and is extensively used throughout the United States. The average leased dedicated line is 56 Kbps or 56 kilobits per second connections. The standard copper voice telephone line in your home can easily carry 9600 Kbps to 28,800 Kbps (38,400 to 115,200 Kbps with compression) connections. When using a modem to connect to remote host or through SLIP or PPP you will see the amount of time you're connected as charges on your telephone bill (unless your service provider provides an 800 number). Fiber optic lines are becoming commonplace which can provide very high speed connectivity. Current testing shows fiber having connectivity speeds in the gigabit range.

Community networking and free-nets

A number of networking projects are facilitating Internet connectivity in local communities, both urban and rural. These projects are helping to bring public access sites to frequently visited locations within a community. These include libraries, schools, county extension offices, and hospitals. Citizens have a wide range of services available within their local community, including e-mail for communications and Gopher for information discovery and retrieval. If you have a community network or free-net in your town be sure to check it out. It may be a cost effective way to access the Internet.

Internet service providers

You'll need to do some comparison shopping to find a service provider that fits your needs. Many providers supply connectivity within a particular region while others offer worldwide coverage. Initial set-up fees, monthly fees, connect time rates including those during peak times, support availability, and user guides are a few things to compare. One of the biggest expenses is the connect time on your phone line, so check if 800 number service or local exchange access is offered. A listing of service providers is available in most Internet books, and check your local library or book store. A listing is available through the Internet by sending an e-mail message to *info-deli-server@netcom.com* with the following one-line command: send PDIAL.

Your driver's license

Using electronic mail (e-mail) to communicate with others has become one of the most popular ways of getting both information and messages to others. It's like having an international driver's license which enables you to drive in any country. E-mail allows individuals all over the world to communicate easily with little expense. A person can send a message to another person or group of people which can be read at a later date. Mail is sent across phone or data lines from one computer system to another. The computers use a common language to transfer the data. Anyone can get an e-mail address by participating in commercial or private Internet services.

What is an Internet address?

An Internet address indicates where an e-mail box is located on the network, much like your U.S. postal address indicates where to send your regular mail. All Internet addresses follow the same format:

userid@domain

Here's an example of an Internet address:

etaricani@psupen.psu.edu

The "userid" is a person's userid or a specific name for their e-mail box and the "domain" is the name of the host computer. An @ character (the "at" symbol) separates userid and domain.

When you send an e-mail message, the computer first looks at the "domain" to see where to send the message. It's similar to city, state, and country in the U.S. Post Office addressing scheme. After the message arrives at it's destination, that computer looks at the "userid" and places the message in the correct e-mail box.

Name	City	State	Country
etaricani	@ psupen	psu	edu

In our example, the domain psupen.psu.edu has three parts, or sub-domains. Reading the address from right to left, "edu" tells us that the computer is located at an educational institution. This is considered the top-level domain and for addresses within the United States other top-level domains include the following.

Domain	Definition
com	commercial organization
edu	educational institution
gov	government
mil	military
net	networking organization
org	non-profit organization

E-mail originating from outside the United States will have two-letter country codes as the top level domain. For example: fr is France, au is Australia, ca is Canada, de is Germany.

Finding e-mail addresses

One of the first questions new users ask is, "How do I find someone's e-mail address?" Although Internet directory tools are available, the best way to get an e-mail address is to ask the person for it. It's common practice to list your Internet e-mail address on your business cards and office stationary. There isn't one single e-mail address registry but a number of directory services. One popular group of services are the "white pages" directories, named after the white pages in your telephone book. If you're looking for a colleague's e-mail address and you know which university they're from, you can check that location's CSO name server. "CSO" refers to the Computing Services Office at the University of Illinois, Urbana, where the software was developed and is a white pages directory. The CSO name servers are very popular among universities and usually contain information about both students and faculty/staff. Using Gopher to connect to a specific university will allow you to access the CSO phone book for that location. Here's an example, selecting the Pennsylvania State University's CSO.

Sample screen

```
Penn State telephone and other directories
-> 1. Penn State telephone directory lookup <CSO>
    2. College Information Numbers.
    3. Index of Personnel by Country of Experience.
    4. Index of Personnel by Language Competence.
    5. Notes on Directory Information.
    6. Phone Dialing Instructions.
    7. Phone books at other institutions.
    8. Telephone Area Codes by State.
    9. Telephone Area Codes in Numerical Order.
   10. Telephone Exchanges of Pennsylvania.
```

The first menu item, Penn State telephone directory lookup <CSO> has the CSO suffix at the end of the line. This represents a CSO name server. After selecting that option you're presented with a directory look-up containing various fields. Typical fields you may find include: name, e-mail, campus address, curriculum, permanent address, and nickname. Each is available for searching. In this example we typed the name, Ellen Taricani, which resulted in the following information.

Sample screen

```
name:          Taricani, Ellen M
alias:         ext2
email:         ext2@email.psu.edu
campus:        University Park
curriculum:    NONE
phone:         +1 814 863 2533
address:       405 AGRICULTURAL ADM BLDG
               : UNIVERSITY PARK, PA 16802
department:    College of Agricultural Sciences
admin_area:    College of Agricultural Sciences
title:         TRNG & SPT SPEC
```

Two other white pages directory services on the Internet are "whois servers" and X.500 directories. Whois servers allow you to search a database of names within an organization. The X.500 directory service was selected by the Organization for International Standardization (ISO) to be the standard for directories on the Internet. For more information on using directories and finding someone's e-mail address on the Internet check any good Internet book or guide.

E-mail mailing lists and discussion groups

Discussion groups, forums, and mailing groups are popular ways to talk with others with similar interests about various topics. The difference with discussion groups or mailing lists is that an e-mail address stands for a group of people rather than just an individual. They are most often created to address a very specific topic. People can join a list for a short time or stay as long as they are interested in the topic. A number of software programs provide discussion group or mailing list capability on the Internet. Popular ones within Extension are listserv, almanac, majordomo and listproc.

Listserv overview

Listservs offer a variety of topics such as many academic and research topics, computers, and many fields of interest. To get a directory of all listservs available, send an e-mail message to *listserv@umdd.umd.edu* (or another listserv site). In the body of the message, type the command: list global. (Be careful, this list is very, very long and may not be one you want to sort through.) It's better to search for a particular topic by adding a search word to the global command e.g., list global dairy.

How to subscribe to and unsubscribe from a listserv mailing group

1. Send an e-mail message to listserv@ followed by the address. For example, to subscribe to list a located at the University of Maryland you would send a message to list serv@umdd.umd.edu.

2. In the body of your message type the command: SUB followed by the list name and your first and last name. For example, to subscribe to a list called Dairy-L you would type: *subscribe dairy-l Joe Smith*.

3. To post a message to the group, send a message to the list name followed by the address, i.e. *dairyl@umdd.umd.edu*.

4. To unsubscribe from the group, send a message to the listserv address with the command: unsubscribe and the list name. For example, to unsubscribe from the Dairy-L listserv you would send a message to *listserv@umdd.umd.edu* with the command: *unsubscribe dairy-l*.

Almanac overview

Almanac was developed by the Cooperative Extension System through a W. K. Kellogg Foundation grant and is used to manage mailing lists and discussion groups. A number of Cooperative Extension sites throughout the United States operate almanac servers. They are very easy to use because they operate through your current e-mail system. Commands most often used to interact with almanac are: "subscribe," "unsubscribe," and "send."

Extension's current almanac sites

Location	Internet Address
Auburn University	almanac@acenet.auburn.edu
Cornell University	almanac@cce.cornell.edu
CSREES-USDA	almanac@esusda.gov
National Ag Library/CSREES-USDA	almanac@cyfer.esusda.gov
North Carolina State University	almanac@ces.ncsu.edu
Oregon State University	almanac@oes.orst.edu
Purdue University	almanac@ecn.purdue.edu
University of Missouri	almanac@ext.missouri.edu
University of Wisconsin	almanac@wisplan.uwex.edu
Journal of Extension	almanac@joe.org

How to find what's in Almanac

1. Send an e-mail message to *almanac@esusda.gov* or another almanac of choice. Each site maintains a subject catalog for that location.

2. In the body of your message type the command: *send catalog*. Don't include any additional text in your message.

3. Almanac will process the message and return the catalog to your electronic mailbox.

4. Request a new almanac catalog periodically to review new additions or changes to previous entries.

How to get the almanac users guide

1. Send an e-mail message to *almanac@esusda.gov* or another almanac of choice. Each site maintains a users guide for that location.

2. In the body of your message type the command: *send guide.*

3. The guide will be sent to your electronic mailbox.

How to subscribe to an Almanac mailing group

1. Send an e-mail message to *almanac@ces.ncsu.edu* or another almanac of choice. (Some sites do not maintain a catalog for their location.)

2. In the body of your message type the command: *send mail-catalog.*

3. To subscribe to a group, send an e-mail message to the almanac site where the mailing group you wish to join is located. For example, to subscribe to the Food Market News newsletter mailing group send a message to *almanac@oes.orst.edu.*

4. In the body of your message type the command: *subscribe fdmktnews-mg.*

5. To unsubscribe from the group, send an e-mail message to the almanac address of the group and in your message type the command: unsubscribe and the name of the group. For example to remove your name from the Food Market News mailing group, send a message to *almanac@oes.orst.edu* with the command: *unsubscribe fdmktnews-mg.*

Command summary for selected mail servers

Almanac, listproc, listserv, and majordomo operate using similar commands. Following is a summary of the most commonly used commands. One important point to remember is that all commands (subscribe, unsubscribe, etc) must be mailed to the mail server or administrative address, i.e. *listserv@domain, almanac@domain, majordomo@domain.* Users sometimes make mistakes and send adminstrative commands to the listname address which in turns sends it to all list members. For more information on commands request the document, "Discussion Lists: Mail Server Commands by James Milles by sending a message to *listserv@UBVM.cc.buffala.edu* with the line: GET MAILSER CMD NETTRAIN F=MAIL.

Function	Command
Join a list:	
listserv@domain	subscribe listname yourname
	e.g. subscribe dairy-l Debbie Shaffer
listsproc@domain	subscribe listname yourname
almanac@domain	subscribe listname

majordomo@domain	subscribe listname
Leave a list:	
listserv@domain	unsubscribe listname yourname
	e.g. unsubscribe dairy-l Debbie Shaffer
	or SIGNOFF listname
listsproc@domain	unsubscribe listname yourname
almanac@domain	unsubscribe listname
majordomo@domain	unsubscribe listname

Summary of lists supported by the mail server:

listserv@domain	lists - its better to search for LIST SERVS of interest by issuing the command:
	lists global /[keyword]
	e.g. lists global /parenting
listproc@domain	lists
almanac@domain	send mail-catalog or send catalog
majordomo@domain	lists

Help or additional information:

listserv@domain	help
almanac@domain	send guide
majordomo@domain	help

Finding out about new resesarch, education, and extension-related mailing lists

There is no master list of research, education, and Extension-related mailing lists, and it takes time to check each almanac mailing list catalog for changes. The best way to learn about new lists is to talk with colleagues, watch for advertisements during national meetings, and check newsletters from state specialists and national program leaders. Periodically, you may see a list referenced in trade publications. New communications and technology resources available through Internet are listed in *CONNEX*, a bimonthly newsletter from the Communications, Technology, and Distance Education unit within Cooperative State Research, Education and Extension Service-USDA (CSREES-USDA). For *CONNEX* subscription information send a message to *action@reeusda.gov* or Jodi Horigan (*jhorigan@reeusda.gov*).

Frequently Asked Questions (FAQs)

Frequently Asked Questions, or FAQs, are lists of common questions and answers that often arise about a particular network tool, news group, or Internet resource. FAQ lists are accumulated and available to assist those using the Internet. Users find FAQ, very valuable because they help to reduce the amount of redundant information posted on the Internet. Check if a FAQ is available when you join a new discussion group or when learning to use a new network tool.

Following the rules

Acceptable Use Policy

Acceptable Use Policy (AUP) was established by the NSFNET to keep an eye on network activities. One of the main points in the policy is that the transmission of "commercial" information or "commercial" traffic is not allowed across the NSFNET backbone. There are many gray areas with the current list of AUPs, because it is so difficult to judge what is acceptable regarding information exchange. With the advent of many commercial ventures, these are due to change and be restated for the new uses.

Netiquette

Recognizing others and being courteous of them is important to maintain some semblance of civility on the network. Remember that although you are communicating using a computer, you are not communicating *to* a computer. There is a real person reading your message on the other end. The bottomline is to be brief and try to summarize your thoughts – no rambling. Your words become an image of you to others. Your presence is created in the style that you write and the manner that you respond to others.

Think about those who are reading the message.

At times, a scattered use of smileys or abbreviations may be appropriate.

Smileys, a combination of symbols used to create faces, may assist in making a point, i.e. :-) and :-(.

It is important to be careful about copyrights and licenses when using information that is found on the Internet. Cite appropriate resources for any information that is used. Check your style manual for the correct syntax.

At the bottom of e-mail messages, a signature should be added to identify yourself and let others know a little about you. At a minimum, your signature should include your name and e-mail address. One caution is to keep your signature simple, avoid extravagant graphics created from ASCII characters. It's common to see about four or five lines which include a professional title, office address, voice and fax numbers as part of the signature.

Symbols and signs on the road

Many signs on the road help dertermine the correct protocol. There are times that you might see someone responding to you in all caps. This is not friendly fire! All caps implies that the person is yelling at you.

Some other words that you might see and not really understand are btw, fyi, imho, wrt. These abbreviations stand for "by the way", "for your information", "in my humble opinion", and "with respect to." There are others that may be found as you advance in your communication skills and others that you may actually create for your own unique identification.

Life in the "faster" lanes

If you imagine that the Internet is a three lane highway, many drivers spend most of their time cruising in the e-mail lane which has already been described. There are two other

lanes on the Internet highway that provide different services for those who are ready to explore new places. Telnet or "remote login" is the second of the three standard TCP/IP protocols which comprise the basic lanes on the Internet highway. Telnet allows any Internet user to initiate an interactive work session with another computer host on the network. The telnet protocol allows you to have the resources of hundreds of Internet hosts at your fingertips. With a login id and a password on an appropriate host, you visit a library, check the weather forecast, interact with a community bulletin board, or search an on-line information service.

Telnet is similar to making a telephone call. By dialing a phone number you connect your telephone to another telephone; by initiating a telnet session you "connect" your keyboard and monitor to another host computer. In a phone call, the call is completed when someone answers the telephone which is ringing; in a telnet session, the connection is completed when you supply your login id and password. Unless you can provide an appropriate login id and password, the host computer will refuse your connection, in the same way that a phone call is not completed if it keeps ringing and no one answers. But once the phone is answered (and the remote login is completed) you can carry on an interactive, real-time conversation with the person (or computer) at the other end of the connection.

The third lane on the basic Internet highway is the FTP lane. FTP is the acronym for "File Transfer Protocol." FTP is the third of the three basic protocols which comprise the TCP/IP suite. FTP is the process that allows Internet users to transfer all types of files – text files, PostScriptâ files, audio files, graphic images, full motion video files, software, etc.– rapidly between one computer and another computer on the Internet. Just as telnet "connects" your local keyboard and monitor to remote hosts, FTP "connects" your local disk drive(s) to the disk drive of a remote host and allows you to transfer files.

FTP hosts are usually established on the Internet to provide public access to collections of files which can be downloaded at no cost. Although these FTP sites are accessible to the public, they generally require the login id "anonymous" and the user's e-mail address as the password before granting access to the file collection. This practice has lead to the common use of the term "anonymous ftp."

A ride in the country

Sometimes, the life in the fast lanes on the interstate is more than you want to deal with, and a simple quiet ride in the country is where you want to be. Cruising the information superhighway can be just like that – for the fast-moving information adventurer, the basic Internet tools of telnet and ftp satisfy our needs; but for others, some newer tools make the Internet a more pleasant place to work.

Gopher. One of the first widely available information discovery tools on the Internet is Gopher. Gopher was developed at the University of Minnesota to provide a simple mechanism for multiple hosts on the Internet to share information easily with a widely disbursed community of users. The Gopher developers at the University of Minnesota Computer & Information Services Gopher Consultant service define the term "Gopher" in this way:

Gopher n.
1. Any of various short tailed, burrowing mammals of the family *Geomyidae*, of North America.
2. (Amer. colloq.) Native or inhabitant of Minnesota: the Gopher State.
3. (Amer. colloq.) One who runs errands, does odd jobs, fetches or delivers documents for office staff.
4. (computer tech.) Software following a simple protocol for tunneling through a TCP/IP internet.

The Internet's Gopher uses a simple client/server protocol that can be used to publish and search for information held on a distributed network of hosts. The major advantage of using Gopher to navigate along the back roads of the Internet is that Gopher clients have a seamless view of the information anywhere in the Gopher world. You don't need a login id, password, machine name, or IP address to find information when using Gopher; the Gopher software does all the navigating through the Internet for you even though the information is distributed over many different hosts. The other advantage of Gopher is that it presents a very simple interface to the user. Gopher clients have two choices to move around in "gopherspace." The first choice is to navigate through a straightforward menu which is structured like a standard outline. In the menu, you can move through a hierarchy of directories and documents.

The process of navigating through menus is often simplified by the presence of a second option, an index server. An index server will often present the user with an option like "Search the contents of .... <?>". After a keyword is specified by the user, the index server will return a list of all documents that contain one or more words. Since the index server does full-text searches, every word in every document is a keyword. This option is particularly helpful when searching on-line phone books or catalog listings. If you want to test a gopher client without setting up your own gopher server you should configure the client to talk to *gopher.micro.umn.edu* at port 70. This will allow you to explore the distributed network of Gopher servers at the University of Minnesota. You can try the Unix client by telneting to *consultant.micro.umn.edu* and logging in as "Gopher".

Veronica. As Gopher servers expanded in popularity and use, it became increasingly difficult to find specific information without the tedious process of examining all of the menus on each Gopher server. The solution to this problem is the information discovery tool developed at the University of Nevada-Reno called Veronica – "Very Easy Rodent-Oriented Net-wide Index to Computerized Archives." Veronica offers a keyword search of most gopher-server menu titles in the entire gopher web. As archie is to ftp archives, veronica is to gopherspace. A keyword search can be done using Veronica, and the result is a customized menu of Gopher items, each of which is a direct pointer to a Gopher data source containing reference to the original keyword.

In essence, Veronica collects all Gopher items containing the original keyword and provides them in single gopher menu. Because Veronica is accessed through a Gopher client, it is easy to use, and gives access to all of the types of data supported by the Gopher protocol. To try Veronica, select it from the "Other Gophers" menu on Minnesota's Gopher server, or point your Gopher at:

Name=Veronica (search menu items in most of GopherSpace)
    Type=1
    Port=70
    Path=1/veronica
    Host=futique.scs.unr.edu

World Wide Web–The World Wide Web (WWW) project was started and driven by CERN (the European Laboratory for Particle Physics in Geneva, Switzerland). It seeks to build a worldwide distributed hypermedia system accessible via the Internet. Like Gopher, WWW is also based on a client/server protocol; this protocol is known as the Hyper-Text Transfer

Protocol (HTTP). In the WWW environment, hypertext defined as "text with pointers to other text" and it is transferred through the Internet with the pointer included in the document. In addition to hypertext documents, WWW servers can also server hypermedia files. Hypermedia is a superset of hypertext – it is any medium (audio, motion video, a graphic, etc.) with internal pointers to other media or to text files. This means that WWW clients might display images or sound or animations in addition to text files. WWW servers are accessed by any number of different "browser" programs which operate as clients on the local workstation or Internet host. The browser reads documents or and can fetch documents from other sources. In addition, these browsers work with a number of "helper" programs which enable you to playback audio clips, motion video, animations or display graphics files. The most important function of these browsers is that they let you deal with the hypertext/hypermedia pointers in a transparent way - - you simply identify the embedded pointer with a mouse or keyboard command, and the browser fetches the selected document/file from the appropriate WWW server on the Internet. The browsers can, in addition, access files by FTP, NNTP (the Internet news protocol), Gopher and an ever-increasing range of other methods. On top of these, if the server has search capabilities, the browsers will permit searches of documents and databases. One popular browser currently available on the Internet is Mosaic. Mosaic is an Internet-based global hypermedia browser that allows you to discover, retrieve, and display documents and data from all over the Internet. Mosaic was originally developed at the National Center for Supercomputing Applications (NCSA) at the University of Illinois, Urbana-Champaign. An important component in understanding the concepts of the WWW is the URL. URL stands for "Uniform Resource Locator." It is a draft standard for specifying an object on the Internet, such as a file or newsgroup. URLs look like this:

- file://wuarchive.wustl.edu/mirrors/msdos/graphics/gifkit.zip
- file://wuarchive.wustl.edu/mirrors
- http://info.cern.ch:80/default.html
- news:alt.hypertext
- telnet://dra.com

The first part of the URL, before the colon, specifies the access method. The part of the URL after the colon is interpreted specific to the access method. In general, two slashes after the colon indicate a machine name (machine: port is also valid) and the specific file of interest (including the path to that file).

To access the World Wide Web, you have two options – either use a browser on your local workstation or telnet to a browser on the Internet. The preferred method of access of the Web is to run a browser at your local workstation. Browsers are available for many platforms, using either a character-based "terminal" interface or a graphical user interface which provides full "point-and-click" functionality. A full list of browsers

is available at *http://info.cern.ch/hypertext/WWW/Clients.html*.

To try out the World Wide Web, you can also telnet to one of the following sites:

- *info.cern.ch*
  No password is required. This is in Switzerland, so continental US users might be better off using a closer browser.
- *ukanaix.cc.ukans.edu*
  A full screen browser "Lynx" which requires a vt100 terminal. Log in as www.

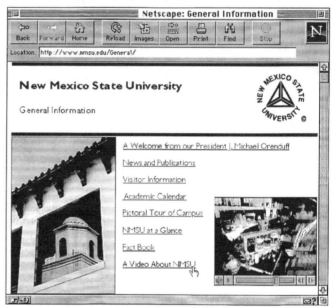

Typical WWW browser.

Resources

Dern, Daniel P. *The Internet Guide for New Users.* New York: McGraw-Hill, Inc., 1994. 570 pp.

Krol, Ed. *The Whole Internet Catalog & User's Guide*, 2nd Edition. Sebastopol, CA: O'Reilly & Associates, Inc., 1994. 543 pp.

Hahn, Harley and Stout, Rick. *The Internet Yellow Pages.* California: Osborne McGraw-Hill, 1994. 447 pp.

Hahn, Hahn and Stout, Rick. *The Internet Complete Reference*. New York:Osborne McGraw-Hill, 1994. 818 pp.

Fisher, Sharon and Rob Tidrow. *Riding the Internet Highway.* Carmel, IN: New Riders Publishing, 1993. 266 pp.

"Entering the World-Wide Web: *A Guide to Cyberspace*," Kevin Hughes, *kevinh@eit.com*. URL: *p://www.eit.com/web/www.guide/* or FTP to *ftp.eit.com* and cd pub/web.guide/.

The Incomplete Guide to the Internet and Other Telecommunications Opportunities Especially for Teachers and Students, *K-12*. FTP *zaphod.ncsa.uiuc.edu* or *ftp.ncsa.uiuc.edu* and look in the education directory. In there is a directory called Education_Resources. or contact: Chuck Farmer *cfarmer@landrew.ncsa.uiuc.edu* NCSA Education Group, 605 E. Springfield Ave., Champaign, IL 61820.

Strategic Communication Planning

Strategic planning is a systematic process used by organizations and firms to assess their strengths and weaknesses; revisit their mission statements; reflect on future economic, demographic and social changes that may affect their operations; and develop strategies to ensure their continuation and future success. Strategic communication planning is an important component of an organization's overall strategic plan. A strategic communication plan may also provide the operating framework for a communication unit.

Historically, strategic plans set medium - and long-term goals and adjust the near-term goals of an organization. Today, however, given the rate and constancy of change, projecting much beyond five years is not only difficult but frequently counterproductive. Of necessity, strategic thinking now has become a way of life. The process is ongoing, and the key questions that affect organizational survival are asked repeatedly. Nevertheless, many organizations continue to find it useful to regularly engage in a more formalized strategic planning process at regular intervals.

Position your organization and your communication unit

What are the benefits of engaging in strategic planning activities? Strategic planning can stimulate organizational renewal, assist the organization make decisions in light of future prospects and trends, and improve its ability to compete against stiffening competition.

As a result, the organization should be better positioned economically and politically and become more accountable and relevant and better able to achieve improved results.

A strategic plan can be a useful tool for monitoring progress in goal attainment, serving as a framework for action. But some organizations indicate that the benefits derived from the strategic planning process – organizational introspection, environmental scanning, mission and goal clarification, team building, strategy development – are of more lasting value than the actual plan that comes out of it.

Though communications have always been considered in an organization's strategic plan, communication systems and delivery alternatives increasingly are shaping the directions taken by

firms and non-profit and educational organizations. Both products and services offered are being re-engineered to better meet the needs and preferences of Information Age consumers. Consequently, greater attention is, and needs to be, given to strategic communication planning. The expertise and skills of communications professionals have never been needed more than they are today.

Unique opportunity for communication professionals

What can communication professionals contribute as members of the strategic planning team? For many years, communicators have been seeking new and better ways of packaging and distributing messages and informational products. In so doing, they have increasingly conducted market research and environmental scanning activities. They have also conducted readership surveys, explored information-seeking behaviors of customers, evaluated the cost effectiveness of various delivery systems and tracked demographic trends. These are all important dimensions of environmental scanning.

While communicators have practiced these information-gathering techniques, their undertakings have sometimes been sporadic, unfocused and perhaps lacking in rigor. Rarely have the findings led to the establishment of measurable objectives or been integrated as a part of organizational strategic planning.

Becoming full partners

For communicators to be full and welcome participants in organizational strategic planning, their scanning activities must be more formally structured and directed toward acquiring insights that will be useful to their partners in the planning process. Their queries should be designed to gather information that can assist planners in making decisions and designing future strategies.

For example, suppose an educational organization is considering making a shift in its product line – producing CD-ROM discs and instructional videotapes instead of printed instructional materials. Communicators on the planning team should be able to provide reliable information concerning projected future use of these technologies, learning preferences and behaviors of the target audiences, availability and market share of similar competing products, and approximate production, packaging and distribution costs of the new products. Then, based on hard information provided by the communicators, the organization can decide on the appropriate goal and implementation procedures to include in the strategic plan.

A strategically thinking organization also may be considering goals related to increased marketing of programs and products, improved internal and external communications or greater staff competency in the use of technology – all of these fall within the domain of communication professionals.

Increasingly, as organizations and their administrators realize that communicators and communication units are an untapped resource, communicators are being called upon to play more proactive roles in organizational planning and consultative services. Communicators have long worked for this kind of recognition, and many have eagerly sought opportunities to act as consulting communicators, professionals contributing knowledge and counsel in addition to the skills needed to produce bulletins, press releases, exhibits, and other products. Strategic planning offers them an excellent entry point to a broader and perhaps more satisfying role in the organization.

Make your unit the R&D arm

In a sense, the communication unit can become a research and development arm of the organization. If that is the direction to be taken, then the strategic plan of the communication unit must embody that change and include goals that will enable communicators to be viewed as credible in the new capacity. Thus, communication units also must revisit their mission statements and set goals that will enable them to take on new roles and responsibilities while continuing to perform more traditional roles in perhaps different and more cost effective ways.

Communication strategic planning, like more generic strategic planning, must be aimed at developing long-term strategy. How can the communication unit get from where it is to where it sees itself being in the future? What functions will no longer be needed? Are there new and different roles and responsibilities to be undertaken? What skills and competencies will be required to perform effectively in the future? What new technologies must be explored and integrated into unit as well as organizational operations? How can new initiatives be staffed and funded?

Organization/communication unit survival linked

The strategic plan of the communication unit must include strategies designed to accomplish the goals set forth and to provide communicators with the expertise needed in organizational

strategic planning. Though the strategic plan of the communication unit must complement that of the organization, it must not be limited to those considerations. The plan is, after all, intended to provide a blueprint for the unit's continuing survival and success.

Therefore, in addition to laying the groundwork for an expanded role in the organization, the plan must ensure the continuing viability of the unit as an entity that conducts excellent media and organizational relations, produces and expands markets for quality informational products, engages in results – producing promotional activities and capitalizing on the availability of new technologies. Goals set forth in the communication strategic plan will include strategies to benefit both the organization and the communication unit.

Find time!

Finding the time to engage in strategic thinking and planning may appear impossible, given the heavy load of production work most communication units carry. But failure to make the time for this worthwhile activity could jeopardize the unit's survival.

A communication unit may feel the need to involve an external consultant in its communication planning efforts, or staff members may feel comfortable facilitating the process themselves, using the following step-by-step process:

STEP 1: Review and refine the unit mission in light of the mission of the organization being served. Are the two in sync?

STEP 2: Identify the values of communication staff members, in both their personal and professional work lives. Are those values compatible with those of the unit and the organization?

STEP 3: Clarify the unit's vision of itself in the future. How does that perception differ from today's reality? How does the organization view the communication unit of the future?

STEP 4: Assess unit strengths and weaknesses. In what ways will they assist, or be barriers to, the unit's moving in desired directions in the future?

STEP 5: Identify external factors and trends that will affect the communication unit and how it does business in the future. In what ways could these forces affect the organization being served?

STEP 6: Develop a list of goals that enables the unit to be futuristic while maintaining essential, ongoing services in a cost-effective manner and discarding non-essentials that have outlived their usefulness. Have unit and organizational needs been adequately accommodated?

STEP 7: Prioritize the goals. What can the unit adequately undertake, given available resources, expectations of funders and unexpected happenings?

STEP 8: Develop measurable objectives for actualizing the goals and spell out the enabling activities that will make accomplishment possible. Does the plan clearly state what resources will be assigned to each objec tive and who will be responsible for making sure the work gets done?

STEP 9: Spell out a strategy for monitoring progress. What yardsticks will be used to measure success?

STEP 10: Identify innovative ways to change directions or redirect efforts if time and circumstances warrant a different scenario. Is the plan a flexible road map or a one-way, dead-end street?

Strategic planning requires leadership, unitwide commit-ment and willingness to engage in the process. It also requires a certain degree of risk. Despite these formidable prerequisites, the payoff can be tremendously rewarding to the individuals participating, the unit and the larger organization affected by the endeavor.

Effective Communication In Crisis

In modern business, whatever the field, a crisis of some type is inevitable. Crises are never convenient and they are always disruptive. An alarming phone call, a damaging headline, a negative radio report, or a detrimental news account could signal the start of a crisis. It is critical that communications professionals be prepared to handle a crisis. Even if the crisis cannot be foreseen, an awareness of crisis management and proper planning can mean the difference between being in control of the situation or being controlled by it, which can lead to disaster.

Your organization should stand ready to respond on a moment's notice, because that may be all the time you have. Your plans must be made well in advance, and be ready to implement, because although you are not in complete control over the crisis, you are in control over your communication about the crisis to the public.

This chapter will analyze types of crises, discuss crisis management and crisis communications and will present techniques that communications professionals need to develop an action plan. Such a plan will allow their organization not only to survive the crisis, but to emerge in a positive condition.

What is a crisis?

Basically, a crisis is anything that suddenly threatens the stability of your organization. David Bastien, writing in MCQ, defines it as a major, unpredictable event that has potentially negative results. The event and its aftermath may significantly damage an organization and its employees, products, services, financial condition, and reputation.

It can erupt from a negative perception about an event or statement, an exaggerated claim by a disgruntled employee, a valid claim by a whistleblower in your organization, management succession, hostile takeover, product defect, or a violent external event. A crisis can be as large as the meltdown at Three Mile Island, the Union Carbide gas leak in Bhopal, India, the Exxon Valdez oil spill, or be as local as an employee charged with sexual harassment or an animal rights protest outside a company facility.

At a college or university, a crisis can be brought about by a fire, explosion or flood on campus; a murder, rape, robbery, assault, suicide; an accident, natural disaster or environmental crisis; a civil disturbance or protest; a negative news report involving a member of the college community; or any myriad of unexpected situations which affect the safety of people or property on campus or which involve students or employees.

A crisis will distract you from your daily routine and divert your focus from important projects, goals, and deadlines. More importantly, it can create serious doubt about the worth or credibility of your organization in the eyes of the public.

A crisis can distort perceptions about your organization. It may involve allegations that tell only part of the story and stimulate negative impressions by the public about your company or institution.

A crisis may polarize or divide your organization by causing employees and management to choose sides, not necessarily based on facts or the best interests of the organization.

An important facet of crisis management is identifying how the crisis is likely to disrupt your organization so that you can strike a balance between handling it and maintaining at least some of your normal work load.

Except in situations where you have taken a calculated risk, a crisis will generally take you by surprise – it will produce a situation to which you must react. Even prudent managers cannot always predict a crisis, but they can understand the elements that comprise a crisis and develop a plan to deal with one when it happens. The quality and thoroughness of the plan will determine the positive or negative outcome.

Types of crises

There are many kinds of crises; knowing which type you are dealing with will enable you to respond to it most effectively.

When a crisis is caused by a dissatisfied employee in your organization spreading false rumors, you must uncover the truth and use it to clarify the misinformation.

A crisis caused by statements taken out of context or made in haste may occur because employees in your organization fail to evaluate the consequences of their comments. They may speak to a reporter without realizing that their comments are always "on the record." They may say more than they can comfortably support with facts or research, then place themselves or you in a position where the communication must be disclaimed, explained or qualified.

Organizations engaging in controversial practices or espousing controversial viewpoints, activities or policies are at greater risk of running into a crisis. Research using animals, radioactive materials or chemicals are examples. In such instances, potential disaster can be caused by a misstatement, a careless act or a misdeed. A crisis manager's job is to know about these hidden calamities and chart the organization's course accordingly. Planning for disasters in advance of the crisis will allow you to positively frame policies, attitudes, and practices to avoid major misperceptions and damaging public opinion.

The most dangerous and potentially damaging crisis of all is the one that takes your organization completely by surprise. Disclosure of such a problem triggers different aspects of the crisis with each new fact that surfaces, with eruptions occurring in all directions. The key to successfully managing the totally unexpected crisis is to gain control through systematic but rapid fact-finding. Your organization should have in place a means to separate truth from fiction. Utilizing accurate information, you may be able to quickly correct the unexpected disaster into a predictable situation and so control the intensity, frequency, and direction of the explosion.

Anticipate issues that could spark a crisis

One of the best ways to anticipate crises is to have key individuals in your organization meet periodically to discuss potential problem areas. Establishing an issues anticipation team comprised of a cross section of the organization's management, employees and stakeholders well in advance of a crisis is an effective preparation. They should identify anything that could possibly go wrong, plan for ways to prevent these events from occurring, and develop policies and procedures to minimize and manage disastrous events if they do occur.

The issues anticipation team members should examine potential problem areas that occur in similar organizations and fields. They should discuss whether company conditions are similar to other organizations where trouble has already occurred. They should look for warning signs from employees and other stakeholders or signs in the external environment that might signal a possible crisis situation.

If warning signs are identified, heed them. Act to prevent potential crises from becoming full-blown ones. To do this, the issues anticipation team should develop strategies and begin dialogue with known or suspected critics. The organization cannot deal with opposing opinions if it has made no effort to find out what they are.

Minimizing and preventing crises

Through thorough self-examination and awareness of what could trigger a crisis, organizations can identify problems and possibly correct or avert some of them. By communicating with

critics before an issue erupts, the organization lessens the chance for misunderstandings. If there are opposing factions, they should be brought together to discuss their differences, to establish rules, and for mediation if necessary. It is easier to understand another person's point of view when you have met and discussed it face to face beforehand. These discussions must take place in an atmosphere of respect. If you don't respect your opponents' right to differ with you, surely they will mistrust and disrespect you. This only leads to heightened tensions and makes crisis resolution more difficult.

Consider the impact of upcoming policy changes on those affected by the changes. Convening focus groups to analyze and test new policies prior to implementation not only can avert problems but also enhances a cooperative – as opposed to confrontational – attitude.

Developing a crisis communications plan

One of the best tools for crisis management is a well conceived crisis communications plan ready to be activated when needed. This plan should address several key issues:

Identify crisis points. Every organization has them: controversial personnel, products or services; internal philosophical conflicts; weak managers; known instances of communication breakdowns; and changing public attitudes in relation to your organization. Examine these carefully ahead of time.

Ask "What if?" Identifying problem scenarios and model solutions based on your organization's vulnerable spots can remove surprise as an element in the next crisis, giving you a head start in dealing with it. The more crisis situations and possible solutions you can propose, the better prepared you will be.

Fact-find during non-crisis periods. As you identify crisis points and construct scenarios, you should routinely gather, sort, classify, and update known information relevant to your organization—including rumors.

Classify the information into categories, such as facts and myths. Facts should be routinely updated; rumors should be verified or exposed as myths.

Catalog relevant positive information to offset negative charges that arise during a crisis. For example, if your college has had no rapes on campus, or your manufacturing plant has had no accidents in five years, or your industrial plant has a record of no chemical pollution, have these facts ready to be presented during the next crisis. Use them carefully, however. Use them to support your case, not to divert attention away from the issue at hand.

Select your team. Your organization needs a crisis management team, a group of pivotal players who perform key functions during a crisis. Your chief public relations or communications officer should be a member of every crisis team. The team must be prepared to work around the clock or to operate from their homes or a remote site, if necessary. Each member should receive routine crisis management training and should be updated regularly on potential crisis points, facts and myths.

Choose a spokesperson. Generally, you will want only one spokesperson to represent the entire organization. This person should not be the crisis team manager, because each will be completely occupied with different responsibilities. The spokesperson will spend most of his or her time planning and working with the media, and one person cannot do justice to both managing the crisis and effectively communicating about it. Having one spokesperson also lessens the possibility of having to explain public contradictions.

Your spokesperson, usually the chief public relations officer, should be able to communicate effectively the facts in a believable and credible manner. In their 1988 *Handbook for Effective Emergency and Crisis Management*, Nudell and Antokol advise, "Your spokesperson should be articulate, well-informed, and personable...with knowledge of the operations of the working press and/or contacts among them." In addition, the ability of your spokesperson to remain calm is critical. Avoid choosing a spokesperson who feels intimidated by close questioning or confrontations; who might use the forum for his or her own agenda; who exhibits signs of unpredictability or insensitivity; or who might feel compelled to reveal confidential information about the organization. Your chief public relations officer presumably has none of these attributes.

Many times, the organization's chief executive officer will serve as the spokesperson during a crisis. Sometimes, however, the CEO may be absent or may need to work behind-the-scenes to end the crisis. The crisis team manager and designated spokesperson must have free and immediate access to the CEO at all times for the duration of the crisis, and also must have authority themselves. All senior managers and potential spokespersons should be trained in dealing with the media should they find themselves having to face reporters.

In certain situations more than one spokesperson may be needed. By developing a list of qualified personnel in different areas of your organization who could serve in this role, you improve your flexibility to respond to the crisis. You benefit from a variety of people who can be called on to respond best to a variety of issues. In such cases the spokespersons must be in constant communication, coordinating the information presented.

Fine-tune your communications networks. Keeping internal and external lines of communications open helps your organization maintain its integrity. If this is done in times of non-crisis, it can help prepare for – and possibly prevent – crises.

Your external communication networks – how you maintain dialogues with your public and/or clientele – should be tested routinely to ensure that all links function properly; that information you want passed along gets disseminated without

distortion of facts and manipulations of meaning; and that you get accurate feedback.

You must also fine-tune your internal tools and networks for effective communication. Be flexible to allow for changes in how information is disseminated in the future. Ensure that the internal links of your organization reflect accurately the true attitudes and opinions of employees. Verify that your internal newsletters are reaching their audiences.

Prudent crisis management teams routinely test all networks, evaluate tools, and fine-tune relationships to ensure that in periods of crisis they can guarantee an effective dialogue with the people the organization serves. The crisis team manager should always have certain things readily available: the annual report; biographies and photos of key organization personnel; names, addresses and phone numbers of crisis management team members as well as senior managers and communications staff; names, addresses and phone numbers of key media contacts; up-to-date fact sheets; fax and copy machines; access to a 24-hour messenger service; and a procedures manual that details all of the things to do in a crisis.

Develop good relationships with the media. Establish and maintain strong relationships with reporters, and work to build rapport with difficult or skeptical ones. Strive to enhance your reputation as a straight-shooter, a person whom a reporter can depend on as an accurate source of facts or tips.

Prepare for the worst. Despite your best efforts, any number of things can go wrong during a crisis. You may face information leaks, disloyalty in the ranks, violent incidents, even defeat. Certainly, you will face incessant media intrusion. However difficult the preparations are, the organization will fare far better if managers have a preview of the gruesome realities and learn how best to cope with substantial disaster.

Strategies for surviving a crisis

However unpleasant a crisis may be, it will eventually end. Your hope, of course, is that it will end quickly with a minimum of damage to your organization. A crisis actually can have a positive outcome. Effective crisis management can solidify the mission of an organization or clarify its role. It can lead to new opportunities for your crisis management team or your organization to consider. And, if top management is willing to deal with it openly, how the crisis is managed often can promote positive opinions about your organization in the minds of the public and among your organization's employees.

How do you survive a crisis and profit from the experience? How can you control the crisis and take a proactive role in managing events to foster positive public opinion? You can accomplish these things if your top priorities are rapid resolution and effective communication. Ending a crisis as quickly as possible, while maintaining integrity and credibility, helps turn the crisis from a negative to a positive experience for your organization.

There are four basic strategies for dealing with a crisis. They are:

- Do nothing.
- Respond and defend
- Block and delay.
- Take the opportunity to act in the public interest.

Do nothing. Some organizations refuse to admit that a crisis exists. By their non-action, they let the crisis take its toll and run its course. Such organizations may mistakenly believe they are insulated from public opinion. The do-nothing approach is the least desirable of any alternative, since a major crisis will ultimately divide the organization and erode its integrity. For example, the Exxon Corporation denied blame in the Exxon Valdez oil spill disaster, which inspired public loathing and severely damaged its reputation.

Block and delay. In a block and delay strategy, management refuses to respond externally to the crisis on the basis of not wanting to dignify what it considers erroneous or improper allegations. They will block attempts from outsiders to seek information and delay resolution, perhaps feeling that the passage of time will work in their favor. An organization using this approach runs the risk of negative public attitudes and trial by media. Often, the public interprets silence as guilt, arrogance or an unwillingness to compromise on an issue. Stonewalling is ineffective also because reporters will get the story anyway, with or without your help.

However, in some instances, the block and delay tactic not only is acceptable, it is the only desirable course of action. Such instances include personnel matters involving disciplinary action deemed confidential under state or federal laws, or a situation to be resolved in a court of law.

Respond and defend. Organizations that face a crisis head-on and work positively and aggressively for a rapid resolution enjoy a higher survival rate than those that either do nothing or stonewall. With your input, the damage can be minimized; continually refusing to confirm or deny is seen by some as an admission of guilt. Thus, responding and defending can be a successful crisis management technique.

The keys to developing a response and preparing a defense include communicating factual information and selecting the proper spokesperson to represent the organization. Your spokesperson should be able to respond proactively, presenting the truth in the most advantageous way. For example, the positive side of laying off 100 workers is saving the jobs of 1000 others who would have been unemployed had the plant been forced to close down altogether, an alternative which had been considered but dismissed as not in the best interest of the company and the community.

Take the opportunity to act in the public interest. This strategy involves using the crisis as an opportunity to create positive public opinion of your organization and its employees. It focuses on a worst case scenario during planning, and utilizes ways to take actions that exceed people's expectations. A crisis is a perfect opportunity to show the public how much your organization is willing to do to address the situation and interpret its responsibilities broadly. An example is the way Johnson and Johnson handled the Tylenol poisoning crisis; they became heroes in the process and increased their market share.

Reaching resolution

Most crises can be resolved – one way or another – through the foregoing strategies. Imagine the long-term effects of your organization's actions, and plan your strategies accordingly. Whether you decide to respond and defend or act in the public interest, your best strategy is having accurate information. As you develop your response to accusations, prepare a rebuttal to a negative event, or plan your offensive, remember that reporters and members of an informed public who ask questions may have or believe they have the answers before they ask the questions.

People respect honesty. Your best defense, therefore, is a factual response. An organization that stretches the truth when developing and issuing responses to a crisis will lose credibility and heighten the crisis. Truthful statements, verifiable and unclouded by value judgements and emotional provocation, enhance credibility and will lead to the most successful end to the crisis. Shouldering blame and taking responsibility nearly always fare better than denial and unwillingness to admit mistakes.

Handling a crisis

When a crisis erupts the crisis team needs to be assembled for an immediate meeting. The team will review the situation, discuss actions to be taken, go over pertinent instructions, and determine the need for additional meetings.

It is important to keep the internal community informed and to use every means before and after the event to tell the employees what is happening and what has occurred. Internal communications are often as vital as dealing with the media. In the event of an accident, a site should be designated where employees can get the freshest information, such as an emergency plan or an outline of their responsibilities.

Effective crisis response is based on several common principles. The crisis management team must be able to:

- get and verify the facts, including the cause of the crisis;

- develop a position, carefully consider the legal aspects, and agree on a strategy;

- keep internal and external lines of communication open;

- deal with the media; and

- evaluate the response and plan for the next crisis.

Getting the facts. Miscommunication heightens a crisis and can result in exaggerations, half-truths, distortions, and negative perceptions. The first step in crisis management is to get the real story and understand the elements of the crisis. Accurate information is critical. It is the responsibility of the management team to gather as much information as possible in order to verify the truth and understand what caused the crisis.

Developing a position and agreeing on strategy. Once the facts are known, the crisis management team can develop a position and agree on a strategy to handle the crisis. The key here is to base your position and strategy on facts. The team should take care to ensure accurate, consistent and relevant statements.

When crisis management involves response strategies, the organization's spokesperson must be well prepared to face the media and respond to the public.

Good internal communication is necessary both for the success of the crisis response and for the success of the spokesperson's efforts. Everyone involved must know the identity of the spokesperson and be willing to allow the spokesperson to assume that role.

Communicate with employees first, if possible. Everyone involved in the crisis and everyone in the organization should receive the same information. If pressed, they all will reveal the same information. It is very important that the organization has its facts and strategy straight – no matter who is speaking.

Keeping communications lines open. Awareness, flexibility and dialogue form a critical triad for crisis management. If you are central to the crisis, stay in touch and keep informed. During the crisis, you may need to postpone ongoing projects and devote your full attention to crisis management.

During a crisis, additional things may go wrong as well. By staying informed, involved and flexible, the crisis manager is in the best position to respond to changing conditions as quickly as possible. An inflexible mindset or inability to respond can create a more serious crisis by inhibiting compromise.

Effective dialogue is critical for successful crisis management. You must be skilled at accurately expressing a viewpoint in a manner consistent with the needs and characteristics of differing audiences or clientele. Crisis spokespersons often deliver the message in the same form to all audiences. Rather, a variation of the message that does not change its overall meaning may be beneficial to communicate clearly to different publics.

The crisis manager also should be a skilled listener to understand your organization's progress – or lack of it – in a crisis. Crises can be prolonged inadvertently because the crisis management team fails to understand that the crisis was ready for resolution and did not take the steps needed for closure. In crisis situations, overheated rhetoric can mask true feelings and opportunities for resolution. Through careful listening you can truly understand opposing viewpoints.

Dealing with the media. All media inquiries must be received courteously. Communications should be timely, open and truthful to maintain public confidence. Log all inquiries and responses. Prepare a media center including telephones and fax machines for the media's use. Information provided to the media must be factual and objective. At all times it is important to resist inclinations – your own or others' – to fragment, manipulate, slant or distort the truth. Partial or unchecked facts must not be given to the media. No speculation should be offered, and only established verifiable facts about the crisis given. Additionally, positive facts about the organization should be included if they are relevant. Avoid irrelevant facts since they distract everyone from the focus and can appear diversionary.

While complete disclosure is the goal in crisis communications, you do not always have to tell the media everything you know, particularly if the information is not necessary for the safety of the public and could potentially harm the company's continued operations. Whatever information you do provide must be accurate, honest and must not mislead.

In many crises, until the facts are available, media inquiries should be deferred tactfully and courteously. In others, the media become the organization's invaluable communication link with the public. For example, in the World Trade Center bombing, communication management through the media was vital in providing information to get people out of the building with minimal loss of life and property. In more relatively benign crises, where loss of life may not be threatened, conclusions should be reached cautiously, yet in a timely manner. The wise communicator will try to anticipate possible media questions and formulate reasonable responses including procedures to be followed in case of certain dangers. Communications should be developed to counterbalance overreactions on the part of the public. If false or misleading information is unknowingly disseminated to the media, the crisis spokesperson must act quickly to correct the erroneous communication. Information sheets and prepared statements, including press kits, should provide a balanced perspective by mixing bad news with good. The organization's good reputation, earned over many years, should not be forgotten in a crisis.

Remember that the reporter's job is to get the story. Some reporters may use deceptive techniques rather than face an editor empty-handed. This is less likely to be a problem if your relationship with the media is in good stead before the crisis occurs. Steven Fink, in his book *Crisis Management*, points out the value of good relations with the media: "Your company's credibility should be high, your company's management should be accessible to the media, your communicator should arrange media briefings, interviews, plant tours, and so on...when there is no crisis and when it is possible to create a reservoir of good will." During the crisis, you must be available to reporters, and you must tell the truth.

Return phone calls even when you have nothing to add. Saying "We have no additional information at this time," is an effective means of maintaining an open, honest relationship, but saying "no comment" is not. When a reporter hears "no comment," he or she might find another source of information, regardless of how well or poorly informed the other source is. "No comment" is alienating and makes the organization appear guilty. If you need additional time to respond to a question, offer to check into it and get back to the reporter when the information is available. Or if the topic is sensitive and you really cannot comment, explain that this is an area that you are not at liberty to discuss. If you have been candid about the things you can talk about, the reporter will generally respect the areas you cannot discuss. If a reporter tells you that your response will be "off the record," be aware that everything is really "on the record." Instead, repeat your offer to get back to them when you have more information, and then do so, or risk losing credibility.

When your spokesperson makes a statement to the media, prepare the statement in writing and give it to the reporter. Written statements formally put you on record and signal that you are prepared. Before facing the press interview, work on your statement so that you can express it accurately and conversationally. Deliver it along with positive information about the organization and/or events.

If you grant an interview in addition to delivering the basic statement, you run the risk of having a statement taken out of context, since you have no control over which quote or sound bite will be used. Nevertheless, interviews are often necessary to dispel myths and correct erroneous information. Your best defense is to develop a few summary statements based on your prepared statement. Each should last 20 to 30 seconds. Know them cold, avoid being cute, and use everyday language that is easy to understand.

Practice so you can repeat your statements without unnatural pauses. The public often will remember your answer, not the question, so find a way to respond to or reshape media questions with the facts you want to emphasize. Do not obfuscate facts in doing so, however. Repeat the central points often during the interview. Do not allow the interview focus to shift from your central theme; keep realigning the discussion with your statements. You have now imposed some degree of control in the interview. You can also use this time as an opportunity to be proactive, correct misinformation, and personify your company's openness, honesty and desire to act in the public interest.

You cannot anticipate every question, and there may be some answers that you don't have. If that is the case, the best response is, "I don't know, but I will try to find out." When you do learn the answer, contact the reporter and supply it. If you can't divulge the information, be courteous enough to contact the reporter to say you can't talk about it. Sometimes a reporter will want background information, where you will not be quoted (you must make this agreement in advance of your response). The general sense of the conversation can be attributed in a credible way without specifically identifying you – for example, 'department official,' 'diplomatic source,' 'industry executive,' and so forth.

To inject your own agenda into the interview process, you can use such techniques as acknowledging the question, but prefacing your response with: "Before trying to answer that question, I feel the people need to know...," or, "Of course, that's one way to look at it, but it may be helpful to first examine the situation this way...," or "Usually when I'm asked a question on that subject, people want to know..." Make sure, though, that you don't just deflect the reporter's question; answer the question as part of or after your statement.

You can also turn a negatively worded question into a positive one, by proactively bringing up the other side of the story – for example, pointing out that a layoff of 100 people enabled you to save the jobs of 1000 others. Mention what you are doing to help the workers find other jobs, and that you hope to be able to rehire them when economic conditions improve.

Getting angry when interviewed will not help your cause, so remain calm. If the reporter asks convoluted questions, or several questions at once, bring clarity and calm to the process by choosing which question or part of the question you will respond to first. If the reporter phrases a question in a way that puts words in your mouth, clarify by explaining that that was not what you said, and rephrase it to say it your way. If the reporter interrupts you, use those moments to sharpen your reponse and think of other proactive statements. To give yourself a few extra seconds, begin your response with short phrases such as, "That's a good question," or "Let me see if I understand what you're asking," or "I'd like to clarify what I think you're asking," or "Let me say this," or something that buys you some additional thinking time.

Stylistic distinctions. Crisis communications managers can benefit from knowing how the media reports on crises. In their *Handbook for Effective Emergency and Crisis Management*, Nudell and Antokol cite a study that points to different areas of emphasis by the three major TV networks when covering crises. "...CBS tends to rely on official sources and its coverage seems to emphasize the manageability of the crisis. ABC concentrates on ordinary people and stresses the hardships of the event on the affected persons, along with the unmanageability of the crisis. NBC's coverage appears to accept crises as an inevitable fact of life, emphasizing that the particular event will pass and things will return to normal." Although CNN was not included in the study, as a 24-hour news network, CNN's "appetite for information is insatiable, and ...it is constantly on the alert for sensational pieces to keep its viewers interested."

Forms of communication. Depending on the nature of the crisis, and the need for immediacy, you can choose many different means of communication. These include telephone calls, electronic mail, first-class mail, overnight mail, teleconferences, establishing a toll-free hotline, news conferences, news releases, interviews, videotapes, and advertising. Even suspending advertising can convey sensitivity, as when McDonald's removed advertising after several patrons were killed by a gunman in San Ysidro, California.

Who to communicate with. Each crisis requires that you inform the people who need to know and have a right to know. This could include the general public, your employees, your customers, your investors, community leaders, the government, insurance companies, families of victims, attorneys, and corporate offices in other locations.

Planning for the next one. When the dust clears and the crisis is over, it is important that the management team does more than simply sit back and wait for the next one. A postcrisis evaluation and astute review of its causes, the quality of the communication effort, the way in which both the crisis and the communications were handled, and a discussion about how the crisis could have been avoided will be effective exercises for future crises. It is important to evaluate whether poor or insufficient communication could have been the cause of the crisis or if it contributed to the continuation of the crisis.

Assessing vulnerabilites, role-playing about the worst that can happen, developing checklists and rehearsing, testing, and revising crisis plans around hypothetical situations will help in avoiding or minimizing future crises. A re-evaluation of crisis points, developed scenarios, the fact-finding process and your communications networks will help you gauge your level of success in dealing with past crises and your state of readiness for the next one. You should also insist that the performance of each member of the crisis team be evaluated to strengthen your ability to respond to crises.

Conclusions

During your career, your organization very likely will experience a crisis. Crises do not have to rage out of control; they can be managed and can leave the organization stronger than it was before the crisis took place. The organizational mindset must include an understanding that crisis management is a continual process that does not end when one crisis is over. The more an organization anticipates and prepares for the next crisis, the less vulnerable it will be to it. Organizations that pay attention to warning signs can limit the duration of a crisis and may be able to prevent it from ever beginning.

Effective crisis management is built upon openness, honesty and a set of principles and techniques that you can learn and apply for the benefit of you and your organization. Always keep in mind that you must communicate truth effectively to your concerned publics, demonstrate good will, and responsibly use communication to continue positive rapport with your concerned publics and elicit behavior compatible with the organization's mission.

Organizational And Product Marketing

What is marketing?

Marketing has taken on many different meanings over the years. Early usage referred to the act of selling or bartering a product, a likely reference to the taking of farm or craft products "to market." Businesses expanded the idea of marketing to include learning what perspective buyers wanted, in addition to what they (the businesses) wanted to offer. This has carried into a broader usage today that includes references to a "marketing approach" to problem-solving encompassing the development and selling of programs, services and ideas, and products. It works equally well for non-profit organizations and individuals as well as those with profit motives.

Marketing today has become synonymous with selling, promotion, and advertising. But they are not the same. Nearly all businesses and organizations sell, promote or advertise, but they may not be marketing. What they may be missing is a formal process that takes into account the desires of the intended audience.

Two definitions of marketing will help you understand it better. The first says that marketing is "a formalized system or process of organized thought and action that helps you achieve

Marketing Tactical Plan Form

Plan Title:				
Messages:			Target Audiences(s):	
Activity	Responsible Person	Date Due	Date Done	Evaluation

Example of a marketing tactical plan form used to organize the process of developing a product or service the consumer desires and will accept.

product or organizational goals." It's a process, not a product or goal in itself. When applied to selling, the marketing definition becomes "a process of developing products or services the consumer desires, and providing those products or services in a place and at a price the consumer will accept."

Foreign automobile manufacturers took over a large share of U.S. sales when they found that Americans wanted smaller, high-performance, low-priced cars, instead of full-sized, high-priced, gas guzzlers. American manufacturers were selling their products, not marketing them.

Public relations practitioners use a marketing approach in "selling" an organization to its many publics. The goal is to create an image that appeals to the interests and desires of certain key audiences. Then, when the audiences are looking for products or services offered by the organization, or when the organization needs support on an issue, the audience will respond favorably.

Those who do advertising and promotion -- tools used in sales and public relations -- use a marketing approach to determine the motivation of potential audiences that may include consumers, clients, or viewers. Much research goes into learning about consumer preferences and interests, likes and dislikes.

The common thread in effective sales, public relations, advertising, and promotion is the attention paid to the market of potential consumers, clients, audiences, viewers, listeners, or readers. Most businesses and organizations exist only because of their markets.

Organizational and product marketing

The techniques and tools described in this chapter are equally applicable for marketing a product, a program, an idea, a service, or an organization (both for-profit and non-profit). From this point on, however, the discussion will be specific to organizational and program marketing in a non-profit setting. Many of the lessons transfer well to a for-profit business, however.

Organizational marketing

Every organization, regardless of its mission, must have the support of its many audiences if it is to survive. Marketing audiences, or markets, for an organization may include: its own staff of employees, volunteers, directors, potential clients, taxpayers, opinion leaders, decision-makers, and, in some cases, the news media.

Marketing goals for an organization usually involve creating visibility or awareness of the organization, or developing understanding and support for the organization's mission and accomplishments. The Red Cross, for example, wants people to be aware of its organization and participate in blood drives. It also wants people to understand and value its work, and to support it with their donations.

Passive marketing. Marketing an organization can be done passively or actively, Passive marketing includes those things that are a part of regular activity of the organization. And it can be incidental or opportunistic.

People, that is, your market, formulate an opinion of an organization based on such things as the way the telephone is answered, the appearance of an office or employees, the way they are treated by employees, the quality or lack of quality of the organization's products; and the effectiveness of the organization's communication pieces. These are incidental marketing opportunities.

To evaluate this aspect of your passive marketing, list all the ways you interact with your market. Then, evaluate each item and identify ways to improve. Develop a system for regular feedback from your markets. Ask clients or customers to fill out a form that evaluates items you identified earlier and leave room for comments on things you may have missed. Everything about an organization can influence the way people feel about it, in either a positive or negative way.

Passive marketing also means looking for ways to increase organizational visibility and support by taking advantage of opportunities created as part of normal activities. This is opportunistic interaction. Does your organization have educational materials that can be handed out when employees or volunteers are dealing with client audiences? Do you have printed signs that can be used by employees or volunteers when giving a talk or conducting a program? Are you taking advantage of every opportunity to get your organization's name and mission before your client markets? Are you getting credit for your organization's successes?

Logos and slogans are one way an organization markets itself passively. The goal is to create a visual or verbal identity for the organization that people will remember.

Logos are distinct visual elements that can be a graphic design or symbol, a name, or the two combined. They should be simple, uncluttered, and designed for use with a variety of media, such as letterhead, flyers, television, publications, or business cards. It's important that logos be used in a consistent manner. That is, the elements in the logo should be kept in the same order. Also, select a color and stick with it. Otherwise, the logo can become unrecognizable.

With repeated use, logo symbols can stand alone, without the name of the organization. Good examples are the golden arches of McDonald's, the Texaco star, Apple Corporation's multi-colored apple with a bite out of it, and the familiar clover of the Extension 4-H program. Logos can be printed on a variety of materials, such as coffee cups, pens and pencils, rulers, and t-shirts as well as on all official organizational materials such as signs, publications, newsletters, and stationery.

Slogans and jingles are brief statements that tell you something about the organization. Usually not more than three to five words, slogans can be used with logos. The advantage of slogans, however, is that they don't have to be seen. They are especially valuable for radio advertising, and if catchy enough, they will be repeated by consumers. And like logos, if repeated enough, slogans do not have to carry the organization's name. Good examples are "You deserve a break today," by McDonald's, "Where's the beef," by Wendy's, and "It's the real thing," by Coca-Cola.

The Cooperative Extension System is one organization that benefits from slogans describing the product. Two slogans being used by state Extension Services are "Helping You Put Knowledge To Work," and "Education That Works For You."

Slogans can help create an image for an organization, but the organization must be prepared to live up to the image created. If the slogan implies your organization is friendly, then make sure your staff behaves that way, Remember, it's easier to build an image than to change one.

Active marketing. Active marketing is more involved than passive marketing. In an active marketing program, you develop a plan for carrying out specific marketing activities. The plan described below forces you to identify target audiences or markets and messages, and develop a strategy for reaching those audiences.

An active marketing program may include such things as a speakers' bureau, a news media campaign, direct mail, exhibits, advertising, events such as an open house, and promotional materials. Each employee or volunteer will be responsible for carrying out specific activities.

Program marketing

An effective effort to market the organization will be of little value if the programs or products of the organization are poorly determined, developed, packaged, or delivered. Stated another way, an organization is only as good as its programs.

It's important here to emphasize that program marketing is not the same as marketing a program. Program marketing is a process designed to make sure your programs are well planned. Don't confuse that with the idea of promotion of or selling a specific program, which is only one element of a marketing plan.

In most cases, your programs will be based on the desires of the market, assuming you do your homework to find out what the market wants. In some cases, however, your programs will be based on what someone has determined the market needs. An example would be an educational program on planning for retirement that you design for your target market of young married couples. You know they need the program, but the market doesn't sense a need or have an expressed interest. Your marketing job will be much more difficult.

Developing a marketing plan

As you identify organizational goals and objectives or problems and opportunities that can be addressed by a logical process of analysis and strategy, you have started the marketing process.

Marketing plans seldom follow steps as closely as you might follow a recipe. There are, however, certain activities that, if accomplished, will help ensure a successful marketing effort.

Sometimes you might start with a formal or informal survey of your market to determine what they want or need. Or, you may already know what the market wants, and you have what they want, but you aren't getting a positive response from the market. Perhaps you haven't even determined who your market is.

How do you know where to start and who to involve in the process? You start by getting organized.

Getting organized

Let's assume somebody in the organization has identified a need to develop a marketing plan. You have a product or program or the organization itself is in need of a market. The first thing you do is form a team or a task force. It helps to have more than one person develop the plan. The team should be appointed by top management to give it credibility. You should also have a representative of top management on the team and the promise of a budget that will allow you to do the job.

The team should represent staff at all levels of the organization who will ultimately be involved in carrying out the marketing plan. At some point, additional staff can be involved in marketing through sub-committees that are given specific responsibilities.

A team or task force leader should be appointed from among those staff who have skills in group process, analysis, and communications. He or she should also have the time to carry out the responsibilities of the position.

If the team also is responsible for overseeing the plan's execution, each member should have a specific assignment and be given the authority to carry it out. If this is a long-term activity, agree on how long members are expected to serve.

Set regular meeting dates for the team. Look for opportunities for team members to participate in staff development activities such as workshops in marketing and strategic planning that strengthen their contributions to the marketing effort.

Now that the team is formed and ready to begin marketing, it's time to start developing the marketing plan. The steps described here are designed to force you to consider all aspects of a marketing approach. In some cases, you will not need to carry out each step, nor will you always follow the steps in the order presented. The important thing is that you understand the value of thoroughly analyzing your situation and base marketing decisions on sound data.

The value of group brainstorming in developing your plan cannot be over-stressed. Take advantage of this process whenever possible. If you have a group of ten or more, break into smaller working groups and share your ideas frequently.

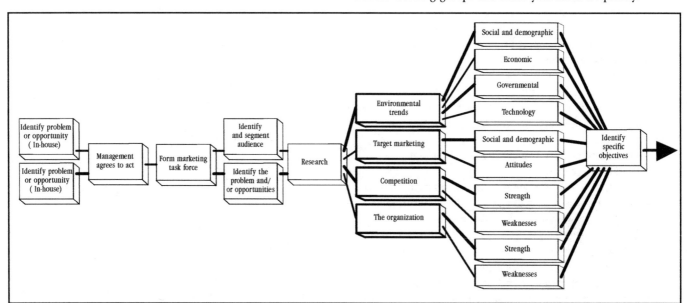

This organizational chart shows steps that can be used in developing a marketing plan. The important thing is that you understand the value of analyzing your situation thoroughly and basing marketing decisions on sound data. Chart continues on next page.

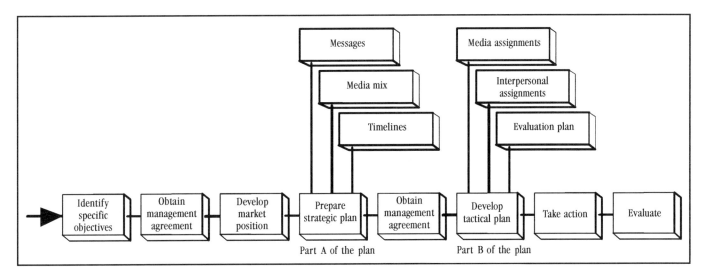

Part A of the plan   Part B of the plan

Develop a form based on the steps described below and keep detailed records.

A seven-step marketing model

Prepare a goal statement

State clearly and concisely the problem, opportunity or need this plan will address.

Prepare a goal statement that all participants in this planning process can agree with. At this point, don't worry about quantifying the results you hope to achieve. And don't spend much time identifying and describing the market you want to address; that comes later. If your goal is organizational marketing, your statement might relate to the image you want the public to have of the organization or a problem with the current image. If you're marketing a program or other product, you might make a goal statement that describes the expected outcome. For example, let's say you want an educational program on teen pregnancy to have an impact on the problem. It is in this step that you describe the problem. Make sure you're not relating to a symptom of the problem instead of the problem itself.

Once you are satisfied with the goal statement, evaluate it against your organization's stated mission. If you don't have a mission statement, have the group attempt to write one. The statement should be less than 25 words and should be clear enough that someone unfamiliar with the organization can understand what you're about. Your goal statement for this marketing plan should clearly fit within the organization's mission.

Identify and segment your market

Identify the audiences, or markets, you want to address. For each market you identify, break the group into smaller groups that have common identifiable characteristics. Then, put these segmented markets in a priority order for addressing, or targeting, in this plan. For each target market, list those people who influence the market. These influencers may be valuable in

your strategy for reaching the target group.

This step is called market segmentation. Brainstorming can be a valuable tool here. The goal is to target a market that has common interests, behavioral patterns, motivations, etc. If you correctly segment, you will have less trouble developing a strategy for reaching this target market. For example, "voters" become "male" and "female" voters; or "low income" and "high income" voters; or "male, low income" or "male, high income" voters.

In another example, let's say you teach a home economics class, and enrollment is dwindling. You want to recruit more students for the class. Your target audience, then, is potential students from among those in the school. Those students are male and female, and your approach to them would be different, so now you have two groups to address. Among the males, one group that might be motivated to get into home economics is athletes because nutrition and health relate to athletic performance. So now, you have segmented the group further

After segmenting the groups, analyze where you might be most effective, that is, have the greatest impact. For example, if athletes take home economics, it might encourage other males to take it also.

Influencers of your target markets can be valuable resources for getting the markets to behave in a certain way. In the pre-

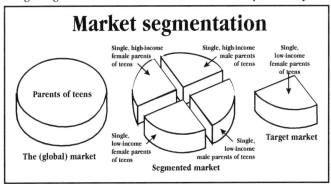

Market segmentation

The goal of market segmentation is to target a market that has common interests, behavioral patterns, motivations, etc. When correctly segmented, you will have less trouble developing a strategy for reaching the specific target market.

vious example, athletic coaches are influencers of the athletes' behavior. So are other respected athletes, for example, the star of a college team. Thinking about these influencers might help you to put your market segments in a priority order.

Note: From this point on you will be addressing your highest priority target market. After you complete the process for one market, you likely will come back and take the second priority market and follow through with the same process.

Research your information needs

There are three sets of data you need to accumulate to develop a marketing strategy. You'll have to learn all you can about your target market, the environment in which you'll be marketing, and the competition you'll have for your target market. Obtain as much information as is practical/feasible in the time you have available.

This is the section where you do the research. The more successful you are in getting appropriate information, the better your strategy will be. Some of the data will come from a market audit where you gather existing information about the target market and the environment in which you'll carry out the marketing plan; other data will require opinion/attitude or behavior surveys.

Surveys can be formal, carried out with a tested questionnaire in a personal, telephone, or mail survey of a representative sample of the target audience; or informal, accomplished by asking a few questions of the target market over the telephone or in person. An example of an informal survey would be to ask every fifth caller to your office where they heard about your organization, how often they call or use your product, and if they are satisfied with what they got. Informal surveys can be good indicators, but the results likely are not reliable data. Your sample of clients may not represent the entire group. Check with a professional survey researcher before attempting a formal survey.

About the target market. Do a demographic and geographic profile of the target audience. Describe it in terms of their age, sex, race, education, marital status, employment status of one or both spouses, religion, family/household composition, income, location of residence, and any other category you think appropriate. Look at lifestyle characteristics: Do they eat out? How often? Do they volunteer? Where and how often do they take vacations? What news media do they use? Do they have a satellite dish? A VCR? What magazines do they read? etc.

If you want to know what the target audience knows and thinks about your organization and its products/programs, you'll need to do an opinion survey.

About the environment. An environmental assessment will identify those things over which you seldom have control, but which may influence your ability to market to your target audience. This function is considered important enough by many companies that they have a full-time manager for

environmental analysis. It's unlikely that all of the categories listed below will be important to your marketing plan, For those that are, be as thorough as possible given the time you have to devote.

- What are the social and demographic trends? Are there patterns -- other than those you already outlined for your target market -- in the way people interact socially? Is the population aging? Are there more working mothers in the job market?

- What are the economic trends? What's happening to incomes, spending patterns, employment, credit availability, public attitude toward funding social services, etc.?

- What are the governmental trends? Any changes in local, state, or federal laws? Political trends, including which party controls government spending? What are the "hot" or "in" programs that seem to get government support?

- What are the technological trends? What's their impact on your target market and your ability to deliver your programs or products through such technologies as satellite communications, home video, office automation, desktop publishing, computer related technologies? Who controls this technology? Who has access to it?

- How does the price of your product or service affect audience acceptance? What can you do about it? What are your resource limitations in people and budget and what can you do about that?

- What other trends should you be aware of if you are to compete for your market share?

About the competition. Do you know who your competition is? Who has a product or service similar to yours? Who else is trying to reach your target market(s)? What do you know about your competition? What are their strengths and weaknesses, and how do they compare with yours? How is the competition positioning itself to the market? You will learn later in this chapter what "positioning" means. How does the price the competition charges for their product/service compare with yours?

Note: At this point you may find that the competition can serve the target audience better than you can. If you don't have the edge or think you can carve out a niche, you might want to find a different target audience, change your product, or change your goals.

One rental car company faced this prospect and decided to change their approach; they indicated that since they were second, they would try harder to win your business.

Identify specific objectives

Develop a series of statements that are very specific in defining what it is you want to accomplish with your target market.

In this section you will quantify your goals. Be very specific. Indicate how much or how many. For an organizational marketing plan, for example, you might want to specify the percentage of your market you want to be aware of the organization's mission. You could then formally evaluate the importance of your organization to that group. For a program, product, or marketing plan, you likely would want to set a goal of a certain number of people who would change their behavior or purchase the product because of the program. Again, you could use a follow-up survey to determine your success.

One way to write your specific objective would be to complete the statement, "This program is a success if..." It's important to be realistic in your objectives. Make sure they are achievable.

Develop your market position

Positioning is a marketing term that refers to how you set yourself apart from the competition. In what way is your organization or your product unique? What advantage does your organization or product have over the competition? Positioning also describes how you want to be perceived by your target market. Does your organization or product meet a perceived need of your target market? Are you perceived as a credible source of the product? List those things about your organization or product that could be used to position it effectively. What audience needs does it meet? What does it have that the competition doesn't have or isn't utilizing?

Positioning is one of the most important elements of your marketing plan. It is the centerpiece for your marketing strategy, which is described later in this chapter. Positioning usually is based on what you learn about your target audience. Understanding human behavior and motivation helps also. If you want to project a certain image to your target market, make sure that image is valid. As was the case in developing a slogan, you had better be able to deliver on what you say, if you position your product, for example, as being ideal for the health conscious, then you should be able to stand behind that claim.

The market position of an organization or product usually is reflected in its promotional materials, including advertising. For example:

- A new California winery, trying to compete against the existing, large wineries, positions its product as being the one to buy "for special occasions, such as anniversaries, birthdays, weddings, and christenings." This company carved its niche in the marketplace and became successful in a very competitive business.

- An insurance company makes you feel safe with television spots showing that "You're In Good Hands With Allstate."

- You don't want to miss out on being a part of "The Pepsi Generation."

- There's one diet soft drink that is made for men, too. Showing a heavyweight boxing champion drinking the product proves it.

- Cooperative Extension Services at many of the land grant universities around the country position themselves as a part of their universities to lend credibility to their educational products. That link with the research base sets them apart from their competition.

- You want to trust products you buy, so many companies use that theme in their products. One tire company positions itself as being the one to buy to make sure your family is safe from harm. A battery company uses the same theme in their advertising.

- Many companies position themselves as providing something you value, such as youth, upward mobility, and power.

Usually, you will position your organization or product differently to different target markets. For example, the same wood stove might be marketed to lower-income consumers as being the one stove that can really save you money on heating bills. For higher-income consumers, you might position your stove based on its aesthetic or status qualities.

The key to getting your market share is to carve out your niche. Find something about your organization or product that can't be or hasn't been utilized by the competition. Think about how you want the market to perceive your organization or product, and use that to develop your market position.

Prepare strategic and tactical plans

Now it's time to develop your marketing strategy. This is the heart of your marketing plan. It's here you will develop the messages, select a mix of media for delivering the messages, and devise a game plan that will help you achieve your objectives.

Start by listing the messages or themes, not the ultimate wording, that will be used in your media plan. Remember, what you're offering is the benefit, not the product or service. Consider your positioning statement(s), and target market motivators.

Next, list the media mix. Consider the media and informal communication networks your target audience might use; you probably developed a list of them when you were researching your target audience.

Finally, develop an informal timeline. Later, you will need to become more specific in your planning by developing a tactical plan that includes a list of assignments and deadlines. The tactical plan will specify who prepares what communication products, by when, and for what delivery time.

Your marketing strategy will influence the degree to which you are successful in your marketing efforts. Keep your target market in mind as you develop your strategy. Identify those people who influence your target market, and market through them. A good example would be to reach state legislators or U.S.. Congressmen by directing your message to the appropriate aides who propose action for the lawmakers to take.

Existing communication networks often are more credible to your target audience. Analyze where they go for information. If your target market is the building trade, for example, then get your message in building trade magazines and newsletters.

Your media mix may include the news media, where you can purchase space or air time for advertising. Or you might try for free space with news or feature articles, or air time with public service announcements. Learn what to expect from the news media. They can be effective in creating awareness and interest, but they are less effective than other media in changing attitudes or behavior. The media mix may also include the use of direct mail such as newsletters or flyers; meetings, workshops, and demonstrations; publications; videotapes; a speakers bureau; exhibits; and any other media discussed in this handbook. Personal, one-to-one contacts is effective if you have the people resources to make it happen.

Your tactical plan will be much more specific. You'll list all the releases, advertisements, exhibits, direct mail pieces, and other communication materials you'll produce for this marketing plan. After each item, you should list who is responsible, when it is due, and when it should be released. If you develop a form for this, leave a column for indicating the date an assignment was completed. You might even go so far as to have gold stars on the form to show that an assignment was done on time. Your tactical plan can change as the situation warrants, so be prepared to take advantage of opportunities that arise.

Make evaluation part of your plan

This is where you build into your plan a means of evaluating how well you've done. At some point you will be able to look back at your specific objectives, and determine if they have been met. But you also need to have several checkpoints where you ask yourself if things are going according to plan. These check points might be in the research stage where you're learning about the target market, the environment, and the competition or during the time the strategic and tactical plans are being executed. If you developed a form for your tactical plan, include spaces with deadlines for checking on your progress. Be prepared to make changes in your plan based on what you learn from the evaluation.

As you develop an evaluation plan, it helps to understand the stages involved in the life cycle of a program:

- The first stage, development, is the time it takes from the inception of an idea to the point where you're ready to execute the plan; this can take anywhere from several days to several months.

- The second stage, introduction, is the period where you are delivering the program, but there has been little time for response; this could last from several weeks to several months.

- The third stage, growth, is the time when the program is maturing and reaching its zenith; this is a major phase of the program and takes anywhere from several months to a year or more.

- The fourth stage, leveling, is the point where interest in the program has peaked and will start to decline unless you introduce some new life into it.

- The final stage, decline, is pretty much defined by its name; the program is winding down and will soon end unless you decide, as in the leveling stage, to introduce some new enthusiasm. The total time for these stages can be less than a year to several years, depending on the nature of your program. If you think about these stages when you plan your evaluation, you'll be ready to take the necessary action to achieve your goals.

The means you use to evaluate your progress or success depends on the resources you want to put into it. As discussed earlier in this chapter, formal evaluations using surveys can be time consuming and expensive. Informal surveys and other feedback can be valuable, but not always reliable.

The value of using a marketing plan like the one above is that it forces you to analyze all those things that can influence how well you market your organization or its products. You may stop with a plan that addresses one target market, or your overall plan may be a compilation of plans developed for several target markets.

Relationship marketing

Many marketers recently have begun to tout the importance and effectiveness of one-to-one or "relationship" marketing. This approach is based on developing a good relationship with individual customers/clients. The goal is to get a greater share of each customer's business by obtaining and using specific information on each individual.

An example of this is the florist who keeps records of what customers purchase for special occasions (birthdays, anniversaries, Mother's Day, etc.) and uses that information to remind them (via a postcard) just prior to those occasions the following year.

Another example is the hotel that keeps records on customer preferences, such as room location (e.g. away from the elevator), special menu items (from room service), and valet needs. This information is used on a return visit to make the customer feel he or she is valued as an individual.

A seven-step marketing model

1. **Prepare a goal statement.** State clearly and concisely the problem, opportunity, or need this plan will address. Do not list specific objectives.

2. **Identify and segment your market.** Identify the audiences (markets) you want to address. For each market you identify, break the group into smaller groups that have common identifiable characteristics. Then, put these target markets in a priority order for addressing in the plan. For each target market, list those people who influence the market. These influencers may be valuable in your strategy for reaching the target group.

3. **Research your Information needs.** There are three sets of data you need to accumulate to help you develop a marketing strategy. You'll have to learn all you can about your target market, the environment in which you'll be marketing, and the competition you'll have for your target market. Obtain as much information as is practical/feasible in the time you have available.

   About the target market: Do a demographic and geographic profile of the target audience. List everything you learn about them.

   About the environment:

   - What are the social and demographic trends? Are there patterns – other than those you already outlined for your target market – in the way people interact? Is the population aging? Are there more working mothers in the job market?

   - What are the economic trends? What's happening to incomes, spending patterns, employment, credit availability, public attitude toward funding social services, etc.?

   - What are the governmental trends? Any changes in local, state, or federal laws? Political trends? What are the "hot" or "in" programs that seem to get government support?

   - What are the technological trends? What impact on your target market (and your ability to deliver your programs or products) do you see from such technologies as satellite communications, home video, office automation, desktop publishing, computer-related technologies? Who controls this technology? Who has access to it?

   - How does the price of your product or service affect audience acceptance? What can you do about it? What are your resource limitations in people and budget and what can you do about that?

   - What other trends should you be aware of if you are to compete for your market share?

   About the competition. Do you know who your competition is? Who has a product or service similar to yours? Who else is trying to reach your target market(s). What do you know about your competition? What are their strengths and weaknesses, and how do they compare with yours? How is the competition positioning itself to the market? How does the price the competition charges for their product/service compare with yours?

4. **Identify specific objectives.** Develop a series of statements that are very specific in defining what it is you want to accomplish with your target market. One way to write your specific objective would be to complete the statement, "This program is a success if ..." It's important to be realistic in your objectives. Make sure they are achievable.

5. **Develop your market position.** "Positioning" is a marketing term that refers to how you set yourself apart from the competition. In what way is your organization or your product unique? What advantage does your organization or product have over the competition? Positioning also describes how you want to be perceived by your target market. Does your organization or product meet a perceived need of your target market? Are you perceived as a credible source of the product? List those things about your organization, or product, that could be used to position it effectively. What audience needs do they meet? What does it have that the competition doesn't have or isn't utilizing?

6. **Prepare strategic and tactical plans.** Now it's time to develop your marketing strategy. This is the heart of your marketing plan.

   It's here you will develop the messages, select a mix of media for delivering the messages, and devise a game plan that will help you achieve your objectives. Develop here your strategy (in broad terms) for how you will go about reaching your target audience(s). On another form, list the specific tactical plan that identifies who will develop what messages for what media on what timeline.

7. **Make evaluation part of your plan.** This is where you build into your plan a means of evaluating how well you've done. At some point you will be able to look back at your specific objectives, and determine if they have been met. But you also need to have several checkpoints where you ask yourself if things are going according to plan. These checkpoints might be in the research stage (where you're learning about the target market, the environment, and the competition) or during the time the strategic and tactical plans are being executed. If you developed a form for your tactical plan, include spaces (with deadlines) for checking on your progress. Be prepared to make changes in your plan based on what you learn from the evaluation.

One-to-one marketing is working for some state Extension Services as well. At least one Extension information/communications office is keeping records on customers who purchase publications and videotapes on certain topics, and sending them promotional flyers when new materials on the same or similar topics are produced.

Relationship marketing works well for high-value products or programs where the return can justify the costs. This includes those situations where goodwill or support from individual is important to the success of the organization.

One way of looking at relationship marketing is that you're doing an especially effective job of segmenting, researching, and targeting your market.

Marketing limitations

Many things can limit the effectiveness of your marketing efforts. Among them are:

- A lack of leadership for marketing. Someone has to have the responsibility and the authority for carrying out a marketing program;

- A lack of credibility for the marketing effort. It has to be clear that the marketing effort is supported at the highest levels of the organization;

- A lack of resources to carry out the marketing plan. You need sufficient people and budget; and

- A lack of staff support for marketing. Everybody in the organization must embrace the marketing concept and be prepared to do their part.

Staff support for marketing will come when they become aware of the benefits to the organization, and ultimately to themselves. They need to realize that marketing isn't an add-on, but a part of everything they do. It makes what they do and the organization itself more effective and successful.

A final note: don't forget the market

In the final analysis, no amount of marketing will ensure organizational success unless everyone in the organization is market oriented. Your customers, clients, readers, listeners, supporters, etc. have to be considered your top priority. Without them, the organization likely will cease to exist.

It's essential that you consider your customers/clients when developing programs and products, and at any time anyone in the organization interacts with them. All the planning in the world will fail if the customer/client is turned off by someone in any level of the organization. One negative interaction, even one so seemingly trivial as a customer on the telephone being left on hold too long, can offset a well-designed marketing plan. Check out your organization, and see if you're really market-oriented.

Further reading:

Creative Marketing, by Dr. William Boldt. Cornell Cooperative Extension. Cornell, New York.

Emerging Communications Issues

Crystal ball gazing in the information age? Very risky business. It's hard to predict the outcome of marriages between huge communication conglomerates or what these unions will mean for consumers. It's even harder to predict the nature of information appliances. Will they be smart computers, smart televisions, or some combination of the two? Despite these uncertainties, we still can raise questions about how these new technologies and trends will affect the way we will do business in the 21st century. What communications issues should we anticipate in light of changing demographics, increased racial and ethnic diversity, and globalization of the economy, all within the context of technological change? How will these factors affect our organizations in the future, relationships between teachers and students, and the ever-widening gap between the information haves and have-nots?

Changing demographics

Changing demographics demand new teaching models to accommodate changing lifestyles and affinities. Traditional face-to-face teaching models will need to be re-evaluated to determine applicability for a rapidly changing student population. People are living longer than ever before in recorded history. Scientists predict that by the year 2000, life expectancy will be 81 years, and 30 percent of the babies born will live to be 100 years old (Farris, 1993).

This trend will have a profound affect on education in this country. A K-12 education, even supplemented with a college degree, will not be adequate for an 80-100 year life span. As a result, multiple careers during each individual's life span will become the norm. Immigration by Hispanics and Asians will continue to increase by record numbers. Statistics predict lower birth rates among Caucasians than among Afro-Americans, Hispanics and Asians. Some estimates indicate that by the year 2000, more than 40 percent of all school children will be non-Caucasian. What does this increased diversity imply for public schools, colleges, and universities whose teachers, faculties and administrators still remain for the most part homogeneous?

Communicating with diverse audiences

"Enlightened self-interest is perhaps the primary motivation behind many of the United States' current attempts to cope with and capitalize on its diversity," states Bowen and Jackson (1992). Demographic trends point to a more ethnically diverse population, with increasing numbers of women employed full-time. To remain competitive in a global economy, America must educate and employ its growing storehouse of rich diversity. Communicating with diverse audiences presents real challenges for many institutions that lack diversity within their own staffs.

Multi-culturalism and organizational pluralism must be cornerstones of future educational programming. Bowen and Jackson (1992) list the following options for educators or communicators working with diverse audences.

- Expect respect and appreciate diversity.

- Have high standards and expectations, regardless of ethnicity.

- Understand, value, and share existing experiences.

- Use culturally-appropriate language and teaching techniques.

- Avoid asking any one person to speak for a whole race of people.

- Use positive role models from ethnic communities.

- Be honest, fair, and consistent in dealing with ethnically diverse audiences.

- Seek "an" answer and not always "the" answer. Use a variety of methods and techniques for ethnically diverse audiences.

- Help end biases that impede the hiring and career advancement of ethnically diverse or female students, teachers, and administrators.

Estela Bensimon (1994) states that effective teaching and learning models of the future must reflect critical multiculturalism. Bensimon defines critical multiculturalism as "curricular and pedagogical approaches concerned with decentering the Western discourse that dominates the curriculum." Empowering students through acknowledging multiple sources of knowledge and critically examining multiple cultures and the forces these cultures bring to bear on classroom experiences will prove challenging for both faculty and students of the 21st century.

New technologies driving change

Powerful new technologies represent a driving force for change among educational institutions. Interestingly enough, these same technologies have not had a broad-based impact on the instructional process yet (Connick, 1994). George Connick, of the University of Maine, a recognized leader in the field of distance education, states that we are at a pioneering stage in distance education and the use of telecommunications. Distance educators don't have a recipe to follow; they're inventing as they go. "In fact, many people are thinking about distance education as an extension of the traditional, campus-based, labor intensive approach to education," says Connick. However, nothing could be farther from the truth.

Even though educational institutions find themselves faced with dwindling resources, demands for greater accountability and productivity, and an unprecedented ethnic diversity in student populations, many of today's colleges and universities are bound by outdated pedagogical models, with teachers as "knowledge gatekeepers." They are constrained by conventional training, budget and social pressures to rely on techniques that are a century old (Connick, 1994).

Many faculty members currently view distance education as peripheral to the mission of colleges and universities (Dillon, 1992). But Connick predicts that distance education by the year 2000 will be viewed as mainstream by those institutions who move to embrace technology and offer education without regard to place or time. Distance education offers increased access to a diverse student population.

Much has been said about technology and distance education, but what about the instructional process? Should faculty teach students at a distance using new technology but traditional teaching methods? This incongruence is the focus of much research and development. New roles for faculty as well as students are emerging. Instruction is being rediscovered and in some cases reinvented as faculty design courses for students at a distance.

Distance education presents many challenges for our current educational system, which was clearly designed for traditional face-to-face instruction. Some such challenges have to do with unanswered questions regarding intellectual property. For example, do faculty members or their universities own the rights to telecourses? Which institution receives credit for courses offered across state lines? Should a student enrolled in distance courses be counted as a full-time equivalent (FTE)? How will this affect funding formulas based on enrollment figures? How about distribution of copyrighted material? The answers to these questions posit distance education as a major-public policy issue involving input from faculty, students, administrators, legislators and policy makers.

Approaching access revolution

Connick (1994) believes we're on the verge of an "access revolution, moving from educational scarcity to educational plenty." The Internet offers free and unlimited access to numerous databases and provides a free network for communicating with any user. Self-directed learners of the future are restrained only by their technological tools and imaginations. With increased access to education, control shifts from the provider to the consumer, bringing about a major paradigm shift for educators. Empowering learners, giving them more responsibility and control over their learning experiences, lends support to the adult learning principles of Malcolm Knowles, collectively referred to as "andragogy." While students need the capacity to become self-teachers, faculty need to work toward being coaches and mentors.

The Clinton Administration's National Information Infrastructure (NII) promises to provide an access revolution for all Americans. Often referred to as the Information Super Highway and compared to the interstate highway system that connects all major cities and towns, the NII promises to provide "universal service" while encouraging private-sector investment. According to Bob Heterick, 1994 president of Educom, the NII will fchange the nation's telecommunications landscape forever. Heterick lists the following five principles guiding current legislative and adminstrative reform:

- Encourage private investment in the NII.

- Promote and protect competition.

- Provide open access for consumer and service providers.

- Advance universal service to avoid creating haves and have-nots.

- Ensure flexibilty to keep pace with rapid technologic and market changes.

Many new issues have arisen as a result of the NII initiative. For example, what constitutes "universal service" in two-way broadband communications? Should certain groups (e.g., rural, low-income, educational and health care users) be subsidized through federal policy? How will society deal with the access vs. security/privacy question? Without protection of intellectual property and individual privacy, there isn't apt to be much information of interest available and shared on our communications networks other than the kind of passive material we find on television (Heterick, 1994). These are deep societal questions that have to do with how much privacy or protection of intellectual property we are willing to sacrifice and what kind of network content and access should be available – and at what cost (Heterick, 1994).

In a recent e-mail conversation, Heterick was asked "what will universal service mean in an era of broadband networks? Heterick's response: "The 1934 Communications Act traded monopoly rights to the telcos in exchange for univeral phone service. (About 97 percent of residences have a telephones because of this act and the major subsidies it created.) Cable passes 80 percent to 90 percent of the residences in the U.S.: and is subscribed to by three-fourths of them. Television is available in more residences than phones are.

About one-third of all homes in the United States have a personal computer with estimates that the number will rise to over 80 percent by the end of the decade. In a world in which we are not granting communication monopolies nor rationing scarce spectrum, how will we achieve universal service and what will universal service mean – simple voice communication? Access to the Internet? Full multi-media, two-way interactive video services? Folks who are not computer literate or don't have network access are increasingly disenfranchised. But disenfranchised from what? How will networked services be charged – by the packet, by the hour, by the end user information appliance type?"

Heterick's response typifies many of the questions currently being raised by policy makers, consumers, and special interest groups.

Conclusion

Of the many issues facing future educators and communicators, most disconcerting is the growing gap between the information haves and have-nots. In the midst of an information age where information is as valuable as any natural resource, those audiences who do not have access to "the electronic supermarket" may find themselves increasingly disenfranchised. Today's educators are challenged to use technology to address the market needs of the customers – students of all ages, ethnicity, national origins, gender, and without regard to time or location. They also are challenged to use multiple formats of delivery to provide access to as many clientele groups as possible, whether the student is disabled, has limited resources, or lives in remote a rural community without access to network capabilities. Rediscovered teaching and learning models designed for a variety of learning styles with seamless technology should help bridge the gap and level the playing field.

Much of the information contained in this section addresses issues associated with teaching and learning in the context of technological change. Technological innovations with unprecedented growth and expansion are difficult to predict, yet higher education must make difficult decisions regarding campus networks, digital platforms, use of wired technologies or wireless air waves.

Another dimension not discussed previously is the politics of telecommunications. More than ever, higher education must play a more active role in shaping the political agendas influencing its access to telecommunication technology. Hopefully, this section raised some issues and clarified others. It is by no means an exhaustive description of the many emerging communications issues. There are many specific issues unique to individual situations and if the past is any indication, there will be many communications issues requiring thoughtful discourse and research in the future.

References

Bowen, B.E. & Jackson, G.B. (1992). "Enhancing diversity in vocational educati*on.*" Columbus, OH: ERIC Clearinghouse on Adult, Career, and Vocational Education, Center on Education and Training for Employment, The Ohio State University, 47 pp.

Connick, G. (1994). "Beyond a Place Called School." Proceedings of the Agricultural Satellite Consortium, February 22-24, 1994, Atlanta, GA.

Dillon, C., Walsh, S., Weintraub, R., & Katz, E. (1992). "The comparative learning benefit of one-way and two-way video conferencing for distance education applications." Proceedings of Eighth Annual Conference on Distance Teaching and Learning (pp. 35-39). Madison: University of Wisconsin-Madison.

Farris, V.K. (1993). No Rear View Mirror on the Electronic Highway. American Association of State Colleges and Universities.

Heterick, R.C. (1994). "First law of change." Educom Review, 29(2), 16-17.

Making Risk Communication Equitable

Life is full of risks.

Why do people often magnify hazards that are slight, while shrugging off risks that pose greater danger? For example, pesticide residues on fruits and vegetables are often perceived as a significant threat to health while improper food handling, generally not of great concern, commonly sickens thousands of people every year through *Salmonella* outbreaks.

When the media, special interest groups and politicians emphasize certain risks, do they warrant as much concern as is implied? The sensational alarm over the accident at the Three Mile Island nuclear plant stands vividly in memory years later, yet deadly accidents in coal mines occur with unfortunate regularity, grabbing headlines for a moment and then passing from the national consciousness. There is no clamor to stop using coal to generate power, and stories about the benefits of nuclear power are rare.

The perception of risk is based too often on incomplete or selective information. Taken out of context, a focus on extreme cases or rare occurrences misleads the public into believing such is the norm. The alarm and fear bred by such misconceptions affect people deeply and are difficult to erase. Faulty policy decisions – which can be burdensome, expensive and unnecessary – are a common result.

While many risks are genuine and deserve wide publicity and public dialogue, others are trivial and alarmist. The challenge is how to tell the difference. Writing in *Newsweek*, Robert Samuelson offers two complicating factors believed by many people:

- identifiable risks should be avoidable risks, and

- anything that raises risk should be outlawed.

Though these may be unrealistic beliefs, they underscore the importance of communicating accurate and complete information to the public and the necessity of understanding how risks can be managed.

This chapter will look at how risks are communicated, examine problems affecting risk communication, and propose alternative strategies that can help reduce anxiety, counter misinformation and enhance people's feelings of control over the risks that inevitably will affect their lives.

What is risk communication?

As normally practiced, risk communication is a process of transmitting information to the public about risk assessment findings and risk management decisions. Conventional risk communication seeks to inform an audience about potential risks and move people to act accordingly, ostensibly to lessen the risk. Risk communication's purpose is to address the issues surrounding the nature and severity of risks inherent in the production or consumption of a product, the delivery of a service or practice of a behavior.

Typically, risk communication situations occur when an organization needs to inform a constituency of a risk about which it has little real knowledge, but potentially skewed perceptions. Information comes from scientific experts, policy makers, government leaders, or industry sources. It is conveyed to a broad range of constituencies, including other government agencies, scientists, media professionals, businesses, special interest groups, professional organizations, trade or labor associations, civic groups, schools, communities in general, and individuals.

Risks cover broad territory:

- environmental health issues such as drinking water contamination, radon gas, hazardous wastes, or pesticide residues;

- consumer products such as lawn mowers, hair dryers, automobiles and computers.

- self-destructive behavior such as smoking, drug use, improper diet, or unsafe sex;

- public safety issues such as wearing bicycle or motorcycle helmets, using seat belts, or gun control; and

- hazardous manufacturing or production practices including nuclear power, chloroflurocarbons (CFCs), coal mining, chemical production, petroleum refining, hormone-enhanced milk production, and genetically engineered food crops.

This somewhat sterile definition of risk communication needs more. If the goal of risk communication is the prevention and reduction of potential risks in people's lives, then the information given to the public must be more than one-sided technical data and pronouncements from authority figures and experts. This type of persuasion is the least effective approach to communicating policy issues, despite its being the most popular approach.

Instead, the information must be diverse, complete, equitable, and reasonable; it should be designed to empower its audience. It should convey how the purported risks realistically affect people's lives, taking into account their social experiences, educational level, cultural milieu, personal values, and predispositions. Risk communication should be a proactive process that enables individuals and communities to appreciate differing viewpoints, beliefs and perceptions about risks, while sharpening the skills necessary to make balanced judgements about them.

The goal of risk communication should be to create a process that respects and encourages divergent outlooks about risks and provides both the public and experts with a solid base of information upon which decisions and actions are based. It should be an interactive process, recognizing the rights of all stakeholders to be involved. This strategy calls attention to existing as well as potential problems, suggests an agenda for discussion, provides a mechanism for information exchange, and both anticipates and sets the pace for resolving future problems.

Problems In communicating risks

There are many problems in communicating risk that interfere with how people perceive hazards and respond to risk information. They are:

- complexity
- the language barrier
- the role of science
- criteria used to assess risk
- trust and credibility
- the role of the media
- the multicultural factor.

Complexity. This is perhaps the greatest obstacle in risk communication. The hazard under consideration in any given risk situation is rarely simple. Rarely is the audience being informed of a risk so narrow and uniform as to allow simple communication. Rarely are the responses to a risk situation few in number or uncontroversial. Quite the contrary, risk situations usually involve a number of factors affecting many people who – depending on their background, abilities and values – may respond in a variety of ways.

Risks are perceived very differently. Technical risk experts focus on hazard, a quantifiable component of how likely a risk is to occur. They rely on statistics, experimental studies and formal risk analysis; they shun nonexpert perceptions embellished by other considerations that may be hard to quantify.

The public focuses on perception, a nontechnical component that encompasses hard-to-quantify issues including process, control, voluntariness, fairness, familiarity, community history, social environment, visibility, vulnerability, and catastrophic potential. Since public perception of risk is based on factors that touch emotions, risks that provoke outrage are less likely to be accepted than risks that don't. Therefore, to reduce overreaction to less serious risks, outrage should be minimized; to increase attention to more serious risks, outrage should be enhanced.

The language barrier. Policymakers and experts often complain that communities are irrational, while communities call government officials and experts insensitive and uncaring. The problem is that each group essentially speaks a different language, making real communication almost impossible. Emotional responses are rarely swayed by facts and figures, while hard data is devoid of emotion. Policy-makers and scientists look at statistics, priorities and standards, while communities want to know how policies will affect them personally. Initiatives, regulations and remedial actions are caught in a gridlock of conflict. To end the stalemate all the stakeholders need to listen to each other and compromise through a process of interactive risk communication.

The role of science. Traditionally, risk assessment has been the domain of experts, with no real role for the public other than doing what the experts recommend. There has been a strong belief that science can provide objective truth based on impartial scientific conclusions. After all, hasn't the scientific method been honed over centuries to be objective and impartial? But, today we understand better that scientific objectivity is always based on some value judgments, personal or environmental influences, and is liable to error.

A second issue underlying public and expert disagreements about risk is the belief that scientific and technical experts are the only sources of valid risk information, and that expert information is more rational than experiential and perceptual judgments of the lay public. This is not true for members of the public, however, for whom risk perception is a social process based on societal norms, moral and ethical values, and power structures.

A third problem is a poor understanding of the limits of scientific information. It is too easy to overextend and generalize scientific findings. Experimental results fit a specific set of circumstances, yet when released and publicized they too often are broadened – for the sake of simplicity – and imply relevance that is unsupported by the data.

Similarly, risk communicators must understand the comprehension level of their audience. Most people have a rudimentary understanding of scientific terms and processes. They are easily confused by jargon. For effective risk communication to occur, it is imperative that the language, terms and concepts being presented must be appropriately tailored to the audience without sacrificing clarity or content.

Criteria used to assess risk. The public and experts use different criteria to assess risk. Some important factors include:

- Voluntariness: the public perceives voluntary risks as safer than forced risks. That is why, for example, sedentary lifestyles, smoking, diets high in fat, unsafe sex, driving without seat belts, biking without helmets, and keeping loaded guns in homes with children are considered more acceptable than involuntary risks such as being limited to purchasing produce with pesticide residues, and meat and milk from animals subjected to antibiotic and hormone injections. According to the 1990 Food Marketing Institute Trends Survey, consumers ranked pesticide and herbicide residues on fruits and vegetables as their most serious food concern, followed by antibiotics and hormones in their meat and poultry. Meanwhile, food safety experts ranked microbiological contamination and naturally-occurring food toxins to be most troublesome.

- Control: the public trusts its own instincts about personal safety more than it trusts others'.

- Process: the public is often willing to accept a higher risk when they are involved in all aspects of the decision-making process.

- Morality: when risks chosen by others are perceived by the public as trade-offs for monetary considerations, the public considers them less acceptable.

- Familiarity: the public tends to regard exotic risks as more hazardous than familiar risks.

- Diffuse impact: the assumption that whatever happens further away will have less effect, therefore making the risk more acceptable.

- Social amplification and memorability: the simple mention of a hazard, no matter how small the risk, tends to give it more importance.

- Media attention: the public generally perceives high profile risks (those conveyed as dramatic or sensational) as less acceptable.

- Simplification tendency: the public prefers decisive, clear-cut determinations of risk and descriptions of appropriate control measures.

- Tendency of association: the public is inclined to assume that roughly similar activities have the same risks.

- Resistance to change: attitudes and beliefs change slowly, even in the face of contrary evidence. However, when people lack strongly held opinions about an issue, they are easily influenced by the way information is presented.

Trust and credibility. Generally, people are more distrustful of authority than they used to be, particularly of govern-ment. Well publicized reports of fraudulent scientific studies have eroded the credibility of all science. The one-sided, often distorted views of special interest groups advocating their cause further confuses people and reduces trust in the veracity of information being presented. Trust and credibility take a long time to build, and can be lost in an instant.

The role of the media. Mass media are the messengers of risk for most people. That special responsibility places the media squarely in the middle of many problems in risk communication. While the media certainly has a mission of public education, its main goal is economic survival. While one of its important roles is to call attention to significant problems, it is not responsible for solving those problems. Yet while the media offers the potential of reaching large audiences, it frequently fails to convey comprehensively the critical complexity necessary for informed risk decisions. This makes the risk communicator's job more complex.

The rise of tabloid journalism and the sensationalism that is its hallmark obscures clarity and further complicates the risk communicator's job. Intense competition among media – the need to sell – leads many media outlets to appeal to emotion rather than take the time, space or distance to explain complex issues in a perspective that both fully covers the issue and helps people make choices about difficult questions. It is a lot easier for the media to call attention to minor risks while ignoring large, complex ones.

The 1989 Alar (daminozide) controversy raised a storm of media coverage and provoked massive outrage. While risk assessment experts estimated the cancer risk of eating apples grown with this chemical growth regulator as extremely low, their assessments did little to calm an alarmed public. Why? In part because of the widespread sensational media coverage. Also, because consumers viewed the risk as involuntary; it affected a particularly vulnerable and emotion-triggering population – children; and one of the people raising the alarm was a glamorous and popular actress.

The multicultural factor. America is no longer the homogenous country symbolized by 1950s television shows such as Ozzie and Harriet. It never was, though people perceived it that way. America of the 1990s is a mixture of diverse cultures, economic classes and special interest groups, each with distinct values, experiences, perceptions, and agendas. Each reacts very differently to risks depending on how they view a risk affecting them. There is no one truth that applies to all, making the job of communicating risk a severe challenge.

Alternative strategies in risk communication

How can risk communicators best inform the public about risk, create more trust, cooperation and awareness as well as an atmosphere conducive to changing behaviors that contribute to risk? Regardless of the causes, responsibilities and complexities in communicating risks, government, regulatory agencies and industry can choose from a number of alternative strategies. They could:

- Continue the present course, that is to defend the traditional system. This strategy, however, is dangerous: it is reactive rather than proactive, and does not educate the public by communicating a broad picture of the strengths, weaknesses and alternatives regarding the risks involved in America's health and safety issues.

- Design and implement a massive public relations campaign aimed at convincing the American public that the U.S. has the world's best health and safety record. The problem with this strategy is that credibility and trust are necessary components of effective strategies, and persuasion campaigns are not effective in such personal and serious issues as health and safety.

- Develop interactive strategies which involve wide segments of the public in discussion of the need for safety and quality. While this is a difficult, complex and threatening alternative, it may be the only one that helps the American public make informed decisions regarding health and safety risks. This alternative calls for the development of a national dialogue by opening up the health and safety system for inspection, exposing its strengths and weaknesses, discussing alternatives and necessary trade-offs.

The following procedures can help resolve the conflict between industry and the American public to balance producer needs with scientific alternatives and public perceptions:

- Develop sophisticated environmental scanning mechanisms to anticipate issues long before they become the focus of media attention.

- Develop a tiered, open information system to allow individuals and groups easy access to information when they need it and want it, and at a level appropriate to their interests and expertise.

- Develop communication systems which allow early discussion of health and safety protection technologies and policies.

- Develop communication systems which do not utilize mass media, thereby allowing for greater control of the message. These systems should enable the complexity of issues to be transmitted, with a full discussion of trade-offs and alternatives. The Internet already exists as a prime example.

- Neither overrate nor underrate the mass media. If organizations seek to utilize the mass media as a means of communication, they must realize that the media cannot be expected to carry the entire content of complex scientific information but can be used to add legitimacy to community-based information and a focus to the interpersonal agenda with the community.

These procedures require a perspective that recognizes the contribution of the public in the discussion of scientific and technical information and policy issues. Often a highly aware and interested public will challenge the conclusions and recommendations of risk assessment experts. The public must be made to understand that government, industry, scientists, and risk assessment experts have a valuable perspective as well. All parties involved must be willing to listen to and be aware of the importance of each other's viewpoints, recognizing that technical and scientific problems require both social and technical solutions.

The proactive strategy involves a credible facilitator who, early in the course of action, processes both scientific risk assessments and public risk perceptions, initiating discussions and making presentations about risk factors. The facilitator works actively to help the public learn about and listen to what the scientific and technical experts say, and, when the mass media is involved, helps reporters understand the context of risk assessments so they can report information about risks in an equitable, precise and comprehensive manner. The proactive strategy allows facilitators to gain insights into how the public incorporates risk factors into their daily lives, and to learn and appreciate the social contexts in which appraisals and perceptions of risk occur. This information is given back to the scientific and policymaking communities.

The interactive, proactive strategy – also called the two-way equity model – is highlighted by cooperation in which experts, policy makers and the public work together in defining the decision-making process, setting the goals, examining the alternatives, clarifying values, and defining outcomes. It emphasizes the need for the scientific community and policy-makers to understand that the public has valuable contributions to make in the discussion of risk policies before they are adopted, recognizing that the public has a right to provide input into policy decisions that will affect them directly. This open and straight-forward presentation of diverse opinions regarding risks is more likely to generate balanced views about the risk issue under discussion and will develop a climate of trust among the participants in the communication process.

While some believe that the issues are too complex for lay members of the public to participate, it should be recognized that an informed public will contribute vital information to risk policy discussions, making determinations based on social judgments of acceptable risk. Public participation is also likely to prevent public resistance, particularly where public behaviors are necessary for effective implementation. This communication strategy, unlike others, equalizes information in the communications process, sending the message that openness, rather than secrecy, is used to make decisions.

If public participation in risk management were encouraged rather than avoided and feared, agencies would have the opportunity to formulate policies that the public would approve more easily. Agencies that decide policy, then announce and defend it, are preempting the ability of citizens and communities to share in making determinations that affect their lives. Inclusive, interactive strategies are also cost-effective: communities allowed to help formulate risk-policy decisions are less likely to cause costly delays by demonstrating, encouraging negative publicity, and initiating litigation.

Soliciting public input goes beyond formal public hearings. Other effective methods of community involvement include task forces, town meetings, telephone contacts, questionnaires, polls, informal communication, hotlines, and using various media outlets to encourage people to give their ideas.

Vincent T. Covello, professor of environmental science and medicine at Columbia University's School of Public Health, has formulated seven key principles of effective risk communication:

- Accept and involve the public as a partner before big decisions are made and be sensitive to the public's concerns and information needs.

- Use different strategies for different goals, audiences, and media. Evaluate the strengths and weaknesses of available information. Classify different subgroups of the audience and target communication to them.

- Listen to your audiences and find out what they know through interviews, focus groups and surveys. Address their concerns and be aware of hidden agendas or broader meanings.

- Be honest and open to gain trust and build credibility. If an answer is unknown or uncertain, acknowledge it. Get back to people with answers, admit mistakes and disclose risk information as soon as it is known; lean toward sharing more information, not less, if in doubt.

- Collaborate and cooperate with other credible sources. Consult with others to learn who is best able to answer questions.

- Meet the media's needs by being open and accessible, respecting deadlines, and providing tailored information. Recognize the media's focuses: political angles rather than scientific validity, simplicity rather than complexity, and danger rather than safety. Establish long-term relationships with news editors.

- Speak clearly and with compassion: use simple language and avoid technical jargon; be sensitive to local speech norms; use vivid, concrete images, anecdotes, and examples that communicate on a personal level; avoid abstract language about death, illness, or injury; be responsive to anxiety, fear, and anger; communicate what cannot be done, promise what can, and do as promised.

Risk communication is a difficult challenge. There are no easy answers, no ready-made procedures. Being responsive to people's perceptions and fears rather than basing policy solely on technical merits, and generating ways of incorporating science with values and social concerns can forestall potential resistance and hostility by the public. The best evidence we have suggests that, in the long run, an open, informed, democratic process of decision-making will most likely succeed in designing effective policies and in communicating them in a manner which will aid in their acceptance.

The Communicator's Handbook
Tools, Techniques and Technology

Reviewer:
Don Ranly
Professor of Journalism
University of Missouri
Columbia, Missouri

Chapter 7
Photography

Authors:
Tom Gentle
Communication Specialist
Oregon State University
Corvallis, Oregon

Bob Rost
Information Representative
Oregon State University
Corvallis, Oregon

Adapted from Second Edition

Photographers:
Fritz Albert, Bill Carnahan, Victor Espinoza, Tom
Gentle, Jeanne Gleason.

Reviewer:
Milt Putnam
Photography Director
Institute of Food and Agricultural Sciences
University of Florida
Gainesville, Florida

Chapter 8
Graphic Design Basics

Author:
Ashley Wood
Coordinator of Educational Media
Educational Media and Services
University of Florida
Gainesville, Florida

Adapted from Second Edition chapter

Chapter 9
Exhibit Design

Author:
Harry A. Carey
Professor of Agricultural Communications

Department of Agriculture and Extension Education
Pennsylvania State University
University Park, Pennsylvania

Reviewer:
Thomas Land
Exhibits/Graphics Specialist
Agricultural Information Services
College of Agricultural Sciences
Pennsylvania State University
University Park, Pennsylvania

Chapter 10
Posters

Author:
Harry A. Carey
Professor of Agricultural Communications
Department of Agriculture and Extension Education
Pennsylvania State University
University Park, Pennsylvania

Reviewer:
Thomas Land
Exhibits/Graphics Specialist
Agricultural Information Services
College of Agricultural Sciences
Pennsylvania State University
University Park, Pennsylvania

Chapter 11
Slides and Slide-tapes

Author:
Karen Cronin
Senior Producer
University Relations
Virginia Polytechnic Institute and State University
Blacksburg, Virginia

Adapted from Second Edition chapter

Photographer:
Bob Veltri
Photography Supervisor
University Relations
Virginia Polytechnic Institute and State University
Blacksburg, Virginia

Chapter 12
Designing Visuals for Presentations

Author:
Karen Lilley
Communication Specialist
University of Minnesota
St. Paul, Minnesota

Graphics:
Tammy Blair
Communication Specialist
University of Minnesota
St. Paul, Minnesota

Editor:
Deedee Nagy
Communication Specialist
University of Minnesota
St. Paul, Minnesota

Chapter 13
Effective Meetings

Authors:
John R. Brooks
Broadcast News Editor
Louisiana State University
Baton Rouge, Louisiana

Julia A. Gamon
Associate Professor
Department of Agricultural Education and Studies
Iowa State University
Ames, Iowa

Chapter 14
Effective Speaking

Author:
M. Virginia Morgan
Extension Communications Specialist
Education Methods
Auburn University
Auburn, Alabama

Illustrator:
C. Bruce Dupree
Extension Communications Specialist
Auburn University
Auburn, Alabama

Chapter 15
Media Relations

Author:
Stanley C. Ernst
Director
North Dakota State Extension Communications
Fargo, North Dakota

Chapter 16
Campaign Communications: Public Information Campaigns

Author:
Janet Rodekohr
Extension Editor
University of Georgia
Athens, Georgia

Reviewer:
Dan Rahn
Extension Editor
University of Georgia
Athens, Georgia

Chapter 17
The ABCs of Working with Volunteers

Author:
John M. (Jack) Sperbeck
Extension Communication Editor
Associate Professor
University of Minnesota
St. Paul, Minnesota

Reviewers:
Melva L. Berkland
Extension Communication Specialist
Iowa State University
Ames, Iowa

Sheryl Nefstead
Extension Educator
Associate Professor
University of Minnesota
St. Paul, Minnesota

Illustrator:
John Mostad
Graphic Designer/Media Artist
University of Minnesota
St. Paul, Minnesota

Photographer:
Donald L. Breneman
Audiovisual Producer
Associate Professor
University of Minnesota
St. Paul, Minnesota

Chapter 18
Radio

Author:
David A. King
Department Head
Agricultural Communication
Purdue University
West Lafayette, Indiana

Reviewer:

John Brooks
Communication Specialist
Louisiana State University
Baton Rouge, Louisiana

Chapter 19
Television News

Author:
Bill Armstrong
Media Specialist
New Mexico State University
Las Cruces, New Mexico

Reviewer:
D'Lyn Ford
Associate Editor
New Mexico State University
Las Cruces, New Mexico

Photographer:
Tomilee Turner
Video Producer
New Mexico State University
Las Cruces, New Mexico

Chapter 20
Video Productions

Authors:
Jeanne Gleason
Supervisor and Video Producer
New Mexico State University
Las Cruces, New Mexico

Patrick Holian
Media Specialist/Video
New Mexico State University
Las Cruces, New Mexico

Reviewer:
David A. King
Department Head
Agricultural Communication
Purdue University
West Lafayette, Indiana

Technical assistance and graphics:
Barbara Copeland
Media Specialist/Multimedia
New Mexico State University
Las Cruces, New Mexico

John "CC" Chamberlin
Programmer/Analyst
New Mexico State University
Las Cruces, New Mexico

Photographers:
Tomilee Turner
Video Producer
New Mexico State University
Las Cruces, New Mexico

Victor Espinoza
Video Producer
New Mexico State University
Las Cruces, New Mexic

Chapter 21
Multimedia

Authors:
Jeanne Gleason
Supervisor and Video Producer
New Mexico State University
Las Cruces, New Mexico

John "CC" Chamberlin
Programmer/Analyst
New Mexico State University
Las Cruces, New Mexico

Barbara Copeland
Computer Operator
New Mexico State University
Las Cruces, New Mexico

Photographer:
Tomilee Turner
Video Producer
New Mexico State University
Las Cruces, New Mexico

Graphics:
Gloria Wood
Graphic Artist
New Mexico State University
Las Cruces, New Mexico

Barbara Copeland
Media Specialist/Multimedia
New Mexico State University
Las Cruces, New Mexico

John "CC" Chamberlin
Programmer/Analyst
New Mexico State University
Las Cruces, New Mexico

Chapter 22
Instructional Design for Distance Education

Authors:
Cathy Bridwell
Distance Education Specialist
USDA, Cooperative State, Research, Education and Extension Service
Washington, DC

Randall Bretz, Ph.D.
Director
Nebraska State-wide Education and Information Service
Nebraska Educational Telecommunications
Lincoln, Nebraska

Henry DeVries, Ph.D.

Electronic Technology Specialist
Cornell Cooperative Extension Service
Cornell University
Ithaca, New York

James W. King, Ed.D.
Associate Professor
Institute for Agriculture and Natural Resources
University of Nebraska
Lincoln, Nebraska

Deborah Shaffer Knapp
Information Technology Specialist
Cooperative State Research, Education and Extension Service
USDA
Seabrook, Texas

Reviewer:
William Murphy, Ph.D.
Distance Education Specialist
Virginia Polytechnic Institute and State University
Blacksburg, Virginia

Chapter 23
Navigating the Internet

Authors:
Henry DeVries
Director
Extension Electronic Technology Group
Cornell University
Ithaca, New York

Deborah Shaffer Knapp
Information Technology Specialist
Cooperative State Research, Education, and Extension Service, USDA
Seabrook, Texas

Ellen Taricani
Information Specialist
Computer Services
Pennsylvania State University
University Park, Pennsylvania

Reviewers:
Eldon Fredericks
Education Technology Specialist
Purdue University
Cooperative State Research, Education, and Extension Service, USDA
West Lafayette, Indiana

Trish Sacks
Assistant Director
Cooperative Extension Service
University of Massachusetts
Amherst, Massachusetts

Gregory L. Parham
Director
Distance Education and information
Technology Extension Service, USDA
Washington, DC

Graphics:
Harry A. Carey, Jr.
Professor
Agricultural Communications
Pennsylvania State University
University Park, Pennsylvania

Chapter 24
Strategic Communication Planning

Author:
Maxine S. Ferris
Director
Outreach Communications
Professor, Department of Agricultural and Extension
Education
Michigan State University
East Lansing, Michigan

Reviewer:
Karen F. Bolluyt
Head
Agricultural Information Services
Iowa State University
Ames, Iowa

Chapter 25
Effective Communication in Crisis

Authors:
Clifford W. Scherer
Associate Professor
Cornell University
Ithaca, New York

Nadine K. Baker
Graduate Student
Cornell University
Ithaca, New York

Chapter 26
Organizational and Product Marketing

Author:
Ken Kingsley
Department Head
Extension and Experiment
Station Communications
Oregon State University
Corvallis, Oregon

Reviewer:
Meg G. Ashman
Publications Editor
University of Vermont
Burlington, Vermont

Chapter 27
Emerging Issues in Communication

Author:
Valorie F. McAlpin
Director
Agricultural communications
North Carolina A&T University
Greensboro, North Carolina

Reviewers:
Janet Poley
CEO
ADEC
Lincoln, Nebraska

Blannie E. Bowen
Rumberger Professor of Agriculture
Pennsylvania State University
University Park, Pennsylvania

Chapter 28
Making Risk Communication Equitable

Authors:

Clifford W. Scherer
Associate Professor of Communication
Cornell University
Ithaca, New York

Nadine K. Baker
Graduate Student
Cornell University
Ithaca, New York

Editor:

Kenn Marash
Cornell University
Ithaca, New York